GENDER HISTORY IN PRAC

GENDER HISTORY IN PRACTICE

§ HISTORICAL PERSPECTIVES ON

BODIES, CLASS & CITIZENSHIP §

by KATHLEEN CANNING

CORNELL UNIVERSITY PRESS *Ithaca & London*

First published 2006 by Cornell University Press
First printing, Cornell Paperbacks, 2005

Printed in the United States of America

Library of Congress Cataloging-in-Publication Data

Canning, Kathleen.
    Gender history in practice : historical perspectives on bodies, class, and citizenship / Kathleen Canning.
        p.   cm.
    Includes bibliographical references and index.
    ISBN-13: 978-0-8014-4357-2 (cloth : alk. paper)
    ISBN-10: 0-8014-4357-1 (cloth : alk. paper)
    ISBN-13: 978-0-8014-8971-6 (pbk. : alk. paper)
    ISBN-10: 0-8014-8971-7 (pbk. : alk. paper)
    1. Women—History.   2. Feminism—History.
3. Women in politics—History.   4. Feminist theory.
I. Title.
HQ1121.C295 2005
305.4'09182'1—dc22

                                        2005025037

Cornell University Press strives to use environmentally responsible suppliers and materials to the fullest extent possible in the publishing of its books. Such materials include vegetable-based, low-VOC inks and acid-free papers that are recycled, totally chlorine-free, or partly composed of nonwood fibers. For further information, visit our website at www.cornellpress.cornell.edu.

Cloth printing   10 9 8 7 6 5 4 3 2 1
Paperback printing   10 9 8 7 6 5 4 3 2 1

CONTENTS

ACKNOWLEDGMENTS

The essays collected here reflect different moments in my scholarly and personal life: they took shape in seminars, at dinner tables, and in libraries and archives too numerous to list individually. The rethinking they pursued received the generous support of the National Endowment for the Humanities and the German Marshall Fund. I am also grateful to the College of Literature, Science, and the Arts and Rackham Graduate School at the University of Michigan, which have provided much-valued research support and release time from teaching for the writing of these essays.

The human debts we incur in the course of projects like these are, of course, never adequately honored, recounted, or remotely possible to repay. My first are owed to Geoff Eley and Sonya Rose, who helped me envision this book in the first place and advised me about its contents along the way. Their own recent books have not only inspired me intellectually, but their collegiality and friendship make it all worthwhile. I had the particular good fortune to be part of the interdisciplinary "Weimar group" at Michigan, which aimed to "rethink Weimar" in ways that were enormously fruitful for many of the chapters in this volume. Each of the group's members—Kristin McGuire, Kerstin Barndt, Elizabeth Otto, Ari Sammartino, and Manuela Achilles—contributed something valuable to my work on bodies and citizenships, through their comments on my work and the completion of their own admirable studies. Libby Otto not only offered brilliant interpretations of Marianne Brandt's photomontages, but she also provided me with the crucial information on permission to reprint them. Many day-to-day conversations shaped the thinking in this book—those with my co-teachers, co-editors, and friends Helmut Puff, Michele Mitchell, and Nancy Rose Hunt: with them I was fortunate to explore geographies and chronologies far beyond modern German history. Scott Spector has been a valued friend and fellow traveler since graduate school: teaching together has not only made us both laugh but enriched my thinking on many of the issues I engage here.

Outside of Michigan I have benefited from the counsel and collegiality of many fellow historians, including Roger Chickering, David Crew, Michael Geyer, Atina Grossmann, Vernon Lidtke, Robert Moeller, and Molly Nolan. In Germany Alf Lüdtke was a generous host and interlocutor at the Max-Planck-Institut für Geschichte in Göttingen and at the University of Erfurt seminar with Hans Medick. I presented earlier versions of the chapters featured here at colloquia and conferences, including those organized by Tina Campt and Jocelyn Olcott at Duke University; Franz Brüggemeier and Sylvia Paletschek in Freiburg; Martin Geyer, Eric Weitz, and Thomas Lindenberger at the Transatlantic Seminar in Munich; Cornelie Usborne in London; Andreas Wirsching in Augsburg; Karen Hagemann and Christine von Oertzen in Toronto; Claudia Opitz and Regina Wecker in Basel; Brigitte Studer in Bern; Jakob Tanner and Angelika Linke in Zürich, Ute Frevert in Bielefeld; Adelheid von Saldern and Barbara Duden in Hannover; Alexandra Binnenkade and Beatrice Bowald in Lucerne; Martina Kessel in Bielefeld; Uta Poiger and Lynn Thomas at the University of Washington; Judith Walkowitz and Vernon Lidtke at Johns Hopkins; Kathleen Brown at the University of Pennsylvania; and Anna Clark at the University of Minnesota. I thank them and their audiences for pushing me on many of the questions I pursue here.

As these essays became a book, I was grateful for the feedback from the anonymous readers for Cornell University Press and from my best critic, Hubert Rast. I also benefited from last-minute consultations with Geoff Eley, Bob Moeller, and Kristin McGuire and from the superb skills of Mary O'Reilly, who took on the Herculean task of assembling the bibliography for this volume under time pressure. I also thank John Ackerman and Teresa Jesionowski at Cornell University Press for editorial wisdom and support.

We all know by now that books would not be written without the sustenance of friends. Kristin McGuire occupies a special place here, as do the wonderful meals and other occasions shared with Jane Burbank and Fred Cooper, Penny von Eschen and Kevin Gaines, Kerstin Barndt and Johannes von Moltke, Susan Douglas and T. R. Durham, David Cohen and Gretchen Elsner-Sommer. Weighing in with good humor and support from afar were Liz Horodowich, Julie Berkowitz, Tom Wolfe, and Sally Silk. During the last year Mary Edmonson, Tim Canning, and Paula Cain Gorman provided something only they understand. Hubert Rast wisely warned me against the sentiment of acknowledgment, while Samuel and Norah Rast thought I should dedicate this book to them.

K.C.

INTRODUCTION

The essays collected in this volume represent distinct moments in my longer-term engagement with the history of bodies, class, and citizenship. One important connection between the essays is the dual objective of theorizing historical analysis and historicizing theoretical concepts. In explicating the workings of keywords and concepts like class, citizenship, and bodies in specific historical settings, I attempt to bring social theory, including feminist theory, into conversation with the archives. This encounter varies across the individual essays presented here. As much as these essays originate in my own research context of modern German history, they are also informed by debates and dilemmas I have pursued in recent years in teaching transnational gender history and as North American co-editor of *Gender & History*. Moving far beyond my own field in both cases has sharpened some of these questions and confirmed the validity of the inquiry, even if I remain acutely aware of their reliance upon literatures that are mainly European and North American, and of my own professional location in the North American academy.

The essays in Part I of this volume examine the encounters between history and theory that have most profoundly informed the practice of gender history in the European field during the last two decades. The first essay pursues a genealogy of gender itself, noting its embeddedness within the field from which it emerged—women's history—as well as the separations it has effected from that legacy. Even as gender became an established field of inquiry, it has been continually interrogated and destabilized by new scholarship on bodies and sexualities, on race, ethnicity, and hybridity. One point in tracing the genealogy of gender is to insist on a clarification of terms instead of the blurriness that has let gender, body, and sexuality be used interchangeably without reflection on the distinct methodologies associated with each. In this essay I also highlight the different patterns of gender's entry into or impact upon individual national, chronological, and thematic fields: while gender was a powerful revisionary force in some, in others it persists as a separate or "partial" inquiry on the sidelines, disconnected from the definitive events and transformations that shape the wider field. In some fields gender's primary effect was critical, even deconstructive—taking apart concepts like class or sex, for example—in order to establish its place in the field. Its task was less combative or subversive in fields where gender was already recognized as significant in the early stages (or where gender was formative of a new wave of inquiry)—in the study of consumption, welfare state, and empire, for example. The situatedness of gender inquiry within individual fields—the question of whether it has become integral to the field or continues to struggle for legitimation—has significant methodological consequences for the practices of gender history. In either case gender history has had a crucial partner—feminist theory—so my analysis of the impact of gender on bodies, class, and citizenship illuminates the ways in which their respective critiques coincided with and fueled one another.

Historicizing the practices of gender history itself makes it easier to understand why I wrote the essay that comprises chapter 2 of this volume, "Feminist History after the Linguistic Turn," which was first published in 1994. The debate this article addresses turned around the concept of discourse and its implications for agency and experience, keywords that had been essential in the practices of women's history, in rendering women subjects of their own history. The epistemological crisis that inspired this article has, of course, long since dissipated, but my attempt to analyze the workings of these concepts in specific historical settings and grounded in that history, to posit a more fluid and less binarized relation between them, remains an instructive example of historicizing theory. Probing possible methodologies for histories of both discourse and experience in this piece, I resisted taking "discourse" at face value and sought instead to identify particular discourses that indisputably congealed around a new social question of female factory labor in late nineteenth-century Germany. I probed the discrepant and partially disconnected origins of these discourses, the process by which they concentrated images, metaphors, and ultimately power in order to define and regulate female factory labor. As a second step, I abandoned the presumption of a hierarchy between discourse and experience, probing how subjects might have constituted, contested, and changed the terms of discourses, drawing upon their experience in doing so. Pushing at the limits of discursive power, I hypothesized that some realms of experience—perhaps the body—may have escaped from, defied, or subverted linguistic mediation in certain historical moments. While I acknowledged the difficulty of delineating or defining experience, in my call to historicize not only experience and discourse, but also their contingent relationship to one another, I expressed the optimistic hope that we might fine-tune our skills of historical interpretation in order to listen harder and more creatively, to the ways in which historical subjects "talk back" through our archival sources.

The genesis of chapter 3, "Difficult Dichotomies," was the invitation to give a keynote address at a feminist history conference in Zürich in 2002 on the question: "Experience: Is Everything Now Discourse?" Rather than returning to the debates of the previous decade, my first intention was to determine the fate of experience since the debates of the early 1990s. A quick survey of book titles, journal articles, and dissertation abstracts suggested that experience had virtually vanished from historical inquiry. By contrast with bodies—which were everywhere at this time—experience seemed to have gone underground. I first explored the figurations of experience that the linguistic turn was to overcome, noting that thought or consciousness were essential elements of experience as understood by those who had elevated experience to a "foundationalist" keyword. My excavation of experience soon uncovered it, an unnamed but powerful presence in the flourishing study of historical memory, in body histories, and in the more recent feminist explorations of subjectivity. The point of my excursion was never to resuscitate experience. I was interested, however, in whether its new deployments had perhaps broken the stranglehold of dichotomization that had first tied experience to discourse, only to discredit and then submerge it. The very fact that experience could remain unnoticed and unnamed for so long raised a new question for me about historicization. Raymond Williams's distinction between experience past and experience present, for example, rendered memory a crucial factor in experience. Experience, I postulated, could not be timelessly, universally relevant. Rather, it had an important temporal dimension, that is, its meanings varied according to the historically specific ways subjects lived—and experienced—the passage of time.

Part II of this volume features essays that examine the impact of gender (as opposed to women) in the histories of labor (chapter 4) and the welfare state (chapter 5). In "Beyond Insularity" I take a critical approach to the narrative of labor history's demise, according to which the loss of its "materialist presumptions" had left it without an analytic framework in the wake of the turn towards language and culture. From my perspective, however, a wave of new studies in gender and labor had significantly reinvigorated the history of work precisely at the point of its alleged demise. This reinvigoration was made possible by the very undermining of materialist (and masculinist) presumptions through the more culturally inflected study of labor that often encompassed far more than factories—connecting work to leisure, production to consumption, and identifying the ideological (rather than material) underpinnings of skill, wage, and work ethic. A crucial argument here was that this methodological renovation, the fostering of a less bounded study of labor—because it was propelled by gender—seemed to occur outside of the field of labor history, rather than within it. The boundary drawing that relegated these new studies of gender and labor to women's history and posited labor history as a field in demise disguised the very potential of gender to perform the critical, deconstructive work of rethinking that labor history precisely needed at the time.

While I contend in chapter 4 that gender fostered a less bounded study of labor, my analysis of social policy as body politics in chapter 5 pursues a gender story across several milieus of German history that are usually analyzed separately—industrial crisis, social reform, working class formation, and the founding of the welfare state—and argues that social citizenship was shaped precisely along the gendered lines that connected these arenas. My examination of labor legislation and the welfare state also makes a methodological point about the importance of distinguishing the different work of the analytical categories of women and gender in our historical case studies. For even where feminist activists' mobilizations for social reform were spurned, perceptions of gender crisis prompted social policy interventions and inflected its regulatory practices. This essay's exploration of social policy as body politics situates the female body as a central object of both rhetorical and material intervention, but the body itself remains a rather peripheral, unexplicated category. I thus return to it in chapter 6, probing the meanings of the sudden explosion of interest in the history of the body, especially for gender historians. Did the body, in its apparent materiality, appear to resolve some of the more paralyzing dilemmas of the linguistic turn? Identifying specific bodies—from social and symbolic bodies, to bodies as objects of medical-hygienic intervention, to bodies as sites of experience or subjectivity—makes clear that no one methodology would suffice to analyze all of them. Finally, I wondered, are some periods of history more "embodied" than others? What criteria might we posit for determining the usefulness of body as a lens of historical analysis? In the second half of the essay I seek to historicize the body in the particularly violent twentieth century, exploring the bodily shock of prolonged total war and probing the naming of male and female citizens in explicitly embodied terms.

The critical expansion and redefinition of the concept citizenship, which I undertake in Part III of this volume, is propelled by histories and theories of gender. I consider here whether feminist rethinkings of citizenship in any sense mirror the critical onslaught against class a decade or more ago. When I set out to analyze the absence of citizenship in the analytical vocabulary of German history, I found a category constrained by linguistic limitations: for one, the English term "citizenship" did not map onto either of the common German notions of *Staatsangehörigkeit* or *Staatsbürgerschaft*, both of which were preoccupied with the state as the definitive actor and with citizenship as a legally prescribed status. Another constraint of this terminology was the difficulty in differentiating between citizenship as status and citizenship as practice, or in discerning the meanings of citizenship rights and rhetorics for those excluded from them.

My arguments in these essays about the constraints of concepts were also aimed at feminist historiography for which citizenship also had little resonance beyond the social citizenship at the heart of study of the welfare state. Historians of women and gender had namely approached social citizenship as a success story for German women, as a bundle of rights and duties that German women possessed in the early twentieth century, and presumed that participatory citizenship, political and civic rights, was less relevant because it had remained largely unfulfilled. With this recognition, finding a place for citizenship in Germany became an explicitly gendered undertaking. Yet engendering citizenship also necessitated expanding its terms to those experiential, subjective arenas in which citizenship acquired meaning for those it excluded.

One ambition of these essays is to show how the claims of German women, emboldened by their experiences of war, defeat, and revolution in the years 1916–18, resonated in and reshaped realms of politics that seemed impervious to gender—rhetorics of defeat, negotiations of peace, the crisis of the nation, and the declaration of democracy. At the same time the assignment of citizenship rights to women in 1918 was significant in another sense, for it opened possibilities for the coalescence of new female subjectivities and self-representations that would echo long after 1918, rendering gender a site of continuous contention throughout the history of the republic. That is to say that a certain kind of participatory politics I term "citizenship" helped to generate and sustain Weimar's democratic project while also constituting a crucial site of the contests over gender that beset the republic from its founding moments. Understanding citizenship in its subjective dimensions also makes clear that citizenship mattered not only in the formal realms of politics, but also well beyond them, in the realms of consumption and popular culture; in the practices of welfare, social, and sexual hygiene; in the campaigns of socialists and communists for reproductive rights.

In this case study many of the terms I have analyzed in the previous essays reappear—the experiences of war, the embodying of citizenship, the discourses of democracy, and the agency of those named as citizens. Striking in these last essays is the impossibility of dichotomizing them, of putting them into pairs and reordering history. One outcome of the critical project of gender history, then, may be the postponement of closure that is inherent in both the projects of "mainstreaming" and the construction of binary, oppositional terms—public/private, gender/sex, discourse/experience.

PART I § BRINGING HISTORY TO THEORY

CHAPTER 1 § GENDER HISTORY § MEANINGS, METHODS & METANARRATIVES

A few years ago I was asked to write a short essay for an encyclopedia of the social sciences, defining "gender history." A number of questions framed my initial goals of tracing the lineage and offering an overview of the accomplishments of gender history some fifteen years after it gained currency as an historical concept. In this essay I return to this set of fundamental questions that inform teaching, research, and writing on the history of gender. Did the inclusion of gender history in this kind of authorizing text signal the arrival of a once subversive field of historical inquiry in the "mainstream" of social scientific study? Should gender be understood mainly as a new *object* of historical study—in its dimension as social relation, symbol, or ideology—or did it signify a set of identifiable *practices* or shared *methodologies* that had emerged from the burgeoning body of gender historiography? Furthermore, important questions arose regarding the genealogy and singularity of gender as a keyword of historical and social analysis, which required that gender first be disentangled from the related study of women, body, and sexuality, in which it had been enmeshed since its emergence as historical vocabulary. No sooner had a critical accumulation of scholarship on gender made this possible than gender was destabilized by the growing recognition of its contingency upon race, ethnicity, nationality, generation, and sexual orientation.

The intention of this essay, then, is to analyze the achievements of gender history since its emergence some twenty years ago, while contending with the dissonances, dilemmas, and destabilizing impulses that make the reception and application of gender so uneven across different national historiographies, chronological fields, and thematic areas of inquiry. Approaching gender history as a situated practice means considering its disparate impulses: in fields where the study of gender has succeeded in uprooting and revising keywords or in amending chronologies and synthetic narratives, feminists have begun to wonder whether integrating gender means dissipating its subversive impetus.

This essay represents a significant expansion of my brief contribution on "Gender History" in the *International Encyclopedia of the Social and Behavioral Sciences*, vol. 15, ed. Jürgen Kocka (Amsterdam, 2001), pp. 6006–11.

Others wonder whether the future of gender history is the "overspecialization, overproduction, and fragmentation" that characterize other once marginal and contested thematic fields.[1] In those areas of study where gender has remained peripheral to the mega-events and metanarratives of European histories, the quest for entry, acceptance, and legitimacy within "mainstream" history still fuels scholarly initiatives on gender. The difference in the status of gender history—as "insider" or "outsider" in the wider fields of historical inquiry—is merely one example of what I term here uneven or differential practices. While the vocabulary of gender was "intended to clarify matters and to transcend [the] paradoxes" that had been inherent in women's history, its emergence was beset with controversy and produced new paradoxes of its own.[2]

DEFINING GENDER

Gender is a category of social analysis that denotes the relational character of sexual difference. When this term first gained currency among historians of women in the early 1980s, it mainly signified the social or cultural relation between the sexes.[3] As gender became an increasingly important and visible site of scholarly research and debate across the disciplines, its meaning widened to include the symbolic system or signifier of relations of power in which men and women are positioned differently.[4] The embrace of the concept of gender as a culturally formed set of social relations, distinct from sex, signaled the departure of feminist social scientists from the unchanging and universal notions of biological differences. The word "gender," however, does not exist in some languages, while in others its meaning diverges significantly from the English usage. The German term *Geschlecht*, for example, encompasses both sex and

1. See, for example, Anne Firor Scott, Sara M. Evans, Susan K. Cahn, and Elizabeth Faue, "Women's History in the New Millennium: A Conversation across Three Generations," parts I and II, *Journal of Women's History* 11/1 (1999): 9–30, and 11/2 (1999): 199–220. Also see Joan W. Scott's commentary on this conversation and on the future of feminist history, "Feminism's History," ibid., 16/2 (2004): 10–29.

2. Claudia Honegger and Caroline Arni, eds., preface to *Gender: Die Tücken einer Kategorie* (Zürich, 2001), p. 15.

3. See the use of the term "gender" in *Sex and Class in Women's History*, ed. Judith L. Newton, Mary P. Ryan, and Judith R. Walkowitz (London, 1983).

4. Joan Wallach Scott, "Gender: A Useful Category of Historical Analysis," *American Historical Review* 91/5 (1986): 1053–75. For an important reflection on the passage from women's history to gender history, see Bonnie G. Smith, *The Gender of History: Men, Women, and Historical Practice* (Cambridge, Mass., 1998).

gender and thus blurs the core distinctions of the English term.[5] In French the terms *sexe* or *sexuel* are more commonly used than *genre*, which can refer to either grammatical or literary genre or serve as a classifying category in natural history.[6] The use of the analytical tool, gender, does not per se connote a primacy of gender relative to other forms of inequality, such as race, class, or ethnicity; rather, scholarship of the last decade has amply illustrated the mutual relationships between gender and other categories of difference.

From Women's History to Gender History

The historical study of women, which became a vital field of scholarly inquiry during the 1960s, first sought to recover the ways in which women participated in and were excluded from processes of social transformations and political change. The empirical investigation of the "private" (familial, sexual) and "public" (political) inequality of women in past societies drove the first decade of feminist social science. From its inception, women's history relied upon the disciplinary practices of history but many of the conceptual debates that propelled it forward took place in interdisciplinary settings such as Women's Studies where many early feminist paradigms and methodologies were first formulated and debated.[7]

In this first phase of women's history sex and class often figured as related forms of oppression: the female *sex* was viewed as a subordinate *class*, subjugated by a dominant class of men. In feminist scholarship the embrace of the notion of *patriarchy* marked a new emphasis on sexual exploitation as the primary form of women's oppression.[8] Women's historians located the origins of the patriarchal sexual order in "the private family" and examined how it was reproduced in social modes of production, divisions of labor, and property re-

---

5. Claudia Opitz, "Gender—eine unverzichtbare Kategorie der historischen Analyse: Zur Rezeption von Joan W. Scotts Studien in Deutschland, Österreich und der Schweiz," in *Gender: Die Tücken einer Kategorie,* ed. Honegger and Arni, pp. 95–116.

6. Michelle Riot-Sarcey, "The Difficulties of Gender in France: Reflections on a Concept," *Gender & History* 11/3 (1999): 489–98.

7. See the interesting reflections on the development of Women's Studies in *Women's Studies on the Edge,* ed. Joan W. Scott, special issue of *Differences: A Journal of Feminist Cultural Studies* 9/3 (Fall 1997).

8. See, for example, Gayle Rubin, "The Traffic in Women: Notes on the 'Political Economy' of Sex," in *Toward an Anthropology of Women,* ed. Rayna Reiter (New York, 1975), reprinted in *Feminism and History,* ed. Joan W. Scott (New York, 1996), pp. 105–52. Also see Zillah Eisenstein, *Capitalist Patriarchy and the Case for Socialist Feminism* (New York, 1978.)

lations in a wide range of historical settings.[9] This study of patriarchy's origins, practices, and ideologies laid an important foundation for feminist research on women and family, women and labor, social protest, and social transformation. During this earlier phase of women's history, *sex* was elevated to a keyword of social analysis and female actors began to appear as agents of their own history.

Yet in furnishing a more complete rendering of contemporary and past societies, pioneering scholarship in women's history also revealed the limitations of sex as an analytical category. Unitary analytical categories, such as those of woman/women and man/men, were based on fixed, rather than historically or socially variable, notions of biological sex, thus creating a cohesive history of the oppression of *women* that overlooked the differences of race, class, ethnicity, and sexual orientation. Furthermore, women were frequently studied in isolation from men, which produced a fragmented and partial understanding of the workings of sexual difference in society. As sex became a crucial category of social analysis in the 1970s, its impact on other keywords of social analysis, such as class or race, became a topic of intensive debate. Labor historians and political theorists often attempted to fit women into prevalent notions of class, some by arguing that women formed a separate or parallel class of their own, others by examining the ways in which (female) gender presented an obstacle to the formation of unitary classes. Still others circumvented the dilemma of "sex and class" altogether by ascribing to women the same class positions, social identities, and political interests as those of their fathers or husbands.

In the late 1970s the feminist historian Joan Kelly Gadol sought to transcend this theoretical impasse by formulating a "doubled vision" of society, one that emphasized the ways in which both men's and women's social identities were shaped by sex and class.[10] In emphasizing the inextricable links between sex and class, women's history widened the scope of the political to include family and household, bodies and sexualities, which had been situated until then in the sphere of the "private." As the concept of gender came into currency through this doubled vision of society, feminist scholars began to excavate the ideologies, norms, and symbolic systems that shaped identities, social institu-

---

9. Examples include Joan Kelly Gadol, "The Social Relation of the Sexes: Methodological Implications of Women's History," *Signs* 1/4 (1976): 809–23; and Natalie Zemon Davis, "Women's History in Transition: The European Case," *Feminist Studies* 3/3–4 (1976): 83–103.

10. Joan Kelly Gadol, "The Doubled Vision of Feminist Theory," *Feminist Studies* 5/1 (1979): 216–27. Also see Joan Kelly, *Women, History, and Theory: The Essays of Joan Kelly* (Chicago, 1984).

tions, and social relations. The editors of the pioneering collection *Sex and Class in Women's History,* for example, noted in 1983 that the term gender denoted the systematic ways in which sex differences cut through society and culture and conferred inequality upon women.[11] Thus, even as gender began to emerge from women's history in the early 1980s, women and gender remained highly tangential, sometimes interchangeable concepts.

The intellectual forces driving the shift from women to gender were multiple. The achievements of nearly two decades of scholarship in women's history were significant, but had left the chronological and conceptual framings of history unshaken. Feminist historians delivered powerful critiques of the dualism of public/private and worked to dissolve or transcend the sex/gender distinction as well. Yet the binary pairings of home/factory, production/reproduction, and production/consumption remained tenaciously in place. As feminist historians sought, empirically and theoretically, to overcome or dissolve these dualisms, they began to pose more fundamental challenges to established chronologies, categories, and theories of historical transformation. In the natural and social sciences feminists critiqued biological essentialism as an explanation for sexual inequality, emphasizing instead the power of languages and discourses to define hierarchies of sex and gender and to anchor them in social practices and institutions.[12]

Feminist scholars of race in Britain and the United States also intervened at this juncture with powerful critiques of the categories and practices of women's history. Defining race as a "metalanguage," as the "ultimate trope of difference," Evelyn Brooks Higginbotham explicated the powerful effects of race on the construction and representation of gender, class, and sexuality. Understanding race as a "double-voiced discourse" revealed the ways in which it shaped both the oppression and the self-representation of minorities.[13] These powerful cri-

11. Newton, Ryan, and Walkowitz, introduction to *Sex and Class in Women's History.* For a view of this development in the German field, see Karin Hausen and Heide Wunder, eds., *Frauengeschichte/Geschlechtergeschichte* (Frankfurt a. M., 1992).

12. Sandra Harding, "The Instability of the Analytical Categories of Feminist Theory," in *Sex and Scientific Inquiry,* ed. Sandra Harding and Jean E. O'Barr (Chicago, 1987), pp. 283–302; Ludmilla Jordanova, *Sexual Visions: Images of Gender in Science and Medicine between the Eighteenth and the Twentieth Centuries* (Madison, Wis., 1989); Mary Jacobus, Evelyn Fox Keller, and Sally Shuttleworth, eds., *Body/Politics: Women and the Discourses of Science* (London, 1990); and Donna Haraway, *Simians, Cyborgs, and Women: The Reinvention of Nature* (London, 1991).

13. Evelyn Brooks Higginbotham, "African-American Women's History and the Metalanguage of Race," *Signs* 17/2 (1992): 251–74. Also see Patricia Hill Collins, "The Social Con-

tiques of the unitary categories of "woman" and "sex," of the tendencies of white feminism to homogenize sexual and patriarchal oppression, resonated as well in the debates about "identity politics" that crossed the divide between academia and the public sphere in the United States and Britain. A new generation of feminist scholars of colonialism and empire took a similar approach to the history of Western feminism, calling upon historians to confront its racist and nationalist legacies and its involvement in imperial ideologies, institutions, and practices.[14] The outcome of these critiques was a widespread recognition that race and gender were located distinctly in relations of power, but that they mutually constituted social identities. Race, like gender, came to be viewed as a social construction rather than a genotypic or phenotypic form of difference. As ethnic, racial, national, or sexual identities that had once been viewed as cohesive dissolved, they were increasingly understood as multiple, mutable, and contradictory.[15]

By the mid-1980s a gradual breakdown of the category "woman" had begun to propel the turn to gender. The critical questioning of woman as cohesive historical subject, object, and political identity was one factor that both allowed for and necessitated the arrival of gender as a keyword of historical analysis. Another decisive conjuncture was the gradual severance of the links between sex-gender and biology in feminist thought and the dismissal of the remnants of Marxism that hinged the production of gender to changing economic structures. The 1986 publication of Joan Scott's essay "Gender: A Useful Category of Historical Analysis" in the pages of one of the most influential American historical journals marks the moment at which gender gained an analytic status

---

struction of Black Feminist Thought," *Signs* 14/4 (Summer 1989): 745–73, and the important collection edited by Kum-kum Bhavnani, *Feminism and "Race"* (Oxford, 2001).

14. Vicky Amos and Pratibha Parmar, "Challenging Imperial Feminism," *Feminist Review* 17 (1984): 3–19; Chandra Talpade Mohanty, "Feminist Politics: What's Home Got to Do with It?" in *Feminist Studies/Critical Studies,* ed. Teresa de Lauretis (Bloomington, Ind., 1986), pp. 191–212; Chandra Talpade Mohanty, Ann Russo, and Lourdes Torres, eds., *Third World Women and the Politics of Feminism* (Bloomington, Ind., 1991); Mrinalini Sinha, "Gender in the Critiques of Colonialism and Nationalism: Locating the 'Indian Woman,'" in *Feminists Revision History,* ed. Ann-Louise Shapiro (New Brunswick, N.J., 1994), pp. 246–75.

15. Bonnie Thornton Dill, "Race, Class and Gender: Prospects for an All-Inclusive Sisterhood," *Feminist Studies* 9 (Spring 1983): 131–50; Gloria Anzaldúa and Cherríe Moraga, eds., *This Bridge Called My Back: Writings of Radical Women of Color* (New York, 1982); Barbara Smith, ed., *Home Girls: A Black Feminist Anthology* (New York, 1983); and Elsa Barkley Brown, "'What Has Happened Here': The Politics of Difference in Women's History and Feminist Politics," *Feminist Studies* 18 (Summer 1992): 295–312.

of its own among English-speaking historians, especially in the United States.[16] Scott's intervention not only made explicit the new directions and analytical promise of the flourishing scholarship in feminist history, but also challenged historians in all fields to contend with the emergent category of gender. Her highly theoretical intervention, expanded two years later in her essay collection *Gender and the Politics of History,* analyzed the discursive constitution of gender, which she understood as a system of meanings or symbolic order that signified relationships of power.[17]

Scott's articulation of gender as a challenge to established historical categories and practices was followed by British philosopher Denise Riley's powerful disavowal of "woman" in her book-length essay, provocatively entitled *Am I That Name? Feminism and the Category of 'Women' in History.*[18] Rather than possessing a fixed biological character, woman, Riley argued, was characterized by a "peculiar temporality." The historical contingency of "woman" became evident when the developing human sciences evoked a new and highly modern social category, "women," that was enmeshed with and reliant upon "the histories of other concepts . . . including those of 'the social' and 'the body.'" "Being a woman," Riley contended," is always an inherently unstable state," while feminism constitutes the site at which differences among women are acknowledged and "systematically fought out."[19]

In tracing the genealogy of gender, it is important to remind ourselves that the turn to gender did not bring about an abrupt or immediate shift in analytical vocabulary. Rather, for a decade or more after its emergence, gender and women co-existed as fields of historical study, sometimes differentiated in name only with gender figuring as a more fashionable renaming of women's history. In other cases gender and women denoted distinct methodological approaches and objects of study, which were often related to or even reliant upon one another within a single study. Even in those fields that proved most receptive toward gender, its effect was to transform practices gradually and unevenly. The controversies that swirled around gender created a sense of immediate and revolutionary change, while the actual changes in historical practices, in fact, proceeded in slower motion: gender and its accompanying methodologies first had to be understood before it could be "adopted" or "applied." Joan Scott's

16. Scott, "Gender: A Useful Category."

17. Ibid., pp. 1066–68.

18. Denise Riley, *Am I That Name? Feminism and the Category of 'Women' in History* (Minneapolis, 1988), pp. 7, 14.

19. Ibid., pp. 4–5.

postulation of gender in terms of the cultural, linguistic, or discursive construction of sexual difference placed gender at the forefront of the debates that raged over the "linguistic turn" in the Anglo-Saxon social sciences during the late 1980s and early 1990s. Lines were drawn between social and cultural history, between disciplinary and interdisciplinary approaches, as historians increasingly turned to philosophy, cultural and symbolic anthropology, or poststructuralist linguistic and literary theory to explore how language constituted, rather than merely reflected, historical change and human consciousness.[20] Still other conflicts turned around the prospect that gender might efface or disempower women as subjects in history, which for many represented the first step towards dismantling feminism as a political project. The destabilization of "women" and the growing emphasis on the relational character of sexual difference made clear that the study of gender would remain one-sided without a serious and systematic examination of masculinity.[21] Soon masculinity became for some the most compelling and least understood facet of gender history, while feminists cautioned that men's history or masculinity studies were merely fashionable refigurings of a very familiar male-dominated history.[22] In the view of its skeptics and opponents, gender history had the potential to write

20. John Toews, "Intellectual History after the Linguistic Turn: The Autonomy of Meaning and the Irreducibility of Experience," *American Historical Review* 92/4 (1987): 879–907.

21. Harry Brod, ed., *The Making of Masculinities: The New Men's Studies* (Boston, 1987); Ute Frevert, "Männergeschichte oder die Suche nach dem 'ersten' Geschlecht," in *Was ist Gesellschaftsgeschichte? Positionen, Themen, Analysen,* ed. M. Hettling, C. Huerkamp, P. Nolte, and H. W. Schmuhl (Munich, 1991), pp. 31–43; Michael Roper and John Tosh, eds., *Manful Assertions: Masculinities in Britain since 1800* (London, 1991); and Michael Kimmel, ed., *Changing Men: New Directions in Research on Men and Masculinity* (Newbury Park, Calif., 1987); R. W. Connell, *Masculinities* (Berkeley, Calif., 1995). Historical studies of masculinity include Robert Nye, *Masculinity and Male Codes of Honor in Modern France* (Oxford, 1993); George L. Mosse, *The Image of Man: The Creation of Modern Masculinity* (Oxford, 1996); and Gail Bederman, *Manliness and Civilization: A Cultural History of Gender and Race in the United States, 1880–1917* (Chicago, 1996); Barbara Evans Clements, Rebecca Friedman, and Dan Healey, eds., *Russian Masculinities in History and Culture* (New York, 2002); Dan Healey, *Homosexual Desire in Revolutionary Russia: The Regulation of Sexual and Gender Dissent* (Chicago, 2001); and Thomas Kühne, *Männergeschichte/Geschlechtergeschichte: Männlichkeit im Wandel der Moderne* (Frankfurt a. M., 1996).

22. Gisela Bock, "Challenging Dichotomies: Perspectives on Women's History," in *Writing Women's History: International Perspectives,* ed. Karen Offen, Ruth Roach Pierson, and Jane Rendall (Bloomington, Ind., 1991). On the place of masculinity in gender history, see

history without social actors or sexual oppression, to produce scholarship without the political vision and commitment that drove the first decades of feminist women's history.[23]

The degree to which gender appeared to threaten the established practices of women's history differed according to its advancement and acceptance across various national or chronological fields. Where women's history was still in an early stage of research or had yet to establish its legitimacy, the arrival of gender appeared to cut short a struggle not yet won and one still worth fighting—to discover the place of women in the definitive events and processes that underpin textbook or mainstream history. Ironically, in some instances those who had long castigated women's history for its preoccupation with "special interests" took a more positive stance towards gender, which emphasized relations between the sexes and a new attention to masculinity. Yet, regardless of the particular reception gender received in individual fields, almost nowhere did the turn to gender actually preclude or undermine the study of women. Most common was perhaps a new coupling of gender *and* women's history, whereby gender signaled the embrace of new methodological approaches to women, who remained the primary objects of study. Gender history became a more theoretically inflected history of female subjects, whereby the process of becoming of a subject itself became part of the investigation. This is still the case today in many fields, whereas in others, the study of gender increasingly encompasses attention to both sexes. These are perhaps the two most familiar faces of gender history today, yet both tasks remain exceedingly difficult to fulfill. Two decades after the first controversies over gender began, "doing gender" is still a highly contextualized practice, inflected by sources and archives, by na-

---

Joy Parr, "Gender History and Historical Practice," *Canadian Historical Review* 76 (1996): 354–76; Lynn Hunt, "The Challenge of Gender: Deconstruction of Categories and Reconstruction of Narratives in Gender History," in *Geschlechtergeschichte und allgemeine Geschichte,* ed. Hans Medick and Ann-Charlott Trepp (Göttingen, 1998), pp. 78–79.

23. Honegger and Arni, *Gender: Die Tücken einer Kategorie,* p. 15. Joan W. Scott, *Gender and the Politics of History* (New York, 1988). See the review of Scott by Claudia Koonz in *Women's Review of Books* 6/4 (1989): 19–20. Also see the forum "Women's History—Gender History: Has Feminist Inquiry Lost its Critical Edge?" in *Journal of Women's History* 5/1 (Spring 1993). Other influential articles on the methodological implications of the "linguistic turn" include Mary Poovey, "Feminism and Deconstruction," *Feminist Studies* 14/1 (Spring 1988): 51–65; Isabel Hull, "Feminist and Gender History Through the Literary Looking Glass: German Historiography in Postmodern Times," and Jane Caplan, "Postmodernism, Poststructuralism, and Deconstruction: Notes for Historians," *Central European History* 22 (1989): 260–78, 279–300.

tional legacies, temporal specificities, and the political valences of the analytical vocabulary it set out to critique.

GENDER AND THE KEYWORDS OF SOCIAL ANALYSIS: CLASS, CITIZENSHIP, CIVIL SOCIETY

Historians of women critically engaged the concept of class almost from the beginning of feminist study of the Industrial Revolution. From the publication of Louise Tilly and Joan Scott's ground-laying *Women, Work, and Family* in 1978, which analyzed men and women's different experiences and interests in the legendary "transition from home to factory," much of the scholarly energy in women's history (through the 1980s) and even in early gender history (in the 1990s) concentrated on studies of work place, family, and workers' movements[24] Over the years nearly every aspect of industrial transformation was rewritten, as feminist historians studied specific industries and regions, producing a wealth of empirical material that changed understandings of skill and sexual divisions of labor, career patterns, productivity, and protest.[25] The cumulative outcome of this scholarship was not a new paradigm for the workings of gender in industrial change, but instead the recognition that sexual divisions of labor emerged from complex interactions of traditions and technologies, of ideologies and imperatives of capital, and were thus highly variable across factories, industries, towns, and regions.[26]

24. Joan W. Scott and Louise Tilly, *Women, Work, and Family* (New York, 1978).

25. Some of the influential studies of the 1980s include: Charles Sowerwine, *Sisters or Citizens? Women and Socialism in France since 1876* (New York, 1982); Patricia Hilden, *Women and Socialist Politics in France, 1880–1914* (New York, 1986); Temma Kaplan, "Female Consciousness and Collective Action: The Case of Barcelona, 1910–18," in *Feminist Theory: A Critique of Ideology,* ed. Nannerl O. Keohane, Michelle Z. Rosaldo, and Barbara C. Gelpi (Chicago, 1981), pp. 55–76; Maxime Berg, *The Age of Manufactures: Industry, Innovation, and Work in Britain, 1700–1820* (Totowa, N.J., 1985); Barbara Franzoi, *At the Very Least She Pays the Rent: Women and German Industrialization, 1871–1914* (Greenwood, Conn., 1985); Gay Gullickson, *Spinners and Weavers of Auffay: Rural Industry and the Sexual Division of Labor in a French Village, 1750–1850* (Cambridge, 1986); Jean H. Quataert, "The Shaping of Women's Work in Manufacturing: Guilds, Households, and the State in Central Europe, 1648–1870," *American Historical Review* 90 (December 1985): 1122–48; Judy Lown, *Women and Industrialization: Gender at Work in Nineteenth-Century England* (Cambridge, 1990); and Barbara Evans Clements, Barbara Alpern Engel, and Christine D. Worobec, eds., *Russia's Women: Accommodation, Resistance, Transformation* (Berkeley, Calif., 1990).

26. Joy Parr, "Disaggregating the Sexual Division of Labour: A Transatlantic Case Study," *Comparative Study of Society and History* 30/2 (1988): 511–12. Parr's synthesis shows

While early studies of women's work often tried to fit female subjects into existing categories of social analysis, the turn to gender prompted more fundamental critiques and redefinitions of the keywords of social analysis. The notion of class, for example, was at the heart of debates about both gender and the linguistic turn, leading some feminist scholars to call for an emancipation from class as a "privileged signifier of social relations and their political representations," while others approached both middle-class and working-class formation as processes of differentiation in which gender was always centrally implicated.[27] Eschewing models of class formation that posited causal links among economic, social, cultural, and political levels or stages of development, historians of gender and class approached class as a political language, the meanings of which were contested across the lines of race, ethnicity, nationality, and generation.[28] The vocabulary of class had rather different meanings in the study of bourgeois or middle-class formation. Middle "class" was a notably more fluid and culturally-inflected category than working-class, which despite the powerful influence of E. P. Thompson's study of the cultural making of the working class, remained tied to material structures and relations of production. At the heart of the exploration of the history of the middle classes, then, were the practices of consumption, the ideology of domesticity, and the meanings of religion and ethnicity in shaping "home and hearth," each of which more centrally implicated gender than the categories of labor history.[29]

———

that jobs that were "clearly and exclusively women's work in one factory, town or region may be just as exclusively men's work in another factory, town or region."

27. Sally Alexander, "Women, Class, and Sexual Differences in the 1830s and 1840s: Some Reflections on the Writing of a Feminist History," *History Workshop* 17 (Spring 1984): 125– 149. Exemplary studies here are Leonore Davidoff and Catherine Hall, *Family Fortunes: Men and Women of the English Middle Class, 1780–1950* (Chicago, 1987), and Anna Clark, *The Struggle for the Breeches: Gender and the Making of the British Working Class* (Berkeley, Calif., 1995).

28. Joan W. Scott, "On Language, Gender, and Working-Class History," *International Labor and Working-Class History,* no. 31 (Spring 1987): 1–36; William H. Sewell, Jr., "How Classes are Made: Critical Reflections on E. P. Thompson's Theory of Working-Class Formation," in *E. P. Thompson: Critical Perspectives,* ed. Harvey Kaye and Keith McClelland (Philadelphia, 1990), pp. 50–77; Ava Baron, ed., *Work Engendered: Toward a New History of American Labor* (Ithaca, N.Y., 1991); Laura Levine Frader and Sonya O. Rose, eds., *Gender and Class in Modern Europe* (Ithaca, N.Y., 1996); and Kathleen Canning, "Gender and the Politics of Class Formation: Rethinking German Labor History," *American Historical Review* 97/3 (1992): 736–68.

29. The works that defined this field include Martha Vicinus, *Suffer and Be Still; Women*

Critical feminist studies of gender and class had an important role in undermining the "materialist presumptions" of class as an analytical category and of labor history as a scholarly practice. Although historical interest in labor, workers, and class appeared to wane at the end of the 1980s, a wave of studies on gender and labor in Europe and North America not only revived this field during the 1990s, but pushed labor into arenas well beyond the shop floor with analysis of such related thematics as bodies and hygiene, consumption and leisure, and welfare and citizenship, to name a few.[30] This new scholarship on

---

in the Victorian Age (Bloomington, IN, 1972); Carol Christ, "Victorian Masculinity and the Angel in the House," in A Widening Sphere: Changing Roles of Victorian Women, ed. Martha Vicinus (Bloomington, IN, 1977); Bonnie G. Smith, Ladies of the Leisure Class: The Bourgeoisie of Northern France in the Nineteenth Century (Princeton, 1981); Karin Hausen, "Family and Role-Division: The Polarisation of Sexual Stereotypes in the Nineteenth Century," in The German Family, ed. Richard J. Evans and W. R. Lee (London, N.J., 1981), and Barbara Alpern Engel, Mothers and Daughters: Women of the Intelligentsia in Nineteenth-Century Russia (Cambridge, 1983). A second wave of innovative studies include Davidoff and Hall, Family Fortunes; Jane Lewis, ed., Labour and Love: Women's Experience of Home and Family, 1850–1940 (London, 1986); Ruth-Ellen B. Joeres and Mary Jo Maynes, eds., German Women in the Eighteenth and Nineteenth Centuries: A Social and Literary History (Bloomington, IN, 1986); Nancy Armstrong, Desire and Domestic Fiction: A Political History of the Novel (New York, 1987); Mary Poovey, Uneven Developments: The Ideological Work of Gender (Chicago, 1988); Ute Frevert, ed., Bürgerinnen und Bürger: Geschlechter-Verhältnisse im 19. Jahrhundert (Göttingen, 1988); Marion A. Kaplan, The Making of the Jewish Middle Class: Women, Family, and Identity in Imperial Germany (New York, 1991); and Catherine Hall, White, Male, and Middle-Class: Explorations in Feminism and History (Cambridge, 1992). Also see Judith L. Newton, "History as Usual? Feminism and the 'New Historicism,'" in The New Historicism, ed. H. Aram Veeser (New York, 1989), pp. 152–67.

30. See, for example, Sonya O. Rose, Limited Livelihoods: Gender and Class in Nineteenth-Century England (Berkeley, Calif., 1992); Deborah Valenze, The First Industrial Woman (Oxford, 1994); Tessie Liu, The Weaver's Knot: The Contradictions of Class Struggle and Family Solidarity in Western France, 1750–1914 (Ithaca, N.Y., 1994); Barbara Alpern Engel, Between the Fields and the City: Women, Work, and Family in Russia, 1861–1914 (Cambridge, 1994); Laura Lee Downs, Manufacturing Inequality: Gender Division in the French and British Metalworking Industries, 1914–39 (Ithaca, N.Y., 1995); Clark, The Struggle for the Breeches; Judith Coffin, The Politics of Women's Work: The Paris Garment Trades, 1750–1915 (Princeton, N.J., 1996); Kathleen Canning, Languages of Labor and Gender: Female Factory Work in Germany, 1850–1914 (Ithaca, N.Y., 1996); Frader and Rose, Gender and Class in Modern Europe; and Nancy L. Green, Ready-to-Wear and Ready-to-Work: A Century of Industry and Immigrants in Paris and New York (Durham, N.C., 1997); Clare H. Crowston, Fabricating Women: The Seamstresses of Old Regime France, 1675–1791 (Durham, N.C.,

labor and class flourished, as it took up the challenges of the linguistic turn, seeking to explore empirically the criss-crossing of ideologies and experience, of discourses and material transformations, in shaping sexual difference in the realms of waged work. Fifteen years later, the concept of class remains salient for feminist history, but it no longer occupies the definitive place it once did in the analysis of social identities. It figures instead as one among several key social categories and identities, including race, ethnicity, sexuality, and generation, which inform and shape one another in ways that are always contingent and historically specific.[31]

Scholars of gender have also contributed importantly in recent years to rethinking keywords like "public sphere," "civil society," and "citizenship."[32] Just as class took shape within the socio-economic structures of capitalism, the frameworks for the exploration of citizenship were the legal and constitutional grids of nations, republics, and democracies. Studies of citizenship and gender may overlap or rely analytically on the study of the nation and nationalism, while examinations of citizenship in terms of rights, duties, and claims of individuals or collectivities in relation to states are more likely contiguous with histories of civil societies and public spheres. Much of critical feminist theoretical work on citizenship was aimed at T. H. Marshall's classic model of citizenship in Western democracies, formulated half a century ago, which posits the progressive acquisition of citizenship rights, parallel to the advance of modernity. So the eighteenth century was marked by advances in civil rights, the nineteenth by the acquisition of political rights, and the rise of twentieth-

---

2001). Also see Barbara Hanawalt, Thomas Dublin, E. Patricia Tsurumi, and Louise A. Tilly, "*Women, Work, and Family* after Two Decades," *Journal of Women's History* 11/3 (Autumn 1999): 17–30.

31. Joan W. Scott, "The 'Class' We Have Lost," *International Labor and Working-Class History,* no. 57 (Spring 2000): 69–75 (reply to Geoff Eley and Keith Nield, "Farewell to the Working Class?" ibid., pp. 1–30).

32. On gender and the public sphere, see the essays by Nancy Fraser, "Rethinking the Public Sphere: A Contribution the Critique of Actually Existing Democracy," and Mary P. Ryan, "Gender and Public Access: Women's Politics in Nineteenth-Century America," in *Habermas and the Public Sphere,* ed. Craig Calhoun (Cambridge, MA, 1992), pp. 109–42, 259–88; see also Judith Walkowitz, *City of Dreadful Delight: Narratives of Sexual Danger in Late-Victorian London* (Chicago, 1992). Joan Landes, *Women and the Public Sphere in the Age of the French Revolution* (Berkeley, Calif., 1992), sparked many of the initial debates about civil society and gender. The most notable texts on civil society include Carole Pateman, *The Sexual Contract* (Stanford, Calif., 1988) and Isabel V. Hull, *Sexuality, State, and Civil Society in Germany, 1700–1815* (Ithaca, N.Y., 1996).

century welfare states by the expansion of rights of social citizenship.[33] This linear trajectory was based on the presumption of white men's progress toward full citizenship in republican democracies. and failed to consider, as feminists pointed out, the differential experiences of women, ethnic and racial minorities, or colonial subjects, for whom social citizenship in the form of state protection or welfare benefits often preceded the acquisition of political rights.[34]

The main impulse of feminist critiques of citizenship, as in the case of class, has been to critique and dismantle existing categories rather than to assemble alternative paradigms or models.[35] They have thus excavated the contradictions between universalism and particularism, freedom and order, individual rights and collective responsibilities, identity and difference, nation and individual.[36] Probing the boundaries of belonging, the entitlements and exclusions that are inherent in citizenship, feminist scholars have differentiated between citizenship as legal status and as lived practice, and have emphasized the fact that not only formal citizens, but also those excluded from citizenship rights take up languages of citizenship in order to stake claims upon states.[37] Ex-

33. T. H. Marshall with T. Bottomore, *Citizenship and Social Class* (London, 1992).

34. Feminist critiques include Ruth Lister, *Citizenship: Feminist Perspectives* (New York, 1997); Sylvia Walby, "Is Citizenship Gendered?" *Sociology* 28/2 (May 1994): 379–95; Pnina Werbner and Nira Yuval-Davis, eds., *Citizenship: Pushing the Boundaries,* special issue of *Feminist Review* 57(Autumn 1997).

35. On the difference between citizenship as status and as practice, see Ruth Lister, "Citizenship: Towards a Feminist Synthesis," in *Citizenship: Pushing the Boundaries,* ed. Werbner and Yuval-Davis, pp. 28–48. Also see Gisela Bock and Susan James, eds., *Beyond Equality and Difference: Citizenship, Feminist Politics, and Female Subjectivity* (London, 1992).

36. The classic essay in this regard is Iris Marion Young, "Polity and Group Difference: A Critique of the Ideal of Universal Citizenship," in *The Citizenship Debates: A Reader,* ed. Gershon Shafir (Minneapolis, 1998), pp. 263–90. Also see Uday Mehta, "Liberal Strategies of Exclusion," in *Tensions of Empire: Colonial Cultures in a Bourgeois World,* ed. Frederick Cooper and Ann Stoler (Berkeley, Calif., 1997), pp. 59–86.

37. See Kathleen Canning and Sonya O. Rose, "Gender, Citizenships, and Subjectivities: Some Historical and Theoretical Considerations," in *Gender, Citizenships, and Subjectivities,* ed. Kathleen Canning and Sonya O. Rose (London, 2002), pp. 1–17, first published as a special issue of *Gender & History* 13/3 (November 2001). Examples of recent empirical historical research on women, gender, and citizenship include Linda Kerber, "The Meanings of Citizenship," *Journal of American History* 84/3 (December 1997): 833–54; Nancy Cott, "Marriage and Women's Citizenship in the United States, 1830–1934," *American Historical Review* 103/5 (December 1998): 1440–74; William H. Sewell, Jr., "Le citoyen/la citoyenne: Activity, Passivity, and the Revolutionary Concept of Citizenship," in *The French Revolution and the Creation of Modern Political Culture,* vol. 2: *Political Culture of the French*

panding the notion of citizenship to encompass "a politics of desire," feminist scholars have underscored that citizenship is more than a legal or national category of belonging, but also a subject position that "encapsulates specific, historically inflected, cultural and social assumptions about similarity and difference."[38]

One significant outcome of critical feminist thinking on citizenship and its spatial location in civil societies and public spheres is the critical analysis and ultimate rejection of the presumed opposition between private and public spheres which was at the core of both liberal and republican traditions of political thought. For "public" had usually designated a "realm of homogeneity and universality,"[39] of "the people as a whole," while "private" was signified as a closed and exclusive site of difference, particularity, even inequality.[40] Practitioners of women's history had early on found the distinction between private and public useful: first in establishing the importance of women's "private lives," of marriage, family, and motherhood as formative of female identities and worthy objects of historical research, and then in identifying the potential for women to wield power and influence within female "separate spheres."[41]

Revolution, ed. Colin Lucas (Oxford, 1988), pp. 105 23. Also see Sonya O. Rose, Which People's War? National Identity and Citizenship in Wartime Britain, 1939–1945 (Oxford, 2003); and Laura Nym Mayhall, The Militant Suffrage Movement: Citizenship and Resistance in Britain, 1860–1930 (Oxford, 2003).

38. Werbner and Yuval-Davis, introduction to Women, Citizenship, and Difference, pp. 2–3. Also see Canning and Rose, introduction to Gender, Citizenships, and Subjectivities, pp. 6–7; and Barbara Hobson, ed., Gender and Citizenship in Transition (London, 2000).

39. Chantal Mouffe, "Feminism, Citizenship, and Radical Democratic Politics," in Feminists Theorize the Political, ed. Judith Butler and Joan W. Scott (New York, 1992), pp. 379–80; and Anne Phillips, "Citizenship and Feminist Theory," in Citizenship, ed. Geoff Andrews (London, 1991).

40. Joan Landes, introduction to Feminism, the Public and the Private, ed. Joan Landes (Oxford, 1998), pp. 1–2.

41. Leonore Davidoff, "Gender and the 'Great Divide': Public and Private in British Gender History," Journal of Women's History 15/1 (Spring 2003): 11–27; Leonore Davidoff, "Regarding Some 'Old Husbands' Tales': Public and Private in Feminist History," in Worlds Between: Historical Perspectives on Gender and Class (Cambridge, 1995); and Jane Rendall, "Women and the Public Sphere," in Gender & History: Retrospect and Prospect, ed. Leonore Davidoff, Keith McClelland, and Eleni Varikas (Oxford, 2000), pp. 57–70. The legendary article on the power of women within their separate sphere is Carroll Smith-Rosenberg, "The Female World of Love and Ritual: Relations between Women in Nineteenth-Century America," Signs 1/1 (1975): 1–29. Also see the forum on this article, "Women's History in

Yet public/private quickly became a kind of master trope, by which other oppositions, such as home/work (in histories of the middle classes), family and factory (in studies of laboring women) or home and world (in histories of colonialism and empire) came to be figured as mere variations of a gendered fault line of public/private that ran through the history of the West. Underlining this trope was a pronounced tendency to understand public and private as distinct spatial domains, starkly divided along gender lines, so that male authority and influence were situated exclusively in the public sphere, while the private sphere of family and household was the only conceivable site of female agency or power.[42]

Public/private became one of the keywords in feminist debates of the 1980s and 1990s, as historians and political theorists began to distinguish between the normative or ideological notions of public and private and the ways each was experienced by citizens of past and present. Critical feminist engagement with these terms intensified with the publication of Jürgen Habermas's *The Structural Transformation of the Public Sphere* in English in 1989, as feminist critics from an array of disciplines responded vigorously to Habermas's notion of a bourgeois public sphere, constituted through rational communicative behavior among private individuals whose shared interests (rather than differences of gender, class, or ethnicity) prompted them to join together to form a public in order to assert these interests vis-à-vis the state.[43] Habermas's emphasis on *common* rather than *discrepant* interests as formative of the public sphere, his presumption of rational discourse as the mode of articulation of these interests, disregarded conflicts between multiple or competing publics or the possible mobilization of "subaltern counterpublics," for example, of women who "constructed access routes to public political life despite their exclusion from the official public sphere" in nineteenth-century North America.[44] The partic-

———
the New Millennium: Carroll Smith-Rosenberg's 'The Female World of Love and Ritual' after Twenty-Five Years," with contributions by Molly McGarry, Kanchana Natarajan, Dása Francíková, Tania Navarro Swain, and Karin Lützen, in *Journal of Women's History* 12/3 (Autumn 2000): 8–38.

42. Davidoff, "Gender and the 'Great Divide,'" pp. 13–16; Sandra Lauderdale Graham, "Making the Private Public: A Brazilian Perspective," *Journal of Women's History* 15/1 (Spring 2003): 28–42.

43. Jürgen Habermas, *The Structural Transformation of the Public Sphere: An Inquiry into a Category of Bourgeois Society,* trans. Thomas Burger with Frederick Lawrence (Cambridge, Mass., 1989).

44. See Seyla Benhabib, "Models of Public Space: Hannah Arendt, the Liberal Tradition, and Jürgen Habermas"; Nancy Fraser, "Rethinking the Public Sphere: A Contribu-

ular meanings Habermas assigned to the public/private dichotomy "imposed a neutralizing logic" on identities of difference "by establishing qualifications for publicness as a matter of abstraction from private identity."[45] In response to Habermas, feminists posited the fundamental inextricability of public and private life-worlds, tracing the multiple lines of difference that divided public spheres, and probing the relations of power that enabled and authorized the very designation or division between public and private.[46]

Another strand of this debate turned around the political philosophy of the Enlightenment, the inception of civil society, and its particular manifestations in revolutionary France. Redefining the Rousseauian social contract as a "sexual contract," the political scientist Carole Pateman posited civil society as a patriarchal or masculine order, the key features of which—freedom, equality, reason, and contract—"encapsulate all that women lack." The rise of the civil demarcated a new space, a "private world of particularity, natural subjection, ties of blood, emotion, love and sexual passion," inhabited by women but ruled by men.[47] While feminist political theorists sought to establish public/private as an ideological rather than spatial divide, feminist historians delivered numerous examples of the proliferation of publics into which women could and did "venture with varying shades of gender connotation."[48] So scholars of the Enlightenment and French Revolution attested to women's vibrant presence in the marches to Versailles or in the storming of the Bastille, to their adoption of the symbols of the republic, culminating in the impassioned evocation of female citizenship in Olympe de Gouges' "Declaration of the Rights of

———

tion to the Critique of Actually Existing Democracy"; Mary P. Ryan, "Gender and Public Access: Women's Politics in Nineteenth-Century America"; and Geoff Eley, "Nations, Publics, and Political Cultures: Placing Habermas in the Nineteenth Century," in *Habermas and the Public Sphere,* ed. Craig Calhoun (Cambridge, Mass., 1992), pp. 73–98, 109–42, 259–88, 289–339.

45. Craig Calhoun, "Habermas and the Public Sphere," in *Habermas and the Public Sphere,* p. 35. Also see the definitive article by Dena Goodman, "Public Sphere and Private Life: Towards a Synthesis of Current Historiographical Approaches to the Old Regime," *History and Theory* 31/1 (1992): 1–20.

46. Nancy Fraser, "Sex, Lies, and the Public Sphere: Reflections on the Confirmation of Clarence Thomas," in Landes, *Feminism, the Public and the Private.* In her introduction Landes offers a helpful summary of Fraser's important point that "some have more power than others to draw and defend the line" between public and private (pp. 3, 11).

47. Pateman, *The Sexual Contract,* pp. 10–11. Also see Pateman, "The Fraternal Social Contract," in *Civil Society and the State,* ed. John Keane (London, 1988), pp. 101–28.

48. Davidoff, "Gender and the 'Great Divide,'" p. 19.

Women."[49] Although women were a vital force in discrediting and dismantling the Old Regime, the work of the next phase—the crafting of civil society and the revolutionary republic—began with the rhetorical, and then the juridical, removal of women from the sphere of citizenship.[50] The subordination of women, their relegation to the ranks of passive citizenship, was a common feature of early republican politics, which Joan Landes contends not only took shape in the absence of women, but more fundamentally excluded the possibility of women's participation.[51] The activities of women on both the intellectual and the political fronts of the French Revolution, and the recurrent public conflicts over gendered rights, boundaries, and citizenship claims has rendered this historical episode the case study par excellence for the gendering of civil society and the inextricability of public and private.

While public garnered the most attention from political theorists, historians also investigated the so-called private practices within marriage, family, household, and associational networks, examining the salience of the private for male historical actors and exploring how these customs situated individuals and families in exchanges of capital and goods, in processes of class formation, and in the expansion of state power in metropoles and empires.[52] As public spheres and private domains came under increasingly empirical scrutiny by historians, the Victorian model of separate spheres, which had gained iconic status through studies of middle-class domesticity and class formation in Britain and North America, was recognized as only one variation of many possible public/private distinctions rather than a prescriptive or repre-

49. Joan W. Scott, "French Feminists and the Rights of 'Man': Olympe de Gouge's Declarations," *History Workshop* 28 (Autumn 1989): 1–21.

50. Harriet Applewhite and Darlene Levy, *Women and Politics in the Age of the Democratic Revolution* (Ann Arbor, Mich., 1990); Carol Blum, *Rousseau and the Republic of Virtue: The Language of Politics in the French Revolution* (Ithaca, N.Y., 1986); Dorinda Outram, *The Body and the French Revolution: Sex, Class, and Political Culture* (New Haven, Conn., 1989); Dominique Godineau, *The Women of Paris and Their French Revolution*, trans. Katherine Streip (Berkeley, Calif., 1998), first published in French as *Citoyennes tricoteuses: Les femmes du peuple à Paris pendant la Révolution française* (Aix-en-Provence, 1988).

51. Landes, *Women and the Public Sphere*. Also see her more recent book *Visualizing the Nation: Gender, Representation, and Revolution in Eighteenth-Century France* (Ithaca, N.Y., 2001).

52. See, for example, Davidoff and Hall, *Family Fortunes;* and Amanda Vickery, "Golden Age to Separate Spheres? A Review of the Categories and Chronology of English Women's History," *Historical Journal* 36/2 (1993): 383–414.

sentative model that could be generalized to other historical settings[53] Recognizing the historical specificity of public/private distinctions and their normative/ideological character has enabled recognition that public and private, like class and citizenship, are part of the lexicon of historical actors in some of our studies and as such, deserve attention and analysis. Breaking apart the sense of spatial realms, divided and dichotomized along gendered lines, allows us to take up Elizabeth Thompson's call to engage in a "more extensive experimentation with public and private as *lenses* of historical analysis" by interrogating these terms in "local historical contexts" and undertaking transnational comparisons in new terms that do not presume the prevalence of one or the other particular model.[54]

GENDER, SEXUALITIES, BODIES

In addition to critiquing and dismantling keywords of historical analysis like class, citizenship, and experience, the theoretical impulses associated with gender history sharpened the distinctions among and between gender, body, and sexuality. Sexuality and body, once regarded as the material or natural foundation of "woman," gained an analytical status of their own, separate from a presumed biology of the sexes, in the course of the paradigm shift from women to gender. While *sexual systems*—heterosexual, homosexual, bisexual, or transsexual—indisputably inflect and produce *gender*, feminist scholarship on sexuality has categorically rejected simplistic dyads by which sexuality is a phenomenon of nature, biology, or body, and gender a contingent cultural construct.[55] Although the gender/sex binary is no longer tenable, sexuality, body, and gender remain difficult to disentangle from one another in certain areas of inquiry, such as studies of prostitution,[56] where representations of gen-

53. Elizabeth Thompson, "Public and Private in Middle Eastern Women's History," *Journal of Women's History* 15/1 (Spring 2003): 52–68; Graham, "Making the Private Public"; and Mary P. Ryan, "The Public and the Private Good: Across the Divide in Women's History," *Journal of Women's History* 15/1 (Spring 2003): 14–15.

54. Thompson, "Public and Private in Middle Eastern History," p. 52; and Ryan, "The Public and the Private Good," p. 14.

55. See, for example, Judith Halberstam, *Female Masculinity* (Durham, N.C., 1998) and Jay Prosser, *Second Skins: The Body Narratives of Transsexuality* (New York, 1998).

56. Older histories of prostitution, in which state regulation of women is a central concern, include Judith R. Walkowitz, *Prostitution and Victorian Society: Women, Class, and the State* (New York, 1980); and Mary Gibson, *Prostitution and the State in Italy, 1860–1915* (New Brunswick, N.J., 1986). For more explicit attention to sexuality, see Alan Corbin,

der or race aim to regulate sexual identities or disseminate assumptions regarding normal and abnormal bodies.[57] Nonetheless I will offer brief suggestions here of how sexuality and body have been delineated from gender.

Sexuality, like body, is a concept that has been debated across disciplines; its study usually involves the consideration of both pleasure/desire and physiology as constitutive of erotic relations, so sexuality is shaped in both "the realm of the psyche and the material world."[58] In a classic essay of 1975, "Traffic in Women," the anthropologist Gayle Rubin pointed out that "human sexual life ... will never be completely 'natural,' if only because our species is social, cultural, and articulate."[59] Rubin's analysis emphasized the particular ways in which sexuality worked in fundamental social structures, such as kinship systems, to effect the subordination of women. The feminist philosopher Judith Butler has considered the prospect of a "radical discontinuity between sexed bodies and culturally constructed genders," by which ". . . *man* and *masculine* might just as easily signify a female body as a male one, and *woman* and *feminine* a male body as easily as a female one."[60]

In scholarship of the last decade sexuality encompasses sexual activity—*having sex*—as well as the phenomenon of having a sex or inhabiting a *body that is sexed,* whereby the dichotomy between male/female, homosexual/het-

Women for Hire: Prostitution and Sexuality in France after 1850 (Cambridge, Mass. 1996); and outside of the field of European history, the excellent studies by Luise White, *The Comforts of Home: Prostitution in Colonial Nairobi* (Chicago, 1990); and Gail Hershatter, *Dangerous Pleasures: Prostitution and Modernity in Twentieth-Century Shanghai* (Berkeley, Calif., 1997).

57. Two examples in which this kind of imbrication of sexuality, body, and gender is already indicated in the titles, are Jill Matus, *Unstable Bodies: Victorian Representations of Sexuality and Maternity* (Manchester, 1995); and Prosser, *Second Skins.* An older example might be Leonore Davidoff's field-defining article on Arthur Mumby and his servant/wife, Hannah: "Class and Gender in Victorian England," in Newton et al., *Sex and Class in Women's History,* pp. 17–71.

58. Quotations here are from Joseph Bristow, *Sexuality* (London, 1997), pp. 2–5. Also see David M. Halperin, "Is There a History of Sexuality?" in *The Lesbian and Gay Studies Reader,* ed. Henry Abelove, Michele Aina Barale, and David M. Halperin (New York, 1993), pp. 416–31. Also see Franz X. Eder, Lesley A. Hall, and Gert Hekma, eds., *Sexual Cultures in Europe,* vol. 1: *National Histories,* vol. 2: *Themes in Sexuality* (Manchester, 1999).

59. Rubin, "The Traffic in Women," p. 137.

60. Judith Butler, "Subjects of Sex/Gender/Desire," chap. 1 of *Gender Trouble: Feminism and the Subversion of Identity* (London, 1990), reprinted in *Feminism and Politics,* ed. Anne Phillips (Oxford, 1998), p. 279.

erosexual *sexed beings* has been complicated by increasing attention to bisexuality and transsexuality. Influenced by Michel Foucault's *History of Sexuality,* scholars in an array of disciplines probed the production of sexual behaviors, characteristics, and types in the domains of medicine, moral philosophy, and social reform.[61] Sexualities were discursively constituted, for example, with the advent of late nineteenth-century sexology, which scientized notions of normality and deviance, while feminist studies and Queer Studies have been particularly interested in the experiences, performances, and subversions of sexualities.[62] Scholars of race, nation, and empire have argued that sexuality, as "the most salient marker of Otherness," is intrinsic to *any* racist ideology and to the definition and enforcement of racial boundaries. On slave plantations and in colonies sexuality was racially embedded in the sense that "'the sex act itself served as a ritualistic reenactment of the daily pattern of social dominance.'"[63]

Following upon and advancing the deconstructive impulse that the term "gender" once unleashed upon the master narratives of Western history, attention to sexuality has highlighted previously neglected dimensions in the history of civil society and the public sphere. Isabel Hull's study of *Sexuality, State and Civil Society in Germany* is exemplary in its analysis of the specific kind of publicity/publicness that drove the emergence of German civil society, namely the mobilization of male experts who honed their role as "practitioners of civil society" through the creation of a "modern sexual system" that formed when citizens qualified themselves (and thus displaced state and religious bodies) as regulators and codifiers of sexual behavior. Civil society and citizenship, then,

61. Michel Foucault, *The History of Sexuality,* trans. Robert Hurley (New York, 1986); Halperin, "Is There a History of Sexuality?"; Bristow, *Sexuality.* Also see Frank Mort, *Dangerous Sexualities: Medico-Moral Politics in England since 1830* (London, 1987); Jeffrey Weeks, *Sexuality and Its Discontents: Meanings, Myths, and Modern Sexualities* (London, 1983); Angus McLaren, *Twentieth-Century Sexuality: A History* (Oxford, 1999); Roy Porter and Mikulás Teich, eds., *Sexual Knowledge, Sexual Science: The History of Attitudes to Sexuality* (Cambridge, 1994); Carolyn Dean, *Sexuality and Modern Western Culture* (New York, 1996); and Robert Nye, *Sexuality* (Oxford, 1999).

62. See for example Laura Engelstein, *The Keys to Happiness: Sex and the Search for Modernity in Fin-de-Siècle Russia* (Ithaca, N.Y., 1993); and Dan Healey, *Homosexual Desire in Revolutionary Russia: The Regulation of Sexual and Gender Dissent* (Chicago, 2001).

63. Ann Laura Stoler, "Carnal Knowledge and Imperial Power: Gender, Race, and Morality in Colonial Asia," in Scott, *Feminism and History,* pp. 214–15. Stoler cites Sander Gilman, *Difference and Pathology: Stereotypes of Sexuality, Race, and Madness* (Ithaca, N.Y., 1985), p. 25.

both indisputably male in this case, coalesced around debates on the pleasures and dangers of sex in early nineteenth-century Germany.[64]

Recent scholarship in the field of Queer Studies both recognizes the sexual oppression of heterosexual dominance, yet at the same time understands sexuality as a realm of infinite possibilities and pleasures, constituted not least by desire. Histories of homosexualities, viewed by many as the site of the most "energetic and ambitious work on sexual relations," have similarly revealed the variable meanings of same-sex relationships across disparate historical periods. The more radical contention of scholars in the field of Queer Studies has been to presume a diversity of sexual types that defies categorizations or that suggests that "sexuality itself should no longer be seen as an unified term."[65] Others have emphasized the fluid and contingent definitions of both homosexual and heterosexual sexual behaviors and the tenuous delineations between sexual and social interplay. Early modern historians in particular have shown that homosexuality is not confined or fixed in one social or discursive space, but constructed and contested across distinctions of social status, religion, politics, ethnicity, and locality.[66] The impact of Judith Butler's interventions, by contrast, has been a sharper distinction between homosexualities and hegemonic heterosexuality, which she regards as "intrinsic" to the construction and enforcement of gender difference.[67] Certainly the history of homosexualities constitutes one field in which gender, sexuality, and body may remain entwined, but for the most part the history of women is no longer in the foreground.[68]

64. Hull, *Sexuality, State and Civil Society.* For a different exploration of how sexuality informs "high politics" see Anna Clark, *Scandal: The Sexual Politics of the British Constitution* (Princeton, N.J., 2004).

65. See the helpful review essay by John Kucich, "Heterosexuality Obscured," *Victorian Studies* 40/3 (Spring 1997): 475–77. Also see Stephen O. Murray, *Homosexualities* (Chicago, 2000); and the review essay by Dan Healey, "(Homo)sex in the City Only? Finding Continuity and Change in the Gay Past," *Gender & History* 16/1 (April 2004): 198–204.

66. Helmut Puff, "Männergeschichten/Frauengeschichten: Über den Nutzen einer Geschichte der Homosexualität," in Medick and Trepp, *Geschlechtergeschichte und allgemeine Geschichte,* pp. 160–61. Also see David Halperin, "How to Do the History of Male Homosexuality," in *Gay and Lesbian Quarterly* 6/1 (2000): 87–124; Robert G. Moeller, "The Homosexual Man Is a 'Man,' the Homosexual Woman Is a 'Woman': Sex, Society, and the Law in Postwar West Germany," *Journal of the History of Sexuality* 4/3 (January 1994): 395–429; Victoria Thompson, "Creating Boundaries: Homosexuality and the Changing Social Order in France, 1830–70," in Scott, *Feminism and History,* pp. 398–428.

67. Kucich, "Heterosexuality Obscured," pp. 475–76. Also see Lisa Duggan, "The Theory Wars, or Who's Afraid of Judith Butler?" *Journal of Women's History* 10/1 (1998).

68. One striking example is Lisa Duggan, *Sapphic Slashers: Sex, Violence, and American*

Of all of the concepts in the toolbox of gender history, "body" was perhaps the most closely bound to biologism and essentialism: in early Women's Studies, the female body constituted the basis for the shared experiences and identities of "women." The work of "making women visible" in history imparted a certain hegemony to the materiality of female bodies—the experiences of pain, trauma, and pleasure that had been effaced in previous history. The study of sexualities also presumed the existence of a sexed body as a physical, tangible location of sex before the linguistic turn began to force these terms apart.[69] The "discursivation" of the body, which took place in the course of the linguistic turn, not only detached the body from unchanging notions of sexual difference, but also cast it as a site of inscription—of disciplinary measures, discourses, medical norms and pathologies—and thus as an instrument of variable cultural meanings.[70] The liveliest debates about the analytical status of body took place in literary studies or philosophy, while in the field of modern history bodies were most frequently studied by historians of science and medicine.[71] While the advent of the discursive body delivered the final blow to biological determinism, it left unsettled the thorny issue of the body's materiality. Many who readily conceded that bodies were constituted through webs of discourses or were only knowable through language nonetheless sought to grasp that very process of mediation, the positioning of bodies in discourses, of selves in bodies. Some remained perplexed by the unspeakability of bodily experiences that marked and transformed bodies in times of crisis—war, maiming, torture, sexual violence—and in the more everyday arenas of bodily trauma, such as pregnancy and childbirth or injury and invalidity in the workplace, and sought to consider how gender inflected the process by which bod-

---

Modernity (Durham, N.C., 2000). Also see Nan Enstad, "Partners in Crime? Writing the Social History of Women and the Poststructural History of Gender," *Journal of Women's History* 14/3 (Autumn 2002): 177–82.

69. An influential book in this regard is Thomas Laqueur, *Making Sex: Body and Gender from the Greeks to Freud* (Cambridge, Mass., 1990).

70. Judith Butler, *Bodies That Matter: On the Discursive Limits of "Sex"* (London, 1993), especially the introduction.

71. At the same time the body had different resonances across disciplines and historical periods. See the article by Caroline Bynum, "Why All the Fuss about the Body? A Medievalist's Perspective," *Critical Inquiry* 22 (1995): 1–33; also see Londa Schiebinger, *The Mind Has No Sex? Women in the Origins of Modern Science* (Cambridge, Mass., 1989) and *Nature's Body: Gender in the Making of Modern Science* (Boston, 1993). Also see Colin Blakemore and Sheila Jennett, eds., *The Oxford Companion to the Body* (Oxford, 2001).

ies became discursively constituted. Taken less abstractly, this formula called for reflection on the ways in which differently gendered subjects read/heard/accessed/made/participated in/transformed discourses as they experienced and tried to make sense of their bodily experiences. The notion of *embodiment,* explored in recent years most fruitfully by feminist philosophers, helped to overcome the posited opposition between discourse and materiality in the history of bodies, shifting attention to the assignment of meanings to bodies by subjects.[72]

In the discipline of history the body gained a startling new presence in the 1990s, but few of these studies were informed by the theoretical debates about body/bodies taking place in other disciplines. Perhaps that is why the titles and book jackets of so many recent studies let the body stand in, often uneasily, for sexuality, reproduction, or more generally for gender, without distinguishing explicitly between them or making clear the ways in which they might inform one another. In the last decade histories of the body have most often studied the "body politics" of states and the milieus of social reform, moral reform, and medicine-hygiene-eugenics. Yet in many cases "body politics" are nearly indistinguishable from "sexual politics," for example when institutions of power seek to regulate individual bodies and to enforce codes that inhibit realms of illicit sexual activity, such as prostitution, illegitimate birth, birth control, or abortion.[73] Cultural histories of the body have examined its significance as a symbol for nation, ethnicity, or race, or as a metaphor for modernity, although the dissemination of these symbolic bodies through society remains difficult to trace.[74]

The history of bodily experiences represents an area in which research is far from abundant, not least because the sources most historians rely upon seldom

72. See Moira Gatens, *Imaginary Bodies: Ethics, Power, and Corporeality* (London, 1996); Elizabeth Grosz, *Volatile Bodies: Toward a Corporeal Feminism* (Bloomington, Ind., 1994); and Londa Schiebinger, ed., *Feminism and the Body* (Oxford, 2000). Diverse approaches to body histories are provided by Thomas Laqueur and Catherine Gallagher, eds., *The Making of the Modern Body: Sexuality and Society in the Nineteenth Century,* special issue of *Representations* 4 (Spring 1986); and Michael Feher with Ramona Nadoff and Nadia Tazi, eds., *Fragments for a History of the Human Body,* 3 vols. (New York, 1989–91).

73. Excellent books on body politics include Cornelie Usborne, *The Politics of the Body in Weimar Germany* (Ann Arbor, Mich., 1992); Atina Grossmann, *Reforming Sex: The German Movement for Birth Control and Abortion Reform, 1920–1950* (Oxford, 1995); Philipp Sarasin and Jakob Tanner, eds., *Physiologie und industrielle Gesellschaft: Studien zur Verwissenschaftlichung des Körpers im 19. und 20. Jahrhundert* (Frankfurt a. M., 1998); Philipp Sarasin, *Reizbare Maschinen: Eine Geschichte des Körpers 1765–1914* (Frankfurt a. M., 2001); and Ute Frevert, ed., *Körpergeschichte,* special issue of *Geschichte und Gesellschaft* 26/4 (2000).

offer insight into the meanings individuals assigned to their bodies. The anthropology of the body has made further headway in investigating how contemporary subjects interpret everyday as well as transformative bodily experiences.[75] Barbara Duden's study *Woman beneath the Skin* has remained a classic in this field because she charts the "discovery, description, categorization, and administration of the inner female space from which the 'body politic' had to emerge" on the basis of transcribed conversations between a German physician, Johann Storch, and his female patients.[76] Although Storch's notes are representations of his patients' bodily experiences, Duden exposes a fascinating underworld of communication between patient and doctor in which two different dynamics of embodiment were at play. As patients "embodied themselves" through their narratives of pain, blood, and blockage, Storch, in turn, served as a rare "witness to an orally transmitted popular concept of the body," instead of seeking to discipline or medicalize his patients' bodies.[77]

New histories of the body have added new dimensions both to the history of twentieth-century wars, prompting inquiry into the experiences of trauma on the part of combatants and civilians, and also to the body as a powerful new symbol in the crafting of historical memory in war's aftermath. While Elaine Scarry's widely read study, *The Body in Pain,* may have sparked a wave of interest in embodied violence inflicted by states and militaries, the growing interest in the history of masculinity has spurred a renewed interest in cultural and gendered histories of men at war, of the experiences and social significa-

74. This is a very broad category, which includes diverse studies of symbolic bodies in modern social transformations, such as Lynn Hunt's *The Family Romance of the French Revolution* (Berkeley, Calif., 1992) and her *Eroticism and the Body Politic* (Baltimore, 1991); Anson Rabinbach, *The Human Motor: Energy, Fatigue, and the Origins of Modernity* (Berkeley, Calif., 1990); and Katherine Verdery, *The Political Lives of Dead Bodies: Reburial and Postsocialist Change* (New York, 1999).

75. See Emily Martin, *The Woman in the Body: A Cultural Analysis of Reproduction* (Boston, 1987). For an interesting newer study, see Jane Caplan, ed., *Written on the Body: The Tattoo in European and American History* (Princeton, N.J., 2000).

76. Barbara Duden, *Woman beneath the Skin: A Doctor's Patients in Eighteenth-Century Germany,* trans. Thomas Dunlap (Cambridge, Mass., 1991), pp. 17–18. On the meanings of the bodily experiences of abortion, see Cornelie Usborne's new work, "Female Voices in Male Courtrooms—Abortion Trials in Weimar Germany," in *Coping with Sickness: Medicine, Law and Human Rights—Historical Perspectives,* ed. John Woodward and Robert Jütte (Sheffield, UK, 2000), pp. 91–106.

77. Duden, *Woman beneath the Skin,* pp. 15, 36, 62–66.

tion of injury, dismemberment, and death in histories of postwar reconstructions.[78] The apparent significance of the body in the history of total war would suggest that certain eras may lend themselves more than others to body histories. Other "body" epochs beyond the First World War might include: the 1920s in which welfare states, public spheres, and popular cultures politicized both male and female bodies; the eras of fascism and Nazism, when individual bodies were indispensable to the remaking of race; and the 1960s, when social protest made bodies both subjects and objects of sexual politics and social utopias. In these epochs of history transformations of bodies were a crucial part of their definitive events and processes; taking bodies into account alters the tasks of interpreting both the history and the historical memory of the particular forms of twentieth-century violence. As a methodological strategy, exploring the bodily stakes of history is often the most effective means for uncovering the place of gender in transformative events. Moreover, understanding bodies as another layer of experience, site of subjectivity, or representation of self and social collectivity enriches the history of everyday life in the milieus of popular culture, fashion and advertising, social hygiene and sexual politics.

CONSUMPTION, WELFARE STATES, EMPIRE, NATION

Labor, class, citizenship, and civil society are thematic areas in which feminist criticism overturned and revised key concepts in the process of illuminating what they had ignored or concealed. Gender had quite a different role to play in the study of consumption, welfare state, empire, and nation. In these fields its impetus was directed less toward disassembling established categories or narratives than toward serving to map out new research terrain in fields that were still relatively young when the turn to gender began. Innovative research on gender energized areas of research that counted as new (consumption) or that appeared to become "hot topics" through or coincident with the reception of gender (empire, welfare state, nation). A foundational force in these fields,

78. Elaine Scarry, *The Body in Pain: The Making and Unmaking of the World* (New York, 1985). One widely reviewed history of bodies and war is Joanna Bourke, *Dismembering the Male: Men's Bodies, Britain, and the Great War* (Chicago, 1996). Also see the recent work of Sabine Kienitz, especially "Body Damage: War Disability and Constructions of Masculinity in Weimar Germany," in *Home/Front: The Military, War, and Gender in Twentieth-Century Germany,* ed. Karen Hagemann and Stefanie Schüler-Springorum (Oxford, 2002), pp. 181–204.

research on gender could draw on a far smaller accumulation of research on women, but also stirred up considerably less controversy than in those fields where its first task was to dismantle and dethrone an established analytical apparatus. In fact, because women's history had hardly made inroads before the turn to gender took place, the line between women and gender is relatively fluid in the study of consumption, welfare state, empire, and nation.

Consumption

There were several prerequisites to the arrival of consumption as a historical topic in its own right. First, it followed decades of exhaustive research on the spheres of production in which the social spaces and patterns of consumption were viewed as depoliticized sites of private (and implicitly feminine) behavior. Rising interest in material cultures, in leisure and mass culture, in social movements outside of the workplace, focused attention on consumption as a vital site of social allegiances and identities, as did the critical engagement of feminists with the very boundaries between public and private that underpinned and were frequently mapped onto the opposition between production and consumption. Feminist scholarship of the 1970s and 1980s left in place the premise that consumption was a mainly feminine arena, even if it succeeded in fostering an understanding of consumption as a sphere of labor, recognizing the agency in women's decisions to scrimp, save, or spend frugally, which were of vital importance to families' survival in times of unemployment or economic downturn.[79] Consumption had a different place in middle-class households, where the ideology of domesticity was materialized through the purchase, utilization, and presentation of goods.[80] The consumption practices of middle-class women fostered the representation of respectability to the world beyond home and hearth, crucial in the cultural distinctions the bourgeoisie drew between itself, the aristocracy, and the urban working classes. Female consumers negotiated identities of class, race, ethnicity, and gender in the acts of shopping, gazing, longing, saving, buying, displaying, and donning the goods, acts that were sometimes complicit with dominant ideologies of family and gender and at other times represented resistance against them.[81]

79. Lewis, *Labour and Love.*

80. Davidoff and Hall, *Family Fortunes,* remains a field-defining study on this topic. Also see Victoria de Grazia with Ellen Furlough, *The Sex of Things: Gender and Consumption in Historical Perspective* (Berkeley, Calif., 1996), pt. 2; and Smith, *Ladies of the Leisure Class.*

81. The classics on this topic are Rosalind Williams, *Dream Worlds: Mass Consump-*

Besides the reproduction of daily life through the work of shopping for, utilizing, or displaying goods, the sphere of consumption expanded during the early twentieth century to encompass leisure activities and mass entertainment.[82] The joint impulses of cultural studies and gender history helped illuminate the changes in the cultural and symbolic meanings of commodity goods over time and the ways in which consumption shaped social relations and gender hierarchies. Scholarship on consumption offered its own critical view of the public/private dichotomy, weaving connections between the acts of production, purchase, use and display which linked "private" households to the public spaces of markets and mills.[83] The design, acquisition, location, and exhibition of goods also helped to fashion iconographies of gender, whether in the realm of high politics (the "diamond necklace" affair of Marie Antoinette) or in everyday encounters with commodities, such as the ivory soap that signified white femininity in British advertising during the age of empire, or the cigarettes and hosiery that recast femininity amidst the rubble of German cities at the end of the Second World War.[84]

As much as the history of goods involved the congealing of norms and standards—of hygiene, beauty, or fashion—or the crafting of images and identities, feminist study of consumption also explicated its deeply political character.[85] At the level of state, for example, the moral and hygienic codes of

tion in Late Nineteenth-Century France (Berkeley, Calif., 1982); and Susan Porter Benson, Counter Cultures: Saleswomen, Managers, and Customers in American Department Stores, 1890–1940 (Urbana, Ill., 1986).

82. Dana Frank, "Consumerism and Consumption," in Reader's Companion to U.S. Women's History (Boston, 1998). On consumption as leisure, see the exemplary study by Kathy Peiss, Cheap Amusements: Working Women and Leisure in New York City, 1880 to 1920 (Philadelphia, 1986).

83. Mary Lynn Stewart, For Health and Beauty: Physical Culture for Frenchwomen, 1880s–1930s (Baltimore, 2001); and Kathy Peiss, Hope in a Jar: The Making of America's Beauty Culture (New York, 1998).

84. See, for example, Sarah Maza, Private Lives and Public Affairs: The Causes Célèbres of Prerevolutionary France (Berkeley, Calif., 1993); Anne McClintock, Imperial Leather: Race, Gender, and Sexuality in the Colonial Movement (London, 1995). Also see de Grazia and Furlough, The Sex of Things; Green, Ready-to-Wear; Erica Carter, How German Is She? Postwar West German Reconstruction and the Consuming Woman (Ann Arbor, Mich., 1997); Elizabeth Heinemann, What Difference Does a Husband Make? Women and Marital Status in Nazi and Postwar Germany (Berkeley, Calif., 1999); and Maria Höhn, GIs and Fräuleins: The German-American Encounter in 1950s West Germany (Chapel Hill, N.C., 2002).

85. See Carole Turbin and Barbara Burman, eds., Material Strategies Engendered, spe-

social policy and social reform of the late nineteenth century sought not only to remedy the conditions of labor for women and youths, but also to combat their purportedly extravagant habits of consumption.[86] Consumption has become indispensable to the study of class, now seen as formed across a range of milieus of social interaction and cultural exchange in which women and men intermingled—from households to hallways, corner markets to consumer coops, department stores to dance halls.[87] Consumption was no less a field of conflict than production, if we consider the fact that the capacity to consume was a crucial aspect of struggles over wages, prices, and work hours, or that the ability to participate in the exchange of goods in capitalism was equally constitutive of social status as occupation or earnings. That consumption was an intensely political field of conflict was most evident perhaps in periods of war, revolution, or economic crisis, when states' decisions to ration, tax, or stockpile often determined the fate of regimes or the resolution of crises.[88] "Consumer regimes," in turn, shaped "the stakes of citizens in politics," particularly once welfare states were founded and minimal standards of living or well-being established.[89] The Cold War was itself characterized not only by the competition of arms and ideologies, but also by the enactment of different consumer regimes on either side of divided Europe.[90] By the time we can speak

---

cial issue of *Gender & History* 14/2 (November 2002), on fashion and gender in transnational comparison.

86. See Coffin, *The Politics of Women's Work*, and Warren Breckman, "Disciplining Consumption: The Debate about Luxury in Wilhelmine Germany, 1890–1914," *Journal of Social History* 24/3 (Spring 1991): 485–505.

87. See Victoria de Grazia and Lizabeth Cohen, "Class and Consumption," *International Labor and Working-Class History*, no. 55 (1999): 1–5; and Mary Nolan, *Visions of Modernity: American Business and the Modernization of Germany* (New York, 1994), especially chap. 6 on gender and women.

88. An important study of consumption in wartime is Belinda J. Davis, *Home Fires Burning: Food, Politics, and Everyday Life in World War I Berlin* (Chapel Hill, N.C., 2000).

89. Judith Coffin, "The Politics of Things: New Directions in the History of Consumption," *Journal of Modern History* 71/1 (March 1999): 177, review essay on de Grazia and Furlough, *The Sex of Things* and Leora Auslander, *Taste and Power: Furnishing Modern France* (Berkeley, Calif., 1996). Also see Judith Coffin, "A 'Standard' of Living? European Perspectives on Class and Consumption in the Early Twentieth Century," *International Labor and Working-Class History*, no. 55 (1999): 6–26.

90. Barbara Einhorn, *Cinderella Goes to Market: Citizenship, Gender, and Women's Movements in East Central Europe* (London, 1993); Hannah Schissler, ed., *The Miracle Years: A Cultural History of West Germany, 1949–1968* (Princeton, N.J., 2001); and Katherine

of an age of "consumerism" in the postwar United States or western Europe, consumption had not only become a fetish, but had taken on the status of a civil or political right and was thus broadly encompassed in the notion of citizenship in Western democracies.[91]

Welfare State

Consumption is closely related to the study of welfare states in the sense that welfare is often defined in terms of the capacity of a governing body to regulate the reproduction of social life, of which the capacity for consumption is a vital component. The early study of welfare states in women's history identified female actors on both sides of this social space. On the one side, bourgeois feminists envisioned and enacted welfare in its many varieties, from the abolitionist agitation of early feminists through petitions for poor relief, campaigns against child labor and for the protection of women in factories, to mass mobilizations against social scourges like alcohol and tobacco, prostitution and venereal disease, premarital sex and unwed motherhood.[92] On the other side were the objects of their reform efforts: mothers working long hours in mills and shops; women with alcoholic husbands, sick children, unhygienic households; war widows in despair; women chronically unemployed or temporarily on the dole; women deported, displaced, or driven out of their homes by wars or revolution.

Pence, "Labours of Consumption: Gendered Consumers in Post-War East and West German Reconstruction," in *Gender Relations in German History,* ed. Lynn Abrams and Elizabeth Harvey (Durham, N.C., 1997), pp. 211–38. Pence's forthcoming book makes clear that the Berlin Wall was built, in part, to enforce the divide between capitalist and socialist consumer regimes. Also see David F. Crew, ed., *Consuming Germany in the Cold War* (New York, 2003).

91. Susan Strasser, Charles McGovern, and Matthias Judt, eds., *Getting and Spending: European and American Consumer Societies in the Twentieth Century* (Cambridge, 1998); and Lizabeth Cohen, *A Consumer's Republic: The Politics of Mass Consumption in Postwar America* (New York, 2003).

92. For a sampling of books on these themes, see Seth Koven and Sonya Michel, eds., *Mothers of a New World: Maternalist Politics and the Origins of Welfare States* (New York, 1993), especially "Introduction: Mother Worlds"; Paul Weindling, *Health, Race, and German Politics between National Unification and Nazism, 1870–1945* (Cambridge, 1989); Ulla Wikander, Alice Kessler-Harris and Jane Lewis, eds., *Protecting Women. Labor Legislation in Europe, the United States and Australia, 1880–1920* (Urbana, Ill., 1995); Mary Lynn Stewart, *Women, Work, and the French State: Labour Protection and Social Patriarchy, 1879–1919* (Kingston, 1989); and Sabine Schmitt, *Der Arbeiterinnenschutz im deutschen Kaiserreich: Zur Konstruktion der schutzbedürftigen Arbeiterin* (Stuttgart, 1995).

In many instances the vulnerability of women and children in the spheres of production and reproduction set the apparatus of social intervention in motion, while the broader goals of social policy were usually not women and children per se, but a more fundamental restoration of the family unit—its health, stability, or economic well-being, the realignment of relations between men and women and of the reproductive and productive capacities of families.[93]

Female experts in the sphere of social reform, many already in possession of impressive academic credentials, represented a lively segment of the public that mobilized around the various "social questions" during the late nineteenth and early twentieth century.[94] European middle-class women left their distinct stamp on this realm of the social through the ideology of maternalism, a social language in which feminism learned to speak for itself.[95] Studies of bourgeois maternalists suggest that welfare states formed and expanded not only or not mainly out of their own internal imperatives to secure social peace; rather they also coalesced in response to the sustained pressure of the public sphere upon the state. Female social reformers, for example, did much of the "leg work" for revision of the labor code in France and Germany, gathering empirical evidence of the needs of working mothers and offering expert testimony to assembled bureaucracies or legislators.[96] The activities of bourgeois feminists in these realms rendered the boundary between state and civil society more fluid, as they agitated and brought their expertise to bear in both realms. The welfare state was therefore a crucial site at which bourgeois feminism crafted its world-

93. Jacques Donzelot, *The Policing of Families* (New York, 1979). For examinations of women as clients of welfare states, see David F. Crew, *Germans on Welfare: From Weimar to Hitler* (Oxford, 1998) and Ute Frevert, "'Fürsorgliche Belagerung': Hygienebewegung und Arbeiterfrauen im 19. und frühen 20. Jahrhundert," *Geschichte und Gesellschaft* 111 (1985): 420–46.

94. Koven and Michel, *Mothers of a New World*. Also see chapter 5 in this volume.

95. Young Sun Hong, *Welfare, Modernity and the Weimar State, 1919–1933* (Princeton, N.J., 1998); Ann Taylor Allen, *Feminism and Motherhood in Germany, 1800–1914* (New Brunswick, N.J., 1991); Christiane Eifert, *Frauenpolitik und Wohlfahrtspflege: Zur Geschichte der sozialdemokratischen "Arbeiterwohlfahrt"* (Frankfurt, 1993); Kevin Repp, *Reformers, Critics, and the Paths of German Modernity: Anti-Politics and the Search for Alternatives, 1890–1914* (Cambridge, Mass., 2000); and Andrew Lees, *Cities, Sin and Social Reform in Imperial Germany* (Ann Arbor, Mich., 2002).

96. Stewart, *Women, Work, and the French State;* Andrew Lees, *Character Is Destiny: The Autobiography of Alice Salomon* (Ann Arbor, Mich., 2004); Christoph Sachße, *Mütterlichkeit als Beruf: Sozialarbeit, Sozialreform and Frauenbewegung 1871–1929* (Frankfurt a. M., 1986); Schmitt, *Der Arbeiterinnenschutz.*

view. Yet the fact that many different groups of female reformers staked claims in the name of the "social question" across Catholic, Protestant, Jewish, socialist, and nationalist milieus makes clear that neither feminism nor maternalism were ideologically cohesive.[97] Bourgeois feminism accommodated the contradictory positions of liberal, radical, conservative, religious, nationalist, and racist organizations, while socialist feminists confronted the "proletarian antifeminism" of their own male comrades and resisted the custodial claims of bourgeois women in the realm of the social.[98] Radical feminists, like Ellen Key or Helene Stöcker, envisioned a future in which social reform, and later social work, would lay the groundwork for women's citizenship and for sexual freedom.[99] Nationalist and colonial women pursued a vision of the future as a maternal fantasy of national regeneration, one that was inflected with eugenics and hierarchies of race in the age of empire.[100]

Interestingly, the study of welfare states is one of the few fields of history in

97. See Koven and Michel, *Mothers of a New World,* especially Christoph Sachße, "Social Mothers: The Bourgeois Women's Movement and German Welfare-State Formation," pp. 135–58; and Jean H. Quataert, "Woman's Work and the Early Welfare State in Germany: Legislators, Bureaucrats, and Clients before the First World War," pp. 159–87; Gisela Bock and Pat Thane, eds., *Maternity and Gender Policies: Women and the Rise of the European Welfare State* (London, 1991); Allen, *Feminism and Motherhood in Germany;* and Irene Stoehr, "'Organisierte Mütterlichkeit': Zur Politik der deutschen Frauenbewegung um 1900," in *Frauen suchen ihre Geschichte,* ed. Karin Hausen (Munich, 1983), pp. 221–49.

98. On the "proletarian antifeminism" of the German socialist movement, see Jean H. Quataert, *Reluctant Feminists in German Social Democracy 1885–1917* (Princeton, N.J., 1979); Werner Thönnessen, *Frauenemanzipation: Politik und Literatur der deutschen Sozialdemokratie zur Frauenbewegung 1863–1933* (Frankfurt, 1969); and Mary Nolan, "Proletarischer Anti-Feminismus, dargestellt am Beispiel der SPD-Ortsgruppe Düsseldorf, 1890–1914," in *Frauen und Wissenschaft: Beiträge zur Berliner Sommeruniversität* (Berlin, 1976), pp. 356–77.

99. Also see Karen Offen, *European Feminisms, 1700–1950: A Political History* (Stanford, Calif., 2000); Sylvia Paletschek and Bianka Pitrow-Ennker, eds., *Women's Emancipation Movements in the Nineteenth Century: A European Perspective* (Stanford, Calif., 2004); Richard J. Evans, *The Feminists: Women's Emancipation Movements in Europe, America and Australasia, 1840–1920* (London, 1977); Christl Wickert, *Helene Stöcker: 1869–1943: Frauenrechtlerin, Sexualreformerin und Pazifistin. Eine Biographie* (Bonn, 1991).

100. Anna Davin, "Imperialism and Motherhood," *History Workshop* 5 (1978): 9–65, reprinted in Cooper and Stoler, *Tensions of Empire,* pp. 87–151; Lora J. Wildenthal, *German Women for Empire, 1884–1945* (Durham, N.C., 2001); and Christopher Lawrence and Anna-K. Mayer, eds., *Regenerating England: Science, Medicine and Culture in Interwar Britain,* Wellcome Institute Series in the History of Medicine, vol. 60 (Amsterdam, 2000).

which the methodology of comparison has been critical in deepening our understanding of the disparate connections between welfare states and gender regimes, between maternalist ideologies and natalist practices of state, between male breadwinners and female dependents as gendered social citizens.[101] Gender history has probed the place of the welfare state in the genesis of modernity, attending to the prescriptions for a "scientification of the social" in the last third of the nineteenth century and charting the embrace of eugenicist body politics in the decades that followed.[102] Comparative study has helped to elucidate how and why the "spirit of science," embodied in welfare states across Europe, ended in the eliminationist racism of the Nazi and Fascist regimes.[103]

Empire/Nation

In the study of empire and nation no definitive lines separate women from gender, gender from sexuality or body. Initial explorations of the place of women in the histories of empire and colonialism uncovered not only their significance as objects or victims of colonial rule, but also made explicit the active participation of women who enjoyed the manifold privileges of race and shared "positions of decided—if borrowed   power, not only over colonized women, but also colonized men."[104] Studies of popular nationalism, which cut

---

101. Koven and Michel, *Mothers of a New World;* Bock and Thane, *Maternity and Gender Policies;* Susan Pedersen, *Family, Dependence and the Origins of the Welfare State: Britain and France, 1914–1945* (Cambridge, 1993); Linda Gordon, ed., *Women, the State and Welfare* (Madison, Wis., 1990) (see especially Gordon's introduction, "The New Feminist Scholarship on the Welfare State"); Theda Skocpol, *Protecting Soldiers and Mothers: The Political Origins of Social Policy in the United States* (Cambridge, 1992); Birthe Siim, *Gender and Citizenship: Politics and Agency in France, Britain, and Denmark* (Cambridge, 2000); Theresa Kulawik, *Wohlfahrtsstaat und Mutterschaft: Schweden und Deutschland 1870–1912* (Frankfurt, 1999); and Barbara Hobson, Jane Lewis, and Birte Siim, eds., *Contested Concepts in Gender and Social Politics* (Cheltenham, UK, 2002).

102. Martin Hewitt, "Bio-Politics and Social Policy: Foucault's Account of Welfare," *Theory, Culture, and Society* 2/1 (1983): 67–84; Mary Poovey, *Making a Social Body: British Cultural Formation, 1830–64* (Chicago, 1995); and David Horn, *Social Bodies: Science, Reproduction, and Italian Modernity* (Princeton, N.J., 1994).

103. On the spirit of science, see Detlef J. K. Peukert, "The Genesis of the 'Final Solution' from the Spirit of Science," in *Reevaluating the Third Reich,* ed. Thomas Childers and Jane Caplan (New York, 1993), pp. 234–52. Also see Lesley A. Hall, "Women, Feminism and Eugenics," in *Essays in the History of Eugenics: Proceedings of a Conference Organised by the Galton Institute, London 1997,* ed. Robert A. Peel (London, 1998).

104. McClintock, *Imperial Leather,* pp. 6–7. Antoinette Burton, *At the Heart of the Em-*

across the themes of both nation and empire, have highlighted the activities of nationalist women on behalf of militarist and colonialist associations. In late nineteenth-century Germany, for example, the ideology of maternalism criss-crossed the boundary between nation and empire, fostering specifically female fantasies of national regeneration and empire and prompting many colonialist women to travel to the colonies themselves, as tourists or settlers, as social mothers or adventurers, each with a shared stake in the outcomes of imperial rule.[105]

Studies of colonialism and empire in the late 1980s and early 1990s shifted attention from colonies and colonial practices to the mutual shaping, the "intimate engagement, attraction, and opposition" between colonies and metropoles.[106] Historians began to approach the two sites of colonies and metropoles as formed reciprocally, documenting how the colonial experience transformed politics, culture, and everyday life in the metropoles, thus redefining "what it meant to be European, Western and capitalist."[107] Once policies pertaining to marriage and family, citizenship and consumption, health and hygiene, reproduction and race were instituted in the setting of colonies, they also acquired new significance for welfare practices "at home" in the metropoles.[108] Gender-

---

pire: Indians and the Colonial Encounter in Late Victorian Britain (Berkeley, Calif., 1998); Mrinalini Sinha, "Gender in the Critiques of Colonialism and Nationalism"; Wildenthal, German Women for Empire; and Nupur Chaudhuri and Margaret Strobel, eds., Western Women and Imperialism: Complicity and Resistance (Bloomington, Ind., 1992).

105. See, for example, Roger Chickering, "'Casting Their Gaze More Broadly': Women's Patriotic Activism in Imperial Germany," Past & Present, no. 118 (February 1988): 156–85; and in a somewhat different vein Renate Bridenthal, "'Professional Housewives': Stepsisters of the Women's Movement," in When Biology Became Destiny, ed. Renate Bridenthal, Atina Grossmann, and Marion Kaplan (New York, 1984), pp. 153–73, which inspired later work on German colonialism, such as Lora Wildenthal, "'She is the Victor': Bourgeois Women, Nationalist Identities, and the Ideal of the Independent Woman Farmer in German Southwest Africa," in Society, Culture and the State in Germany, 1870–1930, ed. Geoff Eley (Ann Arbor, Mich., 1996), pp. 371–95; and her book German Women for Empire. More recent scholarship on a different kind of imperial and racialized gaze includes Elizabeth Harvey, Women and the Nazi East: Agents and Witnesses of Germanization (New Haven, Conn., 2003).

106. Harvey, Women and the Nazi East, p. viii. Also see Catherine Hall, Civilising Subjects: Metropole and Colony in the English Imagination 1830–1867 (Chicago, 2002); and Catherine Hall, ed., Cultures of Empire: Colonizers in Britain and the Empire in the Nineteenth and Twentieth Centuries: A Reader (New York, 2000).

107. Cooper and Stoler, preface to Tensions of Empire, pp. vii–viii.

108. McClintock, Imperial Leather; Stoler, "Carnal Knowledge and Imperial Power,"

historical analysis of the framing and fulfillment of colonial visions as they moved fluidly from the metropoles to the colonies and back, gender was never very far removed from sexual politics in the enforcement of labor practices, the organization of domestic spaces, and the social demarcations of caste, class, or race. The concepts of gender, class, and nation worked together to explicate the transformation of "indigenous patriarchies" and their replacement by middle-class codes of domesticity and morality.[109]

As a relational category encompassing social and symbolic dimensions of sexual difference, gender has proven a far more effective tool than women for capturing the fluidity between nation and empire. Gender illuminates—in ways that woman cannot—the multiple, rather than unitary, femininities or masculinities that were always mutually constituted across the divide metropole-colony, colonizer—colonized.[110] In the study of empire more than that of nation, the analytic of gender is entwined with that of race as "an organizing principle and a powerful rhetorical theme" that infiltrated every layer of the

------

pp. 209–10, and *Her Carnal Knowledge and Imperial Power: Race and the Intimate in Colonial Rule* (Berkeley, Calif., 2002); Susan Pedersen, "National Bodies, Unspeakable Acts: The Sexual Politics of Colonial Policy-Making," *Journal of Modern History* 63 (December 1991): 647–80; Nancy Rose Hunt, *A Colonial Lexicon of Birth Ritual, Medicalization, and Mobility in the Congo* (Durham, N.C., 1999); Elizabeth Thompson, *Colonial Citizens: Republican Rights, Paternal Privilege, and Gender in French Syria and Lebanon* (New York, 2000); White, *The Comforts of Home;* and Lynn Thomas, *Politics of the Womb: Women, Reproduction, and the State in Kenya* (Berkeley, Calif., 2003). Also see Antoinette Burton, *Dwelling in the Archive: Women Writing House, Home, and History in Late Colonial India* (Oxford, 2003).

109. This is Mrinalini Sinha's summary of Mohanty's field-defining overview of 1991. Chandra Mohanty, "Cartographies of Struggle," in *Third World Women and the Politics of Feminism*, p. 15, as cited in Sinha, "Gender in the Critiques of Colonialism and Nationalism," p. 498. Also see Mrinalini Sinha, *Colonial Masculinity: The "Manly Englishman" and the "Effeminate Bengali" in the Late Nineteenth Century* (Manchester, UK, 1995); Partha Chatterjee, *The Nation and Its Fragments: Colonial and Postcolonial Histories* (Princeton, N.J., 1993); and Catherine Hall, "The Rule of Difference: Gender, Class, and Empire in the Making of the 1832 Reform Act," in *Gendered Nations: Nationalism and Gender Order in the Long Nineteenth Century*, ed. Ida Blom, Karen Hagemann, and Catherine Hall (Oxford, 2000), pp. 107–36. Also see Ian C. Fletcher, Laura E. Nym Mayhall, and Philippa Levine, eds., *Women's Suffrage in the British Empire: Citizenship, Nation, and Race* (London, 2000).

110. See Stoler, *Carnal Knowledge and Imperial Power*, and Hall, *Civilising Subjects*. Among other influential works in this field is Julia Clancy Smith and Frances Gouda, eds., *Domesticating the Empire: Race, Gender, and Family Life in French and Dutch Colonialism* (Charlottesville, Va., 1998).

colonial interface.[111] The general instability of subject positions in the landscape of empire meant that the work of defining and maintaining otherness was continuous, as sexual difference was reordered in relation to shifting categories of race, class, or caste.[112] So, for example, colonial women who were indisputably subordinate to colonial men nonetheless claimed moral hegemony over male colonizers while also asserting solidarity with colonized women on matters such as mixed marriage or sexual violence against indigenous women.[113]

Not all nations possessed empires, however, so the designations "gender and nation" vs. "gender and empire" do continue to suggest somewhat different scholarly pursuits. Sometimes the distinction between the two is mainly temporal, so nation or nation-state signifies a period of history *before* its expansion into empire, while in other instances, nation remains a vital analytic for understanding the dynamics of imperial rule, including the coalescing of *new nations* in response to colonialism or other forms of hegemonic rule (fascism or postwar state socialism).[114] Also challenging is the conceptual distinction between nation and nationalism, for in some historical cases nations coalesced as a direct outcome of nationalist mobilizations, while in others popular nationalism drove nations into imperial expansion and competition. In still others the aim of popular nationalism was to defend indigenous cultures against the encroachments of empire without a vision of nation-state as the necessary outcome. The identification of nation as discursively constituted or "imagined," along with the post–Cold War realignments of nations and nationalisms in

111. Cooper and Stoler, "Between Metropole and Colony: Rethinking a Research Agenda," introduction to *Tensions of Empire,* pp. 10–11.

112. Cooper and Stoler, "Between Metropole and Colony," pp. 6–7. See also Sinha, *Colonial Masculinity.*

113. Lora J. Wildenthal, "Race, Gender, and Citizenship in the German Colonial Empire," and Ann Laura Stoler, "Sexual Affronts and Racial Frontiers: European Identities and the Cultural Politics of Exclusion in Colonial Southeast Asia," in Cooper and Stoler, *Tensions of Empire,* pp. 198–237, 263–86. Also see Chaterjee, *The Nation and Its Fragments,* chap. 6, "The Nation and its Women," and chap. 7, "Women and the Nation," pp. 116–57; and his "The Nationalist Resolution of the Women's Question," in *Recasting Women: Essays in Indian Colonial History,* ed. Kunkum Sangari and Sudesh Vaid (New Brunswick, N.J., 1990), pp. 233–53.

114. See Antoinette Burton, *After the Imperial Turn: Thinking with and through the Nation* (Durham, N.C., 2003), especially her "Introduction: On the Inadequacy and the Indispensability of the Nation"; Geoff Eley, "Culture, Nation, and Gender," in *Gendered Nations,* ed. Blom, Hagemann, and Hall, pp. 27–40; and Geoff Eley and Ronald G. Suny, eds., *Becoming National: A Reader* (New York, 1996).

eastern and southern Europe, led to a virtual explosion of scholarship on this topic across the disciplines in the 1990s.[115] Study of the re-formation of post-colonial societies as nations or the remaking of states and nations in eastern Europe since the end of the Cold War concentrated particularly on the process of nation-state formation and the terms in which belonging and exclusion were defined.[116] In most of these scholarly arenas women, gender, and sexuality all figured at best peripherally throughout the 1980s and early 1990s.[117]

In recent years the concept of gender has certainly revitalized the study of nation through the comparative study of topics alternatively termed "gender and nation," "gendered nationalism," and "gendered nations."[118] Building upon

115. See Eley, "Culture, Nation, and Gender," who points to the important influence of Eric Hobsbawm, Stuart Hall, Benedict Anderson, Paul Gilroy, and Edward Said on re-thinking nation and nationalism. Of foremost importance here is Benedict Anderson, *Imagined Communities: Reflections on the Origin and Spread of Nationalism* (London, 1983).

116. Eley, "Culture, Nation and Gender," pp. 31–33; see Beth Baron, "The Making of the Egyptian Nation"; Jitka Malecková, "Nationalizing Women and Engendering the Nation: The Czech National Movement"; and Irina Novikova, "Constructing National Identity in Latvia: Gender and Representation during the Period of National Awakening," in *Gendered Nations,* ed. Blom, Hagemann, and Hall, pp. 137–58, 293–334; and Malgorzata Fidelis, "'Participation in the Creative Work of the Nation': Polish Women Intellectuals in the Cultural Construction of Female Gender Roles, 1864–1890," *Journal of Women's History,* 13/1 (Spring 2001): 108–31. A definitive study of the dynamics of inclusion and exclusion in nation-state formation is Chaterjee, *The Nation and Its Fragments.*

117. Ruth Roach Pierson, "Nations: Gendered, Racialized, Crossed with Empire," in *Gendered Nations,* ed. Blom, Hagemann, and Hall, pp. 41–62. See also Ruth Roach Pierson and Nupur Chaudhuri, eds., *Nation, Empire, Colony: Historicizing Gender and Race* (Bloomington, Ind., 1998). Also see Frauen und Geschichte Baden-Württemberg, *Frauen und Nation* (Tübingen, 1996); Ute Planert, ed., *Nation, Politik und Geschlecht: Frauenbewegungen und Nationalismus in der Moderne* (Frankfurt a. M., 2000); Patricia Herminghouse and Magda Mueller, *Gender and Germanness: Cultural Productions of Nation* (Providence, R.I., 1997); and Sarah Friedrichsmeyer, Sarah Lennox, and Suzanne Zantop, eds., *The Imperialist Imagination: German Colonialism and Its Legacies* (Ann Arbor, Mich., 1998).

118. Blom, Hagemann, and Hall, eds., *Gendered Nations.* In this volume see particularly the preface for a brief discussion of the state of research on gender and nation in the late 1990s and Geoff Eley's discussion of the importance of cultural studies for the study of gendered nations in Eley, "Culture, Nation, and Gender." Also see Catherine Hall, Keith McClelland, and Jane Rendall, eds., *Defining the Victorian Nation: Class, Race, and Gender and the British Reform Act of 1867* (Cambridge, 2000); and Andrew Parker et al., eds., *Nationalisms and Sexualities* (London, 1992).

previous study of movements of nationalist women, historians with an interest in gender began to probe the deep connections among nationalism, anti-modernism, anti-Semitism, and antifeminism at the turn to the twentieth century when the specter of women's emancipation rallied nationalists behind campaigns to consolidate and protect nations against perceived internal and external threats.[119] European nation-states pursued programs to "nationalize the masses" in a longer-term sense and in terms that diverged from the reactive campaigns of popular nationalists. Expansionist states sought to sustain and deepen positive popular identifications with the nation through national monuments, celebrations, and rituals and in the institutional settings of schools, the military, and museums. The analytic gender and nation thus encompasses the symbolic rendering of nations through male and female iconic figures and has become a particularly fruitful site of masculinity studies in recent years.[120] These projects often involved their own national sexual or body politics, from the training and strengthening of militarized male bodies to the sanctioning of specific sexualities by states, such as those invoked by natalist visions of fertility and maternity or in campaigns against prostitution and venereal disease.[121]

119. See, for example, Nancy R. Reagin, *A German Women's Movement: Class and Gender in Hanover* (Chapel Hill, N.C., 1995); Jean H. Quataert, *Staging Philanthropy: Patriotic Women and the National Imagination in Dynastic Germany, 1813–1916* (Ann Arbor, Mich., 2001); Julie Gottlieb, *Feminine Fascism: Women in Britain's Fascist Movement, 1923–1945* (London, 2000); Elizabeth Harvey, "Pilgrimages to the 'Bleeding Border': Gender and Rituals of Nationalist Protest in Germany, 1919–39," *Women's History Review* 9/2 (2000): 201–29; Raffael Scheck, "Women against Versailles: Maternalism and Nationalism of Female Bourgeois Politicians in the Early Weimar Republic," *German Studies Review* 22/1 (February 1999): 21–41; Scheck, *Mothers of the Nation: Right-Wing Women in Weimar Germany* (Oxford, 2004); and Ute Planert's excellent monograph *Antifeminismus im Kaiserreich: Diskurs, soziale Formation und politische Mentalität* (Göttingen, 1998).

120. See the work of George Mosse: *The Image of Man, Nationalism, and Sexuality: Respectability and Abnormal Sexuality in Modern Europe* (New York, 1985), and *The Nationalization of the Masses: Political Symbolism and Mass Movements in Germany from the Napoleonic Wars through the Third Reich* (New York, 1975). Also see Karen Hagemann, *"Männlicher Muth und Teutsche Ehre": Nation, Militär und Geschlecht zur Zeit der Antinapoleonischen Kriege Preußens* (Paderborn, 2002); and Parker et al., *Nationalisms and Sexualities.*

121. Karen Offen, "Depopulation, Nationalism and Feminism in Fin-de-Siècle France," *American Historical Review* 9/3 (June 1984): 648–76; Alisa Kraus, "Depopulation and Race Suicide," in *Mothers of a New World*, ed. Koven and Michel; Ute Planert, "Der dreifache Körper des Volkes: Sexualität, Biopolitik und die Wissenschaften vom Leben," in *Körpergeschichte*, ed. Ute Frevert, special issue of *Geschichte und Gesellschaft* 26/4 (2000): 539–76.

A confluence of women and gender persists in the research on female actors and gender ideologies in popular and state nationalism. Nation/nationalism remains a large and unwieldy rubric, one in which the methodologies of political history, with their emphasis on the organization and mobilization of popular nationalism and nation-states, may favor the study of women both as subjects and objects of these forces, while cultural histories of nation are more interested in the ideologies and symbolics of both gender and sexuality.

THE GENDER OF WARS AND POSTWAR RECONSTRUCTIONS

The history of war, revolution, and postwar reconstruction, as well as of memory work and commemoration, spans most of the twentieth century. There is some overlap between the history of war and the thematic area of gender and nation not least because twentieth-century wars were fought over nations and nationalism, empires and colonies. If war was once the purview of military and political history, research of the last two decades has approached the two world wars from nearly every other angle, including social and economic histories of capital and labor, family and workplace; death and birth in the trenches and on the home front;[122] cultural history of ideologies and intellectual life; explorations of trauma and memory, mentalities and mass culture; and of the transformations of experiences and identities in everyday life.[123]

122. The literature on this topic is too vast to survey here. A sampling of important earlier works includes Gerald F. Feldman, *Army, Industry, and Labor in Germany, 1914–1918* (Princeton, N.J., 1966); Jürgen Kocka, *Facing Total War: German Society, 1914–1918* (Cambridge, Mass., 1984); Jean-Jacques Becker, *The Great War and the French People* (Leamington Spa, 1986); Richard Wall and Jay Winter, eds., *The Upheaval of War: Family, Work, and Welfare in Europe, 1914–1918* (Cambridge, 1988); Jay Winter and Jean-Louis Robert, eds., *Capital Cities at War: Paris, London, Berlin, 1914–1919* (Cambridge, 1997); Patrick Fridenson, ed., *The French Home Front* (Providence, R.I., 1992); Arthur Marwick, *The Deluge: British Society and the First World War* (Houndsmills, 1991); Diane Koenker and William G. Rosenberg, *Strikes and Revolution in Russia, 1917* (Princeton, N.J., 1989); and Roger Chickering, *Imperial Germany and the Great War, 1914–1918* (Cambridge, 1998).

123. On the topic of war and historical memory, see Paul Fussell, *The Great War and Modern Memory* (New York, 1975); Modris Eksteins, *Rites of Spring: The Great War and the Birth of the Modern Age* (New York, 1990); Robert Weldon Whalen, *Bitter Wounds: German Victims of the Great War, 1914–1939* (Ithaca, N.Y., 1984); Jay Winter, *Sites of Memory, Sites of Mourning: The Great War in European Cultural History* (Cambridge, 1995); and Joy Damousi, *The Labour of Loss: Mourning, Memory, and Wartime Bereavement in Australia* (Cambridge, 1999).

The history of women in the First World War began with social historical inquiry into the reorganization of family, work, and welfare in wartime and quickly demonstrated that the total wars of the twentieth century were far from "entirely male enterprises."[124] Research, both national and comparative in scope, revealed the significance of women to the conduct of war, from their labor in field hospitals and munitions plants to the reorganization of domestic life on the home front, whether in the public realms of welfare, education, and social hygiene or in the everyday management of individual homes and hearths in a time of prolonged and severe crisis.[125] New scholarship on these topics widened the scope of total war to encompass civil society on the home front and effectively differentiated that society along the lines of class, gender, generation, and ethnicity.[126] War came to be understood as an "activity that ritually mark[ed] the gender of all members of a society," as nation-states called upon both men and women for distinct but mutually dependent tasks in the conduct of war.[127]

The fact that only men in their best years were sent to the battlefields in the First World War, while the ranks of civilian society were both feminized and militarized, led some historians to approach the two fronts as separate spheres or life-worlds.[128] Studies of the home front, for example, emphasized

124. Gail Braybon, *Women Workers in the First World War* (London, 1981); Margaret Randolph Higonnet, Jane Jenson, Sonya Michel, and Margaret Weitz, eds., *Behind the Lines: Gender and the Two World Wars* (New Haven, Conn., 1987); Ute Daniel, *Arbeiterfrauen in der Kriegsgesellschaft: Beruf, Familie und Politik im Ersten Weltkrieg* (Göttingen, 1989), trans. Margaret Ries as *The War from Within: German Working-Class Women in the First World War* (Oxford, 1997); and Angela Woollacott, *On Her Their Lives Depend: Munitions Workers in the Great War* (Berkeley, Calif., 1994).

125. Winter and Wall, *The Upheaval of War*.

126. Winter and Robert, *Capital Cities at War;* Robert Wohl, *The Generation of 1914* (Cambridge, Mass., 1979). A more recent history that undertakes these differentiations impressively is Chickering, *Imperial Germany and the Great War*. Also see Stéphane Audoin-Rouzeau and Annette Becker, *14–18: Understanding the Great War*, trans. Catherine Temerson (New York, 2002).

127. Higonnet et al., *Behind the Lines*, introduction, pp. 4–5. A selection of titles on war and masculinity includes George Mosse, *Fallen Soldiers: Reshaping the Memory of the World Wars* (New York, 1990); Bourke, *Dismembering the Male;* Deborah Cohen, *The War Come Home: Disabled Veterans in Britain and Germany, 1914–39* (Berkeley, Calif., 2001); Paul Lerner, *Hysterical Men: War, Psychiatry, and the Politics of Trauma in Germany, 1890–1930* (Ithaca, N.Y., 2003); and Lerner, "Hysterical Cures: Hypnosis, Gender, and Performance in World War I and Weimar Germany," *History Workshop* 45 (1998): 79–99.

128. Elizabeth Domansky, "Militarization and Reproduction in World War I Germany,"

the transformative effects of prolonged total war upon women, upon their experiences—of labor and loss, family and food provision, protest and propaganda—and on the ways in which they were represented in the new national symbolics of war. The war enveloped ever more nations and armies as it became "total," compelling the new calibration of political economies, state bureaucracies, and social reproduction, revealing a widening of the apparent gulf between the two fronts. At the same time, the recognition that militarization had loosened, even undone the gender order that was in place when the war began seemed to indicate deeper connections between the two fronts as formative and interdependent parts of this gender order. Increasingly, then, studies of the totalizing effects of militarization prompted the call for "a total history," in which the massive mobilizations of "resources and energies" worked to conjoin rather than to divide production and reproduction, war front and home front, high politics and everyday life, so that each became a distinct but related part of the larger process of militarization.[129] Attention to gender in the history of the First World War helped to explicate the dual impulses of total war that dissolved the boundary between public and private space, for example while compelling ever more intricate connections between the home front and the theater of war.[130] The exploration of new ideologies of gender has pro-

in Eley, *Society, Culture, and the State*, pp 427–63; Birthe Kundrus, "Gender Wars: The First World War and the Construction of Gender Relations in the Weimar Republic," in *Home/Front*, ed. Hagemann and Schüler-Springorum, pp. 159–80.

129. Chickering, *Imperial Germany and the Great War*, pp. 65–66. On military history as "total history," see Roger Chickering, "Total War: Use and Abuse of a Concept," in *Anticipating Total War: The German and American Experiences, 1871–1914*, ed. Manfred Boemeke (Cambridge, 1999); and Thomas Kühne and Benjamin Ziemann, "Militärgeschichte in der Erweiterung: Konjunkturen, Interpretationen, Konzepte," in *Was ist Militärgeschichte?* ed. Thomas Kühne and Benjamin Ziemann (Paderborn, 2000), pp. 9–47, 301–14. Also see John Horne, ed., *State, Society, and Mobilization in Europe during the First World War*, Studies in the Social and Cultural History of Modern Warfare, vol. 3 (Cambridge, 1997).

130. On the turn to gender in the history of the military and war see Margaret Higonnet et al., "Introduction"; Joan W. Scott, "Rewriting History"; and Margaret Higonnet and Patrice Higonnet, "The Double Helix"; in *Behind the Lines,* ed. Higonnet et al., pp. 1–17, 19–47. See the definitive essays collected by Hagemann and Schüler-Springorum in *Home/Front*. Also see Christa Hämmerle, "Von den Geschlechtern der Kriege und des Militärs: Forschungseinblicke und Bemerkungen zu einer neuen Debatte," in *Was ist Militärgeschichte?* ed. Kühne and Ziemann; Lerner, *Hysterical Men;* and Sabine Kienitz, *Beschädigte Helden: Kriegsinvalide Körper in der Kultur: Deutschland 1914–1923* (Paderborn, 2005). For

ceeded in close conjunction with the continued investigation of experience; in fact the history of gender and war comprises one field of inquiry in which discourses/ideologies and experience/practices remain purposefully entwined with one another.[131] For the very redefinition of gender ideologies and hierarchies was fueled by the organization of total war, by the wholly unprecedented experiences it forced upon men and women. Similarly, the changing prescriptions of masculinity and femininity, the realignments of production and reproduction, the militarization of bodies and sexualities that took place during the war shaped and informed how civilians and soldiers, women and men experienced these ruptures.

The contention that the First World spawned an unprecedented crisis of masculinity is no longer new, but the work of analyzing the significance of this crisis for relations *between* the sexes has only recently begun. The first wave of studies of shell shock, for example, exposed the psychic and bodily vulnerability of men in industrialized war, while others probed the links between the brutalization of warfare at the front and the violence of interwar politics.[132] More recent research on sexual violence in the conduct of war has offered further evidence of the ways in which masculinities, and the relations between the sexes, were transformed by war, especially in the somewhat unique space of occupation zones, where the military domination often relied upon sexual subjugation.[133] Sexual violence, or the fears and presumptions thereof, also

———

a comparison with Australia, see Joy Damousi and Marilyn Lake, eds., *Gender and War: Australians at War in the Twentieth Century* (Cambridge, 1995).

131. See the very useful review essay by Belinda Davis, "Experience, Identity, and Memory: The Legacy of World War I," *Journal of Modern History* 75 (March 2003): 111–31.

132. Elaine Showalter, "Rivers and Sassoon: The Inscription of Male Gender Anxieties," and Sandra Gilbert, "Soldier's Heart: Literary Men, Literary Women, and the Great War," in *Behind the Lines*, ed. Higonnet et al., pp. 61–69, 197–226; Klaus Theweleit, *Male Fantasies*, vol. 1: *Women, Floods, Bodies, History*, and vol. 2, *Male Bodies: Psychoanalyzing the White Terror*, trans. Stephen Conway (Minneapolis, 1987); and Mosse, *Fallen Soldiers*. Also see Eric Leed, *No Man's Land: Combat and Identity in World War I* (Cambridge, 1979), and Fussell, *The Great War and Modern Memory*.

133. Key studies include Ruth Harris, "The 'Child of the Barbarian': Rape, Race, and Nationalism in France during the First World War," *Past & Present*, no. 141 (November 1993): 170–206; and John Horne and Alan Kramer, *German Atrocities, 1914: A History of Denial* (New Haven, Conn., 2001). Also see Birgit Beck, "Rape: The Military Trials of Sexual Crimes Committed by Soldiers in the Wehrmacht, 1939–1944," and Thomas Kühne, "Comradeship: Gender Confusion and Gender Order in the German Military, 1918–1945," in *Home/Front*, ed. Hagemann and Schüler-Springorum, pp. 233–54, 255–74.

contributed to the racialization of world war, for example, in the Rhineland where the French occupation forces included African soldiers.[134] The symbolic significance of male bodies, both heroic and wounded, to the postwar re-founding of the nation would further suggest that total war embodied men in new ways.[135] In fact, it is at this juncture that one of the most fruitful encounters between "the new military history" and gender history has taken place in recent years, as historians in both fields have considered military service a formative site of masculine citizenship, at which national belonging was instilled and inscribed in male bodies.[136]

In dissolving the line between the male and female fronts and expanding historical knowledges of both, the joint impulses of total history and gender history have made gender, as both experience and ideology, an integral part of the transformations of the period of war and its aftermath, as represented in textbooks and "mainstream" historical narratives.[137] The perception of the First World War as a period of profound transformation in gender relations and

134. On the fears of sexual violence, see Christian Köller's study of the legends and fears surrounding the French-African troops in the Rhineland: *"Von Wilden aller Rassen niedergemetzelt": Die Diskussion um die Verwendung von Kolonialtruppen in Europa zwischen Rassismus, Kolonial- und Militärpolitik (1914–30)* (Stuttgart, 2001). Also see Tina Campt, *Other Germans: Black Germans and the Politics of Race, Gender, and Memory in the Third Reich* (Ann Arbor, Mich., 2004), especially chap. 1, "'Resonant Echoes': The Rhineland Campaign and Converging Specters of Racial Mixture," pp. 31–62; and Christoph Köller, "Enemy Images: Race and Gender Stereotypes in the Discussion on Colonial Troops: A Franco-German Comparison," in *Home/Front*, ed. Hagemann and Schüler-Springorum, pp. 139–58.

135. Bourke, *Dismembering the Male*; Kienitz, "Body Damage"; Cohen, *The War Come Home*; and Whalen, *Bitter Wounds*.

136. Hagemann, *"Männlicher Muth und teutsche Ehre,"* and Ute Frevert, *A Nation in Barracks: Modern Germany, Military Conscription, and Civil Society* (Oxford, 2004), first published as *Die kasernierte Nation: Militärdienst und Zivilgesellschaft in Deutschland* (Munich, 2001). Also see Hagemann and Ralf Pröve, eds., *Landsknechte, Soldatenfrauen und Nationalkrieger: Militär, Krieg und Geschlechterordnung im historischen Wandel* (Frankfurt a. M., 1998); Ziemann and Kühne, *Was ist Militärgeschichte?*

137. One exemplary synthetic text is Chickering, *Imperial Germany and the Great War, 1914–1918*. Also see Marilyn Shevin-Coetzee and Frans Coetzee, eds., *World War I and European Society: A Sourcebook* (Lexington, Mass., 1995); and *Authority, Identity, and the Social History of the Great War* (Providence, R.I., 1995). One example of a textbook that integrates gender into the history of the First World War is Lynn Hunt et al., *The Challenge of the West: Peoples and Cultures from the Stone Age to the Global Age*, vol. C: *Peoples and Cultures from 1787 to the Global Age* (Lexington, Ky., 1995).

gender ideologies has had significant implications for the study of its after-math, as historians explored the extent to which these changes were lasting, reversible, or quickly submerged in the drive for postwar stabilization. Women's historians debated, for example, whether the war had fostered women's emancipation, particularly in Britain, the United States, and Germany, where they won the vote at the war's end.[138] Or had it merely signified an "emancipation on loan" that was quickly negated with the return of the soldiers and the restoration of a familiar gender order?[139] While historians of women undertook comparisons of the gains and losses of women and men in the immediate postwar years, the lens of gender began to complicate the modernizationist trajectory of rupture and restoration, in which patriarchies were broken and then restored, emancipations won and then negated. The concept of gender provided new tools for analyzing the transformations of symbols and subjectivities that underpinned the perception of a postwar gender crisis, of a society that had survived total war only to find itself a "civilization without sexes."[140]

138. Carol Berkin and Clara Lovett, *Women, War, and Revolution* (New York, 1980); Gail Braybon and Penny Summerfield, eds., *Out of the Cage: Women's Experiences in Two World Wars* (New York, 1987); Ute Frevert, *Women in German History: From Bourgeois Emancipation to Sexual Liberation,* trans. Stuart McKinnon-Evans (New York, 1989), first published as *Frauen-Geschichte zwischen bürgerlicher Verbesserung und neuer Weiblichkeit* (Frankfurt a. M, 1986), see pt. 3, chap. 1 on the First World War. For a more recent assessment of the thematic of women and war, see the review essay by Nicoletta Gullace, "Women and War in Comparative Perspective," *Gender & History* 15/1 (April 2003): 140–45.

139. "Emancipation on loan" is Ute Daniel's formulation. See her *The War from Within.* Also see Downs, *Manufacturing Inequality;* Barbara Alpern Engel, "Not by Bread Alone: Subsistence Riots in Russia during World War I," *Journal of Modern History* 69/4 (1997): 696–721; Susan R. Grayzel, *Women's Identities at War: Gender, Motherhood, and Politics in Britain and France during the First World War* (Chapel Hill, N.C., 1999); Deborah Thom, *Nice Girls and Rude Girls: Women Workers in World War I* (New York, 1998); Davis, *Home Fires Burning;* Margaret R. Higonnet, *Nurses at the Front: Writing the Wounds of the Great War* (Boston, 2001); Nicoletta Gullace, "*The Blood of Our Sons*": Men, Women, and the Renegotiation of British Citizenship during the Great War* (New York, 2002); and Robert L. Nelson, "German Comrades—Slavic Whores: Gender Images in the German Soldier Newspapers of the First World War," in *Home/Front,* ed. Hagemann and Schüler-Springorum, pp. 69–86.

140. Mary Louise Roberts, *Civilization without Sexes: Reconstructing Gender in Postwar France, 1917–1927* (Chicago, 1994). For comparisons with Germany and Britain, see Birthe Kundrus, *Kriegerfrauen: Familienpolitik und Geschlechterverhältnisse im Ersten und Zweiten Weltkrieg* (Hamburg, 1995); Susan Kingsley Kent, *Making Peace: The Reconstruction of Gender in Interwar Britain* (Princeton, N.J., 1993).

The figure of the "new woman" or *garçonne*—in some renderings threateningly androgynous, in others glamorous and sexually alluring—became the marker of this gender crisis, especially when read against the iconography of postwar masculinity, from the war invalids and broken beggars to the lady killers and *Lustmörder* in the work of male visual artists.[141] The dissonances in these images of postwar women and men suggest that a deep rupture in gender relations took place at the outset of the optimistic project of rebuilding democracy, one that would remain a recurrent force of disorder until its calamitous end.[142]

The Weimar Republic is one particular historical crossroads at which the social histories of women and more culturally-inflected histories of gender seem to chart two different paths through this period of prolonged crisis. The last three decades of scholarship on women, sexuality, and gender have offered abundant insight into the struggles of the 1920s over women's advances as citizens, workers, consumers, and sexually independent actors. Despite prolific study of these topics, their traces are seldom detectable in synthetic histories of the Weimar Republic and they appear to remain far removed from the center stage on which the high drama of the republic's struggle to survive was waged.[143] The narrative of women's "willing return to traditional gender roles"

141. Maria Tatar, *Lustmord: Sexual Murder in Weimar Germany* (Princeton, N.J., 1995); Rita Felski, *The Gender of Modernity* (Cambridge, Mass., 1995); Sian Reynolds, *France between the Wars: Gender and Politics* (London, 1996); Elizabeth Wood, *The Baba and the Comrade: Gender and Politics in Revolutionary Russia* (Bloomington, Ind., 1997); Tina Campt, "Blacks, Germans, and the Politics of Imperial Imagination, 1920–60," in *The Imperialist Imagination,* ed. Friedrichsmeyer et al., pp. 205–29; Carolyn Dean, *The Frail Social Body: Pornography, Homosexuality, and Other Fantasies in Interwar France* (Berkeley, Calif., 2000); and Elisa Camiscoli, "Producing Citizens, Reproducing the 'French Race': Immigration, Demography, and Pronatalism in Early Twentieth-Century France," in *Gender, Citizenships, and Subjectivities,* ed. Canning and Rose, pp. 167–95. On the postwar effacement of the trauma of women in wartime, see Karin Hausen, "The 'Day of National Mourning' in Germany," in *Between History and Histories: The Making of Silences and Commemorations,* ed. Gerald Sider and Gavin Smith (Toronto, 1997), pp. 127–46.

142. On the "new woman" in the period before the First World War, see Mary Louise Roberts, *Disruptive Acts: The New Woman in Fin-de-Siècle France* (Chicago, 2002).

143. Renate Bridenthal, "Beyond 'Kinder, Küche, Kirche': Weimar Women at Work," *Central European History* 6/2 (1973): 148–66; Grossmann, *Reforming Sex,* and her essay, "*Girlkultur* or Thoroughly Rationalized Female: A New Woman in Weimar Germany?" in *Women in Culture and Politics: A Century of Change,* ed. Judith Friedlander et al. (Bloomington, Ind., 1986), pp. 62–80. Also see Young-Sun Hong, "Gender, Citizenship, and the Welfare State: Social Work and the Politics of Femininity in the Weimar Republic"; Chris-

after the war is a necessary prerequisite, in fact, for this kind of historiographical boundary-drawing.[144] A different interpretation is certainly thinkable, one that might probe the fragility rather than assert the completion of such projects of restoration. Not only would this approach make it more difficult to marginalize gender but it would also help to excavate its place in the key chapters of Weimar history, from its utopian hopes in the founding years to the resurgent nationalism of its years of crisis.

Considering the history of Weimar from this perspective would also inflect the historical interpretations of fascism and Nazism. Specifically, the rise of fascist movements could be read as revitalizing an authoritarian and violent masculinity that took as its target the ambiguities of gender, ethnicity, and race, the freedoms of sex and leisure, earning, buying, and selling that comprised the aura of the new woman and were implicit in her figuration as modern. Scholarship of the last two decades on the Weimar and Nazi periods would suggest that the gender project the Nazis pursued, relentlessly and violently, was a linchpin of the racial state, and that this desire to realign gender and to subjugate sexuality arose in the interstices of Weimar social and sexual politics. Yet this knowledge has not thus far changed mainstream interpretations of Weimar's collapse, the Nazis' rise to power, or their successful mobilization for war and genocide.

---

tiane Eifert, "Coming to Terms with the State: Maternalist Politics and the Development of the Welfare State in Weimar Germany"; Susanne Rouette, "Mothers and Citizens: Gender and Social Policy in Germany after the First World War"; and Geoff Eley and Atina Grossmann, "Maternalism and Citizenship in Weimar Germany: The Gendered Politics of Welfare"; forum on maternalism and the welfare state in Germany in *Central European History* 30/1 (1997): 1–88; Usborne, *The Politics of the Body;* Patrice Petro, *Joyless Streets: Women and Melodramatic Representation in Weimar Germany* (Princeton, N.J., 1989); Andreas Huyssen, "Mass Culture as Woman: Modernism's Other," in *Studies in Entertainment: Critical Approaches to Mass Culture,* ed. Tania Modleski (Bloomington, Ind., 1986); and Birgitte Soland, *Becoming Modern: Young Women and the Reconstruction of Womanhood in the 1920s* (Princeton, N.J., 2000).

144. Katharina von Ankum, introduction to *Women in the Metropolis: Gender and Modernity in Weimar Culture,* ed. Katharina von Ankum (Berkeley, Calif., 1997), p. 6. For other perspectives from the disciplines of German literature and cultural studies, see Kerstin Barndt, *Sentiment und Sachlichkeit: Der Roman der Neuen Frau in der Weimarer Republik* (Cologne, 2003); Richard W. McCormick, *Gender and Sexuality in Weimar Modernity: Film, Literature, and "New Objectivity,"* (New York, 2001); and Vibeke Rützou Petersen, *Women and Modernity in Weimar Germany: Reality and Representation in Popular Fiction* (Oxford, 2001).

The role of women in interwar fascism and Nazism was a crucial test question for women's history of the 1970s and 1980s, which documented female participation in the highly restrictive female spheres of fascist states and societies.[145] Studies of fascist and Nazi social and family policy left no doubt that the visions of new national community, rejuvenated families, expansion of "living space," and purification of race all relied in different ways upon women, particularly on their willingness to serve as "reproducers of the nation."[146] At the same time studies of motherhood and reproduction in the Third Reich helped to expose the fundamental contradictions than ran through Nazi social and family policy. So, for example, the regime's idealization of motherhood and the elaborate sets of rewards it bestowed upon prolific mothers were undermined by the furious drive to rearm and by the labor shortages that ensued, drawing many women back into well-paying sectors of industrial employment after 1936.[147]

In probing the histories of women who were active subjects, not merely objects of fascist regimes, feminist historians complicated the notions of perpetrators and victims. Indeed, one of the most controversial studies of the late

145. Classics that laid the foundation for later scholarship and debates include Jill Stephenson, *Women in Nazi Society* (New York, 1975), and *The Nazi Organization of Women* (Totowa, N.J., 1981); as well as Claudia Koonz, *Mothers in the Fatherland: Women, Family Life, and Nazi Ideology, 1919–1945* (New York, 1986). Stephenson has recently returned to this topic. See her *Women in Nazi Germany* (Harlow, UK, 2001).

146. Timothy Mason, "Women in Nazi Germany," *History Workshop* 1 (1976): 74–113, and "Women in Germany 1925–1940: Family, Welfare and Work," ibid., 2 (1976): 5–32; Claudia Koonz, "The Competition for Women's *Lebensraum* 1928–34," in *When Biology Became Destiny*, ed. Bridenthal et al., pp. 190–236. On Italy, see Victoria de Grazia, *How Fascism Ruled Women: Italy 1922–1945* (Berkeley, Calif., 1992); Perry R. Wilson, "Women in Fascist Italy," in *Fascist Italy and Nazi Germany: Comparisons and Contrasts*, ed. Richard Bessel (Cambridge, 1996), pp. 78–93; and Lesley Caldwell, "Reproducers of the Nation: Women and the Family in Fascist Policy," in *Rethinking Italian Fascism: Capitalism, Populism, and Culture*, ed. David Forgacs (London, 1986). More recent studies of fascist movements in Britain, Vichy France, and Franco's Spain include Gottlieb, *Feminine Fascism*; Miranda Pollard, *Reign of Virtue: Mobilizing Gender in Vichy France* (Chicago, 1998); and Pamela B. Radcliff, *From Mobilization to Civil War: The Politics of Polarization in the Spanish City of Gijon, 1900–1937* (Cambridge, 1996).

147. Annemarie Tröger, "The Creation of a Female Assembly-Line Proletariat," in *When Biology Became Destiny*, ed. Bridenthal et al., pp. 237–70; Mason, "Women in Nazi Germany"; and Carola Sachse, *Industrial Housewives: Women's Social Work in the Factories in Nazi Germany*, trans. Heide Kiessling and Dorothy Rosenberg, ed. Jane Caplan (New York, 1987).

1980s, Claudia Koonz's *Mothers in the Fatherland,* argued against the notion that German women were "peculiarly resistant to National Socialism," pointing to the crucial complicity of women not only with the Nazi party, state, and social vision, but also in the propagation of war and genocide. "Far from remaining untouched by evil," Koonz contended, "women operated at its very center."[148] The swirl of debate surrounding Koonz's book, termed the *Historikerinnenstreit,* represented a fundamental conflict over the degree to which female actors could exercise agency within a system that had stripped women of most parameters of power.[149] Widely followed and discussed among both feminist and "mainstream" German historians, this dispute made women's participation in the Third Reich a decisive "limit case for testing difficult questions" about the attribution of agency to female historical actors, which in this case was bound up with issues of morality, rationality, and relativism.[150]

This heated debate over female agency and complicity helps to explain why the advent of gender history has not effaced women as actors or objects of analysis in the history of fascist regimes. Instead, the two concepts have coexisted in recent historiography without destabilizing one another. To some ex-

148. Koonz, *Mothers in the Fatherland.* See also the more recent book by Vandana Joshi, *Gender and Power in the Third Reich: Female Denouncers and the Gestapo 1933–1945* (Houndsmills, 2003).

149. The debates prompted by Koonz's book are summarized and analyzed succinctly by Atina Grossmann, "Feminist Debates about Women and National Socialism," *Gender & History* 3/3 (Autumn 1991): 350–58. Koonz's chief critic was the German women's historian Gisela Bock, author of a field-defining book on sterilization of women in Nazi Germany: *Zwangssterilisation im Nationalsozialismus: Studien zur Rassenpolitik und Frauenpolitik* (Opladen, 1986). See the volume of essays by daughters of Nazi perpetrators about the role of their mothers in the Third Reich: Lerke Gravenhorst and Carmen Tatschmura, eds., *Töchter-Fragen: NS-Frauen-Geschichte* (Freiburg i. B., 1990). For an excellent more recent summary of these debates, see Adelheid von Saldern, "Victims or Perpetrators? Controversies about the Role of Women in the Nazi State," in *Nazism and German Society 1933– 45,* ed. David F. Crew (London, 1994). For a more recent discussion of women's interests in nationalism and Nazi expansionism, see Harvey, "Pilgrimages to the 'Bleeding Border.'" Also see Elizabeth Harvey, "Remembering and Repressing: German Women's Recollections of the 'Ethnic Struggle' in Occupied Poland during the Second World War," in *Home/ Front,* ed. Hagemann and Schüler-Springorum, pp. 275–96.

150. Caplan, "Postmodernism, Poststructuralism," pp. 274–75. See the recent assessment of this debate and its implications for feminist German history by Ralph M. Leck, "Conservative Empowerment and the Gender of Nazism: Paradigms of Power and Complicity in German Women's History," *Journal of Women's History* 12/2 (Summer 2000): 147–69.

tent, of course, the study of *policies* towards women, family, marriage, and motherhood in both Italian and German fascism has focused more centrally on the construction of women, motherhood, sexuality, and race than on the actions of women who were interpellated in these policies. This is likely the result of the scarcity of sources on women's experiences in the interstices of fascist social policies. Studies of Nazi reproductive politics, in particular of sterilization, compulsory abortion, and coerced childbirth, refrain from clear delineations between and among body, sexuality, and gender. While each constituted a distinct site of reproductive intervention in prefascist states, the success of fascist biopolitics in fact depended upon the regime's ability to blur these very boundaries.[151] This interplay among and between these concepts should not camouflage the fact that these studies of reproductive politics shared a common object of analysis, namely the fascist circumscription of both sexes in rebiologized and newly racialized bodies. A newer branch of body histories of fascism has highlighted the place of fashion in both disciplining and representing the social body through the creation and enforcement of a highly gendered national style.[152]

In recent years the study of both masculinities and sexualities under fascism has gained new visibility and brisance.[153] Historians of the Third Reich have

151. Gisela Bock, "Racism and Sexism in Nazi Germany: Motherhood, Compulsory Sterilization, and the State," in *When Biology Became Destiny,* ed. Bridenthal et al., pp. 271–96, and *Zwangssterilisation im Nationalsozialismus;* Claudia Koonz, "Eugenics, Gender, and Ethics in Nazi Germany: The Debate about Involuntary Sterilization 1933–1936," in *Reevaluating the Third Reich,* ed. Childers and Caplan, pp. 66–85; Gabriele Czarnowski, "'The Value of Marriage for the Volksgemeinschaft': Policies towards Women and Marriage under National Socialism," in *Fascist Italy and Nazi Germany,* ed. Bessel, pp. 94–112; also see *Das kontrollierte Paar: Ehe- und Sexualpolitik im Nationalsozialismus* (Weinheim, 1991), and Henry P. David, Jochen Fleischhacker, and Charlotte Höhn, "Abortion and Eugenics in Nazi Germany," *Population and Development Review* 14:1 (March 1988).

152. For example Irene Guenther, *Nazi Chic? Fashioning Women in the Third Reich* (Oxford, 2004); and Emilia Paulicelli, "Fashion, the Politics of Style, and National Identity in Pre-Fascist and Fascist Italy," *Gender & History* 14/3 (November 2002): 537–59.

153. Geoffrey J. Giles, "'The Most Unkind Cut of All': Castration, Homosexuality, and Nazi Justice," *Journal of Contemporary History* 27 (1992): 41–61, and "The Institutionalization of Homosexual Panic in the Third Reich," in *Social Outsiders in Nazi Germany,* ed. Robert Gellately and Nathan Stoltzfus (Princeton, N.J., 2001); Stefan Maiwald and Gerd Mischler, *Sexualität unter dem Hakenkreuz: Manipulation und Vernichtung der Intimsphäre im NS-Staat* (Hamburg, 1999); and the recent dissertation by Todd Ettelson, "The Nazi 'New Man': Embodying Masculinity and Regulating Sexuality in the SA and SS, 1930–1939"

launched new investigations of the implication of the Nazi state in prostitution, the articulation and prosecution of same-sex desire, and the crusades against racial "defilement" and sexual fraternization with foreigners.[154] The most recent wave of studies has successfully refuted the once-dominant view of sexuality in the Third Reich as "profoundly repressive and intensely preoccupied with sexual propriety," delivering persuasive evidence for both the proliferation of premarital sex among young couples and a pervasive preoccupation with sexual pleasure.[155] Yet this scholarship on sexuality and fascism has remained mainly peripheral to the field-defining debates and public discussions in Third Reich historiography about perpetrators and victims, the role of the German Army in the Holocaust, the deployment of foreign labor, and the intricacies of guilt and collaboration of "ordinary Germans."[156] In fact, the chasm that has separated these thematics from studies of hetero- and homosexualities is even wider than that which banished gender and sexuality to the margins of Weimar history. The special issue of the *Journal of the History of Sexuality* edited by Dagmar Herzog in 2002 aspires to overcome this separation. The individual essays collectively break with the taboos that once worked to in-

(Ph.D. diss., University of Michigan, 2002). On female sexuality see Claudia Schoppmann, *Nationalsoziastische Sexualpolitik und weibliche Homosexualität* (Pfaffenweiler, 1991), and "National Socialist Policies towards Female Homosexuality," in *Gender Relations in German History*, ed. Abrams and Harvey; Erica Fischer, *Aimée und Jaguar: Eine Frauenliebe, Berlin 1943* (Munich, 1996).

154. For an excellent overview of recent research in this area, see Dagmar Herzog, "Hubris and Hypocrisy, Incitement and Disavowal: Sexuality and German Fascism," and Elizabeth Heinemann, "Sexuality and Nazism: The Doubly Unspeakable?" in *Sexuality and German Fascism*, ed. Herzog, special issue of *Journal of History of Sexuality* 11/1–2 (January/April, 2002): 1–21, 22–66. These topics are addressed by contributors to the volume, including Julia Roos (prostitution); Geoffrey Giles (same-sex incidents in the SS and police); Stefan Micheler (homophobic propaganda); Birthe Kundrus (relationships between Germans and foreigners); Erik Jensen (persecution of gays and lesbians); and Annette Timm (prostitution and venereal disease). The new interest in sexuality under Nazism unfolded, according to Elizabeth Heineman, within a complex of thematics, including the scientific basis of Nazi racism, women's history, and the relatively recent history of sexual minorities. See her "Sexuality and Nazism," p. 23.

155. Herzog, "Hubris and Hypocrisy," pp. 7–12. Note that the title of Heinemann's essay in *Sexuality and German Fascism* is "Sexuality and Nazism: The Doubly Unspeakable?" A definitive work about to appear is Dagmar Herzog, *Sex after Fascism: Memory and Morality in Twentieth-Century Germany* (Princeton, N.J., 2005).

156. An exception is Sven Reichardt, *Faschistische Kampfbünde: Gewalt und Gemeinschaft im italienischen Squadrismus und in der deutschen SA* (Cologne, 2002).

hibit serious study of the place of sexuality in fascism or render it "doubly un-speakable," most notably the fears that a focus on sexuality would titillate, triv-ialize, or sensationalize the "grim subject of Nazi Germany."[157] Staking a bold claim to pursue the connections between sexuality and "other kinds of politics" in the Third Reich, the essays in this volume reveal a sexual grid in which anti-Semitism was inextricable from Nazi sexual politics and homophobia insepa-rable from "happy heterosexuality."[158] The volume fills out the history of everyday sex lives under fascism, depicting the Nazis as obsessed with "both re-production and pleasure," while asserting a definitive place for sexuality, not merely in the realms of "politics," but in the operation of racial persecution and annihilation. The essays in this collection emphasize that sexuality in the Third Reich was "also about the invasion and control and destruction of human be-ings."[159]

One of the "peculiarities of German history" is the impossibility of separat-ing the history of Nazism from the study of the Second World War and the Holocaust. In other national histories the second total war either stands alone or is studied on a continuum or in comparison with the First World War. While women feature more prominently than gender or sexuality in the historiogra-phy of the Second World War, gender and sexuality have a more significant place in the study of the war's aftermath. At the end of the First World War women in several European countries acquired the rights of political citizen-ship; as the front lines of warfare moved into cities and towns during the Sec-ond World War several European states (particularly on the Allied side) issued new appeals to their female citizens to partake in the actual conduct of war. In-deed, the extensive bombings of European cities obliterated the distinction be-tween home front and battlefield, drawing civilians in unprecedented numbers into the war—as "combatants" in the ranks of civilian defense, as targets of the air war in the war of morale, and as members of the medical corps or military support units at the front.[160] The antifascist rhetoric of the Allied states inter-pellated women as citizens in another sense as well, for they directed specific

157. Herzog, "Hubris and Hypocrisy," p. 16; Heinemann, "Sexuality and Nazism," p. 25.
158. Herzog, "Hubris and Hypocrisy," pp. 3–4.
159. Ibid., p. 6. Heinemann, "Sexuality and Nazism," p. 24.
160. Rose, *Which People's War*; Pollard, *Reign of Virtue*; Penny Summerfield, *Recon-structing Women's Wartime Lives: Discourse and Subjectivity in Oral Histories of the Second World War* (New York, 1998); Katherine Jolluck, *Exile and Identity: Polish Women in the So-viet Union during World War II* (Pittsburgh, 2002); and Anna Krylova, "Stalinist Identity from the Viewpoint of Gender: Rearing a Generation of Professionally Violent Women-Fighters in 1930s Stalinist Russia," *Gender & History* 16/3 (November 2004): 626–53.

appeals to women to protect their hard-won rights against the viciously antifeminist Nazis and fascists.[161]

The histories of women in the First World War are mostly written within the boundaries of nations. Because the annihilative consequences of the Second World War and the Holocaust fundamentally altered the maps of both western and eastern Europe, this particular chapter in the history of women (in an interesting parallel to the history of empires) requires the crossing of boundaries between spaces national and international, between East and West. This is certainly true for the study of those women who became the indisputably gendered victims of forced labor, or of the genocidal policies toward European Jews, or those who joined the Resistance movements in one of the Nazi-occupied countries.[162] Women also comprised the majority of civilians and refugees in transit across central Europe during and after the war, displaced, exiled, conscripted, or savagely murdered as German and then Russian troops criss-crossed and fought over this terrain between 1942 and 1945. Of course, women are not only found in the ranks of the millions of victims of war and annihilation, but also as active subjects whose own interests, whether in the

161. Susan Gubar, "'This Is My Rifle, This Is My Gun': World War II and the Blitz on Women," in *Behind the Lines,* ed. Higonnet et al., pp. 227–59.

162. On resistance, see Paula Schwartz, "Redefining Resistance: Women's Activism in Wartime France," in *Behind the Lines,* ed. Higonnet et al., pp. 141–53; Margaret C. Weitz, *Sisters in the Resistance: How Women Fought to Free France, 1940–45* (New York, 1995); Padraic Kenney, "The Gender of Resistance in Communist Poland," *American Historical Review* 104/2 (April 1999): 399–425. On the displacement of women during and after the war, see Katherine Jolluck, "'You Can't Even Call Them Women': Poles and 'Others' in Soviet Exile during the Second World War," *Contemporary European History* 10/3 (November 2001): 463–80; and Doris Bergen, "Sex, Blood, and Vulnerability: Women Outsiders in German Occupied Europe," in *Social Outsiders in Nazi Germany,* ed. Gellately and Stoltzfus. On women/gender in the history of the Holocaust, see Sybil Milton, "Women and the Holocaust: The Case of German and German-Jewish Women," in *When Biology Became Destiny,* ed. Bridenthal et al., pp. 297–333; Joan Ringelheim, "Women and the Holocaust: A Reconsideration of Research," *Signs* 10 (Summer 1985): 741–61, and her more recent "The Split between Gender and the Holocaust," in *Women in the Holocaust,* ed. Dalia Ofer and Lenore Weitzman (New Haven, Conn., 1998); Marion Kaplan, *Between Dignity and Despair: Jewish Life in Nazi Germany* (New York, 1998); Ann Taylor Allen, "The Holocaust and the Modernization of Gender: A Historiographical Essay," *Central European History* 30/3 (1997): 349–64; and Judith T. Baumel, *Double Jeopardy: Gender and the Holocaust* (London, 1998).

symbolism of the "Mother Cross" or the "lightning conquest" of Poland, the Nazi regime promised to fulfill.[163]

Even if the distinction between perpetrators and victims must remain so fluid as to encompass the many different gradations of complicity and resistance, the history of this war nonetheless serves as a laboratory for twentieth-century gender extremes, of which there are ample illustrations. The intensely gendered experiences of men took place in the front lines of the war, where "total" took on new meanings amidst new weapons and strategies of warfare and where the annihilation of civilians and Jews formed part of the war plan, whose perpetrators ranged from the hypermasculine SS commanders to the "ordinary men" analyzed by Christopher Browning.[164] Prisoner of war camps became another site of masculine gender extremes, in which the brutality of war was revisited upon those who waged it—through hard labor, starvation, and terror—and in which, amidst the mass death, broken bodies, and forgotten deeds, new postwar masculinities would emerge.[165]

The singularly female gender extremes include a systematic and barbarous body politics that coerced some women into motherhood, forced upon others sterilization or abortion, conscripted still other women—foreign laborers or those living under German occupation—into prostitution, or used rape as a strategy in securing military and national domination. As one example, the mass rapes that accompanied the Soviet march through Germany, especially those extensively documented in Berlin in the early days of May 1945, demar-

163. Harvey, "'Pilgrimages to the 'Bleeding Border,'" and "Remembering and Repressing." Also see Harvey, *Women and the Nazi East.*

164. Christopher Browning, *Ordinary Men: Reserve Police Battalion 101 and the Final Solution in Poland* (New York, 1993). On male camaraderie in the setting of war, see Kühne, "Comradeship"; Wolfram Wette, ed., *Retter im Uniform: Handlungsspielräume im Vernichtungskrieg der Wehrmacht* (Frankfurt a. M., 2002); and René Schilling, *"Kriegshelden": Deutungsmuster heroischer Männlichkeit in Deutschland 1813–1945* (Paderborn, 2002). For a comparison with England, see Graham Dawson, *Soldier Heroes: British Adventure, Empire, and the Imagining of Masculinities* (London, 1994).

165. On postwar masculinities, see Heide Fehrenbach, "Rehabilitating Fatherland: Race and German Remasculinization"; Robert G. Moeller, "'The Last Soldiers of the Great War' and Tales of Family Reunions in the Federal Republic of Germany"; and Uta Poiger, "A New 'Western' Hero? Reconstructing German Masculinity in the 1950s," forum in *Signs* 24/1 (Autumn 1998): 107–27, 128–46, 147–62. Also see Frank Biess, "Men of Reconstruction—The Reconstruction of Men: Returning POWs in East and West Germany, 1945–55," in *Home/Front,* ed. Hagemann and Schüler-Springorum, pp. 335–58.

cated the new space that was to become Germany after the war and represented the first act in its subjugation for many of its victims.[166] The end of the war itself, certainly in Germany but to some extent across Europe, marked a different kind of gender extreme, in which "women standing alone" confronted the traumas of the war's aftermath: the charred remains of European populations and urban landscapes; the displacement and disorientation of millions of Holocaust survivors or others who had lost families and homes; the and occupation of Germany and its division into zones that formed a new East-West boundary at the heart of the continent; and not least, the worldwide wave of shock and abhorrence at Nazi crimes that followed the liberation of the death camps.[167]

The gender stories of the aftermath of the two world wars diverge on many crucial points. For one, the war itself had not appeared to shake the gender foundation of society in the same way as the First World War had, perhaps because that foundation was still in pieces when the Second World War began, or because so many of the other bedrocks of European society were broken at the end of the war. The task of reordering families, women's roles and rights, and their relations to men, who remained absent in many countries for several years, would become urgent once the project of rebuilding Europe had begun. This period of rupture, between fascist terror and war and the founding of new nations, between the war's end and the reestablishment of political and social order, may not have constituted a "zero hour" in Germany or Europe, but it did

166. Atina Grossmann, "A Question of Silence: The Rape of German Women by Occupation Soldiers," *October* 72 (Spring 1995): 43–63. Also see Norman Naimark, *The Russians in Germany: A History of the Soviet Zone of Occupation, 1945–1949* (Cambridge, Mass., 1995); Beck, "Rape"; Andrea Pato, "Memory and the Narratives of Rape in Budapest and Vienna in 1945," in *Life after Death: Violence, Normality, and the Construction of Postwar Europe,* ed. Richard Bessel and Dirk Schumann (Cambridge, 2003), pp. 129–48; and Ruth Seifert, "The Second Front: The Logic of Sexual Violence in Wars," in *Violence and Its Alternatives,* ed. Manfred B. Steger and Nancy S. Lind (New York, 1999).

167. Robert G. Moeller, *War Stories: The Search for a Usable Past in the Federal Republic of Germany* (Berkeley, Calif., 2001); Heineman, *What Difference Does a Husband Make?;* Höhn, *GIs and Fräuleins;* Atina Grossmann, "Victims, Villains, and Survivors: Gendered Perceptions and Self-Perceptions of Jewish Displaced Persons in Occupied Postwar Germany," in *Sexuality and German Fascism,* ed. Herzog, pp. 291–318. Also see Denise Riley, "Some Peculiarities of Social Policy Concerning Women in Wartime and Postwar Britain"; Jane Jenson, "The Liberation and New Rights for French Women"; and Annemarie Tröger, "German Women's Memories of World War II," in *Behind the Lines,* ed. Higonnet et al., pp. 260–99.

mark a moment of rupture, or liminality, in which the meanings of gender and sex broke away from their moorings—national, social, and cultural.[168] Given the millions of dead, displaced, injured, and missing, and the shifting of peoples, goods, and national boundaries, the landscape of gender and sexual relations was experienced in the temporality of the short-term as tenuous, improvised, and momentary. Discourses about women, gender, and sex could be no more quickly reassembled than everyday life, especially as some of those discourses were spoken in unfamiliar languages or imposed by occupation governments, symbolized by men in arms. Gayle Rubin's proposal that sexualities are best understood in terms of traffic in women or sexual trade seems particularly pertinent to this moment in European history when national maps were redrawn, economies were disassembled and rebuilt, when occupation armies helped to reinvent civil society, and individual survival depended on the capacity for exchanging goods and sometimes sex.[169] Moreover, the trade between occupation armies and civilians, best illustrated in the case of "GIs and Fräuleins," who swapped cigarettes and chocolate, sex and the certain sense of safety that accompanied friendship with soldiers, maps out a space of pleasure amidst death and destruction. More importantly, the traffic in sex helped to refigure the symbolic and material terrains of nation, economy, and family. The work of overcoming the gender extremes of the war and postwar period would begin with the drawing of new borders through Europe, the reconvening of national governments, and the institution of welfare states that were to restore the shattered core of civil society.

The paths from the liminal moments of the immediate aftermath of war and Holocaust to the decade of the 1950s were certainly far from straightforward, as recent work on gender, women, and sexuality has abundantly shown. The work of dismantling ideologies left over from Nazism about motherhood, family, and race more frequently took place at the level of high politics, in the drafting of laws and rewriting of constitutions that expanded women's postwar

168. See, for example, Atina Grossmann, "Trauma, Memory, and Motherhood: German and Jewish Displaced Persons in Post-Nazi Germany, 1945–49," and Dagmar Herzog, "Desperately Seeking Normality: Sex and Marriage in the Wake of War," in *Life after Death,* ed. Bessel et al., pp. 93–128, 161–92.

169. See the recent books by Heinemann, *What Difference Does a Husband Make?* and Höhn, *GIs and Fräuleins.* Also see Heineman, "The Hour of the Woman: Memories of Germany's 'Crisis Years' and West German National Identity," *American Historical Review* 101/2 (April 1996): 354–95; and Susanne zur Nieden, "Erotic Fraternization: The Legend of German Women's Quick Surrender," in *Home/Front,* ed. Hagemann and Schüler-Springorum, pp. 297–310.

citizenship rights and sought to reconcile them with motherhood and family. This "refeminization" of women was to redirect the remarkable resourcefulness of "rubble women" amidst the chaos and despair at the war's end towards the rebuilding of families and homes.[170] This marked the beginning of a new domestic politics in which the drawing of new Cold War boundaries between East and West was mirrored in the distancing of families from public and politics, in the reinscription of private, bounded not least by the renewed investment in consumption. Indeed, the revival of domesticity in the 1950s would foster new female expertise in the socialization of children and the practices of consumption, both of which increasingly defined the political border between East and West and informed the political polarizations of the Cold War, especially on its fault line through Germany.[171]

Yet feminist studies of single motherhood, part-time wage labor, popular culture, and peace movements affirm that the "life-feeling" of this Cold War era diverged significantly from its dominant discourses about family and motherhood and the inherent freedoms of consumption. The impulses of "refamilializing" and "redomesticating" women in Germany would remain partial and incomplete as significant numbers of households (40 percent) were headed by single women into the early 1950s and as increasing numbers of women sought part-time employment outside of the home during this decade.[172] At the same time, women became active participants in social movements, both pacifist anti-armaments initiatives and in anticommunist mobilizations in western Europe.[173] The restoration of gender was at the heart of Europe's social, moral, and economic recovery and relied not only upon an implicitly female "refamilialization," but also on the "remasculinization" of men. This process, for which there was no parallel in the aftermath of the First World War, was to dis-

170. The definitive work on this period remains Robert G. Moeller, *Protecting Motherhood: Women and the Family in the Politics of Postwar West Germany* (Berkeley, Calif., 1993).

171. Pence, "Labours of Consumption"; Carter, *How German Is She?*; and Irene Stoehr, "Cold War Communities: Women's Peace Politics in Postwar West Germany, 1945–52," in *Home/Front*, ed. Hagemann and Schüler-Springorum, pp. 311–34.

172. Moeller, *Protecting Motherhood*; Heineman, *What Difference Does a Husband Make?*; Höhn, *GIs and Fräuleins*; Uta Poiger, *Jazz, Rock, and Rebels: Cold War Politics and American Culture in a Divided Germany* (Berkeley, Calif., 2000); Christine von Oertzen, *Teilzeit und die Lust am Zuverdienen: Geschlechterpolitik und gesellschaftlicher Wandel in Westdeutschland, 1948–1969* (Göttingen, 1999); and Irene Stoehr, "Kalter Krieg und Geschlecht: Überlegungen zu einer Friedenshistorischen Forschungslücke," in *Perspektiven der historischen Forschung*, ed. Benjamin Ziemann (Essen, 2002), pp. 133–45.

173. Stoehr, "Kalter Krieg und Geschlecht," and Poiger, *Jazz, Rock, and Rebels*.

solve the militarized masculinities of war and fascism and instill in their place a gentler masculinity of fathers and providers, whose return home from the war became a crucial symbol of the renewal of both nation and family.[174] Yet the now burgeoning studies of European social movements in the 1960s would suggest that these gender realignments were never wholly stabilized, even in the decade of domesticity—the 1950s.[175]

CONCLUSION

The history of war, Holocaust, and postwar reconstruction is inextricable from the work of memory and memorialization that took place in both the public sphere and the annals of historical scholarship. The narratives and life stories that form the raw material in the study of historical memory bring gender strikingly into the open. In the assembly of historical memory, it is unproblematic to posit that men and women experienced and thus remember, represent or tell their stories differently; in history, by contrast, the tenacious claim to objectivity has made it more difficult to excavate gender in historical analysis of world war, genocide, postwar displacements and reconstructions— the very stuff around which the study of memory and memorialization has turned in recent years. This raises the question about whether there is something intrinsic in the genre of historical writing—or perhaps it is a desire for one genre of historical writing—that works against this very work of excavation, compelling the disconnection of gender again and again from the "mega-events" that define historical epochs, even when abundant scholarship has delivered powerful testimony of its relevance.

From the very moment at which the category "gender" began to emerge analytically from the category "women," feminist historians like Joan Kelly envisioned no less than a comprehensive redefinition of categories, chronologies, and narratives of historical transformation. In this essay I have highlighted the different impulses of feminist history—the critique of established categories and narratives in arenas of study like labor, class, citizenship, and public sphere, which had matured and expanded in the 1960s and 1970s without significant input from feminists. Women's history provided much of the impetus and empirical

174. Fehrenbach, "Rehabilitating Fatherland"; Moeller, "'The Last Soldiers of the Great War'"; Poiger, "A New 'Western' Hero?"; and Biess, "Men of Reconstruction."

175. Dagmar Herzog, "'Pleasure, Sex, and Politics Belong Together': Post-Holocaust Memory and the Sexual Revolution in West Germany," *Critical Inquiry* 24 (Winter 1998): 393–444.

groundwork in this critical enterprise, while the turn to gender helped to redefine the keywords of historical analysis in these fields. In the more culturally inflected inquiries of consumption, cultures of colonialism and empire or body
histories, feminist inquiry was present from an earlier stage, occupying an insider
status rather than representing a critical impulse from outside. Where the "new
cultural history" had its home in the early 1990s, research on gender drove and
defined the expansion into new thematics, such as study of the social and symbolic power of consumption, of the standards of fashion and taste, or the exploration of the intimate realms of empires that laid bare new aspects of colonial
projects and their implications for political practices in the metropoles.[176]

The resonances of gender have been uneven not only across national fields,
but also among different thematic areas in modern European history, a point
that I can only make in view of the extraordinary scholarly achievements surveyed here. While the combined effect of research on women and gender has
led to step-by-step revision of turning points and formative events in some areas of inquiry, in most cases the work of actually reassembling an entirely new
narrative remains a challenge for the future. From the Enlightenment and the
French Revolution to the history of postwar reconstructions, attention to gender has recast keywords and written entirely new actors and conflicts into historical narratives. In other fields, however, the study of women and gender has
refigured understandings of the social or everyday life, of those arenas women allegedly inhabited or shaped most forcefully, or in which femininity or
masculinity were particularly contested, leaving the meanings of gender for
epochal events like revolution, state formation, war, or the negotiation of peace
mostly unexplored. The study of the nineteenth century, for example, which
could now include a wide range of feminisms and domestic ideologies, the
emergence of women as a social category and women's waged labor as a social
question, along with the dissemination of ideologies and scientific classifica-
tions that redefined gender and drew new boundaries of race and class through
both nations and empires, could undoubtedly be fashioned into a new historical narrative that would differ markedly from textbook versions of twenty,
even ten, years ago. Rethinking twentieth-century history, while perhaps still a
premature undertaking, is likely to show that gender histories often follow their

176. Three examples that come immediately to mind: de Grazia with Furlough, *The Sex
of Things;* Hunt, *The Family Romance of the French Revolution;* and Stoler, *Carnal Knowledge and Imperial Power.* On the new cultural history, see Lynn Hunt, ed., *The New Cultural History* (Berkeley, Calif., 1989); and Lynn Hunt, ed., *Beyond the Cultural Turn: New
Directions in the Study of Society and Culture* (Berkeley, Calif., 1999).

own temporalities. As the example of Europe between the wars suggests, gender norms and ideologies that rupture at points of political and cultural crisis are not easily reinstated in the course of political reconstruction or stabilization, continuing often to unsettle new formations, such as interwar democracy. The gender history of the future is one that can confidently admit the possibility of disparate temporalities. Rather than attempting to fit gender back into established chronologies and categories, its more productive outcome may be to allow dissonance within grand narratives.

This essay presents a broad template of methodologies and practices in gender history. Is there any way, then, to generalize about the meanings and methods of doing gender history as opposed to the history of women, which has constituted a central preoccupation of this essay? For one, the fears of the early 1990s that embrace of gender would ultimately disable the study of women have not proven true. Rather, the relationship between the two concepts remains uneven, varied, and above all, historically specific. Nor, secondly, is it apt to posit a division of labor or method between these two terms that aligns the study of women with social history and gender with cultural history, not least because the lines between social and cultural history are no longer so sharp, as historians have pursued cultural histories of the social and social histories of the cultural. Third, gender history has not so much left women behind as it has redefined the terms of the inquiry, the lens of analysis. The pursuit of gender calls on its practitioners to work more creatively with silences and absences, so that gender has meaning even where female actors cannot be found. Methodologically speaking, if our sources are limited to archival fragments, to records with blank spaces, to small snapshots and silences, then the disjunctures in these sources are an essential part of the gender story that should be told. If the writing of gender entails an ensemble of such snapshots, then the standpoint of the photographer is at least as important (also in gendered terms) as the subject of the snapshot.

A final and most important point is that the encounter between gender and women profoundly altered the meanings of both. In fact, the most general effect of gender has been its capacity to divest women of the essentialism that characterized earlier feminist scholarship. And, as Joan Scott has recently argued, gender is itself momentarily undergoing a parallel kind of "defamiliarization" in the face of the flourishing production of scholarship on sexuality, Queer Studies, on race, ethnicity, and hybridity.[177] The recognition that the

177. See Joan Scott's commentary on gender's "defamiliarization" in "Feminism's History," p. 21.

keywords of feminist history—women and gender—are mutable and subject to change highlights the necessity of working more self-consciously with categories or concepts, of knowing why one or the other—gender, body, sexuality—is more apt, while also acknowledging and accounting for the historically specific settings where these distinctions are impossible or even ahistorical. Indeed, one conclusion that emerges from this survey of wide-ranging topical and national fields is the necessity of connecting our archives to our categories, of giving the sources a say in deciding which concept—woman or gender, body or sexuality—is most suitable for a particular historical endeavor. Rather than an end goal, this marks a beginning step, one that requires the work of turning the concepts round and round in the archival sand and then widening their context to consider their resonances in other disciplines. This means pushing at our concepts from at least two directions—from the archival ground up and from the interiors of our discipline into the wider field of interdisciplinary dialogue.

Despite the definitive place of gender in the linguistic turn a decade ago and the implicit affinity of gender with the analysis of culture, ideology, symbols, and meanings, there is no one method that defines the historical study of gender, nor need there be. Gender may constitute an object of historical investigation—for example, the articulations of norms and ideologies of masculinity and femininity—or it may be a strategy for excavating the operations of sexual difference in historical texts or processes of actual transformation. The most ambitious definition of gender as historical practice involves its relentless relationality, its claim to study both the social and the symbolic relations between the sexes, conjoining them where possible, and in its positing of a reciprocal relationship between ideologies and experiences of gender that were lived and assigned meaning differentially by male and female actors. Now that gender history has achieved so much, its practitioners are often asked whether the tasks of disassembling terminologies, temporalities, and narratives might soon be replaced by the desire to reassemble. It is doubtful, however, that this will take place in the form of a one-way march from the margins into the master narratives. Rather than fitting gender into the existent mainstream, we might hope that its eventual integration will mean an altogether less truncated history, one that dissolves the distinctions between epochal changes and histories of gender, women, and sexuality.

CHAPTER 2 § FEMINIST HISTORY AFTER THE LINGUISTIC TURN § HISTORICIZING DISCOURSE & EXPERIENCE

PROLOGUE 2005

This essay was first presented as a conference paper in 1992, a moment when the fierce controversies over the linguistic turn had subsided and the sensation of epistemological crisis had begun to fade. Yet many of those who had followed the debates were still trying to figure out their effects on our own historical practices, both in the classroom and in our research and writing projects. Joan Scott's article "The Evidence of Experience," published first in 1991, unleashed another round of debate, perhaps more specifically this time among historians, on the implications of poststructuralist theory for history. In fact, many read Scott's essay as a kind of "how to" guide for the historical analysis of both discourses and experiences—the crucial keywords that had remained largely undefined in the course of the linguistic turn. Scott's dismantling of social historical notions of experience was dazzling and definitive, so much so that the capacity of discourse to position subjects and produce experience appeared immutable and timeless. In fact, the relationship she posed between discourse and experience, their quasi-melding together under the expansiveness of discourse, seemed to foreclose further discussion, not least because it was extremely difficult to refute.

That, in fact, was not the purpose of my critical engagement with Scott's essay. My intention in writing this essay, then, was to push beyond that moment of apparent foreclosure by tracing the workings of these categories in my own study of "the languages of labor and gender" in Germany. I sought to break open the hierarchies instated between these terms, to challenge their constraints and the boundaries they enforced. This meant attempting to pry discourse and experience away from their binary relation, probing and questioning the neces-

This essay was first published in *Signs* 19/2 (Winter 1994) and reprinted in *History and Theory: Feminist Research, Debates, Contestations,* ed. Barbara Laslett, Ruth-Ellen Boetcher-Joeres, Mary Jo Maynes, and Evelyn Brooks Higginbotham (Chicago, 1997). I thank the University of Chicago Press for permission to reprint this article here.

sity and historicity of the dichotomous pairing that seemed to bind them inextricably together. I sought to historicize these categories by questioning the origins and outcomes of discourses, and the contradictions and conflicting positions within them, in order to grasp just how they came to concentrate so passionately, in late nineteenth-century Germany, on the dangers of married women's factory work. While I agreed with Scott that experience was always linguistically informed, I was also curious about the instances of experience when bodies or physical spaces were perceptibly marked or transformed, but in ways that could not be spoken, or when bodies themselves constituted a kind of ruins, a particular kind of evidence of experience—for example during or in the aftermath of war, revolution, or genocide. Thus for me historicizing these categories meant reading theory through my own archives and eschewing thereby the temptation to embrace any particular historical terms or pairings as definitive across historical time and space. The idea that discourse and experience, theory and archives, inflect one another in changeable and historically specific ways perhaps explains the continued resonance of this essay.

§ § §

The starting point of this essay is the ongoing and uneasy encounter between feminism and poststructuralist theory across the disciplines. I explore here the implications of what has come to be termed the *linguistic turn* for the history of women and gender and analyze the controversies among feminists about its far-ranging consequences for historical research and writing. The very interdisciplinarity implied by the term "linguistic turn" constitutes one of the uneasy moments in this encounter: the boundary crossings between disciplines have challenged the foundations of individual fields while at the same time creating new domains of interdisciplinary inquiry that seem to render obsolete the familiar tools, concepts, and epistemologies of the traditional disciplines. Indeed, because much of the provocative rethinking and recasting of these terms has taken place outside of history, attempts to redefine keywords in the vocabulary of social history and women's history—experience, agency, discourse, and identity—must be embedded in debates across disciplines.[1]

1. Gabrielle Spiegel, "History, Historicism, and the Social Logic of the Text in the Middle Ages," *Speculum* 65 (1990): 73, points to the "one-sided nature of the discussion, which has largely been in the hands of literary critics and social theorists rather than historians"—e.g. Chris Weedon, *Feminist Practice and Poststructuralist Theory* (Oxford, 1987); Mary Poovey, "Feminism and Deconstruction," *Feminist Studies* 14/1 (Spring 1988): 51–65; Linda Nicholson, ed., *Feminism/Postmodernism* (New York, 1990); Deborah Rhode, ed., *Theoretical Perspectives on Sexual Difference* (New Haven, Conn., 1991); Jana Sawicki, *Dis-*

However fruitful the fracturing of disciplinary boundaries has been, it has also opened up difficult questions regarding the meanings and methods of historical practice in the wake of the linguistic turn. For this reason it is imperative to grapple with the poststructuralist challenge not only across the disciplines, but also specifically on the terrain of history, by reexamining the historical narratives, concepts, chronologies, and boundaries that have been displaced in the context of our own historical research and writing. In this essay, therefore, I rethink the contested terms *discourse, experience,* and *agency* through a study of gender and the politics of work in the German textile industry during late Imperial and Weimar Germany. I focus in particular on two moments of crisis and transformation in German history that intertwine the histories of experience and discourses: the emergence of female factory labor as a new social question in the late 1890s and the feminization of union politics during the 1920s, when a politics of the body transformed the politics of class.

FEMINIST HISTORY AND THE LINGUISTIC TURN

In the field of history the term "linguistic turn" denotes the historical analysis of representation as opposed to the pursuit of a discernible, retrievable historical "reality." Any attempt to define the linguistic turn should acknowledge that in popular academic usage—in graduate seminars, conference debates, and even in many scholarly papers—the linguistic turn (like the term postmodernism) has become a catch-all phrase for divergent critiques of established historical paradigms, narratives, and chronologies, encompassing not only poststructuralist literary criticism, linguistic theory, and philosophy but also cultural and symbolic anthropology, new historicism, and gender history.[2]

---

ciplining Foucault: Feminism, Power and the Body (London, 1991); Judith Butler and Joan W. Scott, *Feminists Theorize the Political* (London, 1992); and Michèle Barrett and Anne Phillips, *Destabilizing Theory: Contemporary Feminist Debates* (Stanford, Calif., 1992). Joan W. Scott's pathbreaking essay collection, *Gender and the Politics of History* (New York, 1988), and Sonya O. Rose's essay "Text and Context: A 'Double Vision' as Historical Method" (paper presented to the Social Science History Association Annual Meeting, 1991) constitute important exceptions to this rule.

2. See Lawrence Stone. "History and Post-Modernism," *Past & Present,* no. 131 (1991): 217–18. For an insightful discussion of the terminology of the linguistic turn, see Jane Caplan, "Postmodernism, Post-Structuralism, Deconstruction," *Central European History* 22 (1989): 260–78; Weedon, *Feminist Practice,* especially her chapter on "Principles of Poststructuralism," pp. 12–42; William H. Sewell, *Toward a Theory of Structure: Duality, Agency,*

It is difficult to disentangle the complex ways in which each of these strands of inquiry have (depending upon one's subject position) challenged, threatened, or revitalized the discipline of history or to discern how these strands (separately or in convergence with one another) have engendered a sense of epistemological crisis, a "crisis of self-confidence," among social historians in particular.[3] What is new and controversial about the linguistic turn for social historians is the pivotal place that language and textuality occupy in poststructuralist historical analysis. Rather than simply reflecting social reality or historical context, language is seen instead as constituting historical events and human consciousness.[4]

---

and Transformation, CSST Working Paper no. 29 (Ann Arbor, Mich., 1989); Richard Terdiman, "Is There Class in This Class?" in The New Historicism, ed. H. Aram Veeser (New York, 1985), pp. 225–30; and Butler and Scott, introduction to Feminists Theorize the Political. Butler and Scott emphasize, correctly in my view, that "'poststructuralism' indicates a field of critical practices that cannot be totalized," that "poststructuralism is not, strictly speaking, a position, but rather a critical interrogation of the exclusionary operations by which 'positions' are established" (pp. xiii–xiv).

3. On the crisis of self-confidence among historians, see Stone, "History and Post-Modernism," pp. 217–18. For discussions of the challenges of postmodernism to German history, see also Michael Geyer and Konrad Jarausch, eds., German Histories: Challenges in Theory, Practice, Technique, special issue of Central European History 22/3–4; and the provocative volume edited by Saul Friedlander, Probing the Limits of Representation: Nazism and the Final Solution (London, 1992).

4. While some view the linguistic turn as representing the "dissolution of history," others embrace the opportunities it has created for rethinking and recasting historical categories and narratives. See especially Spiegel, "History, Historicism," p. 60; Patrick Joyce and Catriona Kelly, "History and Post-Modernism II," Past & Present, no. 133 (1991): 204–13. Also insightful on the linguistic turn are Joan W. Scott, "Gender: A Useful Category of Historical Analysis," American Historical Review 91/5 (1986): 1053–75; John Toews, "Intellectual History after the Linguistic Turn: The Autonomy of Meaning and the Irreducibility of Experience," ibid., 92 (October 1987): 879–907; Isabel Hull, "Feminist and Gender History through the Literary Looking Glass: German Historiography in Postmodern Times," Central European History 22 (1989): 260–78; Peter Schöttler, "Historians and Discourse Analysis," History Workshop 27 (1989): 37–65; Lenard Berlanstein, "Working with Language: The Linguistic Turn in French Labor History: A Review Article," Comparative Studies in Society and History 33/2 (1991): 426–40; David Mayfield and Susan Thorne, "Social History and Its Discontents: Gareth Stedman Jones and the Politics of Language," Social History 17/2 (1992): 166–88; and Geoff Eley, "Is All the World a Text? From Social History to the History of Society Two Decades Later," in The Historic Turn in the Human Sciences, ed. Terence J. McDonald (Ann Arbor, Mich., 1996), pp. 193–244.

While most historians would likely define the linguistic turn in terms of the influence of Foucault, Derrida, and/or Lacan, I view feminist history as occupying a central place in its genealogy. In fact, women's history began to interrogate and subvert the historical canon before Foucault, or certainly Derrida, had found an audience among social historians. The reception of various strains of poststructuralism, including French feminism, took place in the interdisciplinary arenas of university Women's Studies programs and journals like *Signs* and *Feminist Studies* during the late 1970s and 1980s.[5] Thus, those feminist historians who came to reject biological essentialism as an explanation of the inequalities between the sexes were among the first historians to discover the power of discourses to socially construct sexual difference and to anchor difference in social practices and institutions. In dissolving the myth of "natural" divisions between public and private, between women and men, women's history prepared the way for the shift towards a self-conscious study of gender as a symbolic system or a signifier of relations of power.[6] Together, if not always hand in hand, feminist and poststructuralist critiques of historical master narratives interrogated, disassembled, and recast historical paradigms in light of new histories of women and gender, of race, ethnicity, and sexuality.

The decentering of the Western white male subject and the reformulation of subjectivity as a site of disunity and conflict initially appeared to open up an

5. See Judith L. Newton, "History as Usual? Feminism and the 'New Historicism,'" in *The New Historicism*, ed. Veeser, pp. 152–67, who makes a powerful case for the importance of feminism in the reception of poststructuralism (153–55). Also see Leslie W. Rabine, "A Feminist Politics of Non-Identity," *Feminist Studies* 14 (1988): 11–31; and Linda Singer, "Feminism and Postmodernism," in *Feminists Theorize the Political*, ed. Butler and Scott, pp. 464–75, on the "family resemblance" between feminism and postmodernism. On French feminism, see Elaine Marks and Isabelle de Courtivron, *New French Feminisms* (New York, 1981); and Nancy Fraser and Sandra Bartky, *Revaluing French Feminisms: Critical Essays on Difference, Agency, and Culture* (Bloomington, Ind., 1992). I thank Kali Israel for reminding me of the crucial importance of these interdisciplinary arenas in the genealogy of the linguistic turn.

6. A key text in mapping out a self-conscious study of gender was Judith L. Newton, Mary P. Ryan, and Judith R. Walkowitz, eds., *Sex and Class in Women's History* (London, 1983). On the current relationship between women's history and gender history, see Hull, "Feminism and Gender History"; and Kathleen Canning, Anna Clark, Sonya O. Rose, Marcia Sawyer, and Mariana Valverde, "Dialogue: Women's History/Gender History: Is Feminist Scholarship Losing Its Critical Edge?" *Journal of Women's History* 5/1 (Spring 1993): 89–128.

emancipatory space in which feminist historians could constitute female subjects while exposing and rectifying the historical exclusion of women and the identification of human with male. The relentless uncovering of binary oppositions, of their hierarchies and orders of subordination, helped, in the words of Mary Poovey, to "reveal the figurative nature of all ideology" and to expose the artifices and exclusions inherent in the categories of nature and gender, of class and citizen.[7] Yet the process of unmasking and deconstructing categories and boundaries also meant that the once unitary category *woman* began to fracture. As women of color rose to challenge racism within feminist movements and in the academy during the late 1970s and early 1980s, feminist scholars and activists became increasingly, and often painfully, aware of the ways in which the "feminist dream of a common naming of experience" was illusory, totalizing, and racist.[8] As feminists of color rewrote histories of slavery, colonialism, and feminism from their oppositional locations, they also contested their own colonization in the discourses of Western feminist humanism.[9]

7. Poovey, "Feminism and Deconstruction," p. 58.

8. Donna J. Haraway, *Simians, Cyborgs, and Women: The Reinvention of Nature* (London, 1991), p. 173.

9. Chandra Talpade Mohanty, "Under Western Eyes: Feminist Scholarship and Colonial Discourses," in *Third World Women and the Politics of Feminism*, ed. Chandra Talpade Mohanty, Ann Russo, and Lourdes Torres (Bloomington, Ind., 1991), p. 53. Some of the most provocative readings on gender, race, and the category woman include Gloria Anzaldúa and Cherrie Moraga, eds., *This Bridge Called My Back: Writings of Radical Women of Color* (New York, 1981); Bell Hooks, *Ain't I a Woman? Black Women and Feminism* (Boston, 1981), and *Yearning: Race, Gender, and Cultural Politics* (Boston, 1990); Barbara Smith, ed., *Home Girls: A Black Feminist Anthology* (New York, 1983); Hortense Spillers, *Conjuring: Black Women, Fiction, and Literary Tradition* (Bloomington, Ind., 1985); Trinh Minh-ha, "Not You/Like You: Post-Colonial Women and the Interlocking Questions of Identity and Difference," *Inscriptions* 3/4(1988): 71–76; Patricia Hill Collins, "The Social Construction of Black Feminist Thought," *Signs* 14/4 (1989): 745–73; Aida Hurtado, "Relating to Privilege: Seduction and Rejection in the Subordination of White Women and Women of Color," ibid., pp. 833–55; and Evelyn Brooks Higginbotham, "African-American Women's History and the Metalanguage of Race," ibid., 17/2 (1992): 251–74. It is interesting to note that many theoretically inclined (including post-structuralist) feminists, as well as many feminist historians of Europe, began to grapple with the challenges of women of color within feminism considerably later than scholars of American or "third world" history. See Jane Gallop's remarks on this point: "Race only posed itself as an urgent issue to me in the last couple of years. . . . I didn't feel the necessity of discussing race until I had moved myself out of a French post-structural orbit and began talking about American literary criticism"; Jane Gallop, Marianne Hirsch, and Nancy K. Miller, "Criticizing Feminist

In a related but distinct vein of inquiry, Denise Riley's *Am I That Name? Feminism and the Category of "Women" in History* also interrogated and deconstructed the category women. Riley analyzed the inherent instability of the term women, emphasizing its embeddedness in other concepts such as the "social" and the "body," through several centuries of European history.[10] Grounded in historical analysis, Riley dismissed notions of tangible unities among women, of fixed notions of identities or counteridentities, and sought to redefine feminism as a contested arena in which the instability of the category women would have to be continually fought out.[11] Joan W. Scott also posed a fundamental challenge to the historical profession with her path-breaking essay of 1986, "Gender: A Useful Category of Historical Analysis." This article, together with her essay collection *Gender and the Politics of History* (1988), marked and theorized the shift from women's history to gender history that had been underway for some time and summoned so-called "mainstream" historians to consider gender as an essential category of historical analysis. In introducing poststructuralist theory into women's/gender history, Scott laid the foundation for a critical reinterpretation of concepts such as experience, agency, and identity and placed gender at the heart of nascent historical discussions of poststructuralism. Even though women's history/gender history prepared the ground in many respects for the linguistic turn, the often vitriolic responses to Scott's challenge make clear that it is also a field in which the stakes of the debate are particularly high.[12]

––––––

Criticism," in *Conflicts in Feminism*, ed. Marianne Hirsch and Evelyn Fox Keller (London, 1990), pp. 363–64.

10. Denise Riley, *Am I That Name? Feminism and the Category of "Women"* (Minneapolis, 1988).

11. Ibid., pp. 4–7, 99. On this point see also Nancy Fraser and Linda J. Nicholson, "Social Criticism without Philosophy: An Encounter between Feminism and Postmodernism," in *Feminism/Postmodernism*, ed. Nicholson, pp. 34–35; Leora Auslander's insightful review of Riley: "Feminist Theory and Social History: Explorations in the Politics of Identity," *Radical History Review* 54 (1992): 158–76; Judith Butler, *Gender Trouble: Feminism and the Subversion of Identity* (New York, 1990); and Nancy Fraser, *Unruly Practices: Power, Discourse, and Gender in Contemporary Social Theory* (Minneapolis, 1989). Judith Butler makes a similar point in her essay "Contingent Foundations: Feminism and the Question of 'Postmodernism,'" in *Feminists Theorize the Political*, p. 16: the term "women," she argues, has become "a site of permanent openness and resignifiability." Thus, "the constant riffing" over this term "ought to be safeguarded and prized . . . as the ungrounded ground of feminist theory."

12. Scott, "Gender: A Useful Category," and *Gender and the Politics of History*. See, e.g.,

As a historian of women and gender who came of age during this sea change, it is evident to me that feminist historical scholarship is still contending with the destabilizing effects of the linguistic turn. While it is impossible to do justice here to the diverse and imaginative ways in which feminists have sought to contend with this challenge, I will briefly allude to three possible outcomes of the encounter between feminism and poststructuralism. First, and for numerous complex and diverse reasons, many feminists have resisted what they perceive as the fragmenting and paralyzing effects of multiple and indeterminate female identities. Indeed, attempts to decenter a (female, gay, African-American or Latino) subject whose own subjectivity is still in the process of being historically constituted created profound dilemmas for feminist historians, whose main task until recently was to recover the female subject and render her visible in history. Thus, many have come to see poststructuralism as a particularly disempowering, even dangerous approach for marginalized groups to adopt, as it undermines their efforts to name themselves, to "act as subjects rather than objects of history."[13] These feminists have sought to uphold "the visionary and critical energy of feminism as a movement of cultural resistance and transformation," to emphasize their own agency as well as that of their historical subjects against the poststructuralist axiom of the discursive character of all practices.[14]

Feminist poststructuralists, by contrast, salute this crisis in feminism as fruitful and invigorating in both the scholarly and the political sense. In their

---

Claudia Koonz's energetic critique of Scott's *Gender and the Politics of History* in *Women's Review of Books* 6/4 (1989): 19–20; Jane Caplan's more measured and favorable review, "Gender Is Everywhere," *The Nation* (January 9–16, 1989): 62–65; Catherine Hall's review, "Politics, Post-structuralism, and Feminist History," *Gender and History* 3/2 (1991): 204–210; the review by Mariana Valverde, "Poststructuralist Gender Historians: Are We Those Names?" *Labour/Le Travail* 25 (1990): 227–36; Bryan Palmer's chapter on gender, especially the section "The Scott Files" in his *Descent into Discourse: The Reification of Language and the Writing of Social History* (Philadelphia, 1990); Geoff Eley's discussion of the particular reception of poststructuralism in feminist studies in Eley, "Is All the World a Text?"; and finally, the somewhat acrimonious debate between Scott and Linda Gordon: Joan Scott, review of Gordon, *Heroes of Their Own Lives* and "Response to Gordon," and Linda Gordon, "Response to Scott," *Signs* 15/4 (1990): 848–52, 859–60. Also see Linda Gordon's review of Scott, *Gender and the Politics of History,* ibid., pp. 852–58.

13. Nancy Hartsock, "Foucault on Power: A Theory for Women?" in *Feminism/Postmodernism,* ed. Linda J. Nicholson (New York, 1990), p. 163.

14. Susan Bordo, "Feminism, Postmodernism, and Gender-Scepticism," in *Feminism/Postmodernism,* ed. Nicholson, p. 135.

volume *Feminists Theorize the Political,* Judith Butler and Joan W. Scott address some of their critics' objections by explicating a kind of methodology for feminist poststructuralist inquiry. Thus, a feminist deconstruction of the historical subject or agent suggests not the negation, dismissal, or censorship of the concept but rather requires its "critical reinscription and redeployment." Categories can be reinscribed and redeployed once "all commitments to that to which the term . . . refers" are suspended and the ways in which it consolidates and conceals authority are unmasked. Significantly, Butler and Scott invite feminists to reinscribe concepts like subject or agency, but do not suggest a rewriting of deconstruction or poststructuralism itself.[15] The third group of feminists to which I refer here envisions an encounter, a strategic engagement between feminism and poststructuralism that transforms both sides in significant ways. Nancy Fraser and Linda Nicholson, for example, seek to meld the analytical and critical power of both strands, to "combine a postmodern incredulity toward metanarratives with the social-critical power of feminism."[16] The literary scholar Mary Poovey calls upon feminists to first rewrite deconstruction in order to render it useful, to endow it with tools for analyzing specificity, historicize it, enrich it with a model of change, and finally deploy it upon itself. And because deconstruction challenges feminism in fundamental ways, this act of rewriting will transform not only deconstruction, but also feminism.[17]

Feminist projects of "rewriting," "reinscribing," or "redeploying" key concepts of political and historical vocabulary have emerged as one primary outcome of the encounter between feminism and poststructuralism. In this essay I aim to rewrite the terms experience and discourse and, by implication, the notions of agency, subjectivity, and identity. Specifically, I mean to untangle the relationships between discourses and experiences by exploring the ways in which subjects mediated or transformed discourses in specific historical settings. To do so, I contemplate the sites of subjectivity and agency, in particular the enigmatic place of the body in the making of subjectivity or identity. My own search for answers takes as its starting point the assertion that there is no

15. Butler and Scott, *Feminists Theorize the Political,* p. xiv, and Butler, "Contingent Foundations," p. 15.

16. Nancy Fraser and Linda J. Nicholson, "Social Criticism without Philosophy: An Encounter between Feminism and Postmodernism," in *Feminism/Postmodernism,* ed. Nicholson, pp. 34–35. See also Weedon, *Feminist Practice;* Poovey, "Feminism and Deconstruction"; Sawicki, *Disciplining Foucault;* Singer, "Feminism and Postmodernism," pp. 469–71.

17. Poovey, "Feminism and Deconstruction," pp. 51, 60–63.

turning back to the unreflective use of concepts such as experience or class (although many historians still seem to hope that the power of the poststructuralist challenge will dissipate with time).[18] My inquiry is also grounded in the recognition that the ongoing encounter between poststructuralism and feminism is itself indeterminate and fluid. It is therefore incumbent upon those of us who have found this challenge stimulating to rewrite, reinscribe, and redeploy the concepts we consider crucial in our own work. Because of the importance of Joan Scott's work for my own, I seek here to read two of her most compelling essays—one on experience, the other on discourse—against my own analysis of the discourses of social reform in late Imperial Germany and the experiences of female textile workers in Germany after the First World War.[19]

REREADING AND REWRITING HISTORY: EXPERIENCE AND DISCOURSE

Experience

Experience has been a keyword in social history, particularly in histories of subjugated or invisible groups, since the 1960s. In the narratives of labor history, for example, experience denoted the "vast, multiple, contradictory realm" that lay between the relations of production and the awakening of class-consciousness.[20] One of the most innovative fields of German history, *Alltagsgeschichte* (the history of everyday life) for instance, has focused on everyday life experiences as the site at which "abstract structures of domination and exploitation were directly encountered."[21] Women's history and feminist theory have long relied upon similar notions of experience as mediating between the experiences of sexual oppression and the development of feminist conscious-

18. I argue this point regarding the concept of class in my article "Gender and the Politics of Class Formation: Rethinking German Labor History," *American Historical Review* 97/3 (1992): 736–68.

19. Scott, "'L'ouvrière! Mot impie, sordide . . .': Women Workers in the Discourse of French Political Economy, 1840–1860," in *Gender and the Politics of History*, pp. 139–63; and Scott, "The Evidence of Experience," *Critical Inquiry* 17/3: 773–97.

20. William H. Sewell, Jr., "How Classes are Made: Critical Reflections on E. P. Thompson's Theory of Working-Class Formation," in *E. P. Thompson: Critical Perspectives*, ed. Harvey J. Kaye and Keith McClelland (Philadelphia, 1990), pp. 55–56.

21. Geoff Eley, "Labor History, Social History, *Alltagsgeschichte*: Experience, Culture, and the Politics of the Everyday—A New Direction for German Social History?" *Journal of Modern History* 61/2 (1989): 324.

ness and as creating the basis for unity or identity among women.[22] Dorothy Smith's study of *The Everyday World as Problematic,* for example, views experience as the foundation of a feminist sociology, as "the ground of a new knowledge, a new culture" that is located in "one's bodily and material existence." For Smith, experience constitutes an alternative site at which dominant sociological paradigms and theory can be contested as women's standpoints are usually "situated outside textually mediated discourses in the actualities of our everyday lives" because they are excluded from "the making of cultural and intellectual discourse."[23]

Joan Scott's "The Evidence of Experience" challenges the "authority of experience," that is, "the appeal to experience as uncontestable evidence and as an originary point of explanation." She is interested in not only interrogating the experience of the historical subject but also that of "the historian who learns to see and illuminate the lives of those others in his or her texts." The starting point of Scott's discussion of experience is Samuel Delany's *The Motion of Light in Water,* which she describes as "a magnificent autobiographical meditation . . . that dramatically raises the problem of writing the history of difference, the history, that is, of the designation of 'other. . . .'" Scott's aim here is to critique Delany's focus on his own experience, his "apprehension of massed bodies" in a gay bathhouse as the basis of knowledge, of identity formation, of political power.[24] His mission of documenting the "lives of those omitted or overlooked in accounts of the past"—in this case black gay men—is one that he shares with many historians (especially women's historians), and his tendency to portray knowledge as "gained through vision" and writing as "reproduction, transmission—the communication of knowledge gained through (visual, visceral) experience"—is indeed emblematic of much historical research and writing.[25] For Scott however, the "project of making experience visible" obscures "the workings of the ideological system itself [and] its categories of representation (homosexual/heterosexual, man/woman, black/white, as fixed immutable identities" and in fact *"precludes"* the central task of analyzing "how difference is established, how it operates, how and in what ways it constitutes subjects who see and act in the world."[26] Here Scott constructs the task of analyzing the ex-

22. Chandra Talpade Mohanty, "Feminist Encounters: Locating the Politics of Experience," in *Destabilizing Theory: Contemporary Feminist Debates,* ed. Barrett and Phillips, p. 76.

23. Dorothy Smith, *The Everyday World as Problematic: A Feminist Sociology* (Boston, 1987), p. 107.

24. Scott, "The Evidence of Experience," pp. 775, 777.

25. Ibid., pp. 775–76.

26. Ibid., pp. 777–78.

perience and/or identity of difference as oppositional, rather than comple-
mentary, to the task of examining how difference was constituted in the first
place.

Scott's call to scholars to historicize rather than take as self-evident the identities of those whose experience is being documented is well taken, although
much recent work in the history of women and gender already does this, even
if it is not always explicitly theorized.[27] Scott's agenda might signal a whole new
kind of historical investigation, the history of homosexuality *instead of* homo-
sexuals; of "blackness" instead of blacks; of the construction of the feminine
instead of women. It is the "instead of" that both intrigues and concerns me.
Although Scott does not explicitly posit this, it is implicit in the opposition she
establishes between the discursive construction of difference and the ways in
which people experienced it (and by extension, how identities were formed
based on that experience) and it underlies her assertion that the exploration of
the latter somehow precludes that of the former.[28]

Even if Scott rejects the notion that historians can capture experience in the
sense of "lived reality" or "raw events," she concedes, nonetheless, that "experience is not a word we can do without."[29] The closest Scott comes to a defini-

27. I found some interesting parallels between Scott's argumentation in this article and
Donna Haraway's views of experience as discussed in her essay "Reading Buchi Emecheta"
in Haraway, *Simians, Cyborgs, and Women*, pp. 109–13. Examples of recent feminist historiography that historicize identities in this way include Leonore Davidoff, "Class and Gender in Victorian England," in *Sex and Class in Women's History*, ed. Newton et al., pp. 17–
71; the pathbreaking book by Davidoff and Çatherine Hall, *Family Fortunes: Men and
Women of the English Middle Class, 1780–1850* (Chicago, 1987); and Judith R. Walkowitz,
Prostitution and Victorian Society: Women, Class, and the State (Cambridge, 1980).

28. I cannot do justice to the complex issue of identity formation within the scope of
this chapter. For a recent discussion of this issue that also engages with poststructuralism,
see Laura Downs, "If 'Woman' Is Just an Empty Category, Then Why Am I Afraid to Walk
Alone at Night? Identity Politics Meets the Postmodern Subject," *Comparative Studies in
Society and History* 35/2 (April 1993): 414–37. Margaret R. Somers and Gloria Gibson, "Reclaiming the Epistemological 'Other': Narrative and the Social Constitution of Identity,"
in *From Persons to Nations: The Social Constitution of Identities*, ed. Craig Calhoun (London, 1994), offer an excellent theoretical reading of narrative and the social constitution of
identity. Caulfield's study of "dishonest women, modern girls, and women-men" in Rio de
Janeiro during the 1920s offers an interesting comparison of Scott and Butler on the issue
of gender identity; see Sueann Caulfield, "Getting into Trouble: Dishonest Women, Modern Girls, and Women-Men in the Conceptual Language of *Vida Policial*, 1925–1927, *Signs*
19/1 (1993): 146–76.

29. Scott, "The Evidence of Experience," p. 797.

tion of experience, however, is that it is a "linguistic event" that "doesn't happen outside established meanings": "Experience is a subject's history; language is the site of history's enactment [and] historical explanation cannot, therefore, separate the two."[30] Although many historians would agree that historical analysis should not (and indeed cannot) separate language and experience, even sympathetic readers may find problematic the one-dimensional notion that language or discourses "position subjects and *produce* their experiences."[31] Moreover, Scott's rhetorical strategy allows concepts to flow into one another, making it difficult to disentangle them. "Experience," for example, is a subject's history"; "language is the site of history's enactment"; "discourses produce experiences"; subjects are constituted "through experience." Scott's arguments sometimes appear to follow an almost circular path; at other times they seem to establish new oppositions. In either case it is difficult to imagine what these postulates might mean in concrete historical settings. Scott offers a masterful deconstruction of the concept of experience but stops short of actually redefining or rewriting it. So even if we might agree with her about what experience is *not* (transparent, visceral), we are left unsure as to what it might be.

What traces of experience might we be able to discover in various historical sources then? Labor and feminist historians usually mean by experience more than the mere "living through of events"; the term also encompasses the way in which "people construed events as they were living through them."[32] In his dialogue with Scott, for instance, William H. Sewell, Jr., defines experience as "the linguistically shaped process of weighing and assigning meaning to events as they happen," a process that is embedded in the "cultural understandings and linguistic capacities" of historical subjects.[33] Alf Lüdtke's notion of *Eigensinn*, a key concept in German *Alltagsgeschichte*, likewise signifies a particular way of responding to or making meanings of events as they happen, a "striving for time and space of one's own"; a sense of self-preservation and self-presentation as well as a "self-willed distancing" that facilitates a "reframing," "reorganizing," or a "creative reappropriation of the conditions of daily life."[34] This emphasis

30. Ibid., pp. 792–93.

31. Ibid., p. 779.

32. Sewell, "How Classes Are Made," p. 64.

33. William H. Sewell, Jr., *Gender, History, and Deconstruction: Joan Wallach Scott's Gender and the Politics of History*, CSST Working Paper 34 (Ann Arbor, Mich., 1989), p. 19.

34. Alf Lüdtke, "Organizational Order or *Eigensinn*? Workers' Privacy and Workers' Politics in Imperial Germany," in *Rites of Power: Symbolism, Ritual, and Politics since the Middle Ages*, ed. Sean Wilentz (Philadelphia, 1985), pp. 304–5, 312–15. For more extensive discussions of *Alltagsgeschichte*, see David F. Crew, "*Alltagsgeschichte*: A New Social History

on construing, reframing, and reappropriating implies that subjects do have some kind of agency, even if the meanings they make "depend on the ways of interpreting the world, on the discourses available to [them] at any particular moment."[35] Indeed, experience, as the rendering of meaning, is inextricably entwined with the notion of agency, with a vision of historical subjects as actors who, in Sewell's terms, "put into practice their necessarily structured knowledge."[36]

In her discussion of Delany, Scott acknowledges that "subjects do have agency" and she clarifies that "they are not unified, autonomous individuals exercising free will."[37] Scott circumvents the thorny problem of agency in her discussion of Samuel Delany as subject-in-the-making: she emphasizes the ways in which "agency [is] created through situations and statuses conferred on individuals," but leaves open the question of how subjects mediate, challenge, resist, or transform discourses in the process of defining their identities. While Scott acknowledges the "conflicts between discursive systems and the contradictions within any one of them," the transformations of individual identities take place within discursive systems that remain seemingly fixed.[38] Her skeptical stance towards stories of emancipation in which "resistance and agency are presented as driven by uncontainable desire" not only obscures the ways in which discourse and experience are entwined, but also disregards the fact that desire (a very interesting kind of agency) has figured importantly in many stories of transformation or revolution.[39]

Key, however, in analyzing how discourses change, how subjects contest power in its discursive form, and how their desires and discontents transform or explode discursive systems is the concept of agency. How can discourses fig-

'From Below'?" *Central European History* 22/3–4 (1989): 394–407; Alf Lüdtke, *Alltagsgeschichte: Zur Rekonstruktion historischer Erfahrungen und Lebensweisen* (Frankfurt a. M., 1989); Lutz Niethammer, ed., *Lebensgeschichte und Sozialkultur im Ruhrgebiet zwischen 1930 und 1960*, 2 vols. (Berlin, 1983); and Niethammer and Alexander von Plato, eds., *"Wir kriegen jetzt andere Zeiten"* (Berlin, 1985).

35. Weedon, *Feminist Practice*, p. 79.

36. Sewell, *Toward a Theory of Structure*, p. 5.

37. Scott refers here to Adams and Minson, who qualify *agency* as "subject to definite conditions of existence, conditions of endowment of agents and conditions of exercise." See Parveen Adams and Jeff Minson, "The 'Subject' of Feminism." *m/f* 2 (1978): 91, reprinted in *The Woman in Question*, ed. Parveen Adams and Elizabeth Cowie (Boston, 1990), pp. 81–101.

38. Scott, "The Evidence of Experience," pp. 792–93.

39. Ibid., p. 778.

ure as anything but fixed hegemonic systems without the interventions of
agents who render them contingent and permeable? Now that the linguistic
turn has stripped agency of the "baggage" of the autonomous enlightened individual, it should undergo the same kind of rethinking and rewriting as the
terms experience, identity, and class.[40] Indeed, we might uncover the ways in
which historical subjects mapped, transformed, and "reterritorialized" political locations by heeding Sherry Ortner's call to make room for those on the
other side of our historical or ethnographic texts, to recognize that as "we attempt to push these people into the molds of our texts, they push back."[41] A
conception of agency as a site of mediation between discourses and experiences
serves not only to dislodge the deterministic view in which discourse always
seems to construct experience, but also to dispel the notion that discourses are,
to paraphrase Ortner, shaped by everything but the experiences of "the people
the text claims to represent."[42]

Discourse

Scott's essay "'L'ouvrière! Mot impie, sordide . . .': Women Workers in the
Discourse of French Political Economy, 1840–1860," offers a historically specific

40. Sherry Ortner, "Resistance and the Problem of Ethnographic Reversal," in *The Historic Turn in the Human Sciences*, ed. McDonald, pp. 281–304, examines the "baggage surrounding the term *agency*." The following texts helped me think through the problem of
agency: Poovey, "Feminism and Deconstruction," and her *Uneven Developments: The Ideological Work of Gender in Mid-Victorian England* (Chicago, 1988), and "Domesticity and
Class Formation: Chadwick's *Sanitary Report*," in *Subject to History*, ed. David Simpson,
65–81 (Ithaca, N.Y., 1991), pp. 65–81; Judith R Walkowitz, Myra Jehlen, and Bell Chevigny,
"Patrolling the Borders: Feminist Historiography and the New Historicism," *Radical His-
tory Review* 43 (1989): 23–43; Judith R. Walkowitz, *City of Dreadful Delight: Narratives of
Sexual Danger in Late Victorian London* (Chicago, 1992); Spiegel, "History, Historicism";
Regenia Gagnier, *Subjectivities: A History of Self-Representation in Britain, 1832–1920* (New
York, 1991); Rose, "Text and Context"; and Mohanty, "Feminist Encounters." Particularly
helpful were Donna Haraway's notion of "situated knowledges" in *Simians, Cyborgs, and
Women*, pp. 2–3, 110–11, 188–89; Somers and Gibson's discussion of narrative identity in
"Reclaiming the Epistemological 'Other,'" and Caulfield's comparative reading of Butler
and Scott in "Getting into Trouble."

41. Ortner, "Resistance and the Problem of Ethnographic Reversal," p. 298. Haraway
also suggests that our quest to disentangle discursive construction from experience and
agency might best be served by a view of history, ethnography, or even social theory as a
"conversation" in which "the agency of people studied itself transforms the entire project."
See her *Simians, Cyborgs, and Women*, p. 198.

42. Ortner, "Resistance and the Problem of Ethnographic Reversal," p. 297.

setting in which to examine the workings of "discursive construction," to consider where discourses begin and end, how they are constituted and transformed, how they empower and disempower, engender and deflect resistance. As such, it provides a different kind of forum for debate than her essay on experience. The starting point of the essay is a mid-century discourse of political economy that "define[d] the terms of a new science of economics, . . . codif[ied] its laws and discipline[d] its practitioners."[43] The political economists who shaped this discourse "established the intellectual and institutional power of their science through control of knowledge and access to government [and] were able to provide the conceptual framework within (and against) which those addressing economic questions had to work." Scott argues convincingly that working women figured in their discourses in a dual way, serving "at once as an object of study and a means of representing ideas about social order and social organization."[44]

Scott explores the contradictions within this discourse "by attending to the rhetorical as well as the literal functions of these writings, by examining the contrasts used to constitute meaning."[45] She delivers a fascinating analysis of the ways in which female sexuality was used metaphorically to talk about working-class misery. Women workers came to inhabit a "world of turbulent sexuality, subversive independence and dangerous insubordination" that placed them in close discursive proximity to prostitutes: "The interchangeable uses of *femmes isolées* suggested that all such working women were potential prostitutes, inhabiting a marginal and unregulated world in which good order—social, economic, moral, political—was subverted."[46] I found this instance of "reading Scott reading" particularly valuable for the insight it offers into the significance of "reading" in historical analysis, which is something social and labor historians seldom problematize.[47] The ability to attend to the rhetorical aspects of historical texts, to their contrasts, exclusions, and/or binary oppositions, makes it possible to uncover, for example, the metaphors of female sexuality that might otherwise be difficult to see or interpret. In fact, learning how to read in new ways may be a prerequisite for pursuing the history of experience as a process of making, assigning, or contesting meanings.

43. Scott, "'L'ouvrière! Mot impie, sordide . . . ,'" p. 141.

44. Ibid., p. 162.

45. Ibid., p. 154.

46. Ibid., p. 143.

47. Laura Downs offers a somewhat different reading of Scott's essay. See Downs, "If 'Woman' Is an Empty Category," pp. 422–24.

Yet Scott's arguments foreground the discursive in the construction of women's work while leaving obscure its relationship to the social context in which it emerged. She insists, for example, that "The prominence of the woman worker in the nineteenth century, then, came not so much from an increase in her numbers or a change in the location, quality or quantity of her work, as from contemporaries' preoccupation with gender as a sexual division of labor. This preoccupation was not _caused_ by objective conditions of industrial development; rather it _helped shape_ those conditions, giving relations of production their gendered form, women workers their secondary status, and home and work, reproduction and production their oppositional meanings."[48] She draws the reader into a compelling analysis of the intertextual process, the meanings internal to this discursive system, but resists the urge to pursue the historical question of what this discourse meant or signified in the broader context of nineteenth-century French history. When and why did political economists begin to "see" women workers? What was the outcome of this discursive explosion during the mid-century, of the attempts of political economists to address public opinion and to translate their views into policy?

To answer these questions I offer a reading of the origins and outcomes of discourses of social reform in Germany during the late nineteenth century. My notion of discourse is a modified Foucauldian one of a convergence of statements, texts, signs, and practices across different, even dispersed sites (from courtrooms to street corners, for example).[49] Implicit in the term discourse, as both a textual and a social relation, is a certain expertise, the power and authority to speak, and the existence of a public sphere that transcends local settings.[50] Historical analysis of discourse is complicated by the need to dis-

48. Joan W. Scott, "The Woman Worker in the Nineteenth Century," in _A History of Women,_ vol. 4: _Emerging Feminism from Revolution to World War,_ ed. Geneviève Fraisse and Michelle Perrot (Cambridge, Mass., 1993), pp. 399–426.

49. My own working definition of discourse and discursive domains has been shaped by readings of Michel Foucault, _History of Sexuality,_ vol.1: _An Introduction_ (New York, 1980); Peter Stallybrass and Allon White, _The Politics and Poetics of Transgression_ (Ithaca, N.Y., 1986); Weedon, _Feminist Practice;_ Poovey, _Uneven Developments,_ and "Domesticity and Class Formation"; Walkowitz et al., "Patrolling the Borders"; Walkowitz, _City of Dreadful Delight;_ Dorothy Smith, _Texts, Facts, and Femininity: Exploring the Relations of Ruling_ (New York, 1990); Rose, "Text and Context"; and Richard Terdiman, _Discourse/Counter-Discourse: The Theory and Practice of Symbolic Resistance in Nineteenth-Century France_ (Ithaca, N.Y., 1985), pp. 12, 54.

50. On the dispersed sites of discourse, see Walkowitz, _City of Dreadful Delight,_ p. 6; and Stallybrass and White, _The Politics and Poetics,_ p. 194. Terdiman, in _Discourse/Counter-_

tinguish between singular discourses and the wider discursive systems or domains to which they belong. Chris Weedon explains, for example, that the ideology of "natural" biological difference between the sexes was cast and anchored within a domain of "conflicting discourses, from medicine and sociobiology to radical feminism" during the mid-nineteenth century.[51] While the constitutive and subjugative power of discourses is a central focus of my discussion, I take up Sonya Rose's notion of a "double vision of text and context," and consider Judith Walkowitz's suggestion that material reality is a force that pressures and destabilizes the discursive domain, requiring representations "to be reworked, shored up, reconstructed."[52] Finally, like Walkowitz and Mary Poovey, I examine the multiple subject positions within discourses, the discrepancies in access to social space and power, that are essential to an understanding of both the subjugation and the resistance of individual subjects.[53]

Similar to the political economic texts that Scott analyzes, the discourses of social reform in Germany depicted female factory work as constituting a new "social question" during the last two decades of the nineteenth century, as Germany underwent its rapid second wave of industrialization. The 1890s saw a marked shift from a focus on the generalized "worker question" to that of the woman worker and, in particular, the married woman worker, whom many social reformers sought to exclude from factory labor. Along with growing anxieties about social democracy, social unrest, and imperial expansion came fears about the working-class family, rent apart by the expansion of the female factory work force—children left to fend for themselves, men driven into the pubs by dirty, inhospitable living quarters in the absence of wives and mothers. Reformers sought to preserve the working-class family as an anchor in a rapidly

––––––

Discourse, pp. 44–46, analyzes the relationships between dominant discourses and counterdiscourses in the specific historical context of nineteenth-century France when the emergence of a literate middle-class public, of newspapers, of new disciplines and bodies of knowledge such as statistics, transformed both the "techniques for assuring discursive control" and those of "symbolic subversion." On discourse as a social relation in a new kind of public arena see Smith, *Texts, Facts, and Femininity,* pp. 161–67.

51. Weedon, *Feminist Practice,* p. 127.

52. Rose, "Text and Context," pp. 7–8; Walkowitz et al., "Patrolling the Borders," p. 31.

53. Mary Poovey, "Speaking of the Body: Mid-Victorian Constructions of Female Desire," in *Body/Politics: Women and the Discourses of Science,* ed. Mary Jacobus, Evelyn Fox Keller, and Sally Shuttleworth (New York, 1990), pp. 29, 43; Walkowitz et al., "Patrolling the Borders," pp. 30–31, 43. On the reciprocal relationship between the discursive and material domains, see also Spiegel, "History, Historicism," p. 71; and Walkowitz, *City of Dreadful Delight,* pp. 9–11, 233–41.

changing world, a bulwark against social distress and disorder, some by "regulating" and "protecting" women workers, others by banning them altogether from factories. The narratives of danger about female factory labor ranged from scholarly treatises on *Geschlechtscharakter* (sexual/gender characteristics) to shocking revelations about the effects of women's work—women's bodies ravaged by machines and long hours of labor, infant mortality, filth and squalor in workers' living quarters—that stimulated popular interest in the problem. These narratives evoked dramatic visions of social dissolution that were replete with analogues between the destruction of the social body, the body of the family, and the physical bodies of women workers and the children they bore. As the public sphere expanded and was redefined by mass politics during the 1890s, a wide spectrum of voices shaped this discursive domain: employers, politicians, state bureaucrats, liberals, Catholics, socialists, and feminists, in addition to some of Germany's leading social scientists: Lujo Brentano, Gustav Schmoller, Ferdinand Tönnies, and Max Weber. The voices of the latter, who spoke as "scientific" experts, were juxtaposed with those of the *Betroffene,* those directly affected—male weavers and union leaders who embraced a virulent rhetoric against the feminization (*Verweiblichung*) of factory production and the displacement (*Verdrängung*) of men from their jobs.

The discursive domain of social reform consisted of several overlapping, often competing discourses: medical-biological-eugenicist; bourgeois feminist; industrialist-capitalist; Social Democratic; social Catholic; liberal social reformist; and the paternalist/interventionist discourses of the welfare state. Although located in discrete social spaces, structured by definite languages, and implementing distinct rhetorical strategies, they were nonetheless ordered by what Denise Riley terms "webs of cross-references."[54] Singular discourses converged to form a discursive domain as each sought to resolve the growing discrepancy between the continued expansion of the female work force and dominant notions about the character of the sexes. Furthermore, the discourses examined here were constituted across a range of texts, encompassing "scientific" studies of workplace or household budgets; parliamentary debates; factory inspections and state surveys; protective labor legislation; employers'

---

54. As cited by Scott in "'L'ouvrière! Mot impie, sordide . . . ,'" p. 141. In practice this occurred when a union leader cited a middle-class social reformer's study in a speech to a union assembly or when parliamentary representatives drew upon local stories to enhance their campaigns for restrictions on women's work. The term "webs of cross-references" also applies to counterdiscourses (such as feminist critiques of social reformers' punitive solutions to the social problem of female factory labor).

sanctions and union programs; and even calls to strikes against the hiring of women workers. During the 1890s the agitation at these diverse sites (parliaments, pubs, strike lines) formed a groundswell of social pressure that ultimately prompted the state to mediate, intervene, and sanction an official resolution of the new social question through labor legislation.

My reading of the discourses of social reform differs from Scott's in several respects. First, I am interested in how and why discourses emerge, how the historical world was internalized or inscribed in texts.[55] Particularly interesting are, of course, the moments of inscription that lead to discursive shifts or transformations. Inscribed in the discourses of social reform in late Imperial Germany was a transformation of the labor market, namely the steady and perceptible expansion of the female factory work force during the last quarter of the century. As the economy boomed at the end of the century, employers faced a continuous labor shortage in nearly all industrial sectors, including the so-called "women's industries" of textiles, garments, and cigar-making. The married female work force nearly doubled between 1882 and 1907 and the proportion of married women among adult female factory workers increased from 21 to 29 percent in the four-year period between 1895 and 1899.[56] These social and economic changes were inscribed in the discursive domain of social reform, in the vision of men displaced and "transformed into maidens" by mechanization and feminization, in the widespread perception of a sexual and social order gone awry.[57]

Thus, to embed the discourses of social reform in a specific historical con-

55. Spiegel, "History, Historicism," p. 84.

56. "Married women" here denotes married and formerly married women (widows and women who were divorced or separated from husbands). The married female work force grew by 90 percent, the single female work force by 78 percent between 1882 and 1907. The numbers of unmarried female factory workers increased at a slightly slower pace. Figures here based on Ludwig Pohle, "Die Erhebungen der Gewerbeaufsichtsbeamten über die Fabrikarbeit verheirateter Frauen," *Jahrbuch für Gesetzgebung, Verwaltung, und Volkswirtschaft* 25 (1901): 158–161; Rose Otto, *Über die Fabrikarbeit verheirateter Frauen,* Münchener Volkswirtschaftliche Studien 4 (Stuttgart, 1901), p. 10; Helene Simon, *Der Anteil der Frau an der deutschen Industrie* (Jena, 1910), p. 7; Hanns Dorn, "Die Frauenerwerbsarbeit und ihre Aufgaben für die Gesetzgebung," *Archiv für Rechts- und Wirtschaftsphilosophie* 5 (1911/12): 86–87; Stefan Bajohr, *Die Hälfte der Fabrik: Geschichte der Frauenarbeit in Deutschland* (Marburg, 1979), p. 25.

57. This term is from Robert Wilbrandt, *Die Weber in der Gegenwart: Sozialpolitische Wanderungen durch die Hausweberei und die Webfabrik* (Jena, 1906), p. 31. The implication of the word "maiden" here is also that of "handmaiden" of a machine.

text (in this case the rapid expansion of industry and of the female labor market in Germany) is not necessarily to postulate that they "reflect a reality." While Scott's analysis suggests an opposition between the discourse's "being caused by industrial conditions" or "helping to shape them," these are two central and intertwined aspects of the discourse about female factory labor in Germany. I agree that discourses about social reform and female factory labor helped shape the industrial order in Germany, but certainly the increasing numbers of female factory workers and the transformation of the industrial labor market were not imaginary creations of the minds of social reformers. Understanding the reformers' imaginations is crucial, however, in grasping the meanings they ascribed to these social and economic transformations and in mapping out the emergence of female factory labor as a new social question. Contextualizing or historicizing discourse makes it possible to see both of these things at once. In fact, locating the discourses of social reform in the context of the changing industrial landscape renders more visible the power of discourse to shape a new sexual division of labor.

The second way in which my inquiry differs from Scott's is that I am interested in the material consequences and ideological effects not only of discourses that become hegemonic but also of those that were contested and transformed. The emergence of female factory labor as a new social question in the late 1880s and 1890s marks a discursive shift away from the prevalent acceptance during the 1870s of "the notion that lower-class women had to work, even if this meant outside the home in factories."[58] The representations of men "transformed into maidens," of women "abducted" from home and family, of a morally degenerate and physically declining workers' estate had complex moralizing as well as regulative outcomes.[59] As they came to realize that married women could not be banned from factories, social reformers sought to import the home into the workplace, to instill female factory workers with domestic skills, and to supplant the imagery of disorder, the specter of feminiza-

---

58. Jean H. Quataert, "A Source Analysis in German Women's History: Factory Inspectors' Reports and the Shaping of Working-Class Lives, 1878–1914," *Central European History* 16/2 (1983): 108.

59. Rudolf Martin, "Die Ausschliessung der verheirateten Frauen aus der Fabrik: Eine Studie an der Textilindustrie," *Zeitschrift für die gesamte Staatswissenschaft* 52 (1896): 104–46, 383–418. Here see pp. 399–400. On moralizing and regulative outcomes of discourses of social reform, see Poovey, "Domesticity and Class Formation," p. 65, and Mary Jacobus, Evelyn Fox Keller, and Sally Shuttleworth, eds., introduction to *Body/Politics: Women and the Discourses of Science* (New York, 1990), pp. 1–10.

tion and disintegration of gender roles, with a new order founded upon the division between the male breadwinner and the female "secondary" earner. Thus, a new ideology of women's work emerged around the turn of the century in the discursive domain of social reform that remade the workplace and demarcated its boundaries and hierarchies of gender. It shaped the structures of production: the sexual division of labor and its hierarchies of wage and skill; the design and implementation of textile technology; the factory regime of discipline and punishment; as well as employers' moral regime of charity and tutelage. Moreover, this discursive shift and the ideology it engendered had important implications for the world beyond the mill gate. Not only did it define a new industrial order, but it also marked the female body as a new site of intervention for both the moralizing and the regulatory regimes of industrial paternalism and social reform. It recast the relationship between family and state, between sexual and social order, and in doing so, it shaped the formation and expansion of the German welfare state.

Third, I am interested in both the subjects and the objects of the discourses of social reform. I aim to recover not only the loud and powerful voices of political economists holding forth on the perils of the industrial world, but also to render as subjects those whose labor was inscribed with ideologies of gender. In seeking to break the silence of women workers (however difficult this may be), I resist the tendency of discourse analysis to displace the subject or to reduce her "to a mere bearer of systemic processes" by analyzing the reception, the contestation, the multiple meanings of texts.[60] I attempt in my work to uncover work cultures and work identities, that is, the meanings workers derived from their waged work and the ways this work was embedded in family, neighborhood, and community.[61] Such an examination might uncover the complex ways in which male and female workers interpreted, subverted, or internalized discourses of labor or ideologies of work. Exploration of the expressive cultural practices—the everyday struggles over pride and honor, gossip and respectability, bodies and sexuality, charity and tutelage—through which workers adapted to and subverted ordained locations within the factory regime reveals not only complicity and resistance (including discursive resistance), but also the multiple subject positions which they occupied at any given moment.[62] In

60. Smith, *Texts, Facts, and Femininity,* p. 161.

61. I do not claim to "reconstruct" identities as they somehow might have "really" existed; rather I attempt to "read" them using a variety of sources that can be compared and contrasted with one another.

62. Kali Israel's work has influenced my thinking about multiple subject positions. See

the next section of this essay I explore one moment of profound disruption in German history, when women workers, armed with the consciousness of their multiple subject positions as workers, wives, and mothers, succeeded in contesting the terms of the discourses that defined them.

EXPERIENCE, DISCOURSE, AND THE BODY
DURING THE WEIMAR REPUBLIC

The First World War, the revolution of 1918, and the subsequent realignment of military and civilian society in Germany brought about a profound transformation of women's experiences of citizenship and class, of family and sexuality, as well as a rapid disordering of the discursive domain of gender. The gender imagery of the early Weimar Republic was replete with contradictions: women's newly acquired right to vote, their prominent place in the strikes and bread riots of 1917–18, and in the revolution of 1918 stood in stark contrast to the mass displacement of women from their jobs during demobilization. Soon after the war the castigation of "double-earners" by state, union, and labor councils nullified their wartime salutations of women's sacrifices for the fatherland. The rhetoric of civic equality for the sexes was supplanted by the rapid erosion of women's rights as the new Social Democratic government struggled to stabilize and regenerate the wounded nation. Central to the tasks of reconstituting the national body politic, of dissolving the boundaries between "male" front and "female" home front, was a new attention to the political meanings of male and female bodies.[63]

------

her essay "Writing Inside the Kaleidoscope: (Re)Representing Victorian Women Public Figures," *Gender and History* 2/1 (1990):40–48.

63. Elisabeth Domansky, "Militarization and Reproduction in World War I Germany," in *Society, Culture, and State in Germany, 1870–1930*, ed. Geoff Eley (Ann Arbor, Mich., 1996), pp. 427–63. On the political meanings of the body during the Weimar Republic, see the work of Atina Grossmann, including "The New Woman and the Rationalization of Sexuality in Weimar Germany," in *Powers of Desire: The Politics of Sexuality*, ed. Ann Snitow, Christine Stansell, and Sharon Thompson (New York, 1983), pp. 153–76; "*Girlkultur* or Thoroughly Rationalized Female: A New Woman in Weimar Germany?" in *Women in Culture and Politics: A Century of Change*, ed. Judith Friedlander, Blanche W. Cook, Alice Kessler-Harris, and Carroll Smith-Rosenberg (Bloomington, Ind., 1985), pp. 62–80; and *Re/forming Sex: German Sex Reform 1920 to 1950* (New York, 1995). Also see Cornelie Usborne, *The Politics of the Body in Weimar Germany: Women's Reproductive Rights and Duties* (Ann Arbor, Mich., 1992); and Karen Hagemann, *Frauenalltag und Männerpolitik: Alltagsleben und gesellschaftliches Handeln von Arbeiterfrauen in der Weimarer Republik* (Bonn, 1990), pp. 196–305.

Recent feminist scholarship makes clear that the history of the body is essential to understanding the ruptures in discourses and experiences during the war and the Weimar Republic. Weimar society was haunted not only by visions of male bodies ripped apart or numbed by war, but also by the wounds inflicted on women's bodies, as Elisabeth Domansky has argued: "They [women] did not recall a generalized immiseration, but the ceasing of menstruation, their inability to breast-feed their children, and the erosion of their good looks. They interpreted the loss of weight not simply as a loss of strength and health, but as a loss of attractiveness. War defeminized them and turned them into prematurely old women. War wounded them as it wounded the men."[64] The postwar task of healing the ailing body politic gave the female body a new visibility as a site of discursive intervention. Women's bodies, constructed in the discursive space between medicine and politics, formed a key link in solving physical and social pathologies that were now more acute and widespread than during the 1890s.[65] They figured centrally in both the coercive pronatalism of wartime and the eugenicist population policies of Weimar. The ideology of motherhood was revitalized across the political spectrum after the war: the Socialist and Communist parties repudiated the punitive population policies advocated by the nationalist Right but pursued their own programs of improving the conditions of maternity for working women.[66] The female body was also at the heart of the discourse of the sexually emancipated "new woman," one of the most profound ruptures in postwar culture: she was the woman who could not be sent back into the home, a figure of transgression in the dual sense of economic independence and the pursuit of sexual pleasure.[67]

The female body has also been a key site of contention in the encounter be-

64. Elizabeth Domansky, "World War I as Gender Conflict in Germany" (paper presented to the Kaiserreich conference, University of Pennsylvania, February 1990; published in a revised version as "Militarization and Reproduction"), p. 14.

65. On the social pathologies of body politics during the last quarter of the nineteenth century, see Anson Rabinbach, *The Human Motor: Energy, Fatigue, and the Origins of Modernity* (Berkeley, Calif., 1992), pp. 21–22.

66. Usborne, *The Politics of the Body*, p. 209.

67. On the "new woman" in Germany see Grossmann, "The New Woman," and Usborne, *The Politics of the Body*, pp. 69–101. For a fascinating comparison with interwar France, see Mary Louise Roberts, "'This Civilization No Longer Has Sexes': *La Garçonne* and Cultural Crisis in France after World War I," *Gender and History* 4/1 (1992): 49–69; and her *Civilization without Sexes: Reconstructing Gender in Postwar France, 1917–1927* (Chicago, 1994).

tween feminism and poststructuralism.[68] In much feminist theory and historiography the body has figured as a site of lived experience that serves to ground agency and resistance, to give it concrete origins.[69] Feminists and others who disavow the poststructuralist emphasis on discursive construction have mobilized the body as a tangible limit to the power of representation. Susan Bordo points out that poststructuralist feminists have fashioned a "body whose own unity has been shattered by the choreography of mulitiplicity." Bordo cites the example of Donna Haraway's cyborg as a postmodern body that "invites us to take pleasure in the 'confusion of boundaries,' in the fragmentation and fraying of the edges of the self that have already taken place."[70] I seek to transcend these dichotomies through a historical case study of the female body in both its discursive and experiential dimensions. I also explore Regenia Gagnier's suggestions that examination of material culture (as the social space in which discourses are located, for example) necessarily leads one to the body, that the body is located at a crossroads between material culture and subjectivity, and that bodily experiences of desire and deprivation shape subjectivity in important ways.[71] My focus here is on a new "moment of inscription," when women workers enunciated their own embodied experiences of work, war, and revolution within the segmented realms of formal politics (the fragmented labor movement and the myriad coalition governments that comprised "the state") and across the terrain of diffuse and often contested discourses about the body. It was a moment when women's experiences of wartime and postwar disjunctures were inscribed in the discourse of class, when a politics of the body transformed the politics of class.

The convergence during the early years of Weimar of a crisis of nation with a crisis of class—the fracturing and (re)formation of the working-class—also

68. Jacobus et al., *Body/Politics*, pp. 3–4, contend that there has been "no issue more vexed" in contemporary feminist theory than that of the female body. See also Sawicki, *Disciplining Foucault*, pp. 13–14, 70–83, 107; Butler, "Contingent Foundations," p. 17; Brian Turner, *Regulating Bodies: Essays in Medical Sociology* (London, 1992).

69. Haraway, *Simians, Cyborgs, and Women*, p. 134, and Riley, *Am I That Name?* p. 104, make this point. On the "lived experiences" of the body in history, see Barbara Duden, *The Woman beneath the Skin: A Doctor's Patients in Eighteenth-Century Germany* (Cambridge, Mass., 1991); and Dorinda Outram, *The Body and the French Revolution: Sex, Class, and Political Culture* (New Haven, Conn., 1989).

70. Bordo, "Feminism, Postmodernism," p. 144, and Haraway, *Simians, Cyborgs, and Women*, p. 151.

71. Gagnier, *Subjectivities*, pp. 10–11, 57–58.

altered the political landscape of the Social Democratic textile union, the DTAV. The extent to which both were also crises of gender became clear during the sudden and powerful transformation of the social climate surrounding women's work during demobilization. This rupture posed particular dilemmas for the DTAV as female membership in the union increased by over 450 percent between 1918 and 1920.[72] It formed the basis for the "feminization" of union politics, for a rewriting of class by gender, as women responded to the rapid discursive shifts about gender and women's waged work after the First World War.

The DTAV, founded in 1891 under the shadow of the protracted transition from home weaving and spinning to mechanized mills, was a site of gender contest from the outset. The profound anxiety of male weavers and spinners about women's waged work in textiles, their perceptions of feminization, dislocation, and displacement, formed an essential subtext of official Social Democratic theories of women's emancipation. Thus, while the first Social Democratic weavers' associations granted women the right to vote and to be elected for office, union members frequently raised public demands for legal sanctions against women's work in textile mills.[73] Until 1908, when the revised Prussian Law of Association permitted women to join political associations, the DTAV's policies toward women were unofficial, localized, and lacked an administrative backbone in the union bureaucracy. A marked dissonance prevailed between the DTAV's endorsement, on the one hand, of "equal pay for equal work" and a shorter working day for women, and its evocation, on the other hand, of threatening visions of female competitors (or "wage-cutters") who displaced male breadwinners from their jobs and then acquiesced in their own exploitation. Nonetheless, by 1908 some forty-eight thousand women belonged to the DTAV, comprising over one-third of its membership and the largest female contingent among the industrial unions.[74]

In the political culture and practice of the DTAV between 1908 and 1914 the "woman question" signified contests about men's wages and female competition, about the meanings of female *Eigenart* for union politics. *Eigenart* became

72. Deutscher Textilarbeiterverband (DTAV), *Jahrbuch 1927* (Berlin, 1928), p. 147.

73. See Lilly Hauff, *Die Arbeiterinnen-Organisationen* (Halle, 1912), pp. 11–13. The Internationale Gewerksgenossenschaft der Manufaktur-, Fabrik- und Handarbeiter, founded in Saxony in 1869, had one thousand female members in 1870, who constituted 15 percent of its membership.

74. Kathleen Canning, "Class, Gender, and Working-Class Politics: The Case of the German Textile Industry, 1890–1933" (Ph.D. diss., Johns Hopkins University, 1988), pp. 317–20.

a complex political slogan that designated the particularities of female needs, activities, sentiments, and consciousness.[75] Female union activists in the DTAV sought recognition of *Eigenart* in their everyday struggles in the textile mills—for higher wages and a shorter work day, for greater protection of pregnant workers—and through their campaigns to create space within the union for separate women's meetings, a women's column in the union paper, and better training for female union functionaries. The fact that female particularities were embedded in working women's bodies was seldom acknowledged explicitly: at this juncture the politics of *Eigenart* did not represent a new body politics. In emphasizing that female particularities made women different from but not inferior to men, women activists opposed the universalist (male) claims of class and repudiated the possibility of seamless integration of women into male spheres of work or politics.[76] They implemented the vocabulary of *Eigenart* to subvert the social identity and the discourse of class by staking political claim to the multiple subject positions women workers inhabited simultaneously, by refusing the assignment of one or the other socially sanctioned subject position ("mother" to the detriment of "worker," for example, or vice versa, depending upon historical circumstances).[77] Male labor leaders, by contrast, utilized their own rhetoric of *Eigenart* to disparage women's needs and experiences and warn against the burdens they might represent for the labor movement. Female *Eigenart* undermined the universalist claims of class and refuted the assertion of DTAV leaders that the union had already achieved equality between the sexes.

The struggle for a social and discursive space for women in the DTAV was suspended by the outbreak of the First World War. The experiences of war, in both their social and discursive dimensions, are crucial to understanding the feminization of union politics that took place during the mid-1920s. First, the fixed boundaries between *Frauen-* and *Männerindustrien* (women's and men's industries) dissolved during the war as women ventured into previously male

75. I define *Eigenart* more extensively in "Gender and the Politics of Class Formation," pp. 761–63.

76. Irene Stoehr, "'Organisierte Mütterlichkeit': Zur Politik der deutschen Frauenbewegung um 1900," in *Frauen suchen ihre Geschichte,* ed. Karin Hausen (Munich, 1983), pp. 228–29.

77. DTAV, *Protokoll der 9. ordentlichen Generalversammlung, abgehalten 1908 in Leipzig* (Berlin, 1908), p. 214; *Protokoll der 10. Generalversammlung, abgehalten 1910 in Berlin* (Berlin, 1910), p. 227. See also DTAV, "An unsere Kolleginnen," *Der Textilarbeiter* 22/30 (July 29, 1910).

sectors of production and acquired new skills.[78] The discursive construction of women's work also shifted as employers, factory inspectors, union leaders, and the militarized state acknowledged that the mobilization of female workers was of critical importance to the war effort. Women's paid labor for the fatherland was imbued, if only for a few years, with the honor and esteem that had otherwise been reserved for skilled male breadwinners.

A parallel process took place in the DTAV as thousands of men left for the front and women took their places at local union posts.[79] Within a few years, the DTAV became a predominantly female union: by 1916 women comprised some 60 percent of members and by 1918, 74 percent, forcing the DTAV leadership to acknowledge that women had become "the core of the organization."[80] Indeed, the politics of *Eigenart* seem to have flourished in the spaces vacated by the union men during the war.[81] Outside the unions, women workers recast civil society as they negotiated the confusing terrain of consumption restrictions and rations. After the turning point of the "turnip winter" of 1916–17, they played a vital role in fracturing the "civil peace" between unions and state by waging illegal strikes.[82]

Although the DTAV had become a predominantly female union by 1918, fe-

78. Hauptstaatsarchiv Düsseldorf, Regierung Düsseldorf 33581, "Bericht der Gewerbeinspektor für Crefeld Stadt und Land und Kreis Kempen von 30.3.1917." According to this report, many women received specialized job training, including some who learned to repair machines. Ute Daniel dispenses with the myth that the majority of women who went to work in factories during the war were housewives employed for the first time. Her work demonstrates that most of the women employed in armaments production during the war had worked before the war in other industrial sectors, above all textiles. See Ute Daniel, *Arbeiterfrauen in der Kriegsgesellschaft: Beruf, Familie und Politik im Ersten Weltkrieg* (Göttingen, 1989).

79. The number of women who held union posts grew from some eighteen hundred in 1913 to three thousand in 1917. DTAV, *Jahrbuch 1914–1915* (Berlin, 1916), pp. 282, 307, *Jahrbuch 1917* (Berlin, 1918), pp. 72–74. By 1915, 25 percent of 316 locals were headed by women.

80. DTAV, *Protokoll der 13. Generalversammlung, abgehalten 1917 in Augsburg* (Berlin, 1917), pp. 127–29.

81. DTAV, "Frauenversammlungen während des Krieges," *Der Textilarbeiter* 27/5 (January 29, 1915): 19; "Kriegszusammenkünfte der Arbeiterinnen," ibid., 27/38 (September 17, 1915):, 152; DTAV, *Jahrbuch 1914–1915*, p. 283.

82. DTAV, *Jahrbuch 1916* (Berlin, 1917), pp. 95–97; *Jahrbuch 1917*, pp. 63–71. In 1916 women comprised 62 percent of striking textile workers and in 1917 they represented 75 percent. Only 26 percent of those involved (male and female) in 1916 and only 36 percent in 1917 were unionized. See, for example, Domansky, "Militarization and Reproduction," and Belinda Davis, "Gender, Women and the 'Public Sphere' in World War I Berlin," in *Society, Culture, and State,* ed. Eley.

male activists faced new challenges when the war came to a close. In 1918 unemployment among textile workers exceeded that of the worst months of the war, as military production ceased and all available raw materials remained under control of the War Ministry.[83] At the same time, men began returning from the front, hoping to reclaim their former jobs. The demobilization decrees, drafted by the state and supported and enforced by unions and factory labor councils, sought to restore social stability by returning newly discharged veterans to their jobs as quickly as possible. The decrees stigmatized thousands of women as "double-earners" (those whose husbands, fathers, or brothers were employed and could presumably provide for them) and forced them to relinquish their jobs in favor of men.[84] By 1920 the DTAV confirmed that some eighty-one hundred married women had been dismissed from their jobs in the textile industry in order to make room for men.[85] Despite the relatively small numbers of demobilized women, the decrees can be viewed as the first step toward a postwar realignment of sexual and social order.

In the meantime a kind of political demobilization took place within the union as men returned after the war to dominate its bureaucracy and to reclaim their former posts on the local level. Although women joined the union in unprecedented numbers between 1918 and 1921, the dissension within the union among Majority Socialists, Independent Socialists, and Communists, as well as the spread of politically charged labor unrest and general strikes during 1920, meant that union leaders scarcely took note of the new female majority.[86]

83. DTAV, *Jahrbuch 1918* (Berlin, 1919), pp. 72–73.

84. We still know too little about demobilization, particularly about its effect on women workers. See Richard Bessel, "'Eine nicht allzu große Beunruhigung des Arbeitsmarktes': Frauenarbeit und Demobilmachung in Deutschland nach dem Ersten Weltkrieg," *Geschichte und Gesellschaft* 9 (1983): 211–29; and Susanne Rouette, "Die sozialpolitische Regulierung der Frauenarbeit: Arbeitsmarkt- und Fürsorgepolitik in den Anfangsjahren der Weimarer Republik. Das Beispiel Berlin" (Ph.D. diss., Technische Universität Berlin, 1991), published as *Sozialpolitik als Geschlechterpolitik: Die Regulierung der Frauenarbeit nach dem Ersten Weltkrieg* (Frankfurt a. M., 1993).

85. DTAV, *Protokoll des 14. Verbandstages des Deutschen Textilarbeiterverbandes, abgehalten 1921 in Breslau* (Berlin, 1921), pp. 91–92.

86. Female membership in the DTV increased by over 450 percent, as some 260,000 women joined the union between December 1918 and the end of 1920. Male membership increased by an even faster rate of 740 percent between 1918 and 1920 as men returned to their jobs and to the union after the war. DTAV, *Protokoll der 13. Generalversammlung,* pp. 53, 77; DTAV, *Jahrbuch 1919* (Berlin, 1920), p. 3; DTAV, *Protokoll des 14. Verbandstages,* pp. 100–101, 108, 130.

In 1919 the DTAV executive even voted to dismantle the Women's Bureau when its members concluded "that a special type of training for women was unnecessary."[87] Male leaders now invoked women's experiences of war, revolution, and democracy as proof of their "equal" abilities and status, as testimony against the politics of *Eigenart*. Female activists, however, quickly renewed their efforts to recast union policies and programs. Drawing on the presence by 1920 of nearly half a million female members, female activists were now empowered to speak more openly and forcefully in the arena of national union conventions and in the union press. Embracing the new democratic rhetoric of rights, they disrupted the union's congress in 1921 to demand restoration of the Women's Bureau and the appointment of a salaried female member of the executive branch, insisting also that "in view of the strength of our female membership, we have a right to have a representative here at this congress."[88] The fulfillment of women's postwar demands was delayed by the political upheavals of 1920 and 1921 and then by the crisis of 1923–24, when their concerns were again submerged while the union contended with the effects of economic collapse and drastic unemployment.[89] The new crisis, like that of 1918–20, was inscribed by gender conflicts as state and unions alike revived the rhetoric of "double-earners" and as women were subjected to *Bedürftigkeitsprüfungen* (means tests) in order to receive unemployment benefits. Indeed, the shift toward a feminization of politics began in the wake of this crisis, during which the DTAV lost nearly 60 percent of its female members.[90]

This crisis served as a turning point in the history of gender politics in the DTAV. As the discursive field of body politics widened during the mid-1920s, female union activists embedded their own bodily experiences of pregnancy, birth control, abortion, and housework in their political demands. The backdrop for the emergence of the female body in the arena of class politics after 1925 was formed by the discourses of national population policy, racist eugenics, and feminist and socialist sexual reform which sought to discipline sexuality and reproduction, as well as by the revitalized science of work, which sought to rationalize and maximize the body's productivity. This shift is remarkable

87. DTAV, *Protokoll des 14. Verbandstages*, p. 146.

88. DTAV, *Jahrbuch 1920* (Berlin, 1921), pp. 90–91.

89. DTAV, *Protokoll des 15. Verbandstags des Deutschen Textilarbeiterverbandes, abgehalten 1924 in Cassel* (Berlin, 1924), p. 60.

90. According to my calculation the male membership declined by 46 percent between 1923 and 1925, while female membership declined by 57 percent during the same period. Although the percentage of women declined steadily after 1923, women continued to constitute the majority of DTAV members.

not only because it represented a fundamental transformation of the discourse of class within the German labor movement, but also because it occurred in a predominantly female union that was led until 1927 almost exclusively by men. It attests to the ways in which women workers broke the silence about their bodies in a public arena and in doing so contested the oppositions between production and reproduction, public and private that underlay the politics of class.

The opening act in the DTAV's politics of the body was the battle it initiated with textile mill owners over the protection of pregnant women at work in 1925.[91] The union launched an inquiry into the effects of factory employment on pregnant textile workers: of the 1,110 surveyed, some 70 percent (or their babies) had experienced prenatal or postnatal complications.[92] Later that year the DTAV presented its shocking findings to the Reichstag in the form of a petition, speaking now not primarily in the name of class but on behalf of its 330,000 female members (40 percent of whom were married) and particularly for the 90,000 pregnant women who were working full-time in the mills in 1925. The physician Max Hirsch issued a pamphlet endorsing the DTAV petition and confirming its claim that some two-thirds of pregnant textile workers experienced complications in childbirth, including very high rates of miscarriage and stillbirth.[93] With this survey, published as a brochure in 1925, the DTAV shifted the terms of the anxiety-ridden discourse about sexual emancipation and the declining birth rate and brought into sharper focus the conditions of birthing and motherhood, transforming what Thomas Laqueur calls "the statistical body" into "the lived (female pregnant) body" which now had a bearing on national politics.[94] Hirsch's brochure (appended to the DTAV's pe-

91. Hauptstaatsarchiv Detmold, Regierung Minden M1IG 172, pp. 256–57: "Offener Brief des Hauptvorstandes des DTV an den Arbeitgeberverband der Deutschen Textilindustrie" (no date); pp. 260–68: "Schreiben des Arbeitgeberverbandes der Deutschen Textilindustrie betr. Antrag des DTAV vom 1. April 1925 auf Erweiterung der gesetzlichen Bestimmungen zum Schutze schwangerer Arbeiterinnen"; pp. 273–300: "Eingabe des Arbeitgeberverbandes der Deutschen Textilindustrie vom 28.10.1926 an die Reichsregierung mit zwei ärztlichen Gutachten beigefügt." See also Max Hirsch, *Die Gefahren der Frauenerwerbsarbeit für Schwangerschaft, Geburt, Wochenbett und Kindesaufzucht mit besonderer Berücksichtigung der Textilindustrie*. special issue of *Archiv für Frauenkunde und Konstitutionsforschung* 2/4 (1925); and DTAV, *Umfang der Frauenarbeit in der deutschen Textilindustrie: Erwerbsarbeit, Schwangerschaft, Frauenleid* (Berlin, 1925), p. 43.

92. DTAV, *Jahrbuch 1923–1924* (Berlin, 1925), and Usborne, *The Politics of the Body*, p. 48.

93. Max Hirsch, *Die Gefahren der Frauenerwerbsarbeit*.

94. Thomas Laqueur, "Bodies, Details, and the Humanitarian Narrative," in *The New Cultural History*, ed. Lynn Hunt (Berkeley, Calif., 1989), pp. 194–95.

tition) visualized these conditions through numerous photographs of pregnant women at work. In each case the task being performed was different—weaving, spinning, winding, finishing—but the shared representation was the woman's swollen belly pressed up against moving machinery. Despite the adamant protests of the employers' association that the DTAV's figures were exaggerated and that many childbirth complications could be attributed to venereal disease, the mill owners conceded that some 25 percent of pregnant textile workers declined the partially paid maternity leave and remained at work until the day of delivery.[95]

The DTAV now sought to create a space within the union for a politics of the body through instituting "women's evenings" and women's conferences. The first was a Conference of Pregnant Workers, held in Crimmitschau in June 1923 in order to organize and outline the planned survey of pregnant women's experiences in the textile mills.[96] Then, galvanized by its results in 1925, the DTAV convened another women's congress in October 1926. The meeting, held in the textile center of Gera, drew some 280 female and 63 male delegates, most of whom were longtime union activists, in addition to factory inspectors, representatives from doctors' and midwives' organizations, the Labor Ministry, and the Prussian Ministry of Commerce and Industry, and officials of the Social Democratic and Communist Parties.[97] Female *Eigenart*—the special needs of pregnant women, new mothers, unwed mothers, and women in need of birth control or abortion—was the theme and preoccupation of the congress. While the delegates heard testimony from mothers who had been forced to stand at their machines until the moment before they gave birth, medical doctors discussed the availability and legality of birth control and presented grim statistics about the epidemic of illegal and dangerous abortion among working-class women.[98] On the last day of the meeting some eight thousand textile workers—mostly women—marched through the streets of Gera, raising banners that linked reproductive issues with the politics of the workplace. They called for a restoration of the eight-hour day; for expanded maternity leave; access to birth control; repeal of Paragraph 218, the law that banned abor-

95. Hauptstaatsarchiv Detmold, Regierung Minden M1IG 172, pp. 256–57: "Offener Brief"; pp. 260–68; pp. 273–300. See also Usborne, *The Politics of the Body*, p. 48.

96. DTAV, *Jahrbuch 1923–1924*, pp. 48–50 and DTAV, *Umfang der Frauenarbeit*, p. 43.

97. DTAV, *Protokoll vom 1. Kongress der Textilarbeiterinnen Deutschlands, abgehalten 1926 in Gera* (Berlin, 1927), pp. 4–12.

98. Ibid., pp. 3, 15, 74–89, 98. Also see Grossmann, "The New Woman," and Julius Wolf, *Mutter oder Embryo: Zum Kampf gegen die Abtreibungsparagraphen* (Berlin 1930).

tion; and finally for the liberation of women from housework.[99] In response to the DTAV's two-pronged campaign, the German government voted in 1927 to sign the Washington Agreement, which extended mandatory maternity leave from eight to twelve weeks, improved maternity benefits, protected pregnant women or new mothers from being fired, and guaranteed women the right to breaks at work during which they could nurse their infants.[100] While motherhood had figured prominently in the rhetoric of *Eigenart* before the war (one element of which had been to appeal to the woman worker as mother), the feminized politics of the 1920s centered on freedom from the *Gebärzwang* (compulsory childbearing). Underlying the new location of the body in DTAV politics was a renewed commitment to gender equality based on recognition of female *Eigenart*.

Entwined with the new politics of the body in the DTAV was the emergence of housework, of the sexual division of the labor in the "private" sphere of home and family, as an issue of debate in the union. Female delegates to the Gera congress had raised demands for daycare and communal laundries, kitchens, and cafeterias in order to liberate women from housework; at the union's 1927 general congress they called upon DTAV members to recognize the benefits of a socialization of housework for women, men, and the union itself.[101] The union undertook its own investigation of the double burden soon after, sponsoring an essay contest for female textile workers on the theme *mein Arbeitstag—mein Wochenende* (my working day, my weekend) in 1928. Like its petition to the Reichstag on pregnancy and work, the DTAV's publication of 150 selected essays in a brochure of the same title inserted the everyday lives of working women into its campaign for expanded health and safety protection, shortened work hours, higher wages, and consumer coops.[102] Despite the abbreviated and edited form in which they appeared, the published essays point to the fluid boundaries between waged work and housework. The main theme of the essays is time, and many recount in minute detail how much time the writer requires for preparing meals, cleaning, darning, walking to and from work, and the scarcity of time for children, husband, parents, leisure, for self-education or for cultivation of new domestic or political skills.[103] While offering power-

99. Protokoll vom 1. Kongress der Textilarbeiterinnen, pp. 39–40, 140.

100. Ibid., pp. 36, 49.

101. Ibid., pp. 51–56; DTAV, Protokoll des 16. Verbandstages, abgehalten in Hamburg (Berlin: DTAV, 1927), p. 142.

102. DTAV, *Mein Arbeitstag—mein Wochenende: 150 Textilarbeiterinnen berichten!* (Berlin, 1930; 2d ed., ed. and introd. Alf Lüdtke, Frankfurt a. M., 1991).

103. See Atina Grossmann's excellent discussion of *Mein Arbeitstag—mein Wochenende*

ful testimony about the ways in which fatigue "defined the limits of the working body," the essays also seem to reflect working women's own internalization of Taylorist norms of efficiency and discipline, of the body as a "human motor."[104] The essays attest to the power of sexual difference as experienced in everyday life in household and neighborhood, even if they efface the sexual or desiring body, the pregnant or nursing body, the body ravaged by frequent abortions. They lack the passion, the urgency of Hirsch's brochure of 1925. Yet they insert a female body into political debate, in particular the campaign for the eight-hour day, that is hassled, hurried, and depleted by the daily double burden.

CONCLUSION: INSCRIPTION/REINSCRIPTION

How does the politicized female body which emerged during the mid-1920s represent the experiences of working women? What is the meaning of the discursively constructed body for women's bodily abjection not only in extraordinary times of war and revolution, but in the everyday sufferings of factory work, childbirth, and back-alley abortions? What are the implications of this analysis of the female body and the politics of class for a rewriting of the contested terms discourse, experience, and agency? First, if the female body appeared at all in union politics prior to the mid-1920s, it was a body that occupied a singular subject position, a body circumscribed by factory work, by its encounters with machines, its submission to production quotas and speedups, its vulnerability to accidents and chronic illness. Second, in representing the multiple subject positions working women simultaneously inhabited, the explicitly politicized female body that emerged during the mid-1920s disrupted the singular social identity of motherhood ascribed to working women through dominant discourses. The female body that appears in the DTAV's petitions to the Reichstag, in Hirsch's brochure on women's reproductive "suffering," in the public demonstration for accessible birth control and abortion, and in the essays featured in *Mein Arbeitstag—mein Wochenende*, marks a discursive shift precisely because it performs different kinds of work

---

in *"Girlkultur,"* pp. 70–75; as well as Lüdtke's introduction to *Mein Arbeitstag—mein Wochenende*, pp. 11–12. The titles of the first two essays are "Die Uhr rückt vor" ("The Clock Ticks On") and "Zicke-zacke die Maschine . . ." ("The Tick-Tock of the Machine"). On rationalized housework in the Weimar Republic, also see Mary Nolan, "'Housework Made Easy': The Taylorized Housewife in Weimar Germany's Rationalized Economy," *Feminist Studies* 16 (1990): 549–77; and Hagemann, *Frauenalltag*, pp. 99–132.

104. Rabinbach, *The Human Motor*, p. 23; Usborne, *The Politics of the Body*, p. 98.

all at once: weaving and spinning, birthing and nursing, cooking, cleaning, and caring for children. Furthermore, in joining rather than severing the different spheres of work, the female body of the 1920s was emblematic of the politics of *Eigenart*. It attests not only to the growing presence of women in the DTAV but also to the ways in which they mobilized their own subjugated and embodied knowledges to contest and recast the dominant meanings of body politics and of class.

My analysis of the feminization of politics suggests that women's embodied experiences of war, revolution, and demobilization—hunger, stealing, striking, demonstrating, birthing or aborting—opened the way for the transformations of consciousness and subjectivities. The erosion of civil society, the escalated policing by the pro-natalist military dictatorship of the spheres of work, consumption, and sexuality, meant that women experienced their bodies as sites of intensified intervention and regulation (and perhaps also as political weapons) during war and demobilization. As the female body became an increasingly unpredictable threat to the success of total war and as military and civilian authorities put new systems of codification and supervision in place, women became acutely aware that "the front was everywhere," that the front was inscribed in their bodies.[105] While the war represented an indisputable turning point in the body's politicization, the accumulated experiences of the female body in all the realms of "work," its day-to-day wounding—the endless cycle of cooking, washing, cleaning, and mending, work without recognition or pay that decided a family's day-to-day survival; the mechanization and depletion of the body by machines in the mills; its vulnerability to illness, injury, or rape; the miscarriages, stillbirths, and pregnancies plagued by pain and complications; the danger and death associated with illegal abortion and the persistently high rates of infant mortality among urban working-class families—was what likely propelled women into the streets of Gera in 1926. Indeed, the insurmountable limits of the body were inscribed in the protests of female textile workers during the 1920s. It was the body stripped of "the natural frontier of the self" which became a site of resistance.[106]

Regenia Gagnier's remarkable study of "Subjectivity, the Body, and Material Culture" explores how female bodies, permeated by discourses and transfigured by the experiences of work and pain, became sites of resistance at certain historical junctures.[107] Her analysis of the ways in which the body fig-

105. Domansky, "Militarization and Reproduction."
106. Gagnier, *Subjectivities*, p. 60.
107. Ibid., pp. 55–98.

ures in the self-representations of working-class women raises important questions about poststructuralist notions of subjectivity. "Reproductive suffering," she argues, "was an essential component of the subjectivity in question: *that* is what it was like to be a working-class woman."[108] In Gagnier's view, women's experiences of "extreme physical abjection or loss of boundaries" shaped their resistance, their transformation into subjects. She invokes their own powerful terminology to explain this loss of boundaries: "They suffered continually from misplacements, womb displacement, falling of the womb, gathered breasts, breasts in slings, childbed fever, husbands' abuse of the organs of reproduction, cold in the ovaries, varicose veins, marble leg, . . . untimely flooding, growth of the afterbirth inside the mother, confinement in body-belts and leg-bands, severe hemorrhaging, . . . white leg, and the psychologically maddening grinding of machinery in the factory," the sense that their bodies were "'going round with the machinery.'" Finally, there was the despair of the "'mother [who] wonders what she has to live for; if there is another baby coming she hopes it will be dead when it is born.'"[109] Gagnier's reading of these working-class women's letters about maternity offers an interesting parallel to my analysis of the feminization of politics in the DTAV. This story of subjectivity is one of transformation from "subjective isolation within their bodies to subjects with claims upon the State," subjects who resisted alienation from their laboring bodies and who learned how to "use their bodies to change culture," in this instance to obtain insurance coverage for maternity benefits and to establish municipal maternity centers.[110]

The notion of the body as a historically contingent site of subjectivity also offers a more complex understanding of the positions female workers assumed within the discourses of class, nation, citizenship, and/or maternity in Weimar Germany. It is important to note that discourses (both those that empower and those that disempower) do not merely constitute the domain in which subjectivities emerge, but also actually create the conditions for this transformation in quite concrete ways. For example, the discourses of the "new woman," sexual reform, and eugenics, the controversies over birth control and abortion, focused the attention of a wide range of political and social groups on female sexuality. At the same time, however, this saturation of the social field created

108. Ibid., p. 60 (emphasis in original). Gagnier's main source here is a collection of 160 letters written by members of the British Women's Cooperative Guild and published in 1915, entitled *Maternity: Letters from Working-Women* (London, 1915).

109. Gagnier, *Subjectivities,* pp. 59–60.

110. Ibid., p. 63.

a social and discursive space in which women were encouraged and empowered to conceptualize their own sexuality.[111] More specifically, the natalist and eugenicist obsessions with population loss and birth rate massed women together as potentially maternal bodies, compelling them to position themselves within this mass. Thus the discursive domain of body politics intruded in women's experiences of their bodies in quite concrete ways during and after the First World War. This intrusion represents one example of how, as Elizabeth Grosz suggests, power in its discursive and material forms "actively marks or brands bodies as social, inscribing them with the attributes of subjectivity."[112] As important as this discursive intervention was in constituting female subjectivities, it comprises only one side of the story.

The emergence of a counterdiscourse about the female body during the 1920s suggests that Weimar body politics was a particularly contested and fractured discursive domain, one that was particularly vulnerable to dispersal, resistance, and transformation.[113] Underlying this formulation is a notion of agency as a site of mediation; here agency signifies the way in which female activists mobilized and recast their embodied experiences within the discursive fields of Weimar body politics. Both Gagnier's poignant reading of British working-class women's letters on maternity and my abbreviated discussion of the emergence of female body in the arena of union politics during the 1920s raise particular questions about the realm of experience embedded in the body. The notion that discourses marked, branded, or massed together bodies should make clear that I do not conceive of the body as an unmediated site of experience. Yet I am fascinated by Grosz's notion of the recalcitrant body, which, because it is capable of being self-marked and self-represented, "always entails the possibility of a counterstrategic reinscription."[114] This is one way of understanding Gagnier's letters on maternity or the female textile workers' demonstration in Gera. When female union members marked their bodies, represented themselves through their bodies—the pregnant bodies pushed up

---

111. On the saturation of the social field by the discursive, see Terdiman, *Discourse/Counter-Discourse*, pp. 42–46). I found Terdiman and Poovey, "Speaking of the Body," pp. 29–30, 43, particularly useful in understanding the specific ways in which the discourses of body politics positioned subjects.

112. Elizabeth Grosz, "Inscriptions and Body-Maps: Representations and the Corporeal," in *Feminine, Masculine, and Representation*, ed. Terry Threadgold and Anne Cranny-Francis (Sydney, 1990), p. 63.

113. Terdiman, *Discourse/Counter-Discourse*, pp. 44–46.

114. Grosz, "Inscriptions and Body-Maps," p. 64.

against the looms, the bodies maimed or made sterile by illegal abortion, the desiring, sexualized bodies—they sought to reinscribe (as a counterstrategy) both the universalist and seemingly disembodied (male) discourses of class politics and the colonizing claims of natalist reproductive politics on female bodies. In the two cases examined here women's embodied experiences proved to be the most compelling means of contesting dominant discourses, of appropriating discursive space, and of altering the discourses that excluded or sought to define them. Thus, the body, if understood as a complex site of inscription and subjectivity/resistance, offers an interesting and intricate way of retheorizing agency. Indeed, the notions of bodily inscription and reinscription seem to defy both the illusion of autonomous agency/subjectivity and the vision of discourse as singularly determinant of subjects and their experiences.

CHAPTER 3 § DIFFICULT DICHOTOMIES § "EXPERIENCE" BETWEEN NARRATIVITY & MATERIALITY

PROLOGUE 2005

A decade ago the notion of experience occupied center stage in the debates about the "linguistic turn." Experience was once a driving force of history from below that authenticated social and political transformations, made them tangible at the level of the everyday. Experience represented the promise of social history to render audible the voices of previously silenced historical actors, to explicate the layers of meaning in their actions and interventions in history. As history turned towards the linguistic, experience, a concept that once marked the crossroads where "social being" and "social thought" coalesced and converged, was drawn into a starkly polarized relationship with discourse. In the course of these debates the category of experience was dislodged from its location at these epistemological crossroads and relegated to the sidelines, where it remained an empty shell stripped of the traces of its past significance. The controversies that constituted the linguistic turn subsided in the mid-1990s and since then experience has been both nowhere and everywhere. Experience, parallel to "work," faded from the center stage of historical productions, rarely featured in book titles, and no longer constituted either an object of investigation or a methodological approach. As the historian Brian Palmer noted in his provocative book, *Cultures of Darkness: Night Travels in the Histories of Transgression*, the "post-project"—encompassing postmodernism, poststructural-

The German version of this essay, "Problematische Dichotomien: Erfahrung zwischen Narrativität und Materialität," was translated by Dr. Hartwin Spenkuch and published in *Historische Anthropologie* 10/2 (July 2002). The genesis of this essay was a keynote address I gave to the eleventh *Historikerinnentagung* in Zürich in February 2002 on the conference theme: "Erfahrung: Alles nur Diskurs?" (Experience: Is Everything Discourse?). I thank Prof. Dr. Rebekka Habermas, editor of *Historische Anthropologie,* and Böhlau Verlag for permission to include this revised version of this essay in this volume. The papers for this conference were collected and published in *Erfahrung: Alles nur Diskurs? Zur Verwendung des Erfahrungsbegriffs in der Geschlechtergeschichte*, Beiträge zur 11. Schweizerischen Historikerinnentagung 2002, ed. Marguérite Bos, Bettina Vincenz, and Tanja Wirz (Zürich, 2004).

ism, postfeminism, and posthistoire—"spiraled inward in actual conceptual denial of ever knowing the experiential subject, let alone locating that solitary being at the powerfully formative conjuncture of self and society where history is ultimately made and remade."[1]

Yet all these years experience was also ubiquitous: historians and anthropologists continued to confront and contend with experience in their research and writing, even if they seldom named it. Experience became the unspoken, the implicitly materialized and oppositional counterpart of the discursive and/ or the narrative. Experience was displaced into areas of research, such as body history, where it was also seldom explicitly named. In English-language study of European history, experience lived on in the guise of everyday life history or *Alltagsgeschichte,* which retained a modest vitality amidst the shifts away from metastructures of economies, politics, and social transformations towards a preoccupation with the power of languages, discourses, and symbols to construct, empower, or silence historical actors and effect everyday hegemonies. Unlike the newfangled German *Kulturgeschichte,* the history of the everyday (more than implicitly involving a notion of experience) has continued to inhabit an enduring place in the formation and practice of North American and British new cultural history/history of cultures.[2] In other instances, historians began to interrogate the ways in which their own experiences had informed the histories they wrote, thus preserving a place for the present-day experiential subject, even as experiences of historical actors faded from central view.[3]

The intention of this essay was not to revisit or reiterate the decade-old debates that surrounded Joan Scott's essay "The Evidence of Experience," which were so definitive for my generation of gender historians. Instead I set out to excavate experience out of its underground, to determine if it was still in use as an analytical category, and to identify the terms that had filled the space it once inhabited. Did the fact that experience had receded from view mean that historians had widely conceded the impossibility of locating it outside of discourses? Had experience perhaps been studied all along without being named? Was it now time to return experience to our historical vocabulary in revised

1. Brian Palmer, *Cultures of Darkness: Night Travels in the Histories of Transgression* (New York, 2000), p. 3.

2. See Alf Lüdtke, "Alltagsgeschichte: Aneignung und Akteure. Oder—es hat kaum begonnen!" *Werkstatt Geschichte* 17 (1997): 83–91; and Philip Sarasin, "Arbeit, Sprache, Alltag: Wozu noch 'Alltagsgeschichte?'" ibid., 15 (1996): 72–85.

3. One example is Leora Auslander, "Erfahrung, Reflexion, Geschichtsarbeit. Oder: Was es heissen könnte, gebrauchsfähige Geschichte zu schreiben," *Historische Anthropologie* 3/2 (1995): 222–41.

terms? In this essay I explore areas of study, like memory, body, and subjectivity, that have continued to rely upon notions of experience. In probing the possible resonances of experience today, I also reflect on the potential and promise of postbinary approaches to historical social vocabulary.

§ § §

FROM 'FOUNDATION" TO BINARY OPPOSITION:
THE CONCEPT OF EXPERIENCE DURING THE LINGUISTIC TURN

In the course of the linguistic turn, experience was rejected as a foundationalist category of social history, as the very basis and epitome of its positivist shortcomings and projects of retrieval. Perceived as a category that was well-worn and in need of renewal, experience was resituated and redefined in terms of its relationship to discourses, languages, and/or rhetorics (depending on the disciplinary or theoretical inclinations of those who sought to redefine experience). The rejection of experience as the sprawling "foundation" of social history resulted in its increasing confinement and circumscription to a relational location in the emergent pair—discourse and experience. As the scope of the concept of experience became narrower, it also became markedly less dynamic and more static.[4] The deterministic relationship between discourse and experience dispelled the very fluidity and unpredictability of history, the ruptures and revolutions that provoked "redefinitions of experience" and "gave rise to new forms of language."[5] This sanitized notion of experience, divested of its complexity, of the layers of memory and emotion, of the passions and positionings that propelled historical change at crucial turning points, such as desire, rage, grief, despair, resistance, was gradually banished from our historical social vocabulary.

The linguistic turn marked a sharp break with previous social historical epistemologies, in particular those that had informed so-called "history from below," above all histories of labor, workers and their social movements, of class and class formation. One historian who was singled out for criticism in the course of the linguistic turn was E. P. Thompson, whose culturalist history of class formation relied upon notions of experience and agency, as implied in his notable opening sentence that the working class "was present at its own making," or in his insistence that class was something embedded in "human rela-

4. Joan W. Scott, "The Evidence of Experience," *Critical Inquiry* 17/3 (Summer 1991): 773–97.

5. Toril Moi, *What Is a Woman? And Other Essays* (New York, 1999), p. 278.

tionships," encompassing a "multitude of experiences."[6] Yet early as well as later histories of labor or women seldom produced tightly defined concepts of experience. Rather, experience was often invoked, drawn upon, or explicated in diffuse or contradictory terms, leaving this term considerably more open and porous than newer framings which rendered experience as that which discourse constructs or acts upon. In the pages of "The Poverty of Theory," in which Thompson debated expansively with Louis Althusser about so many keywords of social theory, including experience, Thompson offered a definition of experience that could not be conceived "independently of its organising concepts and expectations." His contention that "social being [could not] reproduce itself for a day without thought," seems parallel to the formulation of one of his later critics, of experience as a "linguistic event" that "doesn't happen outside established meanings."[7] Experience, Thompson asserted, "exerts pressures upon existent social consciousness," yet at the same time "thought and being inhabit a single space, which space is ourselves. Even as we think, we also hunger and hate, we sicken or we love, and consciousness is intermixed with being."[8]

Raymond Williams, in his legendary *Keywords: A Vocabulary of Culture and Society*, first published in 1976, differentiated between the meanings of "experience present" and "experience past." Williams explained experience in its present sense as "the fullest, most open, most active kind of consciousness, [which] includes feeling as well as thought." He conceived of "experience past" as already including, "at its most serious, those processes of consideration, reflection, and analysis which . . . the most extreme use of the present—an unquestionable authenticity and immediacy—excludes."[9] Interestingly, debates about experience during the linguistic turn did not address the distinct methodological issues that arise once experience is defined temporally and spatially. The impossibility of wholly dismissing experience present, even as experience past faded from historical view, was revealed, for example, in the recurrent texts in which historians or anthropologists sought to analyze the ways in which their own experiences were formative of their research and writing.[10]

6. E. P. Thompson, *The Making of the English Working Class* (New York, 1963), pp. 9–11.

7. E. P. Thompson, *The Poverty of Theory and Other Essays* (London, 1978), p. 8. Scott, "The Evidence of Experience," pp. 792–93.

8. Thompson, *The Poverty of Theory*, p. 18.

9. Raymond Williams, *Keywords: A Vocabulary of Culture and Society* (1983; New York, 1976), pp. 126–29.

10. A few examples might include Renato Rosaldo's introduction, "Grief and a Head-

Experience was also subtly and creatively cast in the theoretical formulations of *Alltagsgeschichte,* a fact that has left many historians of Germany in North America ever perplexed about the wide-reaching embrace of *Kulturgeschichte* amidst the continued disparagement of *Alltagsgeschichte* by more structurally inclined German historians. Placing "human social practice" at the center of the history of everyday life and experience, practitioners of *Alltagsgeschichte* posited understandings of historical change and continuity as "the outcome of action by concrete groups and individuals."[11] Also noteworthy is the preoccupation of *Alltagsgeschichte* with social actors' appropriation of meanings, events, and processes and its focus on "the forms in which people have 'appropriated'—while simultaneously transforming—'their' world."[12] The concept of *Eigensinn,* which the historian Alf Lüdtke defined as self-reliance, self-will, or "the act of reappropriating alienated social relations," has resonated during the last decade far beyond the circles of either *Alltagshistoriker* or the field of modern German history, not least because of the connections it suggests between structures and agents, narrative and experiential realms. *Eigensinn* encompasses both historical subjects' encounter with "constraints and pressures" and their appropriation or *Aneignung* of these structural or discursive pressures.[13] This brief historical overview of the vocabulary of experience suggests that several important valences of the term slipped out of view in the course of the linguistic turn.

---

hunter's Rage," in his *Culture and Truth in Social Analysis* (Boston, 1989), pp. 1–24; Michel-Rolph Trouillot's mapping of his own life story onto his analysis of "Glory and Silences in the Haitian Revolution," in *Silencing the Past: Power and the Production of History* (Boston, 1995); or Leora Auslander's reflections on her own experiences of work and class as informing her interest in furniture-making in her essay, "Erfahrung, Reflexion, Geschichtsarbeit."

11. Alf Lüdtke, "Introduction: What Is the History of Everyday Life and Who Are Its Practitioners?" in *The History of Everyday Life: Reconstructing Historical Experiences and Ways of Life,* ed. Alf Lüdtke, trans. William Templer (Princeton, N.J., 1995), p. 6.

12. Lüdtke, "Introduction," p. 7.

13. Alf Lüdtke, "Organizational Order or *Eigensinn?* Workers' Privacy and Workers' Politics in Imperial Germany," in *Rites of Power: Symbolism, Ritual, and Politics since the Middle Ages,* ed. Sean Wilentz (Philadelphia, 1985), pp. 303–5. The suggested definition as "the act of reappropriating alienated social relations" is from Geoff Eley, "Labor History, Social History, Alltagsgeschichte: Experience, Culture, and the Politics of the Everyday—A New Direction for German Social History?" *Journal of Modern History* 61/2 (June 1989): 323–24. Also see David Crew, "*Alltagsgeschichte:* A New Social History 'from Below'?" *Central European History* 22 (1989): 394–407.

An indisputable outcome of the turn away from experience was a veritable flood of essays and books on histories of discourse(s). The study of discourse, as a new or in some cases, newly designated object of historical research and analysis did far more than uncover an additional layer in the fabric of history. Rather, it served to invigorate and renew the crucially important study of the makings and the workings of ideologies. The task of disassembling discourses and identifying rhetorics, metaphors, and/or tropes expanded the topics and objects of historical investigation and the methodologies for studying them. As scholars launched empirical studies of discourses and meanings, more subtle and fluid notions of discourse emerged, in which human actors came to occupy a place in the discourses they produced, contested, redefined, and replaced. Discourses became less disembodied and more embedded in human practices, even if not in experience per se.

Certainly for some social scientists, the rejection of experience produced a new foundationalist understanding of discourse, which then became as "unquestioned and unquestionable," as transcendent and applicable to all case studies as experience once had been.[14] Recent retrospectives have suggested that the new discursive history that emerged from the linguistic turn, in Anglo-Saxon scholarship at least, represented only a partial break with social historical traditions. In the view of the British historian Gareth Stedman Jones, for example, "Foucauldian" discursive histories now substituted relations of power for the "relations of production" once prevalent in British Marxist historical traditions. Discursive histories, he asserted polemically, continue to be "saddled with the residues" of the radical social history of the 1970s, with its "structuralist reading of mentalité, its reductionism, its functionalism, its dismantling of the subject, [and] its subordination of politics . . ."[15] The French historian Roger Chartier took note of the different resonances and practices associated with the linguistic turn in North America, where it had produced particularly stark dichotomies that, in his view, had dangerously reduced "the social world to a purely discursive construction and to pure language games."[16]

14. Sonia Kruks, *Retrieving Experience: Subjectivity and Recognition in Feminist Politics* (Ithaca, N.Y., 2001), p. 26.

15. Gareth Stedman Jones, "Anglo-Marxism, Neo-Marxism, and the Discursive Approach to History," in *Was bleibt von marxistischen Perspektiven in der Geschichtsforschung?* ed. Alf Lüdtke (Göttingen, 1997), pp. 198–201.

16. See Roger Chartier, *On the Edge of the Cliff: History, Languages, and Practices,* trans. Lydia G. Cochrane (Baltimore, 1997). Citations here are from William H. Sewell's review of Chartier: "Language and Practice in Cultural History: Backing Away from the Edge of the Cliff," *French Historical Studies* 21/2 (Spring 1998): 241–43.

Chartier's observations raised the important but seldom considered point that there was no one linguistic turn, but rather the epistemological shifts and conceptual ruptures it signified were as varied as the national and scholarly traditions and practices it had set out to critique or dismantle.[17]

EXPERIENCE AND DISCOURSE IN THE FIELD OF GENDER AND LABOR HISTORY

The gendering of labor history, a process that produced much of the debate surrounding the linguistic turn, offers an exemplary case study of the displacement of experience in favor of discourse. Despite the swirl of epistemological crisis that swept through social and labor history in the late 1980s and early 1990s, the research and writing of dissertations and historical monographs continued apace, even if these tasks became fraught with new challenges for those who chose to contend with them. One distinguishing feature of the wave of gender/labor scholarship of the early to mid-1990s was the explicit attempt to widen the history of work, workplace, and labor movements to encompass discursive and ideological formations, while still attempting to leave analytical space for interventions and experiences of historical actors.[18] As

17. Sewell, "Language and Practice." Also see the other contributions to this forum on Chartier's *On the Edge of the Cliff* by Bonnie Smith, "One Question for Roger Chartier," pp. 213–20; and Jonathan Dewald, "Roger Chartier and the Fate of Cultural History," pp. 221–40; as well as Chartier's response, "Writing the Practices," pp. 255–64, *French Historical Studies* 21/2 (Spring 1998).

18. A partial list of these books includes: Sonya O. Rose, *Limited Livelihood: Gender and Class in Nineteenth-Century England* (Berkeley, Calif., 1992); Anna Clark, *The Struggle for the Breeches: Gender and the Making of the British Working Class* (Berkeley, Calif., 1994); Tessie Liu, *The Weaver's Knot: The Contradictions of Class Struggle and Family Solidarity in Western France, 1750–1914* (Ithaca, N.Y., 1994); Laura Tabili, *"We Ask for British Justice": Workers and Racial Difference in Late Imperial Britain* (Ithaca, N.Y., 1994); Deborah Valenze, *The First Industrial Woman* (New York, 1995); Laura Lee Downs, *Manufacturing Inequality: Gender Division in the French and British Metalworking Industries, 1914–1939* (Ithaca, N.Y., 1995); Judith G. Coffin, *The Politics of Women's Work: The Paris Garment Trades, 1750–1915* (Princeton, N.J., 1996); Kathleen Canning, *Languages of Labor and Gender: Female Factory Work in Germany, 1850–1914* (Ithaca, N.Y., 1996); Laura L. Frader and Sonya O. Rose, eds., *Gender and Class in Modern Europe* (Ithaca, N.Y., 1996); Leora Auslander, *Taste and Power: Furnishing Modern France* (Berkeley, Calif., 1997); and Nancy L. Green, *Ready-to-Wear and Ready-to-Work: A Century of Industry and Immigrants in Paris and New York* (Durham, N.C., 1997).

much as my own early research was driven by the impulse to discover the ways in which female workers had experienced the cultures of work and the politics of class, it also examined the workings of gender ideologies in "the world behind the mill gate." The shift towards a history of meaning, perhaps the most lasting methodological outcome of the linguistic turn, made it possible to consider the workings of gender even where female actors remained elusive, and directed attention to arenas beyond the factory where those ideologies were cast and contested.[19]

The search for a new lens for analyzing the meanings of gender was not a straightforward process. Rather it required methodological improvisation, the matching or layering of methods that seemed at first glance not to match up, for example using statistics and textual analysis to distinguish "structural" shifts in the labor market from rhetorical invocations of crisis and change in the history of "feminization." This strategy laid bare the dissonances between different archives and sources—local and national, numerical and textual— enabling no singular source to speak for itself. Attempts to write a history of the meanings of work led me not only to analyze how discourses "constructed" divisions of labor or notions of wages and skill, but also to pursue the representational strategies of the individuals who participated in them, the ways they read, wrote, spoke or visually depicted the social question of female factory labor in order to propel changes in ideologies and practices.

Although this posits an ideal world of rich and abundant source materials of different types, in a study like mine it is also necessary to confront the limitations of archives, which are far richer in evidence about discourses than about anything we might recognize as "experience." Indeed, the existence of only fleeting testimony from women workers forced me to rely, problematically, on sources that recorded the views of those who observed and interpreted the actions and visions of workers who spoke so rarely for themselves. A case in point is the social scientist Marie Bernays, student of Alfred Weber, who spent several months disguised as a "mill girl" in the weaving and spinning mills of the Lower Rhine. The evidence she gathered for Weber's far-reaching project on the "psychophysics of work" offered invaluable suggestions of the camaraderie and conflicts on the shop floor, and the meanings female workers assigned to their labor.[20] Testimony of an observer like Bernays, the occasional petition or

19. Canning, *Languages of Labor and Gender.*

20. Marie Bernays, *Auslese und Anpassung der Arbeiterschaft der geschlossenen Groß-industrie, Dargestellt an den Verhältnissen der Gladbacher Spinnerei und Weberei AG zu*

letter to a newspaper editor, factory inspector's reports on rape or sexual coercion, offer only modest snapshots of women's experience in which the photographer must be at least as carefully considered as the subject of the image. It is perhaps worth reminding ourselves at this juncture that both histories and theories of experience, in their older guise of "history from below," were encumbered by an impossible burden of presumed completeness. My own conclusion is that the history of experience, particularly gendered experiences, more often than not must remain incomplete, written on the basis of archival fragments, of disjunctures and silences in records. The very unevenness of these sources is a fundamental part of the history of gender, especially of its experiential dimensions.

DISSOLVING DICHOTOMIES

By the mid-1990s the sense of acute epistemological crisis had subsided, although not necessarily because any one position had prevailed. This was not the kind of controversy that was eventually resolved; nor did the issues fought over become irrelevant. Rather, they remained relevant for many historians, who went on with their research, contending with the contested categories in their own research projects as well as in the classroom. Yet there was also a sense among those who participated in these debates that the practice of gender history had fundamentally changed, on one level by its increasingly sharp distinction from the category women and on another, complexly related level, through the emphasis on textual and visual representations. Even if there was no common pathway out of the crisis, there was also no return to previous concepts and methods. So, for example, no renewed phase of theory struggles managed to revive the category of experience by redefining or redeploying it; nor did anyone (to my knowledge) attempt to resuscitate it in its earlier guise. Rather, experience simply receded for a decade or more into the background, where it remained an unnamed presence, a memory of past practices, that no longer served as the oppositional counterpart to discourse.

The decoupling of experience and discourse that resulted from the linguistic turn represented new possibilities for postbinary approaches to history, many of which took shape on the borders between disciplines in fields like new historicism. Mary Poovey's instructive analysis of "the ideological work of

---

Mönchen-Gladbach im Rheinland, Schriften des Vereins für Sozialpolitik, vol. 133 (Berlin, 1910).

gender in mid-Victorian England" had eschewed binary categories, explicating instead the "'fissured,' self-contradictory, and contested nature of Victorian gender ideology."[21] Taking apart the concept of ideology to examine "ideological work" first in terms of "the work of ideology," she emphasized the ways in which systems of interdependent images, encompassing representations of gender, "became accessible to individual men and women." Her second focus was "the work of making ideology"—the simultaneous construction and contestation of ideological systems. When Poovey, citing Althusser, cast ideology as "a set of beliefs—the 'imaginary relationship of individuals to their real conditions of existence,'" she also linked ideology to experience. For in her view "ideologies are given concrete form in the practices and social institutions that govern people's social relations" and thus "constitute both the experience *of* social relations and the nature of subjectivity"[22] Poovey's serious engagement with the discursive constitution of ideology did not necessitate either the effacement or the reification of experience or agency. A similar refusal of oppositional categories characterizes Poovey's later study, *The Making of the Social Body,* which she subtitled provocatively *British Cultural Formation, 1830–64.* Her analysis of "the production of abstract space" as a prerequisite for the emergence of the "social body" and the defining projects of "anatomical realism and social investigation" relies upon the registers of both narrativity and materiality, which far from being merely fashionable terms, were produced, as she argues, by the very cultural formation her book examines.[23]

The field of colonial and postcolonial studies has forcefully disassembled dichotomies of a somewhat different variety in recent years—first and foremost those between metropolitan and colonial cultures. Implicit in many of the debates in this field is a certain caution, skepticism, or more pronounced rejection of discursive power, not least because of the silencing of the agency and subjectivity of colonized people.[24] Scholars of the colonial past and postcolo-

21. Catherine R. Stimpson, foreword to Mary Poovey, *Uneven Developments: The Ideological Work of Gender in Mid-Victorian England* (Chicago, 1988), p. ix.

22. Poovey, *Uneven Developments,* pp. 2–3 (emphasis in the original). For purposes of my argument here, the publication date of Poovey's study—1988, when the first debates about gender had erupted—is less pertinent than the relevance this book has retained as an exemplary study of the making of ideology.

23. Mary Poovey, *Making a Social Body: British Cultural Formation, 1830–1864* (Chicago, 1995). Another excellent study in this regard is Donald Reid's *Paris Sewers and Sewermen: Realities and Representations* (Cambridge, Mass., 1991).

24. See, for example, Ann Laura Stoler and Frederick Cooper, "Between Metropole and Colony: Rethinking a Research Agenda," in *Tensions of Empire: Colonial Cultures in a Bour-*

nial present have also exposed the power of narratives or discourses to distort or dissimulate history and to disinherit a people of its history. The anthropologist Michel-Rolph Trouillot's *Silencing the Past: Power and the Production of History* illuminates the production of historical narratives that erased or unwrote the history of the Haitian revolution of 1790. Trouillot confronts the dilemma of [discursive] constructivism head on: "While constructivism can point to hundreds of stories that illustrate its general claim that narratives are produced, it cannot give a full account of the production of any single narrative."[25] Hence Trouillot points to "the materiality of the socio-historical process," which he terms "historicity 1" and which in turn sets the stage for "historicity 2," namely "future historical narratives."[26] In Trouillot's rendering, the causes of the Haitian revolution were not to be found in discourse(s), for the claims and goals of the revolution were far too radical to be formulated "in advance of its deeds." The revolution, he argues, was "unthinkable and, therefore, unannounced in the West, it was also—to a large extent—unspoken among the slaves themselves. By this I mean that the Revolution was not preceded or even accompanied by an explicit intellectual discourse."[27] Further, the successive events of the revolution were so unthinkable that they were "systematically recast by participants and observers to fit a world of possibilities" and hence "made to enter into narratives that made sense to a majority of Western observers and readers." Finally, Trouillot analyzes the ways in which historians silenced the revolution, first by formulas of erasure that tended to expunge from the record the fact of a revolution, and second through formulas of banalization that emptied events "of their revolutionary content so that the entire string of facts . . . becomes trivialized." The revolution of Haitian slaves thus became a mere appendix to the Parisian revolutionary upheavals of 1789 and the revolutionary claims of the slaves were figured as merely "Jacobinist demands adapted to the tropics."[28] While Trouillot's main concern is

geois World, ed. Ann Laura Stoler and Frederick Cooper (Berkeley, Calif., 1997), pp. 1–56; Partha Chatterjee, *The Nation and Its Fragments: Colonial and Postcolonial Histories* (Princeton, N.J., 1993); Steven Feierman, "Africa in History: The End of Universal Narratives," in *After Colonialism: Imperial Histories and Postcolonial Displacements,* ed. Gyan Prakash (Princeton, N.J., 1995), pp. 40–65; and E. M. Collingham, *Imperial Bodies: The Physical Experience of the Raj, c. 1800–1947* (Cambridge, 2001).

25. Michel-Rolph Trouillot, *Silencing the Past: Power and the Production of History* (Boston, 1995), p. 13.

26. Ibid., p. 29.

27. Ibid., p. 88.

28. Ibid., pp. 95–97, 103–4.

narrative power, his study is a cautionary tale about historians' reliance upon past discourses for the excavation of historical facts, which in the case of the Haitian revolution served to efface, silence, or rewrite collective experiences rather than explicate them. Ultimately, Trouillot redefines history as a social process, involving "peoples in three distinct capacities"—as agents, as actors, and as subjects—"as voices aware of their vocality," which we can interpret as the capacity to mediate and articulate experience.[29]

THE AFTERLIFE OF EXPERIENCE

This essay has thus far (1) charted how the terms experience and discourse came to be cast as dichotomous in the course of the linguistic turn; (2) argued that greater attention to discourses and narratives produced more nuanced analysis of certain historical formations, such as ideologies; and (3) suggested ways in which historians and anthropologists have critiqued and contended with this dichotomy either by widening the notion of discourse to encompass agents, actors, and subjects (Trouillot) or by positing a more fluid relationship between material/experiential and narrative/discursive realms. In none of these instances, though, has experience emerged into the conceptual fore-ground. Rather, it has inhabited a subtextual and unmarked place in the underground of this wider project of rethinking history. Yet the concept of experience has been resituated and redeployed in at least three arenas of historical-anthropological work which have flourished in recent years.

In the first, the thriving field of memory studies, experience has figured as what I might term a lurking keyword, one which is repeatedly invoked but seldom theorized. The study of memory, recently described as the "leading term in cultural history," has become a virtual industry in its own right in the last decade, so vast as not to permit even a representative, much less a comprehensive overview in an essay of this scope; here I can only briefly survey recent debates or thematic reviews in the field of history and memory. Illustrative of the place of experience as a lurking keyword in historical debates about "History and Memory" is a forum of this title in a 1997 issue of the *American Historical Review*.[30] In the view of one of the contributors, Susan Crane, experience is crucial to the distinction between collective memory, defined as "lived experience," and historical memory—the "preservation of lived experience." This

29. Ibid., p. 23.

30. "History and Memory," AHR Forum, *American Historical Review* 102/5 (December 1997): 1372–1412, featuring articles by Susan A. Crane, Alon Confino, and Daniel James.

work of preservation is itself, in Crane's terms, the "lived experience of recalling and remembering the past in the living, active present."[31] Echoing Michel-Rolph Trouillot's critiques of history's narrativization, Crane contends that certain forms of historical representation or historical preservation have worked to destroy the historical vestiges of lived experience. In this assertion she is following the critical impulses of Pierre Nora, whose several-volume study traced the displacement of *milieux de mémoire* by *lieux de mémoire*, whereby the disembodied sites of French national memory had come to supplant "spontaneous memory activity outside the direction of a modern preservationist culture."[32] Crane suggests a more optimistic rendering of the possibilities for collective memory than Nora, whose critical acumen is directed mainly against history's role as an invasive and manipulative "force within collective memory." Turning back to the work of the early twentieth-century French sociologist Maurice Halbwachs, Crane proposes to reinvigorate the notion of collective memory by "relocating the collective back in the individual who articulates it" and by attending to "the ways individuals experience themselves as historical entities."[33]

Alon Confino's contribution to the same forum criticizes the study of "the politics of memory" that has confined the study of memory to those with the power to invent and appropriate (or contest) the "relationship of power within society." In rendering memory a "'natural' corollary of political development and interests," Confino argues, memory—"fundamentally a concept of culture"—has been reduced to the realm of the political.[34] Rather than searching for "memory traces" in the most visible or familiar places, Confino seeks to situate memory in "a whole world of human activities that cannot be immediately recognized (and categorized) as political," such as the family, voluntary associations, and workplaces.[35] Confino also redefines memory as a category that uniquely links "representation and social experience" and connects the construction and/or evolution of specific historical memories (for example,

31. Susan A. Crane, "Writing the Individual Back into Collective Memory," ibid., p. 1373 n. 4. Here Crane refers to the work of Henri Bergson, *Matter and Memory* (Paris, 1896).

32. Crane, "Writing the Individual Back," pp. 1377–79. She refers here to Pierre Nora, "Between History and Memory: Les Lieux de Mémoire," *Representations* (Spring 1989): 7–25; and his *Realms of Memory: Rethinking the French Past*, trans. Arthur Goldhammer. 3 vols. (New York, 1996).

33. Crane, "Writing the Individual Back," pp. 1379–80.

34. Alon Confino, "Collective Memory and Cultural History: Problems of Method," *American Historical Review* 102/5 (December 1997): 1393.

35. Ibid., p. 1395.

the Vichy syndrome) to the public reception (and possible contestation) of these memories.[36] Like Confino, Peter Fritzsche in his recent review of newer literature on "modern memory" highlights the tensions between "local experiences and national understandings," local and national memories, particularly in view of the traumatic events of world war in the twentieth century. Fritzsche assesses Jay Winter's *Sites of Memory, Sites of Mourning: The Great War in European Cultural History* as exemplary of a new approach to memory that "privileges . . . private spheres and local places" and thus insists on the importance of "remembering in private life," of "telling the story of the trauma of twentieth-century war as a history of grieving families."[37] The expansive literature on memory and memorialization of the Holocaust further attests to the powerful place that trauma, as a particular variation of experience, has in this broader field of memory studies.[38]

Finally, recent scholarship on memory work in colonial studies has critiqued the notion of memory as a "repository of alternative histories and subaltern truths" and proposed a renewed study of memory as interpretive labor, probing "not only *what* is remembered but *how*."[39] In their recent essay Ann Stoler and Karen Strassler explore the place of sentiments in the project of colonialism and in the memories thereof. Colonial domestic relations are at the heart of their study, which pursues specifically tactile memories, that is those colors and textures, tastes, smells, and sounds that comprised the "emotional economy of the everyday" in colonialism. Stoler and Strassler investigate how specific experiences within the colonial domestic order—the "concrete and sensory memories of cooking, cleaning and childcare," for example—evoked sensibilities and sentiments "that other ways of telling" or of remembering colonialism, did not.[40]

The second area of study in which experience has been a lurking keyword is

36. Ibid., pp. 1399–1402.

37. Peter Fritzsche, "The Case of Modern Memory," *Journal of Modern History* 73/1 (March 2001): 104–5. The book under review in Fritzsche's essay is Jay Winter, *Sites of Memory, Sites of Mourning: The Great War in European Cultural History* (Cambridge, 1995).

38. Cathy Caruth, *Unclaimed Experience: Trauma, Narrative, and History* (Baltimore, 1996), pp. 3–4, as cited in Fritzsche, "The Case of Modern Memory," p. 112. For older discussions of Holocaust memory and history, see Saul Friedlander, ed., *Probing the Limits of Representation: Nazism and the "Final Solution"* (Cambridge, Mass., 1992).

39. Ann Laura Stoler and Karen Strassler, "Castings for the Colonial: Memory Work in 'New Order' Java," *Comparative Study of Society and History* 42/1 (2000): 4–48 (emphasis in the original).

40. Ibid., p. 5.

the history of the body, a field almost as amorphous and expansive as memory studies: bodies have been studied across even more disparate disciplinary boundaries, from medicine and biology to gender/women's studies, literature, and history, and have similarly lacked a common or rigorous conceptual vocabulary.[41] The premise of a founding text in body history, Barbara Duden's *Woman beneath the Skin* is the rejection of the "natural history of the female body" in favor of a history of "the body as experience." Duden's interest in exploring the voluminous writings of Dr. Johann Storch on women's diseases during the first half of the eighteenth century is to relate the "body image and body experience expressed in it," to connect the "body as the experienced object of women's complaints, anxieties, fears, and self-perception," and "the body as a conception shaping these sufferings."[42] While Duden's study clearly seeks to link images (ideologies, discourses) and experiences of the body, a certain materialized body is tangible in her analysis of the skin as a boundary between "inner body" and the "outside world," in the conception of the body's potential for mediation between external influences upon the body and that which was generated inside the body and discharged.[43]

Feminist disavowal of the consignment of sex/bodies to nature/materiality and of gender to culture certainly underscored the significance of the discursive body in recent years.[44] The presumption that bodily experiences are in some sense material, in the sense of physicality—even if also informed by and mediated through discourses—is still likely to produce charges of essentialism. In her enormously influential *Bodies That Matter* Judith Butler circumvented the binarization of discourse and matter by underscoring the power of regulatory norms and practices to "materialize 'sex' and bodies."[45] From a different

41. On this point, see Caroline Bynum, "Why All the Fuss about the Body? A Medievalist's Perspective," *Critical Inquiry* 22 (1995): 1–33; and Kathleen Canning, "The Body as Method? Reflections on the Place of the Body in Gender History" (chapter 6 of this volume).

42. Barbara Duden, *The Woman beneath the Skin: A Doctor's Patients in Eighteenth-Century Germany,* trans. Thomas Dunlap (Cambridge, Mass., 1991), pp. 23, 66, 181–83. Also see Duden's article "Somatisches Wissen, Erfahrungswissen und 'diskursive' Gewissheiten: Überlegungen zum Erfahrungsbegriff aus der Sicht der Körper-Historikerin," in *Erfahrung: Alles nur Diskurs?* ed. Bos et al., pp. 25–36.

43. Duden, *Woman beneath the Skin,* p. 145.

44. Donna Haraway, *Simians, Cyborgs, and Women: The Reinvention of Nature* (New York, 1991), p. 134.

45. Judith Butler, *Bodies That Matter: On the Discursive Limits of "Sex"* (London, 1993), pp. 1–3.

angle the feminist philosopher Elizabeth Grosz imaginatively sought to dissolve the oppositions between discursive power and bodily experiences. Her notion of "counterstrategic reinscription" emphasizes the body as a "site of self-knowledge and potential resistance"[46] Grosz is primarily interested in the series of processes she terms "material" that "actively brand bodies as social, inscribing them with the attributes of subjectivity as opposed to primarily affecting consciousness." She takes seriously the "inscription of flesh" which in her view shapes consciousness rather than consciousness being the "cause of the inscription of flesh."[47] More recently the concepts of body and subjectivity have been closely entwined in the work of the literary scholar Toril Moi, who finds significant analogies between Grosz's notion of the "lived body" and Simone de Beauvoir's concept of the "body as situation." Moi's point is to offer a historicized understanding of bodies and subjectivities without relying on the sex/ gender distinction that Judith Butler so eloquently disassembled. Moi seeks to resuscitate a Beauvoirian body as one that forms the basis or site of the self but does not determine the experience of the self. Moi points instead to another step in Beauvoir's thinking by which the subject makes the body her own, "turns it into her own . . . through socially situated, conscious choices and activities."[48]

The body as situation "encompasses both the objective and subjective aspects of experience," Moi contends.[49] As part of "lived experience," the body is a "style of being, an intonation, a specific way of being present in the world." Yet Moi emphasizes that the term "situation" is not coextensive with lived experience, nor reducible to it, rather it encapsulates the ways "individuals make sense of their world . . . through their bodies." Hence, according to Moi's rereading of Beauvoir, "to consider the body as a situation . . . is to consider both the fact of having a specific kind of body and the meaning that concrete body has for the situated individual."[50] Conjoining body, subjectivity, and memory, Moi suggests that the body is "a historical sedimentation of our way of living

46. Elizabeth Grosz, "Inscriptions and Body-Maps: Representations and the Corporeal," in *Feminine, Masculine, and Representation*, ed. Terry Threadgold and Anne Cranny-Francis (Sydney, 1990), p. 64. Also see Grosz's essay "Bodies and Knowledges: Feminism and the Crisis of Reason," in *Space, Time, and Perversion*, ed. Elizabeth Grosz (London, 1995), pp. 25–43.

47. Grosz, "Inscriptions and Body-Maps," pp. 63–65.

48. Toril Moi, *What Is a Woman? and Other Essays* (Oxford, 1999), p. 63.

49. Ibid., p. 67.

50. Ibid., pp. 63, 67–68, 81.

in the world," of the experiences of the past.[51] The philosopher Sonia Kruks underscores the category of experience in her reassessment of Beauvoir's and Merleau-Ponty's notions of body, situation, and subjectivity. In her study, entitled *Retrieving Experience,* Kruks aims to "retrieve an act of a self that is embodied and socially situated," that is, to posit the idea of a self that is always embodied, that "can never leap out of its skin."[52]

The third thematic/conceptual area of study in which experience has been a lurking keyword is that of subjectivity, a term that emerged with the foreclosure of the notion of identity in recent years as either overly essentialized or fraught with multiplicity.[53] Subjectivity, by contrast, is understood as an inherently mediative act, encompassing the subject positions assigned in and by discourses on the one hand and the experience of those constructed, interpellated, or positioned by discourses on the other. Subjectivity is closely entwined with the study of both memory and bodies, and in this sense relies upon a notion of experience, usually without naming it explicitly. As Regenia Gagnier argued some years ago, subjectivity encompasses both an "I," as knowing subject and the sense of being subject to and of others.[54] As specified by Sonia Kruks, subjectivity encompasses the "lived aspect of subjectification," in which this process "is taken up by the subject, be it in modes of complicity, of resistance, or both."[55] Finally, subjectivity "defies our separation into distinct selves"— that is, it encapsulates the work of weaving and linking disparate subject positions simultaneously inhabited—and suggests as well that "our interior lives . . . involve other people, either as objects of need, desire or interest or as necessary sharers of common experience."[56]

51. Ibid., p. 67.

52. Sonia Kruks, *Retrieving Experience: Subjectivity and Recognition in Feminist Politics* (Ithaca, N.Y., 2001), p. 51. Also see the interesting reflections by Jakob Tanner in "Körpererfahrung, Schmerz und die Konstruktion des Kulturellen," *Historische Anthropologie* 2/3 (1994): 489–502; and Philipp Sarasin, "Mapping the Body: Körpergeschichte zwischen Konstruktivismus, Politik und 'Erfahrung,'" ibid., 7/3 (1999): 437–51.

53. Rogers Brubaker and Frederick Cooper, "Beyond 'Identity,'" *Theory and Society* 29 (2000): 2–3. Cooper and Brubaker argue that identity no longer productively serves "the demands of social analysis," for it is "too ambiguous, too torn between "'hard' and 'soft' meanings, essentialist connotations and constructivist qualifiers."

54. Regenia Gagnier, *Subjectivities: A History of Self-Representation in Britain, 1832–1920* (Oxford, 1991), pp. 8–9.

55. Kruks, *Retrieving Experience,* p. 57.

56. Nick Mansfield, *Subjectivity: Theories of the Self from Freud to Haraway* (New York, 2000), pp. 3–4.

SITUATING EXPERIENCE: TIME, SPACE, AND METHODOLOGY

In these closing reflections I would like to contemplate the valences and usages of experience for present-day projects of historical research and writing. First, it is important to note that experience was already enmeshed in culture well before the advent of the new cultural history or the linguistic turn. The virtual melding or blending of social and cultural history since the mid-1990s, as well as the growing proximity of cultural and intellectual history in English-language historical scholarship, helps explain how experience has become so thoroughly detached from its field of origin. Once more or less the exclusive purview of social historians, experience now seems to belong to all of the historicizing disciplines. Does this mean that experience has become a kind of transcendental category, unmoored from social or cultural locations or historiographies, and of greater interest these days to cultural and intellectual historians than to those interested in social or political transformations?

While the concept of *Erfahrung* (experience) appears to have become an axis of what is now called *Kulturgeschichte* in German-speaking Europe, English-language intellectual history has offered some of the most intriguing reflections on experience in recent years. So, for example, Martin Jay, in an essay that situates *Alltagsgeschichte* in a nexus of intellectual traditions, breaks the contemporary concept of experience into parts once specified by Wilhelm Dilthey and Walter Benjamin—*Erlebnis* and *Erfahrung*. While *Erlebnis* denotes a "pragmatic and short-term response to the shocks of external and internal stimuli," *Erfahrung* encompasses a "more cumulative, often subconscious weaving together of discrete events into a narrative whole with coherence. . . ."[57] Mapping this distinction onto the period of upheaval following the First World War, Jay suggests that the meanings of experience are not fixed; instead they are closely connected to understandings of time and perceptions of temporality. Following Benjamin, Jay argues that the narrative continuities of *Erfahrung* were "broken by the unassimilable shocks of urban life" after the First World War and displaced by the more "haphazard information and raw sensations" associated with *Erlebnis*.[58]

Suggesting in a similar vein that experience has distinct valences in different temporal and geographic locales, Harry Harootunian, a historian of mod-

57. Martin Jay, *Cultural Semantics: Keywords of Our Time* (Amherst, Mass., 1998). Here see especially chap. 3, "Songs of Experience: Reflections on the Debate over *Alltagsgeschichte*," pp. 44–45.

58. Jay, *Cultural Semantics,* chap. 4, "Experience without a Subject: Walter Benjamin and the Novel," pp. 49–50.

118 BRINGING HISTORY TO THEORY

ern Japan, underlines the particular salience of experience for the period of modernity, itself shaped by a new and acute "awareness of the temporal dimensions of the present and its difference from the pasts that had preceded it." Likewise drawing upon Benjamin, Harootunian contends that experience acquired a new significance in modernity, informed by a sense of the present as a "primary and privileged temporality."[59] Even more intriguing is Harootunian's idea that the conceptualization of everydayness "as a minimal unity of temporal experience" might usefully serve as a "historical optic to widen our understanding of the processes of modernity"—not only of Western modernity, but of those "throughout the world at the same time," suggesting particularly interesting comparisons between modern Europe and Japan. Hence Harootunian conceives of everydayness as a specifically modern variation of experience, as "a form of disquiet, a moment suspended." For him everydayness signifies "a new present," a new historical situation that "violently interrupted tradition and suspended the line and movement of the past."[60]

Recent studies of the particular temporal experiences of war have proposed that the very meanings of experience were transformed in the course of the first total war. In a volume entitled *Die Erfahrung des Krieges*, Nikolaus Buschmann and Horst Carl propose that understandings of experience can transcend the usually fragmented or separate moments, events, or encounters and instead be welded into a longer-term historical process.[61] Ute Planert's essay in the same volume approaches experience as "interpersonal, bound to processes of communication and thereby implicitly public." Experience, according to Planert, "involves the dimension of the senses, is mediated in the realm of specific historical-cultural contexts, is mutable and can objectify itself in institutions." Ultimately, her notion of experience has the capacity to conjoin subject and object, actor and society, agency and structure.[62] This brief discussion indicates

59. Harry Harootunian, *History's Disquiet: Modernity, Cultural Practice, and the Question of Everyday Life* (New York, 2000), pp. 3–4.

60. Harootunian, *History's Disquiet*, pp. 19–21. On the question of experience and temporality, also see Ute Daniel, "Die Erfahrungen der Geschlechtergeschichte," in *Erfahrung: Alles nur Diskurs?* ed. Bos et al., pp. 59–70.

61. Nikolaus Buschmann und Horst Carl, "Zugänge zur Erfahrungsgeschichte des Krieges: Forschung, Theorie, Fragestellung," in *Die Erfahrung des Krieges: Erfahrungsgeschichtliche Perspektiven von der Französischen Revolution bis zum Zweiten Weltkrieg,* ed. Buschmann und Carl (Paderborn, 2001), p. 18. The precise quote is "Erfahrung erschöpft sich also nicht in ihren Inhalten und Gegenständen, sondern wird als Prozess analysierbar."

62. Ute Planert, "Zwischen Alltag, Mentalität und Erinnerungskultur: Erfahrungs-

that scholars in the field of intellectual history, as well as those involved in research on the history of war, each from their own perspective, have sought not to restore to life a defunct concept, but rather to historicize the category of experience itself.

This approach to a history of experience is highly promising, not only because it embeds the notion of experience in specific textual or philosophical discussions and traditions, but also because it situates experience in distinct historical eras and processes of transformation, dispensing with the claim that it must be meaningful as a megacategory that is relevant to each and every historical investigation. On this point the suggestions of both Jay and Harootunian that experience acquires new meaning in the speeded-up time of postwar modernity are particularly provocative. The promise of a rewritten notion of experience calls not only for historically situating this concept, but also for expanded definitions of archives, encompassing a wider array of sources, including fiction, film, and visual arts, in which traces of experience are differentially represented. This may make it possible to fulfill Sonia Kruks's call to study the same experience, either as a discursive effect or as subjectively lived or as both.[63]

Finally, we might pause to consider how and why it has become so commonplace to frame all of our concepts and categories in dichotomous terms rather than questioning the very compulsion of opposition or probing the reasons we have come to rely so heavily on oppositional pairings. This explication of the concept of experience suggests that oppositional modes of thinking are far more effective in dismantling categories and narratives than in reconfiguring them. A notion of sedimented histories, in which the very seepage between the layers defies the very possibility of sustained oppositions, would seem more fruitful in this interdisciplinary age. One complex question that remains unresolved here is that of the implication of binaries in notions of historical causality, indeed as the driving force of causality. It is certainly difficult to consider of some of the themes in this essay—memory, bodies, subjectivities, or experience—in the same causal terms as say, the study of famines, wars, or revolutions. A critical question here is whether gender history can break away from the adherence to binary categories while still fulfilling the task of mapping change over time.

---

geschichte an der Schwelle zum nationalen Zeitalter," in *Die Erfahrung des Krieges,* ed. Buschmann und Carl, p. 54. Also see the excellent essay by Sabine Kienitz in the same volume, "'Fleischgewordenes Elend': Kriegsinvalidität und Körperbilder als Teil einer Erfahrungsgeschichte des Ersten Weltkrieges," pp. 215ff.

63. Kruks, *Retrieving Experience,* p. 141.

PART II § BODIES, THE SOCIAL & LABOR

CHAPTER 4 § BEYOND INSULARITY? § THE RELEVANCE OF LABOR HISTORY AT THE TURN TO THE TWENTY-FIRST CENTURY

PROLOGUE 2005

In its first guise this essay was part of a forum on the future of labor history in the new millennium. The starting point of our discussion was a widely shared sense that labor history had aged or become passé with the turn from social to cultural history that shifted attention to meanings, rhetorics, and languages while seeming to efface the materiality at the core of labor history. Yet today few remember that labor was one of the first arenas of social history to unleash and embrace cultural inquiry. Instead of being a recalcitrant backwater, the history of work constituted a site of vibrant epistemological contention and creativity.[1] In the Anglo-Saxon academy at least, the cultural turn thus marks the heyday of labor history rather than its demise. In Germany, by contrast, the history of work, industrial transformation, and class formation was viewed as exhaustively researched by the late 1980s, so social historians turned to the thus far unexplored *Bürgertum*, thereby closing the book on labor history before it "went cultural" or began to explore gender. On both sides of the Atlantic however, transformations of geopolitics, symbolized in the "fall of the Berlin Wall," appeared to alter the political resonances of work and workers, shifting attention away from struggles of class to those of citizens, civil societies, and governmentality. For a plethora of reasons, some specific to respective national or academic contexts, labor, as a distinct field of inquiry, seemed to vanish from

A somewhat different version of this essay appeared in the journal *Traverse*, 2000/2 (June 2000) under the title "Gender and the Languages of Labor History: An Overview." I thank Chronos Verlag, Zürich, for permission to publish it here in revised form.

1. See, for example, William H. Sewell, Jr., *Work and Revolution in France: The Language of Labor from the Old Regime to 1848* (Cambridge, 1980); Gareth Stedman Jones, *Languages of Class: Studies in English Working-Class History, 1832–1982* (Cambridge, 1983); Steven L. Kaplan and Cynthia J. Koepp, eds., *Work in France: Representations, Meaning, Organization, and Practice* (Ithaca, N.Y., 1986); and Patrick Joyce, ed., *The Historical Meanings of Work* (Cambridge, 1987).

graduate seminars, conference programs, and academic best-seller lists in the course of the 1990s.

In this essay I take a critical approach to the notion of labor history's disappearance and to the litanies of loss that charted this absence. I point instead to the intriguing afterlife of labor history, namely a wave of studies on gender and labor that revitalized the study of work precisely at the point of its alleged decline. Yet these new studies, which culminated in the essay collection *Gender and Class in Modern Europe*, edited by Laura L. Frader and Sonya O. Rose and published in 1996, appeared to have little impact on laments about labor history's premature end.[2] They were viewed instead as evidence of the vitality of women's history/gender history, which contrasted starkly with the impression of labor history as a field in demise. This essay thus illuminates another central concern of this volume, namely the difficulty of seeing gender as integral to, rather than separate from "mainstream" inquiries like labor history. I show here that this was the case even at a crucial historiographical juncture when gender provided the analytical tools for significant renovations of the study of labor, pushing on its boundaries and revising its keywords, while expanding its scope and relevance.

§ § §

At the turn to the twenty-first century it seems that the once vital field of labor history may be relegated to the realm of legacy. One of the crowning achievements of the new social history of the 1960s, the English-language new labor history was driven by the desire to grasp "the authentic voices and authentic experiences of working people" that underlay the metahistories of class formations and class conflicts.[3] Some three decades of innovative scholarship and intensive debate followed the publication of E. P. Thompson's *The Making of the English Working Class* in 1963, during which the history of work, workers' politics, and workers' cultures was at the center of many of the most interesting and fruitful debates in the wider field of social history. In the German scholarly arena of the 1960s and 1970s, studies of labor, industrialization, urbanization, and social movements drove the rise of social science history, the hallmark of which was the analysis of structures and processes of social transformation. Yet the "authentic experiences" and everyday lives of German workers came to figure in German labor history only as an oppositional narrative of

2. Laura Levine Frader and Sonya O. Rose, eds., *Gender and Class in Modern Europe* (Ithaca, N.Y., 1996).

3. Lenard R. Berlanstein, introduction to *Rethinking Labor History: Essays on Discourse and Class Analysis*, ed. Berlanstein (Urbana, Ill., 1993), p. 1.

Alltagshistoriker, whose anthropologically informed critiques and conceptual innovations were widely heralded in the English-speaking academy, but subjected to scathing criticism by leading German historians.[4]

While the politics of labor history may have diverged across these distinct national settings, by the late 1980s the vitality of labor history had begun to wane across western Europe and in the United States. For one, its "materialist common sense" was undermined, as William H. Sewell has argued, by the "massive and fundamental changes in the nature, location, and meaning of work and in the fortunes of labor movements and socialist ideologies all over the globe."[5] At the same time a crisis, internal to the field of labor history itself, was well underway by the mid- to late 1980s. One impetus was the rejection of socioeconomic causality in favor of political languages, ideologies, rhetorics, and representations, the turn away from a notion of class as a "social fact" to one of class as a postulated "social identity," a paradigm shift in which historians of French and British labor clearly led the way.[6] No less destabilizing was the advancement of feminist historical scholarship on women's labor, which delivered powerful challenges to the concept of class "as the privileged signifier of

4. Here it is also important to mention the *Geschichtswerkstätten.* For some of the early debates on *Alltagsgeschichte,* see Hans Medick, "'Missionäre im Ruderboot?' Ethnologische Erkenntnisweisen als Herausforderung an die Sozialgeschichte," *Geschichte und Gesellschaft* 10/3 (1984): 295–319 and the responses in the same issue from Jürgen Kocka, "Zurück zur Erzählung? Pläydoyer für historische Argumentation," pp. 395–408 and Klaus Tenfelde, "Schwierigkeiten mit dem Alltag," pp. 376–94. Alf Lüdtke's essay, "Organizational Order or *Eigensinn?* Workers' Privacy and Workers' Politics in Imperial Germany," in *Rites of Power: Symbolism, Ritual and Politics since the Middle Ages,* ed. Sean Wilentz (Philadelphia, 1985), pp. 303–34, played an important role in the U.S. reception of *Alltagsgeschichte.* See his collection, *Alltagsgeschichte. Zur Rekonstruktion historischer Erfahrungen und Lebensweisen* (Frankfurt a. M, 1989). For incisive overviews see David F. Crew, "*Alltagsgeschichte:* A New Social History from Below?" *Central European History* 22/3–4 (September/December, 1989): 394–407 and Geoff Eley, "Labor History, Social History, *Alltagsgeschichte:* Experience, Culture and the Politics of the Everyday—A New Direction for German Social History?" *Journal of Modern History* 61 (June 1989): 297–343.

5. William H. Sewell, Jr., "Toward a Post-Materialist Rhetoric for Labor History," in *Rethinking Labor History,* ed. Berlanstein, p. 17.

6. See, for example, Sewell, *Work and Revolution in France;* William Reddy, *The Rise of Market Culture: The Textile Trade and French Society, 1750–1900* (Cambridge, 1984), and *Money and Liberty in Europe: A Critique of Historical Understanding* (Cambridge, 1987); Stedman Jones, *Languages of Class;* and Patrick Joyce, *Visions of the People: Industrial England and the Question of Class, 1848–1914* (Cambridge, 1991), and *The Historical Meanings of Work.*

social relations and their political representations."[7] Similarly, historians of minorities, colonialism, and empire interrogated the hegemony of class and analyzed its embeddedness in race, ethnicity, and nationality. Finally, the collapse of socialist governments across eastern Europe rendered class an apparent remnant of a past age, while citizenship became the new terrain of political contest and social scientific debate.

By the late 1980s, then, cultural modes of explanation had already seriously undermined the materialist presumptions of labor history. As a field in the throes of epistemological change, labor history figured centrally in the subsequent controversies surrounding the so-called "linguistic turn," a catch-all concept that signaled the growing significance of the linguistic, discursive, and symbolic dimensions of workers' politics and culture. The stakes of the struggle over the "linguistic turn" were no less than the very keywords of labor and history—experience, agency, and resistance—which many claimed had been rendered invisible by their subsumption into the all-pervasive phenomenon of discourse.[8] As epistemological debates over these concepts raged in the United States and Britain, the intensive study of German labor came rather quietly to a close in the mid-1980s, with a set of synthetic volumes appearing in the early 1990s as a testimony to its accomplishments,[9] as many social historians turned their attention to comparative study of the German *Bürgertum.* In Anglo-Saxon scholarly arenas, labor history was also eclipsed by the early 1990s by innovative studies of gender and sexuality; of race, ethnicity and nationality, colonialisms and empires; of popular culture and consumption. A parallel development was perhaps the displacement of Marxism, including its Gramscian

7. Sally Alexander, "Women, Class, and Sexual Differences in the 1830s and 1840s: Some Reflections on the Writing of a Feminist History," *History Workshop* 17 (Spring 1984): 133–49. See also Frader and Rose, "Introduction: Gender and the Reconstruction of European Working-Class History," in *Gender and Class in Modern Europe,* pp. 1–36; and Kathleen Canning, "Gender and the Politics of Class Formation: Rethinking German Labor History," *American Historical Review* 97/3 (June 1992): 736–68.

8. See chapter 2 in this volume.

9. For additional Anglo-Saxon debates, see *What Next for Labor and Working-Class History?* special issue of *International Labor and Working-Class History,* no. 46 (Fall 1994). The synthetic volumes were edited by Gerhard A. Ritter in a series titled *Geschichte der Arbeiter und der Arbeiterbewegung in Deutschland seit dem Ende des 18. Jahrhunderts.* See in particular Jürgen Kocka, *Weder Stand noch Klasse: Unterschichten um 1800* (Bonn, 1990), and *Arbeitsverhältnisse und Arbeiterexistenzen: Grundlagen der Klassenbildung im 19. Jahrhundert* (Bonn, 1990); Gerhard A. Ritter and Klaus Tenfelde, eds., *Arbeiter im deutschen Kaiserreich, 1871 bis 1914* (Bonn, 1992).

variant, by British cultural studies, which together with Foucauldian notions of power and feminist literary criticism became the crucial theoretical impulse of English-language historiography on these topics.

At the turn to the twenty-first century the dethroning of labor history has been made tangible, for example, in the absence of labor in the curriculum of major graduate history programs in the United States, and in the declining numbers of dissertations in the field of labor history. While it is difficult to deny the impact of the profound transformations of global political economies on the paradigms and practices of labor history, the epistemological shifts of the late 1980s and early 1990s also had a crucial role in the gradual undermining of labor's historiographical salience.[10] At the height of debates about the linguistic turn, for example, critics warned that the melding of social and cultural modes of historical analysis threatened to detach the study of labor from its own material conditions of production and leave it without a historiographical cause or place of its own.[11] William H. Sewell, Jr., has, by contrast, diagnosed the problems of labor history rather differently: in his view the demise of labor history was the result of its insularity *against* culturalist modes of explanation and its tenacious adherence to a "broad and complacent materialist perspective."[12]

The narrative of labor history's demise forms one of the critical preoccupations of this essay. I aim here to complicate this linear story of progressive decline through a close examination of the ways in which labor history has been revitalized and transformed during the last ten years. In this analysis I attend in particular to the shift that took place in the early 1990s from the history of *women's work* to the new field of *gender and labor,* which, I argue, contributed to substantial reinvigoration of labor history at the very peak of its purported decline.

RECONSIDERING THE LABOR-GENDER NEXUS

In his 1993 essay, "Toward a Post-Materialist Rhetoric for Labor History," William H. Sewell, Jr., drew a comparison between the fields of labor history

10. Here I would like to make clear that I do view these two strands of transformation as related, although not deterministically.

11. Sewell, "Toward a Post-Materialist Rhetoric," p. 15. For the most frequently discussed argument against the linguistic turn in social history, see Bryan Palmer, *Descent into Discourse: The Reification of Language and the Writing of Social History* (Philadelphia, 1990).

12. Sewell, "Toward a Post-Materialist Rhetoric," p. 17.

and women's history, which both began to flourish amidst the political and historiographical transformations of the late 1960s and early 1970s. Women's history, he contended, continued to enjoy an "intellectual vitality" and dynamism that labor history had already lost.[13] Yet Sewell's bifurcation between women's/gender history and labor history overlooked the very invigoration of the field of labor history by gender which had begun in the late 1980s. Instead, Sewell established an opposition between two specialized scholarly arenas—on the one hand, the diminishing field of labor history and on the other, the new and cutting-edge study of gender and labor, which he relegated to the field of women's history. Feminist historians of labor, however, clearly took a different view of their own scholarly contributions. So, for example, Gay Gullickson, historian of gender and work in nineteenth-century France, predicted in an essay published in the same volume as Sewell's that labor historians were "poised on the threshold of an exciting new era."[14] Indeed, Gullickson's call suggests a more complicated trajectory for labor history if scholarship on gender and labor are woven into the story of its rise and fall.

By contrast with the "old labor history" and its focus on idealized male workers and their organizations, the "new labor history" of the 1970s offered new insights into ideologies and workers' cultures and collective actions, sociability and leisure, everyday negotiations and self-perceptions. Yet "much of the new labor history," as Laura Frader and Sonya Rose have argued, "was itself a story of exclusions," in that it "rarely included women" or viewed "their work and labor activism through conceptual prisms that highlighted their differences from men."[15] So one of the first and formidable tasks of feminist labor history was to move women from the margins to the center of the histories of production, social reproduction, and politics, and to examine the path by which working women became "agents of their own history."[16] During the 1970s and early 1980s, then, the new labor history and women's labor history pursued parallel paths of investigation and generated their own tropes and terminologies. Proletarianization, for example, figured centrally in histories of men's experiences of industrialization, while the history of women's work relied upon the analytical paradigms of the sexual division of labor or the separation of home and work, which were viewed as formative of women's work, but scarcely relevant in the study of male labor.

13. Ibid., p. 15.

14. Gay Gullickson, "Commentary: New Labor History from the Perspective of a Women's Historian," in Berlanstein, *Rethinking Labor History,* pp. 200–201.

15. Frader and Rose, "Introduction," p. 4.

16. Berlanstein, introduction to *Rethinking Labor History,* p. 8.

Operating within these paradigms, by the mid- to late 1980s the history of gender and labor could claim considerable achievements in the study of female workers' experiences of workplace, neighborhood, and home, in the understanding of "the centrality of sex as well as class to their experiences."[17] Feminist exploration of the "sexual division of labor," which diverged so remarkably among and sometimes within regions, industrial branches, and technologies, suggested that no one "narrative structure or . . . organizing principle" could account for the disparate patterns of industrial transformation.[18] The comparative study by the Canadian historian Joy Parr of the "diverse and fluid" patterns of dividing labor along gender lines made clear that tasks that were "clearly and exclusively women's work in one factory, town or region" were relegated just as exclusively to male workers in other factories, towns or regions.[19] Women's historians who set out to investigate differentials of skill, wage, and career patterns found the toolbox of labor history, in which material conditions and structures had long been primary, woefully inadequate in explicating the ideologies and cultural practices underpinning definitions of masculinity and the "male breadwinner" or of femininity and the female "wage cutter" that had helped to constitute these inequities in the world of work.[20] Thus, by the mid- to late 1980s feminist historians had powerfully demonstrated the significance of women to the history of work and politics, but they had not yet successfully challenged or displaced the keywords or paradigms of labor history.[21]

17. Frader and Rose, "Introduction," p. 19. See also the influential book edited by Judith L. Newton, Mary P. Ryan, and Judith R. Walkowitz, *Sex and Class in Women's History* (London, 1983).

18. Gullickson, "Commentary," pp. 202–3.

19. Joy Parr, "Disaggregating the Sexual Division of Labour: A Transatlantic Case Study," *Comparative Study of Society and History* 30/2 (1988): 511–33. For further discussion of this topic, see Mary Freifeld, "Technological Change and the 'Self-Acting' Mule: A Study of Skill and the Sexual Division of Labor," *Social History* 11/3 (October 1986): 319–43; Sonya O. Rose, "Gender Segregation in the Transition to the Factory: The English Hosiery Industry, 1850–1910," *Feminist Studies* 13/1 (Spring 1987): 163–84; and Kathleen Canning, *Languages of Labor and Gender: Female Factory Work in Germany, 1850–1914* (Ithaca, N.Y., 1996), chap. 2: "'The Man Transformed into a Maiden'? Feminization in the Textile Industries of the Rhineland and Westphalia," pp. 38–84.

20. See, for example, the classic articles by Jean H. Quataert, "The Shaping of Women's Work in Manufacturing: Guilds, Household, and the State in Central Europe, 1648–1870," *American Historical Review* 90 (December 1985): 1122–48; and Sonya O. Rose, "'Gender at Work': Sex, Class, and Industrial Capitalism," *History Workshop* 21 (Spring 1986): 113–31.

21. See Frader and Rose, "Introduction," p. 19, for a similar argument.

The protracted shift toward the study of *gender*, as a symbolic system or as a signifier of relations of power in which men and women are positioned differently, gradually rendered the pursuit of parallel histories of women and men obsolete and drew new attention to the ways in which "feminine" and "masculine" constituted one another in the various arenas of labor history. The fact that contemporaries—employers, union organizers, social reformers, and state policy makers—were more likely to perceive women workers in terms of their bodily capacities for marriage and motherhood than in terms of the conditions or relations of production, meant that women's labor, more than men's, was debated, defined, governed, and protected across a wide array of social and political arenas. The study of discourses as sites of articulation and dissemination of ideologies helped feminist historians to grasp the connections across the diverse milieus—welfare state, social reform, medicine and hygiene, trade unions, and bourgeois feminist associations—in which the social question of female factory labor was cast and its solutions deliberated. Discourse, understood here as "complexes of signs and practices which organize social existence and social reproduction" and which comprise "a culture's determined and determining structures of representation and practice,"[22] proved a significant, even essential, conceptual tool for analysis of the melding and interlocking domains in which the ideologies of women's work were constituted and contested. The embrace of discourse analysis in and of itself did not bring about the abandonment of the study of waged work or workers, as some opponents of the linguistic turn anticipated at the height of that debate. Rather, this concept suggested new exploration of the texts and realms of debate that produced and problematized the ideologies underpinning the "separation of home and work" or the "sexual division of labor."

The turn to the study of gender and labor gradually led to the crumbling of a whole complex of dualisms, upon which both the materialist paradigm and male-centered labor history had balanced. Class, for example, was understood by historians of gender and labor in terms of its rhetorical distinctions between work and "nonwork," production and reproduction, which by definition excluded most female workers. As an alternative to the notion of class as a set of stages or levels (economic, social, cultural, and political), class was increasingly viewed as a contingent and contested social identity, "a series of makings and remakings . . . in which gender appears to constitute a continual point of con-

22. Richard Terdiman, *Discourse/Counter-Discourse: The Theory and Practice of Symbolic Resistance in Nineteenth-Century France* (Ithaca, N.Y., 1985), pp. 12, 54.

test, a renewed disordering of the process of class formation."[23] Another distinguishing feature of gender/labor scholarship was the firm rejection of dichotomies between class and "nonclass" lines of social differentiation, by which gender (along with ethnicity, nationality, and race) belonged to the "nonclass" category.[24] This view has a particular resonance in German labor history.[25]

Indeed, the bold challenges of gender/labor historians to key concepts and paradigms of labor history, such as class, not only propelled labor history in new directions, but also had a central role in the broader paradigm shift from women's history to gender history. Today in the post–linguistic turn era, few remember the centrality of *labor* in Joan Scott's controversial *Gender and the Politics of History* of 1988, a text that had the dual effect of signaling the arrival of gender as a new category of historical analysis and which also sparked the first wave of vitriolic debate about the linguistic turn.[26] Scott's critical reflections on E. P. Thompson's and Gareth Stedman Jones's histories of English class formation, her probing of work identities, labor statistics, and the discourses of political economy in nineteenth-century France, and finally her insightful analysis of the "equality-difference" debate in the legendary court case

23. Canning, "Gender and the Politics of Class Formation," p. 768. Class came under assault from a wide range of scholars in the field of gender and labor. Formative for my own thinking were Alexander, "Women, Class, and Sexual Difference"; Barbara Taylor, *Eve and the New Jerusalem: Socialism and Feminism in the Nineteenth Century* (New York, 1983); Sonya O. Rose's "'Gender at Work,' and her book, *Limited Livelihoods: Gender and Class in Nineteenth-Century England* (Berkeley, Calif., 1992); Joan W. Scott, *Gender and the Politics of History* (New York, 1988); and Anna Clark, "The Rhetoric of Chartist Domesticity: Gender, Language, and Class in the 1830s and 1840s," *Journal of British Studies* 31 (1992): 62–88.

24. Canning, "Gender and the Politics of Class Formation," pp. 745–48. Of course feminist historians of gender and labor were not alone in their critiques of class. The work of male historians already cited in this essay—William H. Sewell, Jr., William Reddy, Gareth Stedman Jones, and Patrick Joyce, for example—also had a crucial role in undermining the stability of the concept of class. See, for example, Kathleen Paul, Marc W. Steinberg, and Ann Farnsworth-Alvear, eds., *Identity Formation and Class*, special issue of *International Labor and Working-Class History*, no. 46 (Spring 1996).

25. On the class and "nonclass" lines of distinction, see Kocka's *Weder Stand noch Klasse* und *Arbeitsverhältnisse und Arbeiterexistenzen*.

26. Debates about the linguistic turn were already under way at this time among scholars of intellectual history. See, for example, John Toews, "Intellectual History after the Linguistic Turn: The Autonomy of Meaning and the Irreducibility of Experience," *American Historical Review* 92 (October 1987): 879–907.

involving Sears Roebuck Co. of the 1980s, render this book a classic in labor history. It is one that not only offered deep and critical interpretations of influential historiography, but also sought to forge analytical links between historical and contemporary conflicts over women's waged labor.[27] The publication of Scott's essay collection in 1988 and the controversies that followed in its wake galvanized a new wave of gender and labor scholarship in the European field, while Ava Baron's *Work Engendered: Toward a New History of American Labor,* published in 1991, had a similar impact in the American history field.[28]

The extent to which the gendering of labor history transformed the study of work more broadly became evident in the course of the 1990s, which saw a swell of new books by younger scholars who entered the profession on the eve of the linguistic turn.[29] This generation of scholars experienced the disorienting clash of social historical training with the theoretical and methodological impulses of literary theory, cultural anthropology, and Foucauldian notions of discursive and capillary power. At the same time, Joan Scott's challenge had special resonances among this generation, which explicitly sought to place gender, as both a social and symbolic system, at the heart of our own historical case studies. While our books, taken together, maintained a shared sensitivity towards the material fabrics of laboring lives, of the transformations of machines, land-

27. Scott, *Gender and the Politics of History.* Part II includes her essays on E. P. Thompson's *The Making of the English Working Class* and Stedman Jones's *Languages of Class: Studies in English Working-Class History;* Part III includes three essays on the representations of women's work in France in the mid-nineteenth century; and Part IV includes the essay on "The Sears Case," which analyzes the resonances of the "equality-difference" debate in the sex-discrimination suit which the U.S. government's Equal Opportunity Commission filed in 1978 against Sears, Roebuck & Company on behalf of its female sales personnel.

28. Ava Baron, ed., *Work Engendered: Toward a New History of American Labor* (Ithaca, N.Y., 1991).

29. A partial list of these books includes Rose, *Limited Livelihoods* (1992); Anna Clark, *The Struggle for the Breeches: Gender and the Making of the British Working Class* (Berkeley, Calif., 1994); Tessie Liu, *The Weaver's Knot: The Contradictions of Class Struggle and Family Solidarity in Western France, 1750–1914* (Ithaca, N.Y., 1994); Laura Tabili, "'We Ask for British Justice': Workers and Racial Difference in Late Imperial Britain* (Ithaca, N.Y., 1994); Deborah Valenze, *The First Industrial Woman* (New York, 1995); Laura Lee Downs, *Manufacturing Inequality: Gender Division in the French and British Metalworking Industries, 1914–1939* (Ithaca, N.Y., 1995); Judith G. Coffin, *The Politics of Women's Work: The Paris Garment Trades, 1750–1915* (Princeton, N.J., 1996); Canning, *Languages of Labor and Gender* (1996); Leora Auslander, *Taste and Power: Furnishing Modern France* (Berkeley, Calif., 1997); and Nancy L. Green, *Ready-to-Wear and Ready-to-Work: A Century of Industry and Immigrants in Paris and New York* (Durham, N.C., 1997).

scapes, architectures, families, and communities, we also were compelled to develop new interpretive strategies, to learn how to decode images, rhetorics, and tropes in textual sources, while many of us continued to work with quantitative evidence on budgets, wages, prices, and career patterns. In Germany a wave of innovative studies on gender and work appeared by scholars grappling with similar epistemological problems, whose productivity made clear that labor history had prematurely been declared passé.[30]

BEYOND LABOR HISTORIES

As scholars in the field of gender and labor worked to dissolve the binary of material and representational evidence, they delivered the final blow to many of the established tropes and master narratives of labor history. More importantly, they also rendered the study of labor a less bounded inquiry, which now had the potential to reach far beyond the factory workshop and forge new interpretations of state, public sphere (both "subaltern" and dominant), and "the social." Indeed, the project of "rewriting" labor history from the perspective of gender significantly widened its scope, as the meanings of work spilled over into the histories of state and social reform, and laid the groundwork for new explorations of the histories of citizenship and consumption, of empires and diasporas, in which labor had a merely peripheral place. While the pessimist might lament the fact that labor history did not withstand intact the assault of culture, language, or gender, the optimist could take pleasure in the new absence of boundaries around the history of work and class. This process by which the pursuit of gendered labor histories spilled over into other areas of inquiry and forged the way to rethinkings of states, citizenships, bodies, and subjectivities was propelled as well by new methodologies in which discourses and languages helped to map the connections between and among arenas that were otherwise viewed as socially or politically distinct.

An example from my own study, *Languages of Labor and Gender,* regarding the "separation of home and work" might help to elucidate this point. In Ger-

30. See, for example, Marlene Ellerkamp, *Industriearbeit, Krankheit und Geschlecht* (Göttingen, 1991); Karin Hausen, ed., *Geschlechterhierarchie und Arbeitsteilung: Zur Geschichte ungleicher Erwerbschancen von Männern und Frauen* (Göttingen, 1993); Brigitte Kerchner, *Beruf und Geschlecht: Frauenberufsverbände in Deutschland 1848–1908* (Göttingen, 1992); Susanne Rouette, *Sozialpolitik als Geschlechterpolitik: Die Regulierung der Frauenarbeit nach dem Ersten Weltkrieg* (Frankfurt a. M., 1993); and Sabine Schmitt, *Der Arbeiterinnenschutz im deutschen Kaiserreich: Zur Konstruktion der schutzbedürftigen Arbeiterin* (Stuttgart, 1995).

man labor historiography the "separation of home and work" has generally served as a crucial marker of the onset of modernization and working-class formation. In approaching this separation as a plot line in the narrative story of German working-class formation, I was able to trace the connections among and between the megaprocesses of industrial transformation, class formation, and the expansion of the welfare state. As the largest factory employer of women in prewar Germany, the mills constituted a complex laboratory for state bureaucrats and academic social reformers who sought to alleviate the abuses of factory labor for women and youths and to resolve the crisis of the family that accompanied the transition from home to factory industry.

The transformations encompassed in the "separation of home and work" in Rhenish and Westphalian textile regions included the erosion of the household as a site of wage labor, the recurrent unemployment or displacement of male hand-weavers from their craft, the fragmentation of the family wage into individual, gender-specific wages, and the final and permanent replacement of the domestic workshop by the factory. Male weavers, as well as the social reformers who took up their cause, understood this separation not only as a profound disruption of the industrial order, but also of the sexual order, as the competition of "cheap" female labor and the inscription of certain sectors of production with female attributes (dexterity) came to signify the feminization of textile production. Male weavers' litanies of loss, then, figured prominently in the coalescence of class identity among textile workers in these regions. The "separation of home and work," as the most poignant of these litanies, left indelible traces on the programs and practices of the textile unions, both Social Democratic and Catholic, and in the collective memories and class identities of union leaders.

The outcry against feminization and displacement as two key consequences of the "separation of home and work" also resonated in the rhetorics of social reform as eminent professors of political economy undertook *Studienreisen* through the textile regions of Germany and produced scholarly investigations of the human costs of this momentous transition. The subsequent discursive and social mobilizations around the social question of female factory labor during the 1880s and 1890s rendered the "separation of home and work" a critical impetus in the expansion of the German welfare state, as bureaucrats and reformers responded to public pressure to solve this problem by extending labor protection to adult women. The interventions of the German state, from the establishment of social insurance to the expansion of labor protection for women and youths in 1891 and again in 1908, helped to define two distinct categories of citizenship for men and women. The dichotomies this process fostered between male breadwinners and female dependents, between independent male citizens and "female organisms" (as the object of both moral and hygienic intervention), reinforced, in turn, the gendered boundaries of class formation in Germany.

The "separation of home and work" forms a narrative thread that links the processes of German working-class formation, the framing of new social identities of citizenship, and the expansion of the German welfare state. This thread, which is not necessarily replicated or mirrored in institutions, helps to uncover the politics and ideologies of gender that shaped each of these processes. The work of tracing this thread not only led my own study of workplaces, unions, and strikes (as originally conceived) to spill over into the histories of state, social reform, and citizenship. It also necessitated attention to the languages of labor, to the tropes and narrative strands, the component elements of discourses, which spanned by definition a broad range of milieus, movements, and institutions and the source materials they produced.

In recent years labor historians have frequently extended their explorations into the realm of citizenship, probing the meanings of the gendered ideologies of work and divisions of labor for the social identities of masculine and feminine citizens.[31] The claim of British Chartists, for example, that men "held property in their labor" made wage labor the cornerstone of citizenship rights for "respectable" men, and as such, elevated gender to a defining element of the new social identity of working-class citizenship.[32] In other cases, citizenship emerges as a social identity after class has already established a certain rhetorical and social power among workers, as in Germany. In such instances, it might be interesting to consider how the new social claims or legal identities of citizenship transformed the vocabularies and practices of class. So, for example, women's acquisition of citizenship rights in Germany and England after the First World War changed the terms of their struggles for equality of skill and wage at work and in the union halls. In the wake of world war, revolution, and the founding of German democracy, female activists cast themselves as newly empowered citizens in order to demand equal representation for women in the

31. See, for example, the "scholarly controversy" in the forum "Women, Work, and Citizenship," *International Labor and Working-Class History,* no. 52 (Fall 1997), pp. 1–71. Contributors include Louise Tilly, Chiara Saraceno, Ann Shola Orloff, Roderick Phillips, and W. Robert Lee.

32. Frader and Rose, *Gender and Class in Modern Europe,* p. 15. For an excellent analysis of the meaning of labor for male citizenship claims, see Keith McClelland, "Rational and Respectable Men: Gender, the Working Class, and Citizenship in Britain, 1850–1867," in *Gender and Class in Modern Europe,* ed. Frader and Rose, pp. 280–93.

Social Democratic unions, thus mobilizing the new multilayered languages of female citizenship to critique the politics of class.[33] Viewing the history of labor through the lens of citizenship certainly does widen its scope to encompass the realms of nation, state (legislative and juridical), and public sphere as spaces beyond the workplace in which citizenship was both defined and contested.

Citizenship is tangentially related to another field of inquiry which emerged at the nexus of labor history and family history, namely that of consumption. While histories of middle-class formation, such as Davidoff and Hall's classic, *Family Fortunes,* highlighted the significance of women's labor as consumers in fashioning the proper middle-class household, feminist histories of proletarian families recognized the dual contributions of women, as wage-earners and as frugal consumers, in working-class households.[34] Not only was "women's wage earning," as Judith Coffin argues in her study of the French garment industry, "crucial to the expansion of popular consumption,"[35] but the narratives of danger about female factory labor also paired the two realms as well. Just as the rapid expansion of the female factory work force appeared to social reformers as uncontrollable, so they were also alarmed by the allegedly unbridled consumer desires of independent wage-earning women for "luxury" goods (such as hats, silks, hairpins, stockings, and lace). Nancy Green's comparative study of the women's garment industry in Paris and New York also creatively links fashion and fabrication, consumption and production, thereby forming the foundation for an even richer exploration of ethnicity and immigration, urban growth and labor politics in the two metropoles from the late nineteenth century through the 1980s.[36]

33. See chapters 6, 7, and 8 in this volume.

34. In addition to Leonore Davidoff and Catherine Hall, *Family Fortunes: Men and Women of the English Middle Class, 1780–1850* (Chicago, 1987), see, for example, Jane Lewis, ed., *Labour and Love: Women's Experience of Home and Family, 1850–1940* (London, 1986); Ellen Ross, *Love and Toil: Motherhood in Outcast London, 1870–1918* (Oxford, 1993); Leora Auslander, "The Gendering of Consumer Practices in Nineteenth-Century France," and Victoria de Grazia, "Empowering Women as Citizen-Consumers," in *The Sex of Things: Gender and Consumption in Historical Perspective,* ed. Victoria de Grazia and Ellen Furlough (Berkeley, Calif., 1996), pp. 79–112, 275–86.

35. Judith G. Coffin, "Consumption, Production, and Gender: The Sewing Machine in Nineteenth-Century France," in *Gender and Class in Modern Europe,* ed. Frader and Rose, p. 121. Also see Coffin's excellent book, *The Politics of Women's Work.*

36. Green, *Ready-to-Wear and Ready-to-Work.*

BODIES, MATERIAL AND THE DISCURSIVE:
SOME FINAL METHODOLOGICAL CONSIDERATIONS

It is perhaps worth noting in conclusion that the process by which labor history has become less bounded has not produced one dominant paradigm or epistemology, culturalist or discursive. Rather, explorations of citizenship have revived inquiry into the relationship between law and social practices, while the history of consumption links the symbolic and the social in its pursuit of the processes of "commodification, spectatorship, and commercial exchanges."[37] Nor has the willingness of "culturalist" labor historians to grapple with new concepts and methodologies like discourses and narratives meant the wholesale neglect of the "material," or of experience and agency.[38] In contending with both the discourses and the experiences of work, the last wave of Anglo-Saxon gender and labor scholarship, for example, helped to dissolve the dichotomies between these terms, to untangle the relationship between the two, and to resist a fixed notion of this relationship by which one of the pair (discourse) always seems to determine or "construct" the other (experience).[39] An emphasis on the changing meanings of work leaves the historical subject at the center of the process of assigning meaning, of transforming the discourses in which those meanings are internalized, deliberated, or contested. Taking discourses as sites of struggle, rather than as fixed formations, necessitates analysis of their mutability and instability across time and place, as creating or encompassing not a singular image or construct, but an array of subject positions.

Bodies, laboring and symbolic, have emerged in the years since the peak of the linguistic turn as an interesting site of debate and potential resolution of some of its dilemmas, including this very relationship between the material and the discursive. While the laboring body has remained remarkably elusive in most labor history, recent interest in body history has produced a groundswell of books, articles, dissertation proposals, and conference panels on various aspects thereof.[40] It may be possible to interpret this fascination with the body as

37. De Grazia, introduction to *The Sex of Things*, pp. 4–5.

38. See Judith Butler's thoughtful comments on the dichotomy between "the material" and "the constructed" in the introduction to her *Bodies That Matter: On the Discursive Limits of "Sex"* (London, 1993). For a discussion of experience and agency, see Joan W. Scott, "The Evidence of Experience," *Critical Inquiry* 17/3 (1991): 773–97; and Canning, "Feminist History after the Linguistic Turn" (chapter 2 of this volume).

39. Canning, *Languages of Labor and Gender*, pp. 10–15.

40. See chapter 6 in this volume.

a reaction to the disorientation that beset both the humanities and the social sciences in the wake of the linguistic turn, in which the physicality of the body—its pain, disease, desire—has served as an oasis of materiality in a swirl of intangible discourses. For the history of gender and labor, however, female bodies can also serve as sites of evidence of the "hybrid character" of women's work, of its "melding of paid (industrial) and unpaid (domestic or household) labor," often defying the legendary separation of home and work in quite graphic terms (birthing on the factory floor, for example).[41] This notion of hybridity might also help to understand bodies as intriguing sites at which the binary opposition between the discursive and the material dissolves, at which discourses and everyday experiences converge, at which women workers encountered and often subverted the meanings imparted to their bodies by idealized visions of motherhood, by the prescriptions of social and reproductive hygiene. The body, as a more explicit presence in labor history, may shed light on its meanings for the formation of women's political subjectivities, for the articulation of their claims as citizens upon states, employers, or labor unions. The body, then, could also figure as yet another analytical strand by which the history of labor reaches considerably beyond its traditional sites and is made meaningful for the arenas of state, citizenship, consumption, hygiene, and medicine.

By now it should be evident that work and workers remain important subjects of historical analysis in labor history even if the factory workplace is no longer its center stage. The process by which labor history has become less confined within notions of class and dichotomies of production/reproduction is certainly a complex one, in which the social and economic transformations that underlay "the condition of postmodernity" are entwined with the epistemological crises and theoretical renovations encompassed in the linguistic turn and the elevation of gender to a central category of historical analysis.[42] If labor history's dispersal across a wider terrain of institutions, movements, and languages has dissolved the dichotomies of the last wave of debate—material and culture, discourse and experience—its effect has not, hopefully, been the instating of new binary terms. Instead, this critical engagement with the narratives of labor history's demise suggests the importance of reconsidering the many arenas in which work had meaning and the multiple subject positions of workers as well.

41. Coffin, *The Politics of Women's Work*, p. 9.

42. David Harvey, *The Condition of Postmodernity: An Enquiry into the Origins of Cultural Change* (London, 1990). Certainly nationally bounded particularities of both labor politics and labor history writing have also had a role in shaping the responses of French, British, and American labor historians to these challenges of the last two decades.

CHAPTER 5 § SOCIAL POLICY, BODY POLITICS §

RECASTING THE SOCIAL QUESTION IN GERMANY,

1875–1900

PROLOGUE 2005

The focus of this essay is the social body that was defined in the interstices of state social policy and the mobilizations of social reformers around perceptions of the social question. The point of this piece was to analyze the feminization of the social question, indeed of the social, in late nineteenth-century Germany as female factory labor came to preoccupy both state and public sphere. At the heart of this analysis are also various bodies, in particular the social body that was evoked and symbolized in the imaginations of social reformers who decried the dangers of women's work, and the material bodies of female workers as sites of hygienic, medical, and moral intervention. As such this essay also offers a case study of the ideological formation of women's work, which was imprinted upon the process of founding and expanding the German welfare state. In this essay I trace the threads linking the social imagination about women's labor to transformations of state politics, the proliferation of social reform associations, and the process of working-class formation in Germany. One key argument here is that the first variation of citizenship made accessible to workers in Germany—the social citizenship embedded within the welfare state—was formed across these arenas and from its outset was cast in both gendered and embodied terms. Yet in retrospect this case study of social policy as body politics left open crucial questions about both bodies and citizenships, to which I return in the essays featured in Part III of this volume.

§ § §

INTRODUCTION

For a prolonged moment in German history the intricate links between social and sexual order, in the guise of female factory labor, became the object of

This essay was first published in *Gender and Class in Modern Europe*, ed. Laura Levine Frader and Sonya O. Rose (Ithaca: Cornell University Press, 1996). I thank Cornell University Press for permission to reprint it here.

national public debate for the first time. As Germany underwent its rapid second wave of industrialization during the last two decades of the nineteenth century, women's work outside of the home, especially married women's factory work and its long-term effects on the working-class family, came to constitute a new social question. Within the expansive body of literature on the history of European welfare states, protective labor legislation has remained relatively unexamined, submerged between the dichotomized male and female streams or strands of the welfare state—the maternal and child welfare strand of poor relief and public assistance and the male stream of social insurance. Social insurance (old age, health, disability), instituted in Germany by Bismarck during the 1880s, is generally regarded as the linchpin of the German welfare state. In seeking to solve one aspect of the social question—economic security for skilled male workers who posed the greatest political challenge to the Bismarckian state—social insurance legislation also demarcated a male stream of welfare that extended a new kind of social citizenship to skilled male workers.[1]

Feminist historians have pointed out that the social insurance system constructed an ideal of the male breadwinner earning a family wage, thus implicitly fostering the dependence of women and children. Moreover, they point out, the systems of poor relief and public assistance served to reinforce and institutionalize women's dependent status.[2] Feminist scholars have delivered even more compelling evidence regarding the bifurcation between the male and female streams of the welfare state, analyzing the maternal/child welfare stream as the result of maternalists' interventions on behalf of women's and children's' "*needs*," while viewing the male stream as the outcome of workers' mobilization for expanded political *rights*. Protective labor laws, however, fit only un-

1. See, e.g., Florian Tennstedt, *Sozialgeschichte der Sozialpolitik in Deutschland vom 18. Jahrhundert bis zum Ersten Weltkrieg* (Göttingen, 1981), pp. 139–92; Gerhard A. Ritter, *Social Welfare in Germany and Britain: Origins and Development*, trans. Kim Traynor (New York, 1986), esp. chaps. 1 and 2; Heide Gerstenberger, "The Poor and the Respectable Worker: On the Introduction of Social Insurance in Germany," *Labour History* 48 (May 1985): 69–70.

2. Linda Gordon, "Social Insurance and Public Assistance: The Influence of Gender in Welfare Thought in the United States, 1890–1935," *American Historical Review* 97 (February 1992): 20–21; Linda Gordon, "The New Feminist Scholarship on the Welfare State," in *Women, the State, and Welfare*, ed. Linda Gordon (Madison, Wis., 1990), pp. 20–22. Also see Barbara Hobson, "Feminist Strategies and Gendered Discourses in Welfare States: Married Women's Right to Work in the United States and Sweden," in *Mothers of a New World: Maternalist Politics and the Origins of Welfare States*, ed. Seth Koven and Sonya Michel (New York, 1993), p. 396.

easily into either strand of the dichotomized welfare state. As a social policy aimed almost exclusively at protecting female and teenage workers, mothers and children at work, labor legislation disrupts the dichotomy between the two streams, for it implicitly erases the boundary between them.

Similarly, the important expansion of welfare state scholarship to encompass and compare the crucial contributions of maternalist visionaries, female social workers, and female clients as a "social and political force which demanded, brought about, influenced, and introduced" reforms has done little to interrogate or defuse the dichotomies between the streams.[3] Pathbreaking comparative studies of the role of women in the rise of European welfare states, for example, have produced models and paradigms that measure the level of bourgeois women's maternalist activism against "the range and generosity of state welfare benefits for women and children." Yet this comparative exploration of the role of female agency in shaping the welfare state has led to some quite contradictory conclusions, suggesting, for example, that there was little correlation between female activism and the implementation of comprehensive social welfare programs for women. Indeed, Seth Koven and Sonya Michel argue convincingly that in the strongest states, defined as those with well-developed bureaucracies and long traditions of government intervention, such as Germany, women's restricted access to political space prevented them from formulating and effecting visions and programs of social welfare. Furthermore, they contend, women's movements were more likely to be effective when their causes "were taken up by male political actors pursuing other goals, such as pro-natalism or control of the labor force."[4]

The history of labor legislation in Germany between 1878 and 1914 suggests, however, that even where women lacked "bureaucratic and political power" (in France and Germany, but not in the United States, according to Koven and Michel), ideologies of gender shaped the definitions and practices of welfare and were in turn recast by state interventions and anchored by state authority.[5] In fact, the history of labor legislation and the welfare state offers an excellent illustration of how the analytical categories of women and gender might shape

3. Gisela Bock and Pat Thane, eds., *Maternity and Gender Policies: Women and the Rise of the European Welfare States, 1880s–1950s* (London, N.Y., 1991), p. 6. Also see Koven and Michel, "Introduction: 'Mother Worlds,'" in *Mothers of a New World*, pp. 1–10.

4. Seth Koven and Sonya Michel, "Womanly Duties: Maternalist Politics and the Origins of Welfare States in France, Germany, Great Britain, and the United States, 1880–1920," *American Historical Review* 95 (October 1990): 1079; Koven and Michel, "Introduction: 'Mother Worlds,'" pp. 26–27.

5. Koven and Michel, "Womanly Duties," 1079–80; "Introduction: 'Mother Worlds,'" p. 26.

two distinct kinds of inquiry, of how different aspects of the welfare state become visible and are highlighted, depending on which of those categories serves as a lens. Put in the simplest terms, social policy, in which the family historically figured as the key site of intervention, sought to fix gender roles, to align the sexual divisions of labor with the social order, and to regulate the social body by policing female bodies, even where bourgeois feminist-maternalists were unsuccessful or inactive.

A similar critique might also apply to those feminist studies that analyze protective labor legislation in terms of its positive and negative effects on women workers, revealing, for example, that protective labor legislation adversely affected women workers across Europe by "barring them from employment without compensatory benefits."[6] Mary Lynn Stewart, for example, deems "perverse" both the failure of the French state to discern the needs of women workers for labor protection and its tendency to regulate female factory labor only in order to prop up women's housewifely role in the patriarchal family. While it may be valid to label protective labor laws "perverse," "paternalistic," or "patriarchal," Stewart's placement of them within a fixed "paternalist tutelary complex" seems to preclude serious inquiry into the ways in which labor protection also figured as a site of contest and negotiation among and between women and men, workers and the state, the outcomes of which were contingent rather than always fixed and predictable.[7] In the work of Sonya Rose and Robert Gray on factory reform and of Mary Poovey on "the sanitary idea," for example, social reform and factory legislation figure as important sites "for renegotiating some of the inherent contradictions of liberal ideology."[8] These authors also explore the particular social publics and social knowl-

6. Koven and Michel, "Womanly Duties," pp. 1091–92.

7. Mary Lynn Stewart, Women, *Work and the French State: Labour Protection and Social Patriarchy, 1879–1919* (London, 1989), pp. 5–6, 12–13. For an interesting contrast to Stewart's view, see Jane Jenson, "Representations of Gender: Policies to 'Protect' Women Workers and Infants in France and the United States before 1914," in *Women, the State, and Welfare,* ed. Gordon, pp. 152–77.

8. See Sonya O. Rose's essay "Factory Reform in Nineteenth-Century Britain: Gender, Class, and the Liberal State," in *Gender and Class in Modern Europe,* ed. Frader and Rose, pp. 193–210; Robert Gray, "Medical Men, Industrial Labour, and the State in Britain, 1830–1850," *Social History* 16 (January 1991): 19–43, and "The Languages of Factory Reform in Britain, c. 1830–1850," in *The Historical Meanings of Work,* ed. Patrick Joyce (Cambridge, 1989), pp. 143–79; and Mary Poovey, "Domesticity and Class Formation: Chadwick's *Sanitary Report,*" in *Subject to History: Ideology, Class, Gender,* ed. David Simpson (Ithaca, N.Y., 1991), pp. 65–81.

edges produced by the discourses of factory reform in England, in particular by reformers' debates about sexual immorality and declining domesticity. In fact, in the German case, the mobilization and intervention of social reform publics mark a key difference between labor legislation on the one hand and the streams of social insurance and poor relief on the other. Unlike the social insurance laws of the 1880s, which Bismarck initiated in the absence of genuine popular demand and in collaboration with employers' associations, protective labor legislation represented the outcome of intense discursive and social mobilization around the social question of female factory labor.[9]

Finally, explicating the ways in which the female body served as a new object of intervention for both the regulatory and the tutelary regimes of state social policy and industrial paternalism in Germany helps to forge intriguing links between and among the histories of the body, labor legislation, the welfare state, and the social identities of class and citizenship. Though the medicalization of state welfare formulated and legitimated individual and collective visions of *Körperlichkeit* (embodiment), most of the literature on medicalization and the welfare state has focused on social insurance as the locus of the late nineteenth-century *Homo hygienicus* or has emphasized the ways in which the system of poor relief and public assistance "coloniz[ed] and assimilat[ed] marginalized classes" through attempts to discipline the body.[10] Protective labor legislation has, perplexingly enough, escaped the gaze of Foucauldian critics of the welfare state, although uncovering and explicating its focus on the female body might well render it emblematic of a Foucauldian kind of "biopolitics."[11] During the late 1870s, for example, the "female organism" became the object of both moral and hygienic concern in Germany, as some reformers relied on statistics or medical diagnostics, while others recounted sensational stories of seduction and sexual abandon in the carnal underworld of the factory.[12]

9. Rüdiger Baron, "Weder Zuckerbrot noch Peitsche: Historische Konstitutions-Bedingungen des Sozialstaats in Deutschland," in *Gesellschaft: Beiträge zur Marxschen Theorie* 12 (1979): 15–18; Monika Breger, *Die Haltung der industriellen Unternehmer zur staatlichen Sozialpolitik in den Jahren 1878–1891* (Frankfurt a. M., 1982), pp. 37, 124, 156, 212.

10. Alfons Labisch and Reinhard Spree, eds., *Medizinische Deutungsmacht im sozialen Wandel des 19. und frühen 20. Jahrhunderts* (Bonn, 1989), p. 13; Alfons Labisch, "Gesundheitskonzepte und Medizin im Prozeß der Zivilisation," ibid., pp. 25–26.

11. Martin Hewitt, "Bio-politics and Social Policy: Foucault's Account of Welfare," *Theory, Culture and Society* 2/1 (1983): 67–84.

12. The vocabulary of "female organism" typified the discussion of women's factory labor across the political spectrum. See, for example, Ludwig Hirt, *Die gewerbliche Thätigkeit der Frauen vom hygienischen Standpunkt aus* (Breslau, 1873), pp. 5–6; Heinrich Herkner,

State legislators went to considerable lengths to ensure that protective measures would not apply to male workers, even inadvertently (say, by virtue of their employment in the same shops as women whose work was restructured by protective codes). For in their view, male breadwinners, by definition, were able to assert and defend their own interests through political association, whereas women and children, deprived of the same political rights, required the protection of the state. Indeed, as Mary Nolan argued some years ago, the incipient German welfare state, in identifying workers as objects of reform or legislation, had a crucial part in demarcating the boundaries of the working class. Specifically, protective labor legislation fixed women's place in production and anchored both class and citizenship in a particular vision of the female body, which became centrally implicated in and representative of the ills of the social body.[13]

Let us explore these links by examining labor legislation across three historical periods. After the "hungry 1840s," the social question of pauperism was gradually supplanted by the *Arbeiterfrage* (worker question) as factories began to transform urban and rural landscapes. Workers launched their first protests against factory regimes during the 1850s and 1860s. Female factory employment became an important topic in social reform circles during the 1870s, one that was discussed and debated mainly among policy makers at the level of government or in social reform associations. During the second phase, from the mid-1880s through the turn of the century, which forms the central focus of this essay, the social question of women's work exploded into a volatile public controversy for the first time in German history as reformers issued strident calls for a legal ban on married women's factory employment, prompting the emergence of new ideologies and social policies toward female factory labor. The third phase, from 1900 through 1914, was marked by attempts to resolve the debates of the 1890s as the expanded German welfare state, in its guise as media-

---

"Zur Kritik und Reform der deutschen Arbeiterschutzgesetzgebung," *Archiv für Soziale Gesetzgebung und Statistik* 3 (March 1890): 226–27; Johannes Wenzel, *Arbeiterschutz und Centrum mit Berücksichtigung der übrigen Parteien* (Berlin, 1893), p. 86; August Bebel, *Woman under Socialism*, trans. Daniel De Leon (New York, 1971), pp. 89–90; 123–24; Clara Zetkin's article in *Die Gleichheit* 7 (1897): 128, 137–38. Mary Lynn Stewart finds a similar emphasis on the female organism in French social reform: see Stewart, *Women, Work, and the French State*, pp. 3, 61–62.

13. Mary Nolan, "Economic Crisis, State Policy, and Working-Class Formation in Germany, 1870–1900," in *Working-Class Formation: Nineteenth-Century Patterns in Western Europe and the United States*, ed. Ira Katznelson and Aristide Zolberg (Princeton, N.J., 1986), pp. 360–61.

tor and regulator of labor and gender relations, assigned a new legitimacy to women's work outside the home.

THE SOCIAL QUESTION, 1848–1880

Between 1848 and 1914 the social question constituted a discursive site at which the relationship between public and private, production and reproduction, factory and family was defined, contested, and reimagined periodically. From the founding of the first social policy organization, the Zentralverein für das Wohl der arbeitenden Klasse (Central Association for the Welfare of the Working Classes), in 1844, reformers focused their attention on the family as they sought to prevent the "impending dissolution of society into two opposing and hostile classes."[14] When Wilhelm Heinrich Riehl made his ethnographic foray into "The Natural History of the *Volk* as the Foundation of German Social Policy" during the 1850s, he lamented the loss of "family consciousness" and family bonds.[15] Gustav Schmoller, a founding member of the Verein für Sozialpolitik (Association for Social Policy) and renowned professor of politics and government, framed the "worker question" as a *sittliche Kulturfrage*, a social problem embedded in issues of morality, culture, and family, rather than one defined mainly in terms of wage inequities or working conditions.[16] Middle-class social reformers such as Schmoller, along with such Catholic reformers as Bishop Wilhelm Ketteler of Mainz, sought to achieve not only a more equitable distribution of goods in the new nation-state but also to repair the moral and cultural fabric of family and community, rent apart by industrial and urban growth, through the intervention of a *Kulturstaat* (cultural state).

The combined efforts of middle-class social reformers, the Catholic Center

14. Rüdiger vom Bruch, "Bürgerliche Sozialreform im deutschen Kaiserreich," in *Weder Kommunismus noch Kapitalismus: Bürgerliche Sozialreform in Deutschland vom Vormärz bis zur Ära Adenauer,* ed. vom Bruch (Munich, 1985), p. 3.

15. Wilhelm Heinrich Riehl's four-volume study *Die Naturgeschichte des Volkes als Grundlage einer deutschen Social-Politik* was published between 1853 and 1869. Volume 3 (Stuttgart, 1897) is on the natural history of the family.

16. Gustav Schmoller, "Die Arbeiterfrage," in *Preußische Jahrbücher* 14 (1864): 393–424, 523–47; 15 (1865): 32–63. On the meanings of *sittliche Kulturfrage,* see vom Bruch, "Bürgerliche Sozialreform," p. 67; Hans Gehrig, *Die Begründung des Prinzips der Sozialreform: Eine literarisch-historische Untersuchung über Manchestertum und Kathedersozialismus* (Jena, 1914), pp. 140–41; Albert Müssiggang, *Die soziale Frage in der historischen Schule der deutschen Nationalökonomie* (Tübingen, 1968), pp. 133–34.

Party, and the Social Democratic Reichstag delegation introduced the issue of women's factory employment and protective labor legislation into the arena of high politics between 1870 and 1885. In 1875, under pressure from the Center Party and social reformers to "tell the German people about workers' conditions," the upper house of the German legislature requested that factory inspectors conduct a survey of factory working conditions to ascertain the dangers they posed to teenage and female workers' health and morality. Although this was not yet an issue of public debate, inspectors undertook a systematic inquiry of employers, local chambers of commerce, doctors, and workers themselves about the desirability and feasibility of restrictions on women's factory employment. This survey, the first official state inquiry into the conditions and effects of women's factory work, was influenced by the social scientists of the Association for Social Policy. When their findings were published in 1878, the inspectors indicated that they had found no overwhelming evidence that women's work outside the home was necessarily detrimental to their families' health and welfare. The Düsseldorf inspector even asserted that working-class families were healthier then than they had been during the era of domestic textile production, because the additional earnings of wife and teenagers provided the family with better nourishment, housing, and clothing. Finally, few of the people interviewed, notably members of several workers' associations, advocated restrictions on the employment of married women in factories. The authors of the survey concluded that there was no compelling need for the state to intervene to stem the growth of the female factory work force. Rather, the inspectors ascertained a general consensus that the harmful effects of women's factory work could best be remedied by the renovation of factory buildings and other technical improvements, not by the imposition of legal limits on women's labor.[17] Thus in the 1870s, as Jean Quataert has pointed out, most factory inspectors and state bureaucrats "still accepted the notion that lower-class women had to work, even if this meant outside the home in factories."[18] Social reformers, however, were not so easily convinced: as a result of their continued demands for government intervention, the labor code of 1878 extended legal protection to women workers for the first time, pro-

17. Reichskanzler-Amt, *Ergebnisse der über die Frauen- und Kinderarbeit in den Fabriken auf Beschluß des Bundesraths angestellten Erhebungen, zusammengestellt im Reichskanzler-Amt* (Berlin, 1878), pp. 42, 67.

18. Jean Quataert, "A Source Analysis in German Women's History: Factory Inspectors' Reports and the Shaping of Working-Class Lives, 1878–1914," *Central European History* 16 (June 1983): 108.

hibiting female labor in mines and providing for three weeks of maternity leave after childbirth.[19] Even more important, perhaps, the new code reorganized the factory inspectorate and widened the scope of its surveillance to include regular inspection of all shops with more than ten employees.[20] Furthermore, working women's bodies, as carriers of the next generation, were at the center of the parliamentary debates about the revision of the labor code during the mid-1870s, as reformers decried the declining health of working women and called for urgent and expansive protection of pregnant workers.[21] At this juncture the female body came to figure as a powerful marker of the dichotomy between independent worker-citizens and workers who required protection by the state.

Although the legislative reforms of 1878 were rather modest, the first wave of protective labor legislation in Germany represents a formative moment in the history of "the social." If "the social" is understood in George Steinmetz's terms, as "an arena of conflicts over the reproduction of labor" which was located between the state and the "realm of markets and property relations,"[22] and if the family was at the heart of the social and the woman "the heart of the family," then it is important to consider how gender inscribed "the social," how women were aligned with "the social," how they came under "the public gaze" that constituted "the social" and were assigned certain tasks within it from its inception.[23] Lujo Brentano's address to the Association for Social Policy in 1872 on German factory legislation suggests that this articulation of sexual difference was crucial in the formation of "the social." First, Brentano sought to differentiate between "those who genuinely require[d] protection"—women and children, who lacked the political rights to assert and defend their own needs—

19. "Die Frauenarbeit als Gegenstand der Fabrikgesetzgebung, von einem Sachverständigen," *Jahrbuch für Gesetzgebung, Verwaltung und Volkswirtschaft im Deutschen Reich* (hereafter *Schmollers Jahrbuch*) 9/2 (1885): 95.

20. Quataert, "A Source Analysis," pp. 100–101, and Franz Hitze, "Zur Vorgeschichte der deutschen Arbeiterschutzgesetzgebung," *Schmollers Jahrbuch* 22/2 (1898): 377. According to Quataert, it was growing interest in lower-class women who were entering industrial and craft occupations that prompted the government to refurbish the factory inspectorate.

21. See, e.g., Hirt, *Die gewerbliche Thätigkeit der Frauen,* pp. 11–12.

22. George Steinmetz, "Workers and the Welfare State in Imperial Germany," *International Labor and Working-Class History,* no. 40 (Fall 1991): 20–21. See also George Steinmetz, *Regulating the Social: The Welfare State and Local Politics in Imperial Germany* (Princeton, N.J., 1993), esp. chap. 3.

23. Denise Riley, *"Am I That Name?" Feminism and the Category of "Women" in History* (Minneapolis, 1988), pp. 50–51.

and male breadwinners, who were able to assert and defend their own interests through political associations. In contrast to his laudatory view of male workers' associations, Brentano contended that women had little "capability for building coalitions." Elaborating his "ethical" objections to female unions or clubs, Brentano argued that a woman could wage successful struggle against her employer only at the price of a "hardened character." By this transformation of her character, however, she would "sacrifice the very qualities that make women a significant force in society, that foster women's moralizing influence on male workers." Ultimately, he concluded, "it would mean poisoning family and society at their very source."[24] "The social," then, became a key site for the articulation of sexual difference, for the formulation of ideologies of gender that would eventually recast state social policy. Intrinsic to but not yet distinct from the broader "worker question," female factory labor was defined as a social problem at the level of high politics during the 1870s. The social investigations, scholarly debates, and legislative initiatives that produced the labor code of 1878 shaped the social knowledges and the mental landscape of the social reform milieu, furnishing it with rhetorical and legislative strategies that it would continue to deploy in the reform campaigns of the 1880s.

DEBATES ABOUT FEMALE FACTORY LABOR DURING THE 1880S AND 1890S

Female factory employment and its long-term effects on the working-class family came to constitute a new social question during the last two decades of the nineteenth century, as Germany underwent its rapid second wave of industrialization. The campaigns of academic social reformers, often waged invisibly through bureaucratic channels, and the persistence of the Catholic Center Party, which had bombarded the Reichstag and the government with numerous motions concerning women and industrial working conditions during the 1880s, culminated in impassioned calls for a legal ban on married women's work outside the home during the late 1880s and early 1890s. The im-

24. Brentano's speech is quoted in Else Conrad, "Der Verein für Sozialpolitik und seine Wirksamkeit auf dem Gebiet der gewerblichen Arbeiterfrage" (Ph.D. diss, University of Zürich, 1906), p. 86, 88; Dieter Lindenlaub, *Richtungskämpfe im Verein für Sozialpolitik: Wissenschaft und Sozialpolitik im Kaiserreich vornehmlich vom Beginn des "Neuen Kurses" bis zum Ausbruch des Ersten Weltkrieges (1890–1914)* (Wiesbaden, 1967), p. 6; James J. Sheehan, *The Career of Lujo Brentano: A Study of Liberalism and Social Reform in Imperial Germany* (Chicago, 1966), pp. 35–44. For his views on male trade unions, see Lujo Brentano, *Die Arbeitergilden der Gegenwart*, 2 vols. (Leipzig, 1871–72).

mediate cause of the heightened interest in and concern with the female factory worker was likely the steady and perceptible expansion of the female factory work force during the last quarter of the century. As the economy boomed at the end of the century, employers faced a continuous labor shortage in nearly all industrial sectors, including the so-called women's industries—textiles, garments, and cigars. Accompanying the steady influx of female workers into factories was the specters of "displacement" of male workers by women and of lowered wages, and the rhetoric against "feminization" of the factories.

The visible expansion of female factory labor had begun to challenge established definitions of masculinity and femininity and the dichotomies of male and female spheres in new and persistent ways.[25] Along with growing anxieties about Social Democracy, social discord, and imperial expansion during the 1880s and 1890s came fears about the working-class family, endangered by the expansion of the female factory work force—children left to fend for themselves, men driven into the pubs by dirty, inhospitable living quarters in the absence of wives and mothers. Reformers sought to preserve the working-class family as an anchor in a rapidly changing world, a bulwark against poverty, disorder, and decay, some by "regulating" and "protecting" women workers, others by banning them altogether from factories. The textile industry, the first to mechanize and the largest factory employer of women, figured prominently in the representations of men "transformed into maidens," of women "abducted" from home and family, and of a morally dissolute and physically declining workers' estate.[26]

This new social question erupted during the late 1880s into a controversy in which the "public," both bourgeois and working-class, was intricately involved. The sites of discussion and debate about the new social question spanned the arenas of high and low politics, encompassing both the sphere of governing— the Reichstag and the Prussian Ministry for Industry and Trade, for example— and that of public opinion, from the associational networks that constituted

25. Karin Hausen, "Family and Role-Division: The Polarisation of Sexual Stereotypes in the Nineteenth Century—An Aspect of the Dissociation of Work and Family Life," in *The German Family,* ed. Richard J. Evans and W. R. Lee (London, 1981), pp. 57–58. See also Claudia Honegger, *Die Ordnung der Geschlechter: Die Wissenschaften vom Menschen und das Weib* (Frankfurt, 1991).

26. Rudolf Martin, "Die Ausschließung der verheirateten Frauen aus der Fabrik: Eine Studie an der Textilindustrie," *Zeitschrift für die gesamte Staatswissenschaft* 52 (1896): 399– 400. The implication of the word "maiden" here is also that of "handmaiden" to a machine. See Robert Wilbrandt, *Die Weber in der Gegenwart: Sozialpolitische Wanderungen durch die Hausweberei und die Webfabrik* (Jena, 1906), p. 31.

the bourgeois public sphere to the weavers' grievance committees and union locals in textile towns and mill villages across the Rhineland and Westphalia.[27] The narratives of danger about female factory labor were constituted across a range of statements, texts, signs, and practices: from academic lectures and scientific surveys, state inquiries and parliamentary resolutions, to union brochures and feminist tracts, employers' sanctions, and even calls for strikes against the hiring of women workers.[28] They encompassed both scholarly treatises on "sexual characteristics" and scandalous revelations about the effects of women's work that stimulated popular interest in the problem: women's bodies ravaged by machines and long hours of labor, infant mortality, filth and squalor in workers' living quarters. These narratives evoked dramatic visions of social dissolution that were replete with analogies between the destruction of the social body, the body of the family, and the physical bodies of women workers and the children they bore.

Some participants spoke with a purported scientific expertise, others as victims who decried the feminization of the factory work force and the displacement of male workers by women. Amidst the din of voices were not only those of prominent politicians and officials of state but also those of Germany's leading social thinkers and social scientists—Gustav Schmoller, Lujo Brentano, Max Weber, and Ferdinand Tönnies, to name a few. These experts sought, many under the auspices of the Association for Social Policy, later others through the *Gesellschaft für soziale Reform* (Society for Social Reform), both to formulate pragmatic suggestions and to conduct academic, "scientific" inquiries into the social impact of industrialization.[29] However disparate their political contexts and political languages, the discourses of social reform were linked not only by "webs of cross-references," but also by a common appeal to the German state as mediator of social and industrial relations.[30] Agitation at the various sites formed a groundswell of social pressure that ultimately prompted the state to sanction a resolution in the form of protective labor legislation in 1890–91 and

27. On discourse as a social relation in a new kind of public arena see Richard Terdiman, *Discourse/Counter-Discourse: The Theory and Practice of Symbolic Resistance in Nineteenth-Century France* (Ithaca, N.Y., 1985), pp. 44–46.

28. On the dispersed sites of discourse, see Judith R. Walkowitz, *City of Dreadful Delight: Narratives of Sexual Danger in Late Victorian London* (Chicago, 1992), p. 6; Peter Stallybrass and Allon White, *The Politics and Poetics of Transgression* (Ithaca, N.Y., 1986), p. 194.

29. See vom Bruch, *Weder Kommunismus noch Kapitalismus*, pp. 13–15, 66–71.

30. The term "webs of cross-references" is Denise Riley's, as quoted in Joan Scott, *Gender and the Politics of History* (New York, 1988), p. 141.

an official state inquiry into married women's factory employment in 1898–99. Both were key in the articulation of a new ideology of women's work which left a lasting imprint on the policies and programs of state, employers, and labor unions.

The fact that the new social question of female factory labor came to preoccupy the public imagination between 1884 and 1894 should also be viewed as part of a growing discontent among factory inspectors, government administrators, legislators, medical doctors, and trade unions with Bismarckian social policy. Widely admired for its unprecedented (in Europe at the time) social insurance legislation, the Bismarckian welfare state refused to intervene in or regulate the "pathogenic" aspects of the industrial workplace. A source of constant friction between chancellor and Reichstag, the parliamentary contests over labor protection reached their pinnacle between 1884 and 1890 as a majority in the Reichstag came to favor state regulation of female factory labor while Bismarck remained stubbornly impervious to the shifting groundswell of parliamentary and public opinion on the issue. By 1887, the Reichstag had assembled a large majority to pass a bill expanding protection for female and teenage workers. Despite the overwhelming consensus in the Reichstag, the upper house of the legislature rejected the bill, and Bismarck as its leading authority asserted that expanded protection would negatively affect both the living conditions of the workers and the profitability of German industry.[31]

Heretofore a domain of social reform expertise, debates about the worker question spilled over into the sphere of public opinion in 1889–90. In the spring of 1889 some 150,000 coal miners in the Rhine and Ruhr regions walked off their jobs after a dispute with mine owners over wages, work time, health, and safety. As the strike quickly spread to the Saar, Saxony, and Silesia, it brought to a head the growing dissension over social policy between Reichstag and government and fueled the tensions between Bismarck and the young

31. Hans-Jörg von Berlepsch, "Neuer Kurs" im Kaiserreich? Die Arbeiterpolitik des Freiherrn von Berlepsch 1890 bis 1896 (Bonn, 1987), pp. 13, 51–52, 143, 152, 161, 182–84. According to Berlepsch, pp. 134–37, 272–77, Bismarckian social policy remained tailored to the needs of industry. Also see Lothar Machtan and Hans-Jörg von Berlepsch, "Vorsorge oder Ausgleich—oder beides? Prinzipienfragen staatlicher Sozialpolitik im Deutschen Kaiserreich," Zeitschrift für Sozialreform 32 (May 1986): 266; Karl-Erich Born, Staat und Sozialpolitik seit Bismarcks Sturz: Ein Beitrag zur Geschichte der innenpolitischen Entwicklung des deutschen Reiches, 1890–1914 (Wiesbaden, 1957), pp. 71–98; Alfred Weber, "Die Entwickelung der deutschen Arbeiterschutzgesetzgebung seit 1890," Schmollers Jahrbuch 21 (1897): 1145–46. On the electoral shifts between 1884 and 1887, see James J. Sheehan, German Liberalism in the Nineteenth Century (Chicago, 1978), pp. 214–16.

Kaiser Wilhelm II, prompting the shift in state social policy known as the "new course" of the early 1890s.[32] The strike revealed the shortcomings of Bismarckian social policy, dramatizing its failure to ameliorate dire working conditions or to forge a bond of genuine loyalty between workers and the state.[33] The largest mass walkout in the history of the Kaiserreich thus far, the strike engaged both working-class and bourgeois public opinion and left a deep impression on the young emperor, who expressed horror at the idea that the beginning of his reign might be stained "with the blood of [his] subjects."[34]

Within a few months Wilhelm and his advisers formulated a new vision of the relationship between the state and the working class: they sought to implement the paternalist, rather than repressive, apparatus of state in order to confront the social problems that had led to the massive strike. The welfare state was reshaped as Wilhelm, responding to pressure from the labor movement and social reform circles, placed an eminent social reformer, Hans Freiherr von Berlepsch, at the head of the Ministry for Industry and Trade, paved the way for lifting the ban on the Social Democratic Party, issued (the February) edicts outlining the protective measures to be incorporated in the revised labor code, and called an international congress on protective measures for workers most endangered by industrial work, which was held in Berlin in March 1890.[35] These policy shifts marked the beginning of the "new course" in social policy, which would last until Berlepsch's firing in 1896. The Kaiser's edicts and the call to the Berlin congress mapped out a new role for the German state as mediator of labor relations, a task that Bismarck had resolutely resisted throughout the 1880s as harmful to the competitive vitality of German industry in an increasingly complex world market.

32. On the strike, see Tennstedt, *Sozialgeschichte der Sozialpolitik,* p. 194; Jürgen Reulecke, "Stadtbürgertum und bürgerliche Sozialreform im 19. Jahrhundert in Preußen," in *Stadt und Bürgertum im 19. Jahrhundert,* ed. Lothar Gall, special issue of *Historische Zeitschrift* 12 (1990): 194; Otto Pflanze, *Bismarck and the Development of Germany,* vol. 3: *The Period of Fortification, 1880–1898* (Princeton, N.J., 1990), pp. 327–45; Vernon L. Lidtke, *The Outlawed Party: Social Democracy in Germany, 1878–1890* (Princeton, N.J., 1966), pp. 294–95.

33. Berlepsch, *"Neuer Kurs,"* pp. 13, 432–33. See also Rüdiger vom Bruch, "Streiks und Konfliktregelung im Urteil bürgerlicher Sozialreformer 1872–1914," in *Streik: Zur Geschichte des Arbeitskampfes in Deutschland während der Industrialisierung,* ed. Klaus Tenfelde and Heinrich Volkmann (Munich, 1981), p. 257.

34. Kaiser Wilhelm II's speech is quoted in Berlepsch, *"Neuer Kurs,"* p. 25; Pflanze, *Bismarck,* 3:358. See also Lidtke, *Outlawed Party,* pp. 294–95.

35. "Zur Erinnerung: Die beiden Erlässe Kaiser Wilhelm II vom 4. Februar 1890," *Soziale Praxis* 7 (October 7, 1897): 7.

The miners' strike had galvanized public opinion around social reform, drawing attention to the poor conditions of work in the mines, to the unruliness of youth and the militance of adult men, which many people linked to the alleged erosion of working women's skills as housewives and mothers. Thus, even though the strikers were overwhelmingly male, the Reichstag debates and the legislative consensus of the late 1880s about the regulation and restriction of female and youth labor framed the response of the state and of social reformers to the climate of crisis surrounding the strike.[36] Extending the purview of the German welfare state to encompass the welfare of German workers and their families, the February edicts laid the groundwork for the revision of the labor code in 1891 and for its further expansion in 1908. From the restoration of the German family envisioned by the Kaiser's February edicts to the consensus underpinning the programmatic demands of the international congress of March 1890, the protection of female and youth labor was the principal aim of the reforms of the "new course."

While extending the scope of protection significantly beyond that of 1878, the revised labor code of 1891—one of the key outcomes of the "new course"— excluded women from night work, mandated an eleven hour day for women workers, and expanded maternity leave from three to six weeks with the provision that women would be permitted to return to work after four weeks with a doctor's permission. Despite the long-term campaign of the Catholic Center to ban married women from factory work, the code differentiated married women and mothers from single women workers only by providing an extra half-hour midday break "for those with households to tend to." Responding to popular sentiment that the factory had become "the source of moral ruin" for female and teenage workers, Paragraph 120 prescribed the separation of the sexes at work wherever possible: on the shop floor, in cafeterias, courtyards, and washrooms.[37] As in the case of youth, the revised code sought to determine more than the mere conditions of work in the mills, drawing the household into the regulatory complex and mapping out the paths women workers traversed between the two. By extending the daily lunch break and curtailing working hours on Saturdays so women could shop and clean, the new legisla-

36. Weber, "Die Entwickelung," pp. 1152–55.
37. Nordrhein-Westfälisches Hauptstaatsarchiv Düsseldorf (hereafter HStAD), Landratsamt Mönchen-Gladbach 710, "Bericht des Gewerbeaufsichtsbeamten Mönchen-Gladbach vom 14.12.1874," p. 108. On Paragraph 120 see HStAD, Jahresberichte der Königlich Preußischen Gewerberäte (hereafter JBdKPG) 1891: Düsseldorf, p. 290, and Quataert, "Source Analysis," p. 107.

tion aimed not to banish women from factories but, as Jean Quataert has argued, "to give the gainfully employed woman more time in the day to learn and perform her crucial household tasks."[38] The new laws also widened the official denotation of "trade schools" and "skill training" to include housekeeping schools for young female workers. Skill training was to instill in young workers the qualities of "order, discipline, and mental stimulation." However, while young women were to complete courses in "female handiwork and housework," young men were to receive instruction in reading, writing, arithmetic, drawing, and trade-specific subjects, such as textile weaves and mechanics.[39] In all of these respects the revised code represented a negotiated compromise between the alarmist visions of social decay conjured up by the rhetoric of social reform, and the growing demand of mill owners, particularly in textiles, for female workers during the late 1880s and 1890s.

While the revised code of 1891 was widely touted as reform "in the interests of the community, i.e. for the health and the well-being of the *whole nation*," in fact, it defined the social identities of class and citizen in highly gendered terms.[40] The new laws delimited the political rights of adult men at work, restricting some (right to quit, right to strike), augmenting others (elected workers' committees in each factory), and generally excluding men from protective measures such as restricted work hours. Thus from the social policy debates of the late 1880s, the mass strikes of 1889–90, and the legislative innovation of 1891 had emerged two distinct social questions and two different categories of citizenship: on the one hand, the state expanded protection of women, adoles-

38. Quataert, "Source Analysis," pp. 111–12; HStAD, JBdKPG 1892: Düsseldorf, pp. 328–30.

39. Kreisarchiv Viersen, Gemeindeamt Grefrath 1154, "Gewerbliche Fortbildungsschule, 1864–1912," pp. 22–23. Also see Marie Elisabeth Lüders, *Die Fortbildung und Ausbildung der im Gewerbe tätigen weiblichen Personen und deren rechtliche Grundlage* (Leipzig, 1912); Berlepsch, *"Neuer Kurs,"* pp. 243–47; Heinrich Herkner, "Der Entwurf eines Gesetzes betr. die Abänderung der Gewerbeordnung," *Archiv für Soziale Gesetzgebung und Statistik* 3 (1890): 575. Attendance at the trade schools, operated by district or city governments, was voluntary until 1891, when it became mandatory in several German states for men, and for both sexes in Baden, Württemberg, and Bavaria.

40. Alice Salomon, *Labour Laws for Women in Germany* (London, 1907), p. 11. Alfred Weber also pointed out that "it is the interest of the *nation* to protect the health and morality of women in particular," "Die Entwickelung," p. 1149. Also see Herkner, "Zur Kritik und zur Reform," p. 229; *Handwörterbuch der Staatswissenschaften, 1890–1894,* s.v. "Arbeiter," "Arbeiterfrage," p. 389; Gerhard A. Ritter, *Staat, Arbeiterschaft und Arbeiterbewegung in Deutschland: Vom Vormärz bis zum Ende der Weimarer Republik* (Berlin, 1980), p. 68.

cents, and children at work, thereby undertaking a thorough reform of family life through intervention on their behalf in the workplace; on the other hand, it established new organs of representation through which adult male workers could assert their claims to economic and civic equality, their rights of representation, association, and expression.

After the revision of the labor code in 1891, the numbers of married women working outside the home continued to expand; they nearly doubled between 1882 and 1907, and the percentage of married women among adult female factory workers increased from 21 to 29 percent in the four years between 1895 and 1899.[41] And the calls for greater state intervention and social disciplining grew more vociferous during the 1890s, as opponents of female factory labor, inspired by the restrictions on women's labor of 1891 and by the newly awakened interest of the public in this issue, launched a renewed and more vigorous campaign for a legal ban on married women's factory employment. Fueling their campaign was the impressive array of empirical studies that reformers had conducted and compiled on household budgets, nutrition, illness, and infant mortality, which purportedly demonstrated the impact of female factory labor on working-class family life. The experts' research furnished opponents of women's factory employment with hard "scientific" evidence to back their heretofore idealistic appeals. For example, H. Mehner's article of 1886 on working-class family budgets, published in *Schmollers Jahrbuch,* calculated carefully that a married woman contributed more to the family income by staying home and managing her household efficiently than by working at a factory job.[42] According to Jean Quataert, Mehner's piece signaled a "transition" in public opinion about married women's factory employment, for it laid poverty at the

---

41. "Married women" here includes the widowed, divorced, and separated. Between 1882 and 1907 the married female workforce grew by 90 percent, the single female work force by 78 percent. The figures cited here are based on Stefan Bajohr, *Die Hälfte der Fabrik: Geschichte der Frauenarbeit in Deutschland* (Marburg, 1979), p. 25; Hanns Dorn, "Die Frauenerwerbsarbeit und ihre Aufgaben für die Gesetzgebung," *Archiv für Rechts- und Wirtschaftsphilosophie* 5 (1911/12): 86–87; Rose Otto, *Über die Fabrikarbeit verheirateter Frauen* (Stuttgart, 1910), p. 10; Helene Simon, *Der Anteil der Frau an der deutschen Industrie* (Jena, 1910), p. 7; Ludwig Pohle, "Die Erhebungen der Gewerbeaufsichtsbeamten über die Fabrikarbeit verheirateter Frauen," *Schmollers Jahrbuch* 25 (1901): 158–61.

42. H. Mehner, "Der Haushalt und die Lebenshaltung einer Leipziger Arbeiterfamilie," *Schmollers Jahrbuch* 1886, reprinted in *Seminar: Familie und Gesellschaftsstruktur,* ed. Heidi Rosenbaum (Frankfurt a. M., 1982), pp. 309–33. See also Quataert, "Source Analysis," p. 112. Certainly the publication of Mehner's piece in such a respected academic journal as *Schmollers Jahrbuch* increased its circulation and its legitimacy.

doorstep of working-class wives.[43] A study conducted in the mid-1880s by Arthur Geissler, a medical doctor and government official in Saxony, determined that the infant mortality rates in textile towns, where a large percentage of married women worked in factories, exceeded those in all other Saxon districts.[44] Geissler's findings, as well as subsequent research on other textile regions, contributed to a growing sense of urgency among opponents of female factory labor that women workers must be enlightened as to the grave consequences of their double burden.

In addition to the perceptible ills of dismal living conditions and poor infant care in working-class families, opponents also associated the widespread employment of women in factories with a fundamental disintegration of social, cultural, and moral order. A highly respected economist and member of the Association for Social Policy, Heinrich Herkner, articulated this sense of disorder in his popular book *Die Arbeiterfrage,* first published in 1890. Herkner first summoned visions of moral decay inside the factory itself. Citing Alfons Thun's classic study of the textile industry on the lower Rhine, he described male and female bodies, sweaty and scantily clad, working side by side in the mills, where "during the work day the way was paved for the excesses of the night." Then Herkner addressed the implications of women's factory work for family and community, pointing to the example of England, where rising income among male workers had enabled many married women to return to the household. He aimed to show that the era of expanding married women's factory employment had left its indelible mark on English working-class family life. Here he drew upon an eyewitness report titled "How the English Worker Lives," by a German miner who had lived and worked for several years in England. Implicitly warning his readers about the consequences of the expansion of married women's work in Germany, Herkner evoked a vision of domesticity turned upside down:

> English workers' wives are often not capable of preparing an ordinary meal. What they do understand however, is how to drink whiskey. . . . It is certain that more women than men are addicted to drink. The factory workers' wives are usually drunkards. As far as morality goes, one can only imagine. Married women offer themselves for sale when they are drunk. . . . Most workers' wives are too lazy to sew, even though every young girl must learn how to sew at school. An outsider who is not familiar with the conditions

43. Quataert, "Source Analysis," pp. 112–13.

44. Geissler's apparently unpublished study is quoted in Martin, "Die Ausschliessung," p. 404.

and who wanders through a working-class quarter at 9 or 10 A.M., would be astonished to see that two-thirds of the women have fastened their clothes together with pins, are unwashed and uncombed.[45]

Replete with such shocking revelations and rooted firmly in scholarly methods and discourse, social reformers' accounts of working-class life stimulated popular interest in the problem of female factory labor. Others elevated the new social question to the more abstract level of women's "true nature," portraying female factory labor as irreconcilable with and destructive of the feminine character, and ultimately of the social order. In his classic *Gemeinschaft und Gesellschaft,* Ferdinand Tönnies, sociologist and member of the Association for Social Policy, gave female factory labor a leading part in his analysis of the dissolution of the *Gemeinschaft* (community) and the formation of modern *Gesellschaft* (society). Tönnies argued that "the home and not the market, their own or a friend's dwelling, and not the street, is the natural seat of [women's] activity." Factory work was inherently incompatible with women's nature:

> As woman enters into the struggle of earning a living, it is evident that trading and the freedom and independence of the female factory worker as contracting party and possessor of money will develop her rational will, enabling her to think in a calculating way, even though, in the case of factory work, the tasks themselves may not lead in this direction. The woman becomes enlightened, cold-hearted, and conscious. Nothing is more foreign and terrible to her original inborn nature, in spite of all later modifications. Possibly nothing is more characteristic and important in the process of formation of the *Gesellschaft* and the destruction of *Gemeinschaft*. Through this development, the "individualism" which is the prerequisite of *Gesellschaft* comes into its own.[46]

Tönnies may not have intended to enter into a discourse about women's nature and women's work, but his views reappeared in the arguments of at least one key opponent of female factory labor. In 1892, Rudolf Martin, junior barrister at the district court in Crimmitschau, Saxony, undertook an independent investigation of factory and family life among married female textile workers

45. Heinrich Herkner, *Die Arbeiterfrage: Eine Einführung,* 4th ed. (Berlin, 1905), pp. 27, 38–40. Herkner cites Alfons Thun, *Die Industrie am Niederrhein und ihre Arbeiter,* vol. 1 (Leipzig, 1879), p. 174, and Ernst Dückershoff, *Wie der englische Arbeiter lebt* (Dresden, 1898), pp. 19, 32–33.

46. Ferdinand Tönnies, *Community and Association,* trans. Charles P. Loomis (1887; London, 1974), pp. 186, 191.

in his vicinity, which was published in 1896 in the *Zeitschrift für die gesamte Staatswissenschaft*. Martin was the first social reformer to link empirical evidence from factories and working-class neighborhoods with theoretical constructs about women's nature. His article represents a critical juncture in the history of the discourse on women's work, for it shifted the emphasis from protective measures for women workers toward consideration of a legal ban on married women's factory employment. Following Tönnies, Martin asserted that in the course of their "abduction" from the home and the domestic workshop, women had become emancipated. But he rendered even more dramatic images of social dissolution than Tönnies when he claimed that women's work would ultimately "ravage the social body." Martin drew a parallel between the destruction of the social body, the body of the family, and the physical bodies of women workers and the children they bore. Women who worked in factories, he argued, harmed the social body in two ways: first through what they did not do—that is, through neglect of their homes, husbands, and children—and second through the mechanical work they performed in the mills. In his view, women's negligence was "one main cause of the mortality rates among children, especially among infants . . . it spoils the human material and damages the labor power of the nation."[47] Here Martin held working women responsible not only for poverty but also for the moral degeneration of the workers' estate and the physical decline of the human (raw) "material." In posing the fundamental question as to why women went to work in factories, Rudolf Martin broke with previous assumptions, such as those that permeated the inspectors' report of 1878, that women had always worked, whether at home or in a factory, and that their employment was compatible with housework and child rearing.[48]

Rudolf Martin's study, which was widely read, furnished the framework for the debate on women's work—the key questions and controversial solutions—which engaged social reformers during the next decade, as the "new course" in social policy was overshadowed and then dismantled during the mid-1890s, not least by the Kaiser's growing desire for an expanded German empire. Martin's investigation inspired numerous subsequent studies and commentaries by social reformers of diverse political persuasions, including Ludwig Pohle, Robert Wilbrandt, and Heinrich Herkner of the Association for Social Policy and the

47. Martin, "Die Ausschliessung," pp. 105, 399–400.
48. According to Jean Quataert, "Source Analysis," p. 115, "To ask . . . why married women worked in factories implied that ideally married women ought not to work, a new assumption, as seen, that accompanied the industrial age."

feminist social reformers Henriette Fürth and Alice Salomon.[49] Fürth, writing in 1902, pointed out that since the publication of Martin's article, "this question [of married women's factory employment], the critical importance of which is recognized by all sides, has not ceased to engage the world of social policy."[50] A new constituency—middle-class feminists—stepped forward during the 1890s to defend the right of women to work outside the home. Banned by the Prussian Law of Association from official participation in most of the social reform associations, educated women, many of whom were students or protégées of the eminent political economists and reformers, perceived many parallels between their own lack of political, social, and economic rights and the plight of working-class wives and mothers. Forging links between the middle-class "woman question" and the "worker question," they challenged the images of working women that filled the texts of conservative social reformers.

THE EMBODIMENT OF THE FEMALE WORKER

As the social question of female factory labor was debated fervently within the Social Democratic and Catholic labor movements and in the milieu of bourgeois social reform, it also continued to engage the Reichstag during the 1890s. The Catholic Center Party, encouraged by the concessions of 1891 regarding the protection of women and minors, and propelled into motion by the growing popularity of Social Democracy among working-class voters, intensified its campaign for restriction of married women's employment soon after the new code became law. Asserting that state social policy had thus far been grounded in a deficient grasp of the workers' conditions, and presuming that social investigation would advance and expand protective legislation, the Center introduced a motion in the Reichstag in 1894 requesting a formal state inquiry, complete with statistical compilations, into the effects of married women's factory work on their families' physical and moral well-being.[51] Al-

49. See Herkner, *Die Arbeiterfrage*, pp. 36–40; Ludwig Pohle, *Frauenfabrikarbeit und Frauenfrage: Eine prinzipielle Antwort auf die Frage der Ausschliessung der verheirateten Frauen aus der Fabrik* (Leipzig, 1900), pp. 47–48, 113; Wilbrandt, *Die Weber*, pp. 146–47; Henriette Fürth, *Die Fabrikarbeit verheirateter Frauen* (Frankfurt a. M., 1902), pp. 9–11, 16; Alice Salomon, "Frauen-Fabrikarbeit und Frauenfrage," *Die Frau* 8 (January 1901): 196–97.

50. Fürth, *Die Fabrikarbeit*, pp. 9–10. See, e.g., Henriette Fürth, "Die Ehefrage und der Beruf: Sozialistische Betrachtungen," *Die Frau* 4 (September 1897): 710–18; Salomon, "Frauen-Fabrikarbeit und Frauenfrage"; and Alice Salomon, "Fabrikarbeit und Mutterschaft," ibid., 13 (1905–6): 365–69.

51. Otto, *Über die Fabrikarbeit*, p. 177; Pohle, "Die Erhebungen," p. 149; Berlepsch,

though the measure failed in 1894, by the late 1890s the debate and agitation around the issue formed a groundswell of social pressure on the German state to investigate further the conditions of female factory labor and their effects on working-class families.

Thus in 1898 the government launched an official national inquiry into married women's factory employment, and the next year in each government district of Germany factory inspectors set out to determine precisely how many married women worked outside the home and why they sought waged work, thereby reiterating the question that Rudolf Martin had raised a few years earlier. On the basis of a study far more extensive than the inspectors' report of 1878, including interviews with workers' and employers' associations, local chambers of commerce, health insurance boards, priests, teachers, doctors, midwives, married women, and male workers, inspectors were to determine the necessity of restrictions on the employment of married women.[52] Furthermore, the government inquired about the consequences of eventual restrictions: How would the loss of women's earnings affect the working-class standard of living? How would it influence male workers and their propensity to marry if their future wives were not allowed to work? Would restrictions harm German industry and would employers be able to replace married women with single women or male workers?[53]

With this inquiry—prepared by the Reichstag, approved by the chancellor, and conducted by factory inspectors—the German state officially recognized the new social question of female factory labor and lent its authority to its resolution. At the same time, the state entered into the discourse about women's factory employment and joined social reformers in the task of delineating male and female spheres of work, of defining a sexual division of labor. According to Alice Salomon, the inquiry marked the peak of the campaign for exclusion of married women from factories and in one sense attested to its success. At the same time, the inspectors' final report, published by the Ministry of the Inte-

---

"*Neuer Kurs*," pp. 431–32; Herkner, "Die Reform der deutschen Arbeiterschutzgesetzgebung," pp. 243–44.

52. According to Pohle, "Die Erhebungen," p. 150, the inspectors employed disparate methods to obtain information and the reports from the various districts were not necessarily comparable. Some, for example, interviewed women workers directly, whereas others asked them to complete questionnaires.

53. Reichsamt des Innern, *Die Beschäftigung verheirateter Frauen in Fabriken, nach den Jahresberichten der Gewerbeaufsichtsbeamten für das Jahr 1899, bearbeitet im Reichsamt des Innern* (Berlin, 1901), pp. 1–2.

rior in 1901, discounted many of the campaign's main tenets and dampened its often inflammatory and ideological overtones; it banished, in Salomon's words, "the threatening phantom" that had "persecuted women struggling for economic independence and social equality." With the intervention of the state and the carefully crafted inquiry, "the ship found safe harbor," Salomon contended. For "women would be certain to find greater understanding for their economic needs and difficulties among these men of the practical world" than in the realm of high politics, which remained remote from what it sought to protect: women workers and their families.[54]

Indeed, Salomon's prediction was accurate in several respects: the inspectors' report of 1901 underscored the economic necessity of female factory labor and imparted to women's factory work a new legitimacy. While acknowledging that a legal ban would, in many respects, be beneficial to women and their families, all but one inspector rejected such a measure as impracticable.[55] These "men of the practical world" viewed married women's factory work as an "irreversible consequence of the material reality among the workers," notably, of the failure of wages to keep pace with the rising cost of living.[56] The inspectors feared that loss of women's earnings would force many families to turn to the public relief system.[57] Furthermore, employers had stressed the inflexibility of the labor market and the impossibility of wide-scale replacement of married women with men or single women. Employers delineated a sphere of "women's work, which men regard as such as beneath their dignity." Women workers, they argued, were more suited than men for many jobs, especially those requiring the dexterity of "female hands."[58]

In defining spheres of male and female labor, the inspectors tacitly sought to legitimate married women's factory employment in the eyes of its opponents. In addition, they proposed a practical alternative to prohibition. Implying that a legal ban would be of little benefit to the many families whose female members were unable to keep house properly, the inspectors recommended that the state institute obligatory housekeeping schools for female factory

54. Salomon, "Frauen-Fabrikarbeit," pp. 193–99.

55. Reichsamt des Innern, Die Beschäftigung, p. 149.

56. Otto, Über die Fabrikarbeit, p. 125.

57. HStAD, JBdKPG 1899: Düsseldorf, p. 521; Reichsamt des Innern, Die Beschäftigung, pp. 150–52, 217–19.

58. Rheinisch-Westfälisches Wirtschaftsarchiv, Handelskammer Duisburg 20:43/6 (Gewerbe und Industrie, vol. I): Verband der Textilindustriellen von Chemnitz und Umgebung, "Schreiben an das Hohe Reichskanzleramt zu Berlin von 9. Dezember 1899."

workers, where young women could learn to cook, sew, and care for infants.[59] In the promotion of *Häuslichkeit* (domesticity), the inspectors defined the social problem of women's factory work in new terms and shifted its solution from the factory to the home.

After the publication of the factory inspectors' findings in 1901, only a few reformers continued to advocate a legal ban on married women's factory employment; most renewed efforts to expand protective legislation.[60] The Catholic Center Party, which still favored a legal ban in principle, settled on a campaign for a reduction of the work day for married women to six hours.[61] Unable to banish married women to the home, social reformers now sought to import the home into the workplace, to instill domestic skills in female factory workers, and to supplant the imagery of disorder, the specter of feminization and disintegration of gender roles, with a new order founded on the division between the male breadwinner and the female "secondary" earner. Underpinning this new order was a consensus among reformers, inspectors, industrialists, and male workers' organizations about the natural basis of this division and about the rightful claim of male breadwinners to higher earnings, skill, and status.

Even as the inspectors' reports mapped out a resolution to the social question of female factory labor at the turn of the century, their survey also compiled new and compelling information regarding the dangers factory work presented to pregnant women; namely, the extraordinarily high rates of miscarriage, premature birth, and infant mortality among female textile workers reported by medical doctors, health insurance officials, and employers.[62] In specifying the site of intervention as the maternal body, they began to widen the scope of the social question from the factory to the nation, to link more explicitly the conditions of work to the conditions of (national) reproduction and the national birth rate.[63] In the course of formulating solutions to the new so-

59. HStAD, JBdKPG 1899: Aachen, p. 607; Reichsamt des Innern, *Die Beschäftigung*, pp. 251–252; and Pohle, *Frauenfabrikarbeit*, p. 110.

60. Otto, *Über die Fabrikarbeit*, p. 179.

61. See Franz Hitze, *Die Arbeiterfrage und die Bestrebungen zu ihrer Lösung* (Berlin, 1900), p. 80.

62. HStAD, JBdKPG 1899: Düsseldorf, pp. 518–20 and Münster, p. 372; the Barmen inspector reported that the rate of illness was 15 percent higher and the average duration of an illness 70 percent longer among married women than among unmarried women. See also Reichsamt des Innern, *Die Beschäftigung*, p. 96.

63. Reichsamt des Innern, *Die Beschäftigung*, pp. 97–99, 210; HStAD, JBdKPG 1899: Aachen, p. 609.

cial question of female factory labor, social reformers also staked out a domain of sexuality, one that was constructed in direct relation to themes of danger, disease, filth, and depravity, thus laying the groundwork for the even more explicit medicalized intervention in women's bodies from the late 1890s until World War I. As Germany launched its quest for empire after 1890, the growing alarm regarding the birth rate placed women's bodies at the center of a hygienicist, natalist enterprise of identifying and eradicating social pathologies, which by now included not only alcoholism, tuberculosis, venereal disease, and infant mortality but also female factory labor. Interestingly, all of these pathologies could be located directly or indirectly in the moral or bodily deficiencies of women who worked outside the home. Thus, during the first decade of the twentieth century, women's embodiment became a more explicit focus of the social question as it was understood not only by employers and trade unionists but also by the welfare state and the popular hygienicist associations (the various leagues to combat tuberculosis, venereal disease, alcoholism, and infant mortality) which mobilized within the expanded civic sphere during the first decade of the twentieth century.[64] At the same time the emergent psychophysics of work and other productivist visions of the body as a "human motor" began to inscribe female bodies with a new kind of disruptive potential that required new interventions aimed more explicitly to improve the productivity and economic utility of bodies at work.[65]

CONCLUSION

The crises that accompanied Germany's transition from an agrarian to an industrial state were understood by contemporaries in highly gendered terms. The discourses about women's work, which both constituted and attempted to resolve the new social question of female factory labor, are crucial in understanding the expansion of the German welfare state during the "new course" of

64. Paul Weindling, *Health, Race and German Politics between National Unification and Nazism, 1870–1945* (Cambridge, 1989), p. 175.

65. On the psychophysics of work, see Anson Rabinbach, "The European Science of Work: The Economy of the Body at the End of the Nineteenth Century," in *Work in France: Representations, Meaning, Organization, and Practice*, ed. Steven L. Kaplan and Cynthia J. Koepp (Ithaca, N.Y., 1986), pp. 475–513, and *The Human Motor: Energy, Fatigue, and the Origins of Modernity* (Berkeley, Calif., 1992); Josefa Ioteyko, *The Science of Labour and Its Organization* (London, 1919); Max Weber, "Zur Psychophysik der industriellen Arbeit," *Archiv für Sozialwissenschaft und Sozialgeschichte* 28 (1909): 219–77, 719–61, and 29 (1909): 513–42.

the early 1890s. Galvanized by agitation in both the bourgeois and working-class public spheres, policy makers prepared inquiries and proposed legislation to counteract the perceived or threatened dissolution of the social order, an order anchored in sexual difference. The German welfare state was structured centrally and explicitly around a gender program not only because women and children became objects of maternalist welfare policies, or because female social reformers emerged on the scene and articulated in a new and powerful fashion the needs of women and children, as much of the recent scholarship on the welfare state would have it.[66] Taking labor legislation as a lens with which to view the history of the welfare state reveals that its central task was to reorder the relations between the sexes, which had gone awry during the rapid wave of industrialization at the close of the century. The revised labor code of 1891 and the factory inspectors' inquiry about married women's work of 1898 codified a sexual division of labor as one means of reordering those relations.

While a purported crisis of the family appears to have preoccupied reformers across industrialized Europe during the 1890s, this particular confluence of concerns in the context of expanding bourgeois and working-class public spheres marks one of the more intriguing "peculiarities of German history."[67] Another peculiarity—and the immediate cause of the heightened interest in and concern with the female factory worker—was the steady and perceptible expansion of the female industrial labor market, which occurred as the pace of industrial growth intensified and industrial employers confronted a continuous labor shortage in nearly all sectors, including the so-called women's industries of textiles, garments, and cigars, during the late 1880s and 1890s. In particular after 1890, the constant labor shortages in industrial regions such as the Rhineland and Westphalia drew married women into the work force in large numbers in Germany, whereas in England the percentages of married women with jobs had been on the decline for at least a decade. Despite the rapid pace of industrial and social change in Germany, closer study of specific re-

66. See Koven and Michel, "Womanly Duties."

67. David Blackbourn and Geoff Eley, *The Peculiarities of German History: Bourgeois Society and Politics in Nineteenth-Century Germany* (New York, 1984). On the crisis of the family during the 1890s, see Eve Rosenhaft and W. R. Lee, "State and Society in Modern Germany: Beamtenstaat, Klassenstaat, Wohlfahrtsstaat," in *The State and Social Change in Germany, 1880–1980*, ed. Rosenhaft and Lee (New York, 1990), pp. 27–29. For an interesting comparison with France, see Judith Coffin, "Social Science Meets Sweated Labor: Reinterpreting Women's Work in Late Nineteenth-Century France," *Journal of Modern History* 63, no. 22 (1991): 230–70; and Jacques Donzelot, *The Policing of Families* (New York, 1979).

gional and local conditions indicates that the sense of crisis associated with the transition from domestic to factory industry lingered well into the early 1890s. Thus the welfare state took shape at a time when a sense of dislocation and disorder were still acutely felt and passionately articulated in both popular demands on the German state and the social scientific language of social reform.[68]

The discourse about female factory labor also raises some interesting questions about the German state at the end of the nineteenth century. Some scholars have taken the existence of a vital welfare state as a basis for critique of the authoritarian model of political rule in German social science history.[69] The agitation around the social question of female factory labor during the 1880s and 1890s, for example, reveals the German state to be a "permeable arena in which contending social and political forces interact[ed]," "a space for struggle and negotiation, rather than an incorporative machine."[70] Read in this light, protective labor legislation becomes an integral part of "the reshaping of the political nation" that occurred during the Wilhelmine period as new structures of public communication changed the very terms in which political life took place. Labor legislation becomes a prime site for analyzing how "opposing publics maneuvered for space" within an expanding public sphere, especially during the 1890s, when the social reform nexus, a cross-section of liberal academics, Catholics, Social Democrats, feminists, and intellectuals, succeeded in dislodging the social question from the sphere of high politics and locating it in the widening sphere of public opinion.[71] Their debates about female factory labor, about the changing relationship between women and family, between family and state, were crucially important parts of the discursive and social

68. Jean Quataert, "Woman's Work and the Early Welfare State in Germany: Legislators, Bureaucrats, and Clients before the First World War," in *Mothers of a New World,* ed. Koven and Michel, p. 166.

69. Berlepsch, *"Neuer Kurs"*; Rüdiger vom Bruch, *Wissenschaft, Politik und öffentliche Meinung: Gelehrtenpolitik im Wihelminischen Deutschland (1890–1914)* (Husum, 1980); Geoff Eley, "German History and the Contradictions of Modernity," in *Society, Culture, and the State in Germany, 1870–1930,* ed. Eley (Ann Arbor, Mich., 1996).

70. Eley, "German History," p. 94; Gray, "The Languages of Factory Reform in Britain, c. 1830–1860," in *The Historical Meanings of Work,* ed. Patrick Joyce (Cambridge, 1989), p. 172.

71. Geoff Eley, "Introduction I: Is There a History of the Kaiserreich?" in *Society, Culture, and the State,* ed Eley, p. 11; and Eley, "Nations, Publics, and Political Cultures: Placing Habermas in the Nineteenth Century," in *Habermas and the Public Sphere,* ed. Craig Calhoun (Cambridge, Mass., 1992), p. 325.

mobilizations that transformed the relationship between civil society and the state and that challenged and ultimately widened the scope of the German welfare state and reconstituted "the social."[72] Granting labor legislation a more central place in the historical narratives of the welfare state also raises a question about the profoundly different ways in which the various parts of the welfare state were made, with labor legislation embedded in the public sphere and the public imagination, while social insurance remained confined to the bureaucratic imagination.

Thus the example of labor legislation affirms not only the permeability of the welfare state but also the importance of discursive struggle as a particular means of recasting it. The debates about women's work analyzed here occurred at a "classic" historical moment of the nineteenth century, when, as Richard Terdiman notes, "the techniques for assuring discursive penetration," as well as those of "symbolic subversion"—newspapers, new disciplines and bodies of knowledge such as statistics and management—"solidified themselves." As social discourses became the locus of "increasingly conscious struggle," Terdiman argues, they also brought into existence a newly influential category of citizens able to use and administer the new mechanisms.[73] Finally, this history of the discursive terrain of labor legislation also complicates the functionalist view of the German welfare state, which explains its origins and outcomes in terms of its ability to legitimate and secure the conditions of capitalist reproduction, by uncovering the diverse coalitions, the claims of professionalism and expertise, the assertion of scientific knowledge, and the contests about gender that shaped state social policy during the 1890s.[74] For the German welfare state sought to anchor that legitimation not merely in the sphere of labor-capital relations but also and perhaps even primarily in the spheres of family and reproduction, while at the same time seeking to align these two spheres with each other.[75]

72. On the significance of the 1890s in German history, see Geoff Eley, *Reshaping the German Right: Radical Nationalism and Political Change after Bismarck* (1980; Ann Arbor, Mich., 1991); Eley, "Introduction I: Is There a History of the Kaiserreich?" pp. 11–15.

73. Terdiman, *Discourse/Counter-Discourse*, pp. 44, 66, 74.

74. For an analysis of the ways in which the German welfare state legitimated and secured capitalist reproduction, see Geoff Eley, "Social Imperialism in Germany: Reformist Synthesis or Reactionary Sleight of Hand?" in Eley, *From Unification to Nazism: Reinterpreting the German Past* (Boston, 1986), p. 161; and Rosenhaft and Lee, "State and Society in Modern Germany," pp. 24, 29–30. For further reflection on this issue, see Michael Hanagan's review of Stewart, *Women, Work, and the French State*, in *International Labor and Working-Class History*, no. 39 (Spring 1991): 98–100.

75. Eley, "German History," p. 96.

Although the expansion of the German welfare state can be viewed as one of the discernible outcomes of the discourses of social reform, the implications of the shifts in state social policy of the 1890s and the emergence of a new ideology of women's work reached far beyond the realm of governing. For both were central in shaping class and citizenship as social concepts and political identities. This is particularly true of the 1890s when the transformation of the public sphere—the emergence of Social Democracy as a mass party, the popular mobilizations of right-wing nationalists, feminists, and liberal social reformers—changed the meanings of both class and citizenship in Germany. While state social policy reinforced the identities of male workers as breadwinners, women workers' relations to class politics were mediated by the discursive and legislative emphasis on their maternal duties and identities. Under the gaze of male mill owners, trade unionists, factory inspectors, medical doctors, and parliamentary legislators, female workers were always embodied. Entwined in these debates about women's work and the protective legislation they produced were concerns about both the health and the moral integrity of women's bodies: the advent of maternity leave in 1878 and its expansion, and the eleven hour limit placed on women's work day in 1891, were necessitated by concerns about high rates of infant mortality and the health not only of pregnant women and new mothers but also of young girls as future mothers. Thus labor legislation fixed women's place in production and hence in class, as it was popularly understood in the German Social Democratic milieu. Labor legislation inscribed class and citizenship with sexual difference in its explicit distinction between women and children, on the one hand, who lacked the political rights to assert and defend their own interests and whom the state was compelled to protect, and male citizens on the other, who enjoyed civil equality with employers, including the right to form political coalitions against them. Finally, rethinking the welfare state from the perspective of labor legislation and reading labor legislation against the grain to find the body may illuminate how the dichotomies of public/private, work/nonwork, and production/reproduction underwrote both middle class and working class as concepts and as particular visions of male citizenship.

CHAPTER 6 § THE BODY AS METHOD? §

REFLECTIONS ON THE PLACE OF THE BODY

IN GENDER HISTORY

PROLOGUE 2005

This essay, originally written for the tenth anniversary issue of the journal *Gender & History* on definitive thematics in gender history, picks up two threads that run through the preceding chapter, "Social Policy, Body Politics"—those of bodies and citizenship as objects and outcomes of German social policy. My main interest in the first part of this essay is conceptual: I assess the explosion of interest in the body during the late 1990s, probing whether it marked an attempt to rematerialize history in the aftermath of the linguistic turn. My second concern is the promise of the body as a category of historical analysis. The crucial questions I pose here are: What does the body enable us to see that might otherwise remain imperceptible without it? To what extent does invoking the body suggest or require new or different methodologies?

In my own work before this essay I, like many others, had introduced the body as a dimension of social policy, industrial hygiene, and struggles over class and citizenship without elaborating its significance, either conceptually or methodologically. In fact, in writing the essay I recognized that several different bodies had coexisted in my previous scholarship—the *social body*, which was defined by the coalescing efforts of social reformers and state officials to quell the growing dangers of women's work; *rhetorical and textual representations of bodies* that symbolized the moral and hygienic perils of industrial society; *bodies as objects of regulation and tutelage* by welfare states and social

This is a revised and expanded version of an essay under the same title which appeared in *Gender & History, Retrospect and Prospect,* ed. Leonore Davidoff, Keith McClelland, and Eleni Varikas (London: Blackwell, 2000; first published as a special issue of *Gender & History* 11/3 (1999). I thank Blackwell Publishers for permission to include the essay here. The original version of this essay benefited from the incisive comments of Leonore Davidoff, Eleni Varikas, and Keith McClelland. I am also grateful to Alexandra Binnenkade and Beatrice Bowald, organizers of the Luzern symposium *Körper/Sinne* (May 2000), for inviting me to make my theoretical reflections on the body more historically concrete and thus prompting me to revise the second section of this essay.

reformers; and finally, *bodies as sites of experience* like pregnancy, childbirth, illness, overwork, and exploitation that marked them indelibly, shaping subjectivities and self-representations.[1] The recognition that invocation of "the body" often blurs the differences among and between these distinct bodies marks the first step towards a more conceptually conscious and historically grounded use of the term. In that spirit the second half of this essay explores the particular salience of bodies for twentieth-century German history. This version has been significantly revised and expanded to include a brief case study of the turning point of 1918–20, when the tasks of founding a democracy involved not only coming to terms with the unprecedented "body damage" of the First World War, but also the definition of new citizenships in gendered and embodied terms.[2]

§ § §

In the course of the past decade we have been faced with a veritable flood of books, articles, dissertation proposals, and conference panels on various aspects of body history, or bodies in history. Many, even most of these studies merely invoke the body or allow it to serve as a more fashionable surrogate for sexuality, reproduction, or gender without referring to anything specifically identifiable as body, bodily, or embodied. In contrast to other keywords in the history of women and gender, such as patriarchy, class, or gender, which have been the subject of intense debate among feminists and across disciplines, body remains a largely unexplicated and undertheorized *historical* concept. Interestingly, the debates surrounding Judith Butler's notable *Bodies That Matter,* for example, have not resounded widely among historians of women, gender, or bodies.[3] Despite the deep involvement of many feminists in interdisciplinary arenas of Women's Studies, it is still more common to seek methodological

1. Kathleen Canning, *Languages of Labor and Gender: Female Factory Work in Germany, 1850–1914* (Ithaca, N.Y., 1996).

2. I discuss this case study in greater detail in my essay "Der Körper der Staatsbürgerin als theoretisches und historisches Problem," which was published in *KörperSinne: Körper im Spannungsfeld von Diskurs und Erfahrung,* ed. Beatrice Bowald, Alexandra Binnenkade, Sandra Büchel-Thalmeier, and Monika Jacobs (Luzern, 2002), pp. 109–33. On "body damage" in the First World War, see Sabine Kienitz, "Body Damage: War Disability and Constructions of Masculinity in Weimar Germany," in *Home/Front: The Military, War, and Gender in Twentieth-Century Germany,* ed. Karen Hagemann and Stefanie Schüler-Springorum (Oxford, 2002), pp. 181–204.

3. Judith Butler, *Bodies That Matter: On the Discursive Limits of "Sex"* (London, 1993).

clarity in the pages of another historical study than in a philosophical text like Butler's.[4] So historians grappling with methodological issues raised by "the body" might be more inclined to turn to more specific case studies of body histories, such as Barbara Duden's imaginative *Woman beneath the Skin: A Doctor's Patients in Eighteenth-Century Germany,* which explores how women "of a vanished world" perceived and experienced their bodies; to the pathbreaking special issue of *Representations,* edited by Catherine Gallagher and Thomas Laqueur, *The Making of the Modern Body;* or to the field-defining Zone Books series, *Fragments for a History of the Human Body,* edited by Michel Feher.[5]

The first part of this essay explores the current fascination with body histories and ponders the simultaneously unspecific and yet seductive invocation of the body in many recent histories. I contemplate the reasons the body has remained an elusive presence in most of our fields of national or chronological specialization until recently and reflect on the potentialities and limitations of the concept of the body, on the methodological implications of placing bodies at the heart of historical investigation. The second part briefly explores the conceptual and methodological implications of recuperating and incorporating the body into my own historical research project on citizenship and the crisis of nation in Germany after the First World War.

BODIES IN HISTORY

Analysis of the body has offered important new insights into the histories of the Enlightenment and the French Revolution, the history of welfare states and

4. The same can be said of other provocative feminist texts on female bodies, including the work of the Australian feminists Moira Gatens and Elizabeth Grosz. See, for example, Moira Gatens, *Imaginary Bodies: Ethics, Power and Corporeality* (London, 1996); and Elizabeth Grosz, "Bodies and Knowledges: Feminism and the Crisis of Reason," in Grosz, *Space, Time, and Perversion* (London, 1995), pp. 25–43. Also see Grosz's *Volatile Bodies: Toward a Corporeal Feminism* (Bloomington, Ind., 1994).

5. Barbara Duden, *Woman beneath the Skin: A Doctor's Patients in Eighteenth-Century Germany,* trans. Thomas Dunlap (Cambridge, Mass., 1991). Although Duden's study relies upon the eight-volume study on the "diseases of women" compiled by the physician Johann Storch of Halle during the period 1721–40, she makes a compelling case that the bodily experiences of Storch's 1,650 female patients were not "medically determined," rendering Storch a witness to "an orally transmitted popular concept of the body." See pp. 23, 36–37, 66. Also see Thomas Laqueur and Catherine Gallagher, eds., *The Making of the Modern Body: Sexuality and Society in the Nineteenth Century,* special issue of *Representations* 4 (Spring 1986); Michael Feher with Ramona Nadoff and Nadia Tazi, *Fragments for a History of the Human Body,* 3 vols. (New York, 1989–1991).

social policy, and more recently of imperialism, the First World War, and the rise of fascism. In some historical studies, bodies, as signifiers, metaphors, or allegorical emblems, promise new understandings of nation or social formation. In others the body, as a site of intervention or inscriptive surface, specifies and expands our grasp of the processes of social discipline or the reach of the interventionist welfare state, of medicalization, professionalization, rationalization of production and reproduction. The body histories that have left a historiographical mark (in the sense of convincing readers that bodies are significant objects of historical investigation) have sought most frequently to analyze bodies as a signifiers—of nation or state power, of social formations or dissolutions, of moral or hygienic visions and dangers, as sites of intervention or inscriptive surfaces "on which laws, morality, values, power, are inscribed."[6]

From Carole Pateman's incisive delineation of the distinct political meanings of male and female bodies in French Enlightenment thought, to Lynn Hunt's "family romance" of the French Revolution and her analysis of the many bodies of Marie-Antoinette, to Dorinda Outram's reading of the "changes in the public presentation and public significance of the bodies of individuals," the history of the body in the Enlightenment and the French Revolution has helped elucidate the transformation of public space, the role of culture in the revolution, and the banishment of women (on the basis of their embodiment, argues Pateman) from the emergent public sphere.[7] Casting a somewhat different light on the relevance of the body to the formation of civil society in Germany, Isabel Hull's masterful study, *Sexuality, State, and Civil Society in Germany, 1700–1815,* regards male rather than female embodiment as a crucial aspect of emergent civil society and of definitions of citizenship in eighteenth-century Germany. "Whereas collective estate, or *Stand,* had once organized society," she argues, "the individual citizen now founded civil society. Stripped of social status and regional inflection, the citizen had to be based on universal principles adhering to the only distinguishing feature he had left: his body."[8]

6. Elizabeth Grosz, "Bodies and Knowledges," p. 33.

7. Carole Pateman, *The Sexual Contract* (Stanford, Calif., 1988), and "The Fraternal Social Contract," in *Civil Society and the State,* ed. John Keane (London, 1988), pp. 101–28; Lynn Hunt, *The Family Romance of the French Revolution* (Berkeley, Calif., 1992); and Dorinda Outram, *The Body and the French Revolution: Sex, Class, and Political Culture* (New Haven, Conn., 1989). Also see the recently translated book by Antoine de Baecque, *The Body Politic: Corporeal Metaphor in Revolutionary France, 1770–1800* (1993; Stanford, Calif. 1997).

8. Isabel Hull, *Sexuality, State, and Civil Society in Germany, 1700–1815* (Ithaca, N.Y., 1995), p. 5.

The study of bodies, particularly symbolic bodies, during the periods of the Enlightenment and the French Revolution, has likely yielded the most sophisticated results thus far in a field we can only vaguely call "body history." In many other areas of gender history—sexuality, reproduction, labor, and welfare state, four crucial areas of inquiry—bodies figured more often implicitly than explicitly. In studies of beauty, prostitution, witchcraft, or female circumcision, for example, the body is so obviously present that it often seems unnecessary to comment upon or theorize its presence.

Attempting to trace the place of the body in the gradual shift from women's history to gender history brings us headlong into a confrontation with the complex sex/gender distinction, which has significant implications for a conceptual-methodological reflection on bodies in history. As Donna Haraway argued some years ago, "the political and epistemological effort to remove women from the category of nature and to place them in culture as constructed and self-constructing social subjects in history" caused the concept of gender "to be quarantined from the infections of biological sex."[9] In a similar vein Moira Gatens contends that the perceived "dangers of biological reductionism" propelled the embrace of gender and the repudiation of sex in feminist analytical vocabulary. In her essay "A Critique of the Sex/Gender Distinction," Gatens seeks to retain a theory of sexual difference while firmly rejecting the notion that all such theories are plagued by essentialism or biologism. In place of a view of the body as a passive mediator of social inscriptions, which accompanied the sharp demarcation of gender and sex, Gatens asserts that "the body can and does intervene to confirm or deny various social significances. . . ."[10] Seeking to define femininity and masculinity in relation to female and male bodies, Gatens makes clear why this relationship is anything but arbitrary: "there must be a qualitative difference," she claims, between the kind of femininity 'lived' by women and that 'lived' by men."[11] Thus the repudiation of sex in favor of gender left sex inextricably linked to body and body stigmatized with biologism and essentialism. This explains in part the apprehension many feminist historians have shown toward a more explicit theoretical or methodological engagement with the body as a historical concept.

As one outcome of the displacement of sex by gender, the discursive body

9. Donna Haraway, *Simians, Cyborgs, and Women: The Reinvention of Nature* (New York, 1991), p. 134.

10. Moira Gatens, *Imaginary Bodies: Ethics, Power, and Corporeality* (London, 1996), pp. 3–4, 10.

11. Ibid., pp. 4, 9.

has figured more prominently in the last decade of gender history than Barbara Duden's "body as experience." Yet it is difficult to overlook the fact that the emphasis on the body's symbolic dimensions has also remained superficial in many instances: the symbolic body remains immaterial/dematerialized, as it grows increasingly difficult to conceive of social relations in terms of associations between bodies as specific loci of experience or identity formation. While the embrace of the discursive body might be traced back to the extraordinary influence of Michel Foucault on the study of both bodies and gender, in the field of history there is also a more practical explanation for its prevalence. Sources that chart the discursive construction of male and female bodies at the levels of state, church, social reform, science, medicine, or law are much more readily accessible than those that might offer insights into the body as a site of experience, memory or subjectivity.

Another legacy of Foucault is the "social body," which emerged according to the anthropologist David Horn at the boundary between the economic and the political, the public and the private, the natural and the discursive in the course of the nineteenth century and was defined in "that modern domain of knowledge and intervention carved out by statistics, sociology, social hygiene, and so cial work."[12] Examinations of "social bodies" therefore often leave obscure the differences between the social bodies of men, women, and children, the distinct experiences of those who inhabited "moral" social spaces and those who inhabited the crowded terrain of "embodied 'others' . . . the sick, the criminal, the mad, the unemployed, the infertile."[13]

If discursive and social bodies have frequently figured as abstractions, studies of individual or collective "material" or bodily experiences often have the reverse problem: they are often problematically concrete, undertheorized, or cast too simply in terms of resistance/subjection.[14] Joanna Bourke's *Dismembering the Male: Men's Bodies, Britain, and the Great War*, which pursued the relatively new topic of male corporeality in war, unfortunately remains limited

12. David G. Horn, *Social Bodies: Science, Reproduction, and Italian Modernity* (Princeton N.J., 1994), pp. 3–4, 10. Also see Martin Hewitt, "Bio-politics and Social Policy: Foucault's Account of Welfare," *Theory, Culture and Society* 2/1 (1983): 67–84.

13. Here I am both citing and entering into dialogue with Horn, *Social Bodies*, pp. 3, 12. Mary Poovey's brilliant study, *Making a Social Body: British Cultural Formation, 1830–64* (Chicago, 1995), suggests that social body is perhaps best understood as an abstraction.

14. These arguments can be traced back to a conversation with Atina Grossmann in a panel discussion, "Reading the Body in the History of the Weimar Republic," at the German Studies Association's Twenty-first Annual Conference, held in September 1997.

within an excessive concreteness, by which "male corporeality" is defined in the most empirical sense of the 722,000 corpses of British soldiers. Also notable is her disavowal of the symbolics of bodily dismemberment and mass death. With respect to those men maimed or disfigured by the war, Bourke argues that despite the "shocking suddenness of wartime disfigurement," a few years after the war had ended the scars and deformities no longer held a unique significance in British society; rather, "they joined a wider population of disabled men, women, and children."[15]

The search for the "material" body reflects, in part at least, an unease with the prevalence of the discursive or Foucauldian body. This unease has led some scholars to pose extraordinarily fruitful questions, for example, regarding the effacement of the specificities of the "bodies of the disciplined" whose corporealities are ultimately subsumed into "a universalized body worked upon in a uniform way by surveillance techniques and practices."[16] N. Katherine Hayles asks, for example, "how actual bodies, in their cultural and physical specificities, impose, incorporate and resist incorporation of the material practices he [Foucault] describes." Hayles points out that the Foucauldian body marks the "absorption of embodiment into discourse" while the hallmark and still influential study by Elaine Scarry, The Body in Pain, emphasizes "that bodily practices have a physical reality which can never be fully assimilated into discourse."[17] Yet Scarry's main pursuit is the intricate relationship between bodily pain and language, or more specifically, the political consequences of pain's resistance to "objectification in language."[18] While Bourke's study of dismembered male bodies sheds light on what Scarry terms "the most radically embodying event in which human beings ever collectively participate," Scarry's attention to the material body is somewhat more subtle than Bourke's. For Scarry probes how the deep alterations of the bodies of massive numbers of participants "are carried forward into peace," how "the record of war survives in the bodies, both alive and buried. . . ." She asks how the soldier's "unmaking" or deconstruction of himself, his consent "to empty himself of civil content 'for his country'" reverberates in the rebuilding of the nation. Ultimately

15. Joanna Bourke, *Dismembering the Male: Men's Bodies, Britain, and the Great War* (Chicago, 1996), pp. 27, 35, 251.

16. N. Katherine Hayles, "The Materiality of Informatics" (unpublished paper), p. 9. Professor Hayles shared this paper with me when we were both fellows at the Stanford University Humanities Center (1992).

17. Ibid., p. 10; Elaine Scarry, *The Body in Pain: The Making and Unmaking of the World* (Oxford, 1985).

18. Scarry, *The Body in Pain*, chap. 1.

the body's pain and its unspeakability in the realm of politics has profound meanings far beyond the individual or collective (material) injured body, namely for "immaterial culture," for "national consciousness, political beliefs, and self-definition."[19] Judith Butler's *Bodies That Matter* has persuasively assailed the tendency of feminists to read the body's "materiality" as that which is irreducible, that which "cannot be a construction," and has offered in its place a highly suggestive examination of the genealogy of materiality by which matter is understood "not as site or surface, but as a process of materialization that stabilizes over time to produce the effect of boundary, fixity, and surface we call matter."[20]

A final complexity, if one attempts to define a field of "body history," is that slippage commonly occurs between individual bodies as sites of experience/ agency/resistance and social bodies, formed discursively, or between bodies as sites of inscription/intervention and notions of nation, class, or race as "reified bodies." It is then often difficult to discern how these divergent bodies are contingent upon and constitutive of one another. Summarizing some of these more problematic aspects of body histories in an article provocatively entitled "Why All the Fuss about the Body?" the historian Caroline Walker Bynum argues that the current preoccupation with the body operates on the basis of "totally diverse assumptions" and definitions of the body within and across different fields. In Bynum's view the absence of "a clear set of structures, behaviors, events, objects, experiences, words, and moments to which body currently refers" has rendered current discussions of the body within and across disciplines incommensurate and often mutually incomprehensible.[21]

The work of conceptualizing the body is further encumbered not only by the wholly diverse understandings of the body, even among scholars in the same field, but also by the particular valence of the body in popular culture, which infiltrates into our academic discussions and renders the task of defining a conceptual frame or methodology an even more confusing enterprise. Bryan Turner, author of a number of works on the "sociology of the body," explains the tenacious fascination of social scientists with the body in terms of economic and social shifts towards an emphasis on "pleasure, desire, difference and playfulness which are features of contemporary consumerism." He also points to the influence of the women's movement and the transformation of

19. Ibid., pp. 71, 112–14, 122.

20. Butler, *Bodies That Matter*, p. 9.

21. Caroline Bynum, "Why All the Fuss about the Body? A Medievalist's Perspective," *Critical Inquiry* 22 (Autumn 1995): 5.

the role of women in the public sphere. Others point to the conversion of the "project of the self, as the principal legacy of individualism, into the project of the body."[22] The October 1997 issue of *Lingua Franca* carried a short article, "Pieces of You," that seemed to confirm these views. It declared 1997 the "year of the Body Part," referring not only to Paula Jones' legal deposition describing President Clinton's genitals, but also to the publication in the July *New York Times* of an illustrated article entitled "The Whole Body Catalogue: Artificial Parts to Mix and Match," which included a shopping list of "available body parts."[23] Similarly the January 1997 issue of the intriguing bilingual English-Russian magazine, *Colors: A Magazine about the Rest of the World,* was entitled "Shopping for the Body" and included rubrics on "extensions" (prostheses), "maintenance" (cosmetic surgery), "transformation" (electric shock, seaweed packs, working out), "purification, "recreation, "personal hygiene," and "protection."[24] Scholarship, the *Lingua Franca* article claims, has been similarly "driven by a culture fixed on the fragment," by a characteristically postmodern "rejection of all forms of totality, including the corporeal."[25]

The incommensurability of representations of the body across the lines of popular culture and academe, across and within the individual disciplines, might appear to reinforce this rejection of totality or to encourage a frivolous embrace of the body (or body parts) as mere adornments in our scholarly projects. Indeed, the recognition that the body is, as Bryan Turner describes it, "at

22. Bryan S. Turner, *The Body and Society,* 2d ed. (London, 1996), pp. 2–4, 20–21. Here Turner refers to Chris Shilling's *The Body and Social Theory* (London, 1993).

23. Emily Eakin, "Pieces of You," *Lingua Franca* 7 (October 1997): 21–22.

24. The editorial offices of *Colors* are located in Paris and its editorial staff appears to be strewn across the world, lending it a global character. The editorial introduction reads: "The body. Everybody's got one. But when it comes to having sex, cleaning ears, working out or taking a pee, people treat their bodies differently—and with lots of different products. What can you learn about a culture from all these items? To find out, *Colors* went shopping. We browsed beauty salons in Tokyo, street markets in Bogota, and a bionics laboratory in Edinburgh to discover what people buy for their bodies and why. We hope you find something in your size." The cover photo is of a "pubic wig," a "fluffy clump of recycled human hair" known as a "night flower" in Japan and worn on the vagina. Cost: $270. *Colors,* no. 18 (December 1996–January 1997).

25. Eakin, "Pieces of You," p. 21. Eakin points to the recently published studies Elizabeth Haiken, *Venus Envy: A History of Cosmetic Surgery* (Baltimore, 1997), and David Hilman and Carla Mazzio's *The Body in Parts: Fantasies of Corporeality in Early Modern Europe* (London, 1997). Also see the recent work of Dorothy Ko, *Every Step a Lotus: Shoes for Bound Feet* (Berkeley, Calif., 2001).

once the most solid, the most elusive, illusory, concrete, metaphysical, ever present and ever distant thing—a site, an instrument, an environment, a singularity and a multiplicity" makes the question of "body as method" a particularly daunting one.[26]

Further dilemmas that cannot be resolved within the bounds of this essay include the location of bodies in time and space. Certainly implicit in the discussion thus far has been a presumed but unexplicated "modern" body, one that requires historicization and demarcation from medieval or early modern bodies. Barbara Duden has suggested that "a violent process began in the seventeenth century" by which "the body as the embodiment of localized social vitality was symbolically broken," for example through witch trials. In the course of the eighteenth century the body as "the vague corporeality of popular culture" became offensive and in the last third of the century "the study and cultivation of the body politic" became a matter of state policy. As states, medical professionals, and social reformers began to wield new knowledges of health and hygiene, "the new body assumed a central place in the self-image of the bourgeoisie."[27] This is undoubtedly what Isabel Hull means when she suggests that "a modern person's sense of self . . . must always have a strong bodily anchor to it," that the imbrication of body and self has a particular salience in the phase of history known as "modernity."[28] Locating bodies spatially, nationally, and as inscribed by ethnicity and race, is obviously another critical methodological task. So it may be useful to interrogate the notion or presumption of a nationally bounded body, especially in the wake of a rich and wide-ranging historiography on gender and colonialism/imperialism which has not usually placed imagined or lived bodies in the foreground, but has nonetheless explicated the body projects of empire and traced the links between domesticity in the metropoles and the conquest of "the sexual and labor power of colonized women."[29]

While this brief discussion has highlighted several dilemmas in the theory

26. Turner, *The Body and Society*, p. 43.

27. Duden, *Woman beneath the Skin*, pp. 10–11, 13–15.

28. Isabel Hull, "The Body as Historical Experience: Review of Recent Works by Barbara Duden," *Central European History* 28/1 (1995): 74.

29. Anne McClintock, *Imperial Leather: Race, Gender, and Sexuality in the Colonial Contest* (New York, 1995), p. 3. See here in particular McClintock's chap. 1, "The Lay of the Land: Genealogies of Imperialism," and chap. 2, "'Massa and Maids': Power and Desire in the Imperial Metropolis," pp. 21–131; and Anne Stoler, "Making Empire Respectable: The Politics of Race and Sexual Morality in Twentieth-Century Colonial Cultures," *American Ethnologist* 16/4 (November 1989): 634–60.

and practice of body history—bodies that are singularly discursive or abstract, bodies that are excessively material and undertheorized, bodies that are not made visible at all—feminist scholarship in the disciplines of literary studies and philosophy has effectively critiqued the gender/sex distinction, boldly sought to dissolve the divide between discourse and materiality with respect to bodies, and sought to redefine the key words agency, subjectivity, and positionality in terms of the body. While on the one hand resisting the allure of biological essentialism, the feminist philosopher Elizabeth Grosz, for example, also refuses the "process of sanitization, of neutralization, of decorporealization of the concept 'body'" that accompanied "the discursivation of bodies."[30] The literary scholar Leslie Adelson introduces her *Making Bodies, Making History* with the contention that "there is an assuredly multifaceted reality of human bodies that does not exist outside discourse and is yet not by any means subsumed by it."[31] Acknowledging the powerful influence of Michel Foucault on our understandings of how "power is inscribed on and by bodies through modes of social supervision and discipline as well as self-regulation" and of how bodies are "moulded by a great many distinct regimes," Elizabeth Grosz nonetheless emphasizes that all of those processes that mark the body through specific rituals and practices—punishment, torture, medicalized observations, sexuality, and pleasure—identify bodies that represent "an uncontrollable, unpredictable threat to a regular, systematic mode of social organization." Positing a place for agency in the discursively constituted subject, Grosz contends that the body is not only marked by coercive forces, but is "internally lived, experienced and acted upon by the subject and the social collectivity."[32] Moira Gatens's notion of the imaginary body also creatively bridges the purported gulf between discursive and material bodies: always socially and historically specific, imaginary bodies are constructed by "a shared language; the shared psychical significance and privileging of various zones of the body; and common institutional practices and discourses which act on and through the body." Imaginary bodies, she contends, provide "the key or the code to the decipherment of the social and personal significance of male and female biologies as lived in culture, that is, masculinity and femininity."[33]

30. Elizabeth Grosz, "Bodies and Knowledges," p. 31.

31. Leslie Adelson, *Making Bodies, Making History: Feminism and German Identity* (Lincoln, Neb., 1993), p. 2.

32. Elizabeth Grosz, "Inscriptions and Body-Maps: Representations and the Corporeal," in *Feminine, Masculine, and Representation*, ed. Terry Threadgold and Anne Cranny-Francis (Sydney, 1990), pp. 65, 71–72. Also see Grosz's *Volatile Bodies*.

33. Gatens, *Imaginary Bodies*, p. 12.

Indeed, the notion of *embodiment* may be the most promising outcome of these fruitful debates and interventions. Embodiment, which Adelson terms "crucial to any feminist enterprise," denotes a process "of making and doing the work of bodies—of becoming a body in social space."[34] So embodied practices are always contextual, inflected with class, ethnic, racial, gender, and generational locations, with "place, time, physiology and culture."[35] A far less fixed and idealized concept than body, embodiment encompasses moments of encounter and interpretation, agency and resistance. So as N. Katherine Hayles has argued, "during any given period, experiences of embodiment are in continual interaction with constructions of the body"; and embodied practices engender "heterogenous spaces even when the discursive formations describing those practices seem uniformly dispersed throughout the society."[36] Elizabeth Grosz's notion of "counterstrategic reinscription" offers a perhaps parallel understanding. In her view, the body "as well as being the site of knowledge-power . . . is thus also a site of resistance, for it exerts a recalcitrance, and always entails the possibility of a counterstrategic reinscription, for it is capable of being self-marked, self-represented in alternative ways." The body's recalcitrance, it seems, might be seen as an example of one kind of "embodied practice" imagined by Hayles. Subjects thus produced are not simply the imposed results of alien, coercive forces; the body is internally lived, experienced, and acted upon by the subject and the social collectivity.[37]

Memory represents perhaps another kind of embodied practice, one that is particularly intriguing in that embodied memories are most likely to be both materialized and mediated discursively. Scarry points to Bourdieu's study of "hidden pedagogies," such as "cultural manners" passed from one generation to the next, and his contention that "the principles embodied in this way are placed beyond the grasp of consciousness, and hence cannot be touched by voluntary, deliberate transformation, cannot even be made explicit." Scarry's own study points to the embodiment of "political identity," which "is usually learned unconsciously, effortlessly, and very early, and expressed in gestures, habits, postures and demeanors, which are nearly impossible to unlearn.[38] The concepts of embodiment, bodily reinscription, and bodily memory may help to

34. Adelson, *Making Bodies,* p. xiii; Turner, *The Body and Society,* p. xiii.

35. Hayles, "The Materiality of Informatics," pp. 10–12.

36. Ibid., pp. 11–12.

37. Grosz, "Inscriptions and Body Maps," pp. 64–65.

38. Scarry, *The Body in Pain,* p. 110. Here Scarry cites Pierre Bourdieu, *Outline of a Theory of Practice,* trans. Richard Nice (Cambridge, 1977), pp. 94–95.

make more specific the fluid and porous concept of body and to help chart historical change in and through bodies which the presumed fixity of "body" seems to defy. Mapping a conceptual space in which bodies encounter, incorporate, intervene among, and resist dominant discourses through the notions of embodiment and reinscription should perhaps be accompanied by a rethinking of the term discourse as well. Judith Butler's apt comments on feminist unease with the notion of construction and her suggestion to rethink the prevalent understanding of discourse as that which is always "artificial and dispensable" should help to elucidate the material outcomes of discursive inscriptions, the ways in which they are materialized and embodied.[39]

BODIES AND RUPTURES IN GERMAN HISTORY

In modern German history the body has figured most significantly in the study of the Weimar and Nazi periods, encompassing the highly charged discourses and practices of interwar natalism and sexual reform, the campaigns for birth control and abortion rights, as well as the emergence of the "new woman," the single "women of the metropolis" whose bodies became markers for all that the First World War had transformed in the relations between the sexes.[40] The body is an even more explicit presence in recent studies of the Nazi "racial state," figuring as a signifier of both racial purity (the "Aryan" body) and racial pollution (the Jewish body, the deformed, handicapped, or aging body) in the Nazis' "barbarous utopia," as an object not merely of intervention, but of mutilation and annihilation.[41] As Leslie Adelson notes, reference to the six million Jews the Nazis murdered "signifies in no uncertain terms the ineluctable embodiment of history" (a point that is underscored by the enormous popularity of Daniel Goldhagen's best-selling and intensely graphic account of

39. Butler, *Bodies That Matter*, pp. xi, 4–5.

40. On the history of body and gender during the Weimar Republic, see Renate Bridenthal, Atina Grossmann, and Marion Kaplan, eds., *When Biology Became Destiny: Women in Weimar and Nazi Germany* (New York, 1984). See also Cornelie Usborne, *The Politics of the Body in Weimar Germany: Reproductive Rights and Duties* (Ann Arbor, Mich., 1992); Atina Grossmann, *Reforming Sex: The German Movement for Birth Control and Abortion Reform, 1920–1950* (Oxford, 1995); Maria Tatar, *Lustmord: Sexual Murder in Weimar Germany* (Princeton, N.J., 1995); Katharina von Ankum, ed., *Women in the Metropolis: Gender and Modernity in Weimar Culture* (Berkeley, Calif., 1997).

41. See Michael Burleigh and Wolfgang Wippermann, *The Racial State: Germany 1933–1945* (Cambridge, 1991).

the "face-to-face" extermination of Jews by "ordinary Germans," in which the bodies of both victims and killers are explicitly present).[42] Klaus Theweleit's influential two-volume study of 1978, *Male Fantasies,* offers an intriguing examination of the meanings of female bodies for male fascist subjectivities, suggesting that the violent destruction of bodies and disordering of gender during the First World War is crucial to understanding the exterminationist drive of the Nazi state. While Theweleit's text left little dispute about the salience of bodies to fascist fantasies and practices, it left unexplicated the precise links between male fears of engulfment after World War I and the perpetration of Nazi violence and, ultimately, genocide, a quarter-century later.[43]

In the remainder of this essay I would like to probe the relevance of the body as a method of reading key moments in the transformations of the war and postwar period when both male and female bodies were politicized and inscribed in new ways. As Eve Rosenhaft has suggested, through the collective experience of mobilization, unique to this first total war, the limits of bodily endurance, and the integrity of the material body itself, were tested, stretched, and massively exceeded, both in the trenches and on the home front.[44] The shock of the war's violence towards both national and individual bodies, juxtaposed with the material sufferings of those who remained at the home front—hunger, cold, illness, anxiety, and grief—render this historical moment one in which both bodily inscription—by states and armies—and the reinscriptive, embodying responses of citizens and soldiers—through revolution, political violence, and social protest—were particularly acute. Indeed, this critical moment of rupture, spanning the years 1917 to 1924, was seared into the consciousness and history of the twentieth-century by the violence it spawned in the late 1920s and early 1930s. Theweleit's unconventional masterpiece, with its of the disordering of gender during the war and the fantasies of "women, floods, bodies," of rape, murder, and dismemberment it produced in male

42. Adelson, *Making Bodies,* p. 23; Daniel Jonah Goldhagen, *Hitler's Willing Executioners: Ordinary Germans and the Holocaust* (New York, 1996). Also see Raul Hilberg's poignant analysis of the popularity of Goldhagen's book, "The Goldhagen Phenomenon," *Critical Inquiry* 23/4 (Summer 1997): 721–28.

43. Klaus Theweleit, *Male Fantasies,* vol. 1: *Women, Floods, Bodies, History* (1977; Minneapolis, 1987). Volume 2 is entitled *Männerkörper: Zur Psychoanalyse des Weißen Terrors.*

44. Here I am paraphrasing Eve Rosenhaft's comments on an earlier draft of this paper, delivered to the European Social Science History Conference held in Amsterdam in April 1998.

Freikorps activists, remains highly suggestive in this regard.[45] The recent work of Maria Tatar and Beth Irwin Lewis on the "Lustmord" series by leftist male artists, such as Otto Dix and George Grosz, suggests that the "five years of unchained atavistic impulses" described by the medical doctor and sex reformer Magnus Hirschfeld, the brutalization of sex behind the lines (in brothels in enemy territory, for example), and the "pathological and perverse forms of sex" which Hirschfeld claimed took place in the trenches, spurred fantasies of lustful murder and mutilation even among progressive, let alone prefascist men.[46]

These are among the most dramatic examples of the experiential chasm that likely existed between the war front and home front. In an evocative essay, "Militarization and Reproduction in World War I Germany," Elizabeth Domansky points to the everyday gulf between men, who were to protect the nation against the external enemy, and women, whose task was to protect the "national body" from internal enemies, that is, disease, physical weakness, and immorality.[47] Domansky suggests that the distinct bodily experiences of trenches and home front—dismemberment and death of men at the front; hunger, overwork, illness, and immiseration of women at home—created both important commonalities and disparities in male and female subjectivities after the war, from their shared desires to reclaim traditional roles in the family to the ways they positioned themselves in the new arenas of labor and sexual politics during Weimar.[48]

One outcome of these manifold transformations was the emergence of a new female body—that of the female citizen. The body of the new *Staatsbürgerin* figured prominently during the early years of the republic, from the writing of the Weimar constitution to the campaigns of the reconstituted political parties in 1919 and 1920, to the new arenas of popular culture, consumption, and mass entertainment, and to the visions of an expanded and effective welfare state. Female suffrage was the centerpiece in the revolutionary government's sweeping pronouncement of political citizenship rights, encompassing the annulment of censorship; freedom of expression, assembly, and religious belief; and amnesty for political crimes, alongside new social rights that abol-

45. Theweleit, *Male Fantasies,* vol. 1.

46. Tatar, *Lustmord,* and Beth Irwin Lewis, "Inside the Windows of the Metropolis," in von Ankum, *Women in the Metropolis.* Hirschfeld is quoted by Lewis, p. 219.

47. Elizabeth Domansky, "Militarization and Reproduction in World War I Germany," in *Society, Culture, and the State in Germany, 1870–1930,* ed. Geoff Eley (Ann Arbor, Mich., 1997), p. 455.

48. Ibid.

ished the conscription of wartime labor, reinstated protective labor laws, and held out the promise of the universal eight-hour day.[49] While each of these measures significantly changed the relationship of civil society to state, and of politics to the social body, the proclamation of women's suffrage, and the subsequent debates about its meanings, made gender a transformative force at the height of revolutionary crisis. As surprising as the revolutionary proclamation of female suffrage might have seemed in mid-November 1918, female activists were quick to explain the genesis of their new status as *Staatsbürgerinnen* in their experiences of war. That which women had endured on the home front both enabled and entitled women to claim citizenship rights, argued Adele Schreiber in 1919.[50] In her brochure *Revolution und Frauenrecht,* Schreiber noted that the new democracy was built upon the mound of two million dead men and upon the "suffering and torment of mothers, wives, fiancées, daughters, and sisters."[51] A few months later bourgeois women spoke out as citizens who embraced democracy but deplored the humiliation of the Versailles Treaty. In doing so, they broke the silence surrounding women's experiences on the home front, calling up memories of hunger, illness, fear, and grief, and declaring it unthinkable that more anguish be inflicted by the Allies on those who had not caused the war. Nationalist and right-wing women, who regarded themselves as citizens of the nation more than the republic, also drew upon their patriotic sacrifices in wartime to mobilize mass protests against the treaty, targeting in particular the assignment of war guilt to Germany.[52] In this unusual moment, women's wartime experiences were spoken in order to empha-

49. International Institute of Social History, Amsterdam, Rat der Volksbeauftragten, Protokolle, 14.12.1918–31.12.1918. Here see "Aufruf des Rates der Volksbeauftragten an das deutsche Volk vom 12. November 1918." Also see Susanne Miller, ed., *Quellen zur Geschichte des Parlamentarismus und der politischen Parteien,* vol. 6: *Die Regierung der Volksbeauftragten 1918/19* (Düsseldorf, 1969).

50. Adele Schreiber, "Den Müttern im neuen Deutschland," *Vossische Zeitung,* January 1, 1919. Also see Dr. Ise Reicke, "Frauengedanken zum Krieg," *Die Staatsbürgerin* 6/2 (May 1917): 25–26.

51. Adele Schreiber, *Revolution und Frauenrecht* (Berlin, 1919), pp. 8–9.

52. Ibid.; Raffael Scheck, "Women against Versailles: Maternalism and Nationalism of Female Bourgeois Politicians in the Early Weimar Republic," *German Studies Review* 22/1 (February 1999): 21–41; Elizabeth Harvey, "Pilgrimages to the 'Bleeding Border': Gender and the Rituals of Nationalist Protest in Germany, 1919–39," *Women's History Review* 9/2 (2000): 201–29. Also see Scheck's book, *Mothers of the Nation: Right-Wing Women in Weimar Germany* (Oxford, 2004); and Elizabeth Harvey's *Women and the Nazi East: Agents and Witnesses of Germanization* (New Haven, Conn., 2003).

size that the German nation, embodied in women on the home front, had suffered unbearable misery during the war and could not carry the additional burden of a punitive peace.[53]

While the female citizens of the new republic understood the transformation of their civil and political status as embedded in their past experiences, they were also cognizant of the ways in which it could shape the future. Dr. Agnes von Harnack noted, for example, in 1919 that the postwar *Frauenüberschuß* (excess of women in the German population) of some two million had placed "the fate of Germany in the hands of its women."[54] Indeed, the political potential of the new female electorate became tangible in the campaigns that prepared the way for the first democratic election to the National Assembly in January 1919,[55] as parties campaigned vigorously for women voters. With the convening of the assembly in February 1919, which featured the largest female delegation of any elected body in Europe at the time—41 women from six different parties constituting nearly 10 percent of the deputies—the dreams and desires surrounding citizenship were gradually dissolved by the arduous task of delimiting rights and duties and inscribing them in law.[56] The citizenship that found consensus and was anchored in the constitution six months later differentiated between men and women in terms of the distinct and embodied ways in which the two sexes performed duties and offered sacrifices for the fatherland. This process of embodying citizenship was intensively contested, as delegates fought over the formulation that men and women had the same rights and duties as citizens "in principle" (Article 109), a debate that devolved into acerbic assessments of the distinct "bodily capacities" (*körperliche Veranlagung*) of men and women.[57] Citizenship was also embodied as the National Assembly contemplated the place of the family in new republican society as

53. "Die Friedenslage in der Nationalversammlung," section on "Der Protest der Frauen," *Vossische Zeitung,* May 13, 1919.

54. Helene Lange Archiv, Berlin, 1062, Agnes von Harnack, *Die Frauen und das Wahlrecht* (Berlin, n.d.), published by the Ausschuß der Frauenverbände Deutschlands für die Nationalversammlung.

55. The appeals of the various political parties to women during the Weimar Republic are the subject of Julia Sneeringer's recent book, *Winning Women's Votes: Propaganda and Politics in Weimar Germany* (Chapel Hill, N.C., 2002).

56. Regine Deutsch, *Die politische Tat der Frau: Aus der Nationalversammlung* (Gotha, 1920), appendix, pp. 43–44.

57. Article 109 reads: "Alle Deutschen sind vor dem Gesetz gleich. Männer und Frauen haben *grundsätzlich* dieselben staatsbürgerlichen Rechte und Pflichten" ("All Germans are equal before the law. Men and women have the same rights and duties *in principle*") (em-

well as the relations between the sexes within the family. The new constitution protected marriage, as the site of the "reproduction of the nation."[58] The rights and respectability of unmarried mothers, another legacy of the war, preoccupied several sessions of the assembly, as delegates deliberated the issues of child support and inheritance rights for illegitimate children, along with the right of unmarried mothers to be addressed as "Frau" (instead of "Fräulein").[59]

The drafting of a new democratic constitution, in which female citizenship was qualified and delimited in terms of women's bodily capacities as mothers, while usually interpreted in terms of a restoration of patriarchy, opened a discursive space (and a new legal category) in and from which women could mobilize their embodied experiences to challenge and subvert the rhetorics of class and citizenship. It is also important to consider here the discursive context of Weimar body politics, in which the discourses of sexual reform, natalism, and eugenics criss-crossed with those of the expanded Weimar welfare state. The efforts of female workers and their union during the mid-1920s to expand maternity leave spilled over into mobilizations for the right to birth control and abortion. At times all three demands were raised at once, attesting to the location of Weimar citizenships in bodies. Launched by the German Textile Workers' Union, which represented over 300,000 women workers during the mid-1920s, this action began as an inquiry into the effects of factory work on the pregnant woman's body. Its startling revelation of the high rates of stillbirth, miscarriage, and illness among female textile workers soon transformed the inquiry into a vigorous campaign at the level of the national parliament for expansion of maternity protection. The photographic representations of the pregnant female body at work, compiled by the socialist physician Max Hirsch, showing women workers' swollen abdomens pressed up against moving machinery in each photo, transformed what Thomas Laqueur calls "the statistical body" into "the lived (female pregnant) body" which now had a bearing on national social policy.[60] This campaign marked a shift in labor politics, at least those of this largely female union, toward the foregrounding of the body in its

-----

phasis added). It is worth noting that Hugo Preuß's draft of Part I, "Die Einzelperson," reads: "Alle Deutschen sind vor dem Gesetze gleichberechtigt" ("All Germans are equal before the law") without mention of women or men. See chapter 8 below, p. 228 and note 40.

58. Ziegler, *Die deutsche Nationalversammlung*, pp. 329–30.

59. Ibid.; Gertrud Lodahl, "Die Weimarer Verfassung und die Frauen," *Gewerkschaftliche Frauenzeitung* 4/17 (August 27, 1919).

60. Thomas Laqueur, "Bodies, Details, and the Humanitarian Narrative," in *The New Cultural History*, ed. Lynn Hunt (Berkeley, Calif., 1989), pp. 194–95.

day-to-day political work, as female workers brought the lived (female pregnant) body into the streets of textile towns across Germany and underscored the claims they staked upon both state and labor movement. Of particular relevance here is the genesis of this shift: How did this mobilization relate to the other, middle-class, Social Democratic, and Communist social movements that mobilized bodies around the issues of sexual reform, birth control, and abortion rights during Weimar?[61] To what extent were female union activists the impetus behind these campaigns, exerting pressure from below upon the male leadership? Or was this shift instigated by the predominantly male leadership in order to preempt or thwart dissent or protest within the union or to incite a new battle against employers or the Christian unions?

Beyond the study of embodied subjects and subjected bodies, the history of Germany after the First World War lends itself also to the exploration of symbolic bodies. The most visible and contested symbolic bodies in Weimar Germany were undoubtedly those of the "fallen soldiers," figured as heroes whose masculinity was fulfilled in the bodily sacrifices of war, as well as the broken bodies of the invalid veterans who were a stark reminder of Germany's defeat.[62] During and after the war it is likely that female bodies symbolized the intimate dangers of war—one thinks of the propaganda placard of the rapacious darkened figure (presumably from the East or from Africa) seizing a shapely blond woman around the waist as she seeks to keep her feet within the bounds of Germany—and in its aftermath female figures, usually well-dressed and modern "new women," symbolized the new citizen in the posters and leaflets of nearly every party (see Figures 1 and 2).[63]

A rather different body of the Weimar Republic was that of the Polish Jewish Communist Rosa Luxemburg. The "brilliant and fiery leader" of the prewar Socialist left and one of the founders of the German Communist Party, became the quintessential "red rifle woman" of Theweleit's *Male Fantasies* when she led the Spartacist Revolt in Berlin in January 1919.[64] Her brutal murder, along with

61. Grossmann, *Reforming Sex.*

62. George Mosse, *Fallen Soldiers: Reshaping the Memory of the World Wars* (New York, 1990); Robert Weldon Whalen, *Bitter Wounds: German Victims of the Great War, 1914–39* (Ithaca, N.Y., 1984); Deborah Cohen, *The War Come Home: Disabled Veterans in Britain and Germany, 1914–39* (Berkeley, Calif., 2001); and Kienitz, "Body Damage," pp. 181–204.

63. See Julia Sneeringer's analysis of the visual appeal to women in her *Winning Women's Votes,* and more recently in her article "The Shopper as Voter: Women, Advertising, and Politics in Post-Inflation Germany," *German Studies Review* 27/3 (October 2004): 476–502.

FIGURE 1. *"Women's suffrage is a main goal of the German Democratic Party!"*
Election poster of the DDP for the elections to the National Assembly, Düsseldorf, 1919.
Lithograph, Deutsches Historisches Museum, Berlin, P 64/419.

FIGURE 2. *Participants in a women's suffrage congress, Munich, 1912.*
Photo, Deutsches Historisches Museum, Berlin, F 52/4339.

that of her comrade Karl Liebknecht, not only lived on as the ultimate symbol of the indelible division of Socialists and Communists that fractured Weimar democracy, but was also enshrined in the culture of the Communist Left, which commemorated its leaders' deaths each January with "sacred public rituals that consecrated the militant activism . . . of the party's founding leaders and succeeding generations."[65] Although Luxemburg herself disavowed nearly all particularities of women's politics (or bodies), her mutilated corpse, found six months after her murder at the bottom of the Landwehr Canal in Berlin, left an explicitly gendered legacy for the political culture of the labor movement during the Weimar Republic. Her body was manifestly female (a Jewish body as well), one whose symbolics attested to the violent anti-Semitism, anticommunism, and hatred of women that were woven together in the ideology of the Freikorps. Luxemburg's discarded and disfigured body signified a traumatic rupture in the founding of Weimar democracy.

This brief excursion into historically specific analysis of symbolic, lived, and interpellated bodies makes clear that this concept does very different work in the analysis of constitutions, social policy, and the political symbolics of democracy. My call for historical specificity in analyzing bodies, inscriptions, and embodiment may not instate the body as the stable concept Caroline Bynum desires, one grounded in "a clear set of structures, behaviors, events, objects, experiences, words and moments." Rather, it suggests that bodies sometimes do different work at the same historical moment, as in the early Weimar Republic, when both the symbolism of the body as well as the politicized processes of embodiment shaped the emergent democracy.[66] The body histories I have outlined today, even if broken into fragmentary vignettes, make clear the merits of charting the connections and convergences of the material and the discursive that make bodies such difficult objects of historical analysis and such intriguing sites of memory, agency, and subjectivity.

64. Theweleit, *Male Fantasies,* and Eric Weitz, *Creating German Communism, 1890–1990* (Princeton, N.J., 1997).

65. Weitz, *Creating German Communism,* pp. 179–80.

66. Bynum, "Why All the Fuss about the Body?" p. 5.

PART III § THE GENDER OF CITIZENSHIP IN GERMAN HISTORY

CHAPTER 7 § OF MEANINGS & METHODS § THE CONCEPTS OF CLASS & CITIZENSHIP IN GERMAN HISTORY

THE ORDER OF TERMS

Class, citizenship, and welfare state are three keywords that seem, at first, to signify a familiar historical order of contingent social/political categories (i.e., three different but crucial formations in modern German history). Does the order in which these three terms seem to flow imply a hierarchy or an implicit chronology, whereby class figures as the definitive concept—the genuine megaconcept of the three, perhaps—in German and European social history as it has been studied from the 1960s through most of the remaining twentieth century? Have our historical studies implicitly located class in a historical time period that predates or inflects that of citizenship? Has class not been a far more definitive term in German history than citizenship, especially for the study of the period from 1848 to 1933, in which the emergence of a German labor movement and socialism were shaped by languages of class? It is plausible to view class as informing the research domain of social history, while citizenship, until the 1990s, was more likely to be theorized by sociologists and political scientists than studied empirically by historians.[1]

Citizenship served as a kind of partner concept to class in studies of the

This is a substantially revised and shortened version of an essay, "Class vs. Citizenship: Keywords in German Gender History," which was published in *Central European History* 37/2: 225–44 (June 2004), in a special issue honoring Prof. Vernon L. Lidtke. I thank Kenneth F. Ledford, editor of *Central European History*, for permission to publish this revised version here. I also express my appreciation to the editors of the special issue, Gary Stark and Lawrence Stokes, for their input into this essay. Finally, I also thank Christine von Oertzen who commented on the first version of the paper, which I presented to the conference "Gendering Modern German History: Rewriting the Mainstream," held in March 2003 at the University of Toronto.

1. The work of the historical sociologist Margaret Somers both theorized and historicized the concept of citizenship in British history. See, for example, Margaret R. Somers, "Citizenship and the Place of the Public Sphere, Law, Community, and Political Culture in the Transition to Democracy," *American Sociological Review* 58 (1993): 587–620.

French Revolution, British Chartism, and suffrage reform campaigns, that is, in studies of movements in which class-consciousness was expressed in demands for new or expanded citizenship rights. Yet citizenship, in the sense of participatory rights and claims rather than mere national belonging, has been far less tangible than class in the history of imperial Germany, with the important exception of Margaret Anderson's recent *Practicing Democracy*.[2] Citizenship is also curiously absent in the abundant historiography on the democratic experiment of Weimar.[3] It seems fair to conclude that citizenship has served as a crucial historical category for the history of the Federal Republic since 1949, when democracy was sustained over a longer historical time span. Also noteworthy is citizenship's close affinity with the welfare state, especially in German history. Did the German welfare state, perhaps from its earliest Bismarckian conception, serve as a site at which the hopes of class were refashioned into the rights of citizenship, whether in their Social Democratic or Social Catholic guise? Did the very efficacy of the welfare system depend upon its ability to produce citizenship rights as it gained the capacity to mediate or displace "class" struggle? These questions are meant to reflect on the implicit temporalities of historical vocabulary, by which class seems to dominate the history of Germany's long nineteenth century and citizenship the period after World War II, and the two seem to meld in the guise of the welfare state during the First World War and the Weimar Republic. Finally, does the welfare state constitute the very site at which citizenship appears to transcend or displace class, particularly for the period after the Second World War when consumption and social welfare combined to create the veneer of a *nivellierte Gesellschaft* (an equalized society), in which social equalities were no longer easily signified or defined?

In addition to this implicit temporal positioning, each of these terms carries a certain amount of structuralist baggage, in the sense of invoking processes of structural transformation—of economies (the transition from agrarian to industrial production, for example) and geographies (urbanization), of populations (migrations), social relations (class formation), bureaucratization, and

2. Margaret Lavinia Anderson, *Practicing Democracy: Elections and Political Culture in Imperial Germany* (Princeton, N.J., 2000). See the review essay by Volker Berghahn, "The German Empire 1871–1914: Reflections on the Direction of Recent Research," and Anderson, "Reply to Volker Berghahn," in *Central European History* 35/1 (2002): 75–90.

3. Here recent studies related to citizenship and gender constitute an exception. See Julia Sneeringer's *Winning Women's Votes: Propaganda and Politics in Weimar Germany* (Chapel Hill, N.C., 2002), which examines the constructions of female citizenship by party political propaganda; and Heidemarie Lauterer's *Parliamentarierinnen in Deutschland 1918/19–1949* (Königstein, 2002).

modernization of the state (social welfare, social citizenship). So class and citizenship have mainly been understood as embedded in economic or juridical structures and have only relatively recently been examined as cultural constructs. Thus, in this essay I will explore the place of these terms in epistemological debates of the last decades, comparing how each was recast and probing their significance in the development of German and European gender history. The fact that so many studies in German gender history—on both sides of the Atlantic divide—contend with one or more of these keywords prompts the question as to whether these concepts can viably serve as stepping stones to the "mainstreaming" of gender history, a fantasy of legitimation that seems particularly pronounced in the field of German history.

ENGENDERING CLASS

It is no exaggeration to assert that class has been the definitive term in several waves of historical scholarship, from the new social history of the 1960s to the "linguistic turn" of the late 1980s and early 1990s. The concept of class forms an axis in histories of "the social," of labor, women, and gender, around which many different epistemological debates have turned. Also indisputable is the fact that class, since the linguistic turn, no longer serves as a unitary category designating a lived social experience, definitive social identity, or line of social demarcation. As Geoff Eley and Keith Nield argued some years ago in their article "Farewell to the Working Class?" this transformation does not mark the "death of class," but rather the passing of one particular meaning of class, "one particular *type* of class society."[4] Yet class remains present, even ubiquitous, in our historical vocabulary, as a descriptive term of social belonging (working class, middle class). Class, according to Joan Scott, has become "one way of naming, understanding, and organizing certain forms of social inequality,"[5] that coincides with or jostles against race, gender, nationality, ethnicity, and sexuality, depending upon the object of study. Our reluctance to dismiss class altogether may have more to do more with politics than with history, for even if class is no longer taken as a social fact, global capitalism continues to thrive and reproduce inequalities in new forms for which class remains an important

4. Geoff Eley and Keith Nield, "Farewell to the Working Class?" *International Labor and Working-Class History*, no. 57 (Spring 2000): 1–30. Respondents to this article include Stephen Kotkin, Judith Stein, Barbara Weinstein, Don Kalb, Frederick Cooper, and Joan W. Scott.

5. Joan W. Scott, "The 'Class' We Have Lost," *International Labor and Working-Class History*, no. 57 (Spring 2000): 69–75.

shorthand.[6] Furthermore, there is nothing universal about class, either its salience, its crisis, or its recasting. Because the political and historical resonances of class clearly vary across regional, national, and colonial spaces, this exploration is meant to apply to the field of European, particularly German history, where class enjoyed an incomparable dominance, at least until the (North American) linguistic or (German) culturalist turn. Let us backtrack to see how gender history helped chart the path to this present moment.

For most of the 1960s and 1970s, even into the 1980s, histories of class were informed by disparate methodologies. It is fair to generalize that British and American histories of class, inspired by E. P. Thompson's definitive *The Making of the English Working Class* (1963), tended to be more culturalist than structuralist, in the sense of pursuing "the authentic voices and authentic experiences of working people" that underlay the metahistories of class formations and class conflicts.[7] In Germany, by contrast, studies of labor, industrialization, urbanization, and social movements drove the rise of social science history, the hallmark of which was the analysis of structures and processes of social transformation. The "authentic experiences" and everyday lives of German workers came to figure in German labor history mainly as an oppositional narrative of historians of everyday life (*Alltagshistoriker*), whose anthropologically informed critiques and conceptual innovations were widely heralded in the English-speaking academy, but were subject to scathing criticism and subsequent marginalization by mainstream German historians.[8]

6. Frederick Cooper makes this point elegantly in his response to Eley and Nield: "Farewell to the Category-Producing Class?" in *International Labor and Working-Class History*, no. 57 (Spring 2000): 60–68. Also see Barbara Weinstein's contribution, "Where Do New Ideas (about Class) Come From?" ibid., pp. 53–59.

7. See Lenard R. Berlanstein, ed., *Rethinking Labor History: Essays on Discourse and Class Analysis* (Urbana, Ill., 1993), especially the "introduction," p. 1.

8. For some of the early debates on *Alltagsgeschichte*, see Hans Medick, "'Missionäre im Ruderboot?' Ethnologische Erkenntnisweisen als Herausforderung an die Sozialgeschichte," *Geschichte und Gesellschaft* 10/3 (1984): 295–319 and the responses in the same issue by Jürgen Kocka, "Zurück zur Erzählung? Plädoyer für historische Argumentation," pp. 395–408; and Klaus Tenfelde, "Schwierigkeiten mit dem Alltag," pp. 376–94. Alf Lüdtke's essay "Organizational Order or *Eigensinn*? Workers' Privacy and Workers' Politics in Imperial Germany," in *Rites of Power: Symbolism, Ritual, and Politics since the Middle Ages*, ed. Sean Wilentz (Philadelphia, 1985), pp. 303–34, played an important role in the U.S. reception of *Alltagsgeschichte*. For incisive overviews see David F. Crew, "*Alltagsgeschichte*: A New Social History from Below?" *Central European History* 22/3 and 4 (September/December, 1989): 394–407; and Geoff Eley, "Labor History, Social History, *Alltagsgeschichte*: Experi-

It is safe to say that early labor history, whether structuralist or culturalist, seldom included women or tended to rely upon gendered prisms and paradigms that "highlighted their differences from men."[9] Yet I would contend that the attention to workers' cultures and collective actions, sociability and leisure, everyday negotiations and self-perceptions in English-language labor history of the 1960s and 1970s left more openings for a history of women than did the more structurally oriented German labor histories.[10] Proletarianization, for one, stood for a quintessentially male experience of industrialization, while work had "sexual" meanings and characteristics only for women. The separation of home and work, in turn, could figure as a dramatic rupture only because of presumptions about women's natural location in the home. One outcome of the history of women's work in the 1970s and early 1980s was the powerful evidence it delivered for "the centrality of sex as well as class to women workers' experiences" of workplace, neighborhood, and home.[11] Feminist history managed to force labor history to concede a place to sex next to class, but for long years the recognition of the importance of sex did not fundamentally change the meanings of class. Awkward schemata arose by which historians and theorists worked to fit women into existing models of class, suggested that women formed a separate or parallel class of their own, or concluded that sex presented an inherent obstacle to the formation of cohesive and conscious classes. Joan Kelly Gadol's formulation of a "doubled vision of society" in the late 1970s pointed the way toward a resolution of this theoretical impasse, postulating that sex and class were inextricably linked in shaping social identities of men and women and making clear that models, master narratives, and chronologies would require disruption and redefinition in order to account for this dynamic.[12]

Kelly's postulation of a doubled vision of society also marks the point at

---

ence, Culture, and the Politics of the Everyday—A New Direction for German Social History?" *Journal of Modern History* 61 (June 1989): 297–343.

9. Laura L. Frader and Sonya O. Rose, eds., *Gender and Class in Modern Europe* (Ithaca, N.Y., 1996), introduction, p. 4.

10. Here I recall my own participation as a graduate student in a transatlantic workshop, which Vernon Lidtke organized at Johns Hopkins in 1983, on comparative German and American workers' cultures, in which this very difference led to some heated discussion among the participants.

11. Frader and Rose, eds., *Gender and Class in Modern Europe*, p. 19.

12. Joan Kelly Gadol, "The Social Relation of the Sexes: Methodological Implications of Women's History," *Signs* 1/4 (1976): 809–23. Also see her essay collection *Women, History, and Theory: The Essays of Joan Kelly* (Chicago, 1984).

which the concept of gender came into currency in English-language historiography. Feminist scholarship of the next decade began to devote more attention to the ideologies, norms, and symbolic systems that shaped identities, social institutions, and relations between the sexes. By 1983, with the publication of the pioneering collection of essays *Sex and Class in Women's History*, the category of gender had come to denote the systematic ways in which sex differences cut through society and culture and conferred inequality upon women.[13] First sex, then gender, began to destabilize key terms like class, as some Anglo-Saxon feminists even sought to emancipate feminist history from class as "privileged signifier of social relations and their political representations."[14]

Class was thus at the heart of the wider epistemological crisis that began during the mid- to late 1980s in the social sciences, which over the next decade saw the gradual displacement of notions of socio-economic causality as scholarly interest was reoriented toward representations, languages, and ideologies.[15] Unitary subjects and social identities, including class, were undermined not only by the linguistic turn, but also, perhaps more powerfully, by the interventions of scholars of race and empire whose work made clear the inflection of class through race. At the same time real-life transformations of technologies, relations and locations of production, the feminization and visible racialization of European labor markets, and the collapse of socialist governments and ideologies in the late 1980s seemed to have eclipsed the vocabulary of class.[16] The combined effect of these transformations in social and scholarly arenas was the erosion of a catalogue of oppositional categories, notably structure-agency, materiality-culture, production-reproduction, and public-private, which had formed the conceptual foundation of labor history. The degree to which labor and class had a crucial place in the linguistic turn, and the extent to which feminist scholarship prepared the way for the fundamental rethink-

13. Judith L. Newton, Mary P. Ryan, and Judith R. Walkowitz, eds., *Sex and Class in Women's History* (London, 1983).

14. Sally Alexander, "Women, Class, and Sexual Differences in the 1830s and 1840s: Some Reflections on the Writing of a Feminist History," *History Workshop* 17 (1984): 125–54.

15. Kathleen Canning, "Feminist History after the Linguistic Turn: Historicizing Discourse and Experience," *Signs* 19/2 (Winter 1994): 368–404, republished as chapter 2 of this volume.

16. William H. Sewell, Jr., "Toward a Post-Materialist Rhetoric for Labor History," in *Rethinking Labor History*, ed. Berlanstein, p. 17; Eley and Nield, "Farewell to the Working Class?" p. 3.

ing of these keywords, has been overlooked in many of the retrospectives on this methodological turning point.[17]

German labor history, by contrast, remained quite impervious to this epistemological crisis surrounding labor and class, as orderly models of class formation, broken into stages and levels, remained intact.[18] The fact that women and gender could not be made to fit these models easily led to the conclusion that gender belonged to a category of "nonclass" distinctions, which included race, ethnicity, nationality, and religion.[19] One reason why the impetus to rethink key categories such as class was far weaker in Germany is that labor history was widely declared passé in the early 1990s, at least for the periods of the Kaiserreich, Weimar, and Nazi Germany. Labor history of the post–World War II period was still in its infancy at this time but has since had a significant presence in the newer studies of both the Federal Republic and the former German Democratic Republic.[20] Yet it is important to note that the turn from labor to other social formations, such as the *Bürgertum,* coincided, perhaps not by chance, with an unusually vital moment in the production of feminist labor history in Germany.[21] The practitioners of German labor history had already

17. Debates about the linguistic turn were already under way at this time among scholars of intellectual history. See, for example, John Toews, "Intellectual History after the Linguistic Turn: The Autonomy of Meaning and the Irreducibility of Experience," *American Historical Review* 92 (October 1987): 879–907. As I have argued in chapter 4 in this volume, labor was a central focus of Scott's *Gender and the Politics of History* (New York, 1988).

18. Kathleen Canning, "Gender and the Politics of Class Formation: Rethinking German Labor History," *American Historical Review* 97/3 (June 1992): 745–48.

19. On class and "nonclass" lines of distinction, see Jürgen Kocka's *Weder Stand noch Klasse: Unterschichten um 1800,* 2 vols. (Bonn, 1990), and *Arbeitsverhältnisse und Arbeiterexistenzen: Grundlagen der Klassenbildung im 19. Jahrhundert* (Bonn, 1990).

20. Two excellent examples include Christine von Oertzen, *Teilzeit und die Lust am Zuverdienen: Geschlechterpolitik und gesellschaftlicher Wandel in Westdeutschland, 1948–1969* (Göttingen, 1999); and Annegret Schüle, *"Die Spinne": Die Erfahrungsgeschichte weiblicher Industriearbeit im VEB Leipziger Baumwollspinnerei* (Leipzig, 2001).

21. See, for example, Karen Hagemann, *Frauenalltag und Männerpolitik: Alltagsleben und gesellschaftliches Handeln von Arbeiterfrauen in der Weimarer Republik* (Bonn, 1990); Marlene Ellerkamp, *Industriearbeit, Krankheit und Geschlecht* (Göttingen, 1991); Karin Hausen, ed., *Geschlechterhierarchie und Arbeitsteilung: Zur Geschichte ungleicher Erwerbschancen von Männern und Frauen* (Göttingen, 1993); Brigitte Kerchner, *Beruf und Geschlecht: Frauenberufsverbände in Deutschland 1848–1908* (Göttingen, 1992); Susanne Rouette, *Sozialpolitik als Geschlechterpolitik: Die Regulierung der Frauenarbeit nach dem Ersten Weltkrieg* (Frankfurt a. M., 1993); and Sabine Schmitt, *Der Arbeiterinnenschutz*

closed up shop, so to speak, and had already penned their synthetic volumes showcasing the field's accomplishments, before a critical mass of scholarship on women/gender and labor could be incorporated or mainstreamed, before its critical concepts could be interrogated or redefined.[22] Also noteworthy is the crucial role of crisis in prompting the renovation of concepts and methodologies. On a comparative note, this German turn away from labor toward other historical topics and social strata such as the *Bürgertum,* and the shift soon thereafter to cultural history, took place in the absence of an epistemological crisis such as took place in North America. By the end of the 1980s, then, labor history was widely viewed as in decline and the keyword of class had been dethroned on both sides of the Atlantic divide.

CITIZENSHIP BEYOND THE WELFARE STATE?

The breakdown of class as a unitary category coincided with world historical changes, such as the collapse of state socialism in the Soviet Union and eastern Europe, which imbued citizenship with a new relevance. Yet the process by which class was revised and expanded a decade or more ago has not generated a model for redefinitions of citizenship, which have been cast in rather different contexts—political, philosophical, and historical. Citizenship gained new currency as the concept of class became more porous and labor history less bounded, but this was far from a straightforward path. Citizenship emerged as a thematic within labor history as historians probed how state social policy shaped divisions of labor and gendered ideologies of work. In the German field the differential provisions of the welfare state—social insurance for fully employed male workers, protective labor laws for working women—form the historical foundation for the rights and claims of male and female citizens.[23] In

---

im deutschen Kaiserreich: Zur Konstruktion der schutzbedürftigen Arbeiterin (Stuttgart, 1995).

22. For additional Anglo-Saxon debates, see *What Next for Labor and Working-Class History?* special issue of *International Labor and Working-Class History,* no. 46 (Fall 1994). The synthetic volumes appeared in a series edited by Gerhard A. Ritter titled *Geschichte der Arbeiter und der Arbeiterbewegung in Deutschland seit dem Ende des 18. Jahrhundert;* they include in particular Kocka's two volumes, *Weder Stand noch Klasse* and *Arbeitsverhältnisse und Arbeiterexistenzen,* as well as Gerhard A. Ritter and Klaus Tenfelde, eds., *Arbeiter im deutschen Kaiserreich, 1871 bis 1914* (Bonn, 1992).

23. See, for example, the forum "Women, Work, and Citizenship," *International Labor and Working-Class History,* no. 52 (Fall 1997): 1–71. Contributors include Louise Tilly, Chiara Saraceno, Ann Shola Orloff, Roderick Phillips, and W. Robert Lee. On social in-

some historiographies, citizenship was more contingent and less embedded from its inception in the state. Most of the examples of a fluid boundary between class and citizenship stem from English-language historiography, while in the German case citizenship rights in the realm of the social often seemed to preclude their relevance for politics. The historiography on "negative integration" of the working-class implies, for example, that state welfare provisions were meant to preempt demands of German workers for political rights. German peculiarities—Bismarckian social policy, the discrepant suffrage policies of nation and province in imperial Germany, and the particular politics of German Social Democracy, including its formative phase as an "outlawed party," meant that class politics were seldom conducted in rhetorics of citizenship.[24] Thus, the rights of social citizenship seldom fueled claims for wider political participation.

These specificities of German history, along with the fact that "citizenship" translates only awkwardly into German (its meaning in English is captured neither by *Staatsangehörigkeit* nor by *Staatsbürgerschaft*) may explain the relative absence of the term in most German historiography. One of the most porous concepts in contemporary academic parlance, citizenship can be understood as a political status assigned to individuals by states, as a relation of belonging to specific communities, or as a set of social practices that define the relationships between peoples and states and among peoples within communities.[25] As a legal status bestowed upon a people by the state, citizenship is "bounded and

surance see Greg Eghigian, *Making Security Social: Disability, Insurance, and the Birth of the Social Entitlement State in Germany* (Ann Arbor, Mich., 2000). See also the excellent work on youth and the welfare state by Elizabeth Harvey, *The Politics of German Child Welfare from the Empire to the Federal Republic* (Cambridge, Mass., 1996); and Edward Ross Dickinson, *Youth and the Welfare State in Weimer Germany* (Oxford, 1993).

24. Vernon L. Lidtke, *The Outlawed Party: Social Democracy in Germany, 1878–1890* (Princeton, N.J., 1966). On suffrage, see Thomas Kühne, *Dreiklassenwahlrecht und Wahlkultur in Preußen 1867–1914* (Düsseldorf, 1994), and Anderson, *Practicing Democracy*.

25. See Christoph Conrad and Jürgen Kocka, eds., *Staatsbürgerschaft in Europa: Historische Erfahrungen und aktuelle Debatten* (Hamburg, 2001), especially the introduction, pp. 9–26; Bryan S. Turner, "Contemporary Problems in the Theory of Citizenship," in *Citizenship and Social Theory*, ed. Turner (London, 1993), pp. 2–3; Bryan S. Turner and Peter Hamilton, eds., *Citizenship: Critical Concepts* (London, 1994); and Geoff Andrews, ed., *Citizenship* (London, 1991). On the dual nature of citizenship as a status and a practice, see Ruth Lister, "Citizenship: Towards a Feminist Synthesis," in *Citizenship: Pushing the Boundaries*, ed. Pnina Werbner and Nira Yuval-Davis, special issue of *Feminist Review* 57 (1997): 29–33.

exclusive," demarcating territories and borders: "Every state claims to be the state of, and for, a particular, bounded citizenry, usually conceived as a nation," posits Rogers Brubaker in the preface to his *Citizenship and Nationhood in France and Germany.*[26] *Staatsangehörigkeit,* that is, the status of belonging to a territorially defined state or national formation, has received considerable attention in German historiography since the publication of Brubaker's book. Citizenship in the sense of *Staatsangehörigkeit* had a spatial dimension as well, in that the place of permanent residence conferred citizenship, so elaborate sets of rules applied to those emigrating and immigrating across the boundaries of the various German states.[27] The legal framework of this variation of citizenship changed very little with national unification, as citizenship remained localized in specific German states. Only with the passage of the 1913 citizenship law did the principle of citizenship as a "community of descent" became primary, thus facilitating what Brubaker terms an "ethnicization of citizenship." At the height of German imperial desire and competition, then, citizenship law prescribed the closing of national borders to (Polish and Jewish) immigration from the east and opened the way for émigrés and German minorities living in the eastern borderlands to reclaim lost citizenship status.[28]

26. Rogers Brubaker, *Citizenship and Nationhood in France and Germany* (Cambridge, Mass., 1992), p. x.

27. For histories of *Staatsangehörigkeit* in Germany, see Andreas K. Fahrmeir, "Nineteenth-Century German Citizenships: A Reconsideration," *Historical Journal* 40/3 (1997): 721–52, and his *Citizens and Aliens: Foreigners and the Law in Britain and the German States, 1789–1870* (New York, 2000). Also see Dieter Gosewinkel, *Einbürgern und Ausschließen: Die Nationalisierung der Staatsangehörigkeit vom Deutschen Bund bis zur Bundesrepublik Deutschland* (Göttingen, 2001); and Wolfgang J. Mommsen, "Nationalität im Zeichen offensiver Weltpolitik: Das Reichs- und Staatsangehörigkeitsgesetz des Deutschen Reiches vom 22. Juni 1913," in *Nation und Gesellschaft in Deutschland: Historische Essays,* ed. Manfred Hettling and Paul Nolte (Munich, 1998), pp. 128–41.

28. Brubaker, *Citizenship and Nationhood,* pp. 114–15. Also see Brubaker's essay "Homeland Nationalism in Weimar Germany and 'Weimar Russia,'" in Brubaker, *Nationalism Reframed: Nationhood and the National Question in the New Europe* (Cambridge, 1996), pp. 107–47. Brubaker's schema has been criticized on a number of fronts. See, for example, Lora Wildenthal, "Race, Gender, and Citizenship in the German Colonial Empire," in *Tensions of Empire: Colonial Cultures in a Bourgeois World,* ed. Frederick Cooper and Ann L. Stoler (Berkeley, Calif., 1997); and more recently Dieter Gosewinkel's "Citizenship in Germany and France at the Turn of the Twentieth Century: Some New Observations on an Old Comparison," in *Citizenship and National Identity in Twentieth-Century Germany,* ed. Geoff Eley and Jan Palmowski (Stanford, Calif., forthcoming 2006).

While studies of *Staatsangehörigkeit* have at least been revitalized by the new cultural study of nationalism and nation formation, *Staatsbürgerschaft* has scarcely been creatively rethought. In fact, it has remained a far more static, juridically fixed, and generally unproblematized notion than either civil society or public sphere in the historiography of nineteenth- and twentieth-century Germany. While the dual concepts of *Staatsangehörigkeit* and *Staatsbürgerschaft* provide the indisputable starting points for the study of German citizenships, their very confinement to the realms of law and state has inhibited exploration of the experiential, subjective level of citizenship that has informed Anglo-Saxon study of colonial, cultural, or sexual citizenships.[29] Recent attention to suffrage and the practices of voting in imperial Germany has circled around but not explicitly addressed the issue of participatory citizenship.[30] In modern German history, then, citizenship has most frequently been studied in its guise as *social citizenship* in the contest of the welfare state.

Although social citizenship has been the most visible citizenship in German history, it represents only one rubric of citizenship rights, if we take T. H. Marshall's typology of modern Western citizenship as a grid for this discussion.[31] Marshall's schema, which charts the progressive development of citizenship rights in Western societies, has served more as a point of departure for studies of citizenship than as an actual paradigm. Following its trajectory, white men first became citizens with civil rights in the eighteenth century (in the sense of individual rights within the state and civil society); then they gained the rights of political citizenship (suffrage, representation, participation in the exercise of political power) in the mid- to late nineteenth century; and, third, they acquired expanded rights of social citizenship—state protection and provision

---

29. Among others see Gershon Safir, ed., *The Citizenship Debates: A Reader* (Minneapolis, 1998); Aihwa Ong, "Cultural Citizenship as Subject Making: Immigrants Negotiate Racial and Cultural Boundaries in the United States," in *Race, Identity, and Citizenship: A Reader*, ed. Rodolfo D. Torres et al. (Oxford, 1999); Aihwa Ong, *Flexible Citizenship: The Cultural Logics of Transnationality* (Durham, N.C., 1999); Evelyn Nakano Glenn, *Unequal Freedoms: How Race and Gender Shaped American Citizenship and Labor* (Cambridge, Mass., 2004); Mae Ngai, *Impossible Subjects: Illegal Aliens and the Making of American Politics* (Princeton, N.J., 2003); Elizabeth Thompson, *Colonial Citizens: Republican Rights, Paternal Privilege, and Gender in French Syria and Lebanon* (New York, 2000); and David T. Evans, *Sexual Citizenship: The Material Construction of Sexualities* (London, 1993).

30. Anderson, *Practicing Democracy;* and Kühne, *Dreiklassenwahlrecht.*

31. See, for example, the discussion of Marshall's schema in Turner, "Contemporary Problems in the Theory of Citizenship," pp. 6–9.

of the basic means of social reproduction—with the rise of welfare states in the twentieth century.[32] This evolutionary model has come under frequent, even relentless critique by scholars of gender, race, empires, and ethnicities who have emphasized the impossibility of fitting the citizenship struggles of minorities, women, or colonized peoples into these progressive stages.[33]

A second point about social citizenship is that its imbrication in the welfare state has meant the implicit or explicit presence of family and women in its histories. It has thus been understood from the outset in more gendered terms than, say, class or the labor movement, which enjoyed a long life before studies of women and gender began to question their terms. In fact, citizenship has been a key concept in feminist theory, if not history, for the last quarter-century. Certainly Catharine MacKinnon's writings on women and the state, Jean Bethke Elshtain's *Public Man, Private Woman,* and Carole Pateman's analysis of *The Sexual Contract,* in theorizing the purported "public-private" divide, laid the critical groundwork for theorizing women's citizenship in the 1980s. A second round of theorizing about gender and citizenship involving Nancy Fraser, Iris Marion Young, Seyla Benhabib, and Chantal Mouffe took place in the context of debates about the public sphere, democracy, and difference.[34] Feminist scholars have also had a leading role in conceptualizing global transformations in terms of their implications for the citizenship rights of women and minorities.[35]

32. T. H. Marshall, "Citizenship and Social Class," in *Citizenship and Social Class,* ed. T. H. Marshall and Tom Bottomore (London, 1992). Also see Sylvia Walby, "Is Citizenship Gendered?" *Sociology* 28/2 (May 1994): 379–95.

33. See, for example, Linda Gordon, ed., *Women, the State, and Welfare* (Madison, Wis., 1990), introduction, p. 18; Ruth Lister, *Citizenship: Feminist Perspectives* (New York, 1997); and Ong, "Cultural Citizenship," p. 263.

34. Catharine MacKinnon, *Toward a Feminist Theory of the State* (Cambridge, 1989); Jean Bethke Elshtain, *Public Man, Private Woman* (Princeton, N.J., 1981); Carole Pateman, *The Sexual Contract* (Stanford, Calif., 1988); Nancy Fraser, "Rethinking the Public Sphere: A Contribution to the Critique of Actually Existing Democracy," in *Habermas and the Public Sphere,* ed. Craig Calhoun (Cambridge, Mass., 1992), and "Sex, Lies, and the Public Sphere: Reflections on the Confirmation of Clarence Thomas," in *Feminism, the Public and the Private,* ed. Joan Landes (Oxford, 1998); Iris Marion Young, "Polity and Group Difference: A Critique of the Ideal of Universal Citizenship," in *The Citizenship Debates: A Reader,* ed. Gershon Shafir (Minneapolis, 1998); and Chantal Mouffe, "Feminism, Citizenship, and Radical Democratic Politics," in *Feminists Theorize the Political,* ed. Judith Butler and Joan W. Scott (New York, 1992).

35. Sonya O. Rose and I made this point in our essay "Gender, Citizenship, and Subjec-

Citizenship garnered increasing attention in feminist history only in the last decade, after the linguistic turn was well under way. Indeed, the critical interventions of feminist theorists on the subject of citizenship have remained notably separate from feminist *historical* study of citizenship, certainly in German history.[36] Nor has the previous critical engagement of feminist theorists and historians with the concept of class appeared to lay the groundwork for a similarly critical approach to citizenship.[37] In fact, social citizenship constituted a quasi-feminized realm of research into maternalism, social work, and welfare policies. Collections of essays like Seth Koven and Sonya Michel's *Mothers of a New World*, Gisela Bock and Pat Thane's *Maternity and Gender Policies*, and Linda Gordon's *Women, the State and Welfare* defined this inquiry, offering convincing comparative analysis of the divergent patterns of relations among and between gender, welfare-state formation, ideologies of motherhood, and social citizenship across different national settings.[38] These studies have illustrated the importance of gender in sparking mobilizations of the public in the milieu of "the social," delivering convincing evidence that pressure from the public sphere, including women's social reform organizations, shaped and informed the formation and practices of welfare states. Specific to German history were critical questions about this relationship for Weimar Germany, where German women were offered a wider range of social citizenship rights, even the opportunity to participate in governance, within the expanded welfare state.[39]

---

tivity: Some Historical and Theoretical Considerations," in *Gender, Citizenships, and Subjectivities*, ed. Kathleen Canning and Sonya O. Rose (London, 2002), p. 1.

36. An important and exemplary exception comprises some of the articles in Calhoun, *Habermas and the Public Sphere*, most notably those by Mary P. Ryan and Geoff Eley.

37. See, for example, the scholarly controversy in the forum "Women, Work and Citizenship," *International Labor and Working-Class History*, no. 52 (Fall 1997): 1–71.

38. Seth Koven and Sonya Michel, eds., *Mothers of a New World: Maternalist Politics and the Origins of Welfare States* (New York, 1993), especially "Introduction: 'Mother Worlds.'" Also see Gisela Bock and Pat Thane, eds., *Maternity and Gender Policies:. Women and the Rise of the European Welfare State* (London, 1991); Gordon, *Women, the State, and Welfare*, especially the introductory essay on "The New Feminist Scholarship on the Welfare State"; Susan Pedersen, *Family, Dependence, and the Origins of the Welfare State: Britain and France, 1914–1945* (Cambridge, 1993); Theda Skocpol, *Protecting Soldiers and Mothers: The Political Origins of Social Policy in the United States* (Cambridge, 1992); and Ulla Wikander, Alice Kessler-Harris, and Jane Lewis, eds., *Protecting Women: Labor Legislation in Europe, the United States, and Australia, 1880–1920* (Urbana, Ill., 1995).

39. See, for example, the forum with articles by Geoff Eley and Atina Grossmann, Christiane Eifert, Young-sun Hong, and Susanne Rouette in *Central European History* 30/1

Yet widening the scope of social citizenship in the Weimar Republic, argues the historian Young-sun Hong, came with a price: the "repoliticization" of gender and family and the explicit depoliticization and bureaucratization of the bourgeois women's movement that had envisioned and staffed the founding institutions of welfare before and during the First World War.[40]

Social citizenship represents a vital field of feminist historical inquiry in the German field, not least because it was a variation of citizenship that women *actually possessed,* by contrast with the civic and political citizenship they strove to achieve before 1918 and were forced to defend after the founding of Weimar democracy. Interestingly, studies of the campaigns of bourgeois and Social Democratic women for suffrage rights, and of their mobilizations on behalf of civic equality during the revision of the Civil Code in the late 1890s, have seldom been cast in terms of campaigns for *citizenship,* even if this is a fair characterization of their goals.[41] Perhaps the absence of the concept of citizenship in this historiography reflects the ambivalence of the bourgeois women's movement itself toward political citizenship, which led many of its activists to eschew suffrage or civil rights in favor of the rights and duties of maternalist social citizenship. Certainly these older studies of German women's suffrage campaigns, often linked to analyses of the limitations of women's participatory rights by the Prussian law of association, deliver important evidence of how female activists envisioned political citizenship. Yet modernizationist trajectories have cast these turning points—the repeal of the Prussian law in 1908 and the

(1997): 1–75; Christiane Eifert, *Frauenpolitik und Wohlfahrtspflege: Zur Geschichte der sozialdemokratischen "Arbeiterwohlfahrt"* (Frankfurt a. M., 1993); and David F. Crew, *Germans on Welfare: From Weimar to Hitler* (Oxford, 1998).

40. Young-sun Hong, "The Contradictions of Modernization in the German Welfare State: Gender and the Politics of Welfare Reform in First World War Germany," *Social History* 17 (1992): 251–70. Also see her pathbreaking book, *Welfare, Modernity, and the Weimar State, 1919–1933* (Princeton, N.J. 1998).

41. Richard J. Evans, *The Feminist Movement in Germany, 1894–1933* (London, 1976); Barbara Greven-Aschoff, *Die bürgerliche Frauenbewegung in Deutschland 1894–1933* (Göttingen, 1981); Ute Frevert, *Women in German History: From Bourgeois Emancipation to Sexual Liberation,* trans. Stuart McKinnon-Evans (Oxford, 1989); and Ute Gerhard, *Unerhört: Die Geschichte der deutschen Frauenbewegung* (Reinbek, 1990). Other important older studies include Christel Wickert, *Unsere Erwählten: Sozialdemokratische Frauen im Deutschen Reichstag und im Preußischen Landtag 1919 bis 1933,* 2 vols. (Göttingen, 1986); and Helen Boak, "Women in Weimar Germany: The 'Frauenfrage' and the Female Vote," in *Social Change and Political Development in the Weimar Republic,* ed. Richard Bessel and E. J. Feuchtwanger (London, 1981), pp. 155–73.

granting of women's suffrage in 1918—as short-lived gains that were ultimately overwhelmed by tenacious reassertions of patriarchal power in their aftermath.

Feminist scholarship on social citizenship has been abundant and impressive, but it also seems to have implicitly accepted the gendered boundaries that divided male and female realms of citizenship and distinguished civic and political from social citizenship.[42] It is thus important to investigate the work a term like social citizenship has *not* performed and to pursue the questions it has inhibited or left unanswered. For example, studies of social citizenship have been constrained and caught up in the equality/difference debate, which by now represents a spinning of the wheels of feminist history in the sand. The exploration of social citizenship as the site of women's most meaningful citizenship rights has had the effect of leading to neglect or suppression of the fact that social citizenship has often constituted a de facto "secondary citizenship," reserved for those deprived of political and civil rights.[43] A relational approach to these differential citizenships explicates how, for example, the counterpart to the "feminization of protective labor legislation"—a crucial facet of late nineteenth century social citizenship in Germany—was the "extreme masculinization of political identities."[44]

Advancing the study of citizenship beyond the realm of the welfare state requires thinking beyond some of our own most familiar categories. The critiques by feminist social theorists of the concept of citizenship form one starting point; innovative scholarship from adjacent disciplines, particularly cultural studies, offers another. The most recent feminist theory on citizenship has embraced the dualities, contingencies, and contradictions it encompasses, rendering it "a site of intense struggle," both theoretical and political.[45] The

42. Seth Koven and Sonya Michel, "Gender and the Origins of the Welfare State," *Radical History Review* 43 (1989): 112–19.

43. Geoff Eley and Atina Grossmann pose useful questions about the "connections and overlaps between social and political citizenship" in their essay "Maternalism and Citizenship in Weimar Germany: The Gendered Politics of Welfare," *Central European History* 30/1 (1997): 72. Chantal Mouffe makes a similar point in her critique of Jean Elshtain and Carole Pateman's views of liberal citizenship. See Mouffe, "Feminism and Radical Politics," pp. 374–75.

44. Teresa Kulawik, *Wohlfahrtsstaat und Mutterschaft: Schweden und Deutschland 1870–1912* (Frankfurt a. M., 1999), introduction.

45. Werbner and Yuval-Davis, *Citizenship*. See especially "Introduction: Women and the New Discourse of Citizenship," p. 2. See also Erna Appelt, ed., *Citizenship*, special issue of the Austrian journal *L'Homme: Zeitschrift für feministische Geschichtswissenschaft* 10/1 (1999).

British sociologist Ruth Lister's conception of citizenship as *both* status *and* practice (rather than *either* status *or* practice) underlines the distinction between the legally prescribed and the subjectively lived realms of citizenship, and cites the complex situation of those contemporary women who possess legal citizenship status but who are unable to "fulfill the full potential of that status" by practicing or acting as citizens because of the constraints of caregiving and child-rearing.[46] The American historian Nancy Cott has postulated a similarly fluid notion of women's citizenship in the United States as "not a definitive either/or proposal—you are or you are not—but a compromisable one" that is consistent with the status/practice spectrum Lister proposes.[47]

The sociologists Pnina Werbner and Nira Yuval-Davis define citizenship as a relationship "inflected by identity, social positioning, cultural assumptions, institutional practices, and a sense of belonging." A multidimensional discursive framework, in their rendering, citizenship consists of the languages, rhetorics, and formal categories of claims-making that are accessed and deployed not only by those who are endowed with formal citizenship rights, but also by those excluded from them. The emphasis I place here on claims-making posits an intentional link between the experiential and discursive dimensions of citizenship in order to understand the ways in which they diverged from or were dissonant with one another.[48] The discrepancies between legal prescriptions of citizenship and the historical meanings or experiences of citizenship (or its absence) reveal the importance of the intervening and acting subject in historicizing citizenship. Lauren Berlant's conception of citizenship as a means of viewing the self as public, as "an important definitional frame for the ways people see themselves as public, when they do," implies that citizenship is one of "an ensemble of subject positions."[49] Yet this formulation is not as flexible, porous, or impossible to historicize as it may seem. In proposing an

46. Werbner and Yuval-Davis, "Introduction: Women and the New Discourse of Citizenship," p. 4.

47. Nancy Cott, "Marriage and Women's Citizenship in the United States, 1830–1934," *American Historical Review* 103/5 (December 1998): 1442. For an innovative and important discussion of women's citizenship that works creatively with Cott's suggestions, see Maureen Healy, "Becoming Austrian: Women, the State, and Citizenship in World War I," *Central European History* 35/1 (2002): 1–35.

48. For a fuller discussion of this point, see Canning and Rose, "Gender, Citizenship, and Subjectivity," pp. 1–17.

49. Lauren Berlant, *The Queen of America Goes to Washington City: Essays on Sex and Citizenship* (Durham, N.C., 1997), p. 10; see also Mouffe, "Feminism and Radical Politics," pp. 372–73.

understanding of citizenship as subjectivity, my intention is not to minimize the importance of the realms of law or the policies of states in designating the margins of inclusion/exclusion or in defining the formal rights and obligations of citizens, active or passive. My main preoccupation here is rather the meanings historical actors assigned to the prescriptions and delineations of citizenship as they became subjects in their encounters with citizenship laws, rhetorics, and practices. I understand the process of becoming subjects as an inherently meditative one that considers both the power of law and citizenship discourse and the interventions and interpretations of those who encounter, embrace, or contest them. This approach also presumes that the realms of state and law are a crucial but not singular framework for discursive citizenships, underscoring the importance of the realms of popular culture, consumption, media, and visual arts in defining the parameters and promise of citizenship.[50] Moreover, it necessitates a more careful consideration of the historicity of citizenship. This might mean, for example, differentiating between moments in history when, as Chantal Mouffe has noted, citizenship is "just one identity among others," and those moments when it is "the dominant identity that overrides all others," when it operates as the "articulating principle that affects the different subject positions of the social agent."[51]

This interpretive framework seems pertinent as well for the years after the First World War when republicans, socialists and Catholics fashioned a democracy and new visions of citizenship for women from the standpoints of their disparate traditions. For a time in the history of the Weimar Republic citizenship may have had the capacity to cohere the social identities and affinities that were broken down by the devastation of war and the collapse of the nation. The women who became citizens in the aftermath of the First World War wielded a recognizable language of claims we might call "citizenship" to articulate a "plurality of specific allegiances."[52] At the outset of the republic the advances in political citizenship (suffrage) and the anchoring of social citizenship rights (as mothers and workers) in the welfare state stood in stark contrast to the loss of the right to work and the reinforcement of women's civil subordination to men in the realms of marriage and family. The consideration of this subjective, experiential dimension of citizenship allows for the possibility that political cit-

50. Nick Mansfield, *Subjectivity: Theories of the Self from Freud to Haraway* (New York, 2000), pp. 3–4.

51. Mouffe, "Feminism, Citizenship, and Radical Democratic Politics," pp. 372, 378–79.

52. For a more general discussion of this topic, see Canning and Rose, "Gender, Citizenship, and Subjectivity."

izenship *was* meaningful for women after 1918, even as they seemed to vanish from the arenas of formal politics by 1920. Attention to both the discursive and experiential moments of this period of upheaval provides an analytical framework for grasping both the apparent "return to normal" of gender and family relations during the 1920s and the deeper-going ruptures in families and gender ideologies that occurred in the course of defeat, demobilization, revolution, and the founding of democracy. The gulf between the official pronunciations of citizenship and women's own interpretation or experience of its contradictory catalogue of rights and duties designates the very space for their citizenship claims in the early republic. Even after it had come under assault, not least as the symbol of women's "emancipation," citizenship formed the one common ground for the articulation of distinct subject positions of women in Weimar—as demobilized workers, widowed mothers, newly-endowed voters, consumers of popular culture, and sexually independent negotiators of their private lives. Citizenship not only became a site at which these contradictions were named and contested, but also a new language for the assertion of women's claims upon the state and fellow citizens that resonated across the realms of party politics and welfare state, into the increasingly politicized domains of sexuality, reproduction, and consumption.

CONCLUSION

In this essay I have suggested that the unmooring of class and citizenship from their so-called structural confines is a productive process, one that may be a necessary outcome, even the fulfillment of the project of gender history, as Joan Kelly outlined it some twenty-five years ago. In the case of neither concept—class nor citizenship—have I proposed that these terms be wholly detached from economies, geographies, laws, or state power. Instead such structural formations constitute an important starting point, beyond which histories of meaning and experience remain crucial. Rather than using historical concepts like class or citizenship to seek the kind of closure necessitated by the project of mainstreaming, I propose that a more open-ended understanding of these terms will contribute considerably more to revising or fundamentally recasting historical narratives and chronologies. Instead of seeking to map the analysis of gender and citizenship onto the political history of Weimar, we might consider the ways in which the acquisition of citizenship rights thoroughly altered the perception of women by others in the newly expanded public of Weimar, as well as transformed women's own views and displays of themselves in this arena. A reconsideration of citizenship in these terms may render 1918 a different kind of turning point for gender history than for political history.

While my own work pursues a quite specific historicization of the meanings, experiences, and subject positions of citizenship, it appears that a decade of intensive interdisciplinary conversation, encounter, and debate has, in fact, changed the meaning of historicization itself, at least as understood in the American academy. So the goal of historicizing citizenship for the Weimar period may not be exhausted by a close reading of constitutions and laws, but might productively turn to analysis of women's novels, visual arts, theater, and popular culture in order to gain a fuller sense of the arenas in which citizenship rights were made meaningful or engendered conflict. This point brings me, in closing, to the question of mainstreaming, which seems as if it can only flourish as a stringently *disciplinary* exercise. The more interdisciplinary our queries and research projects become, the less likely they are to fit back into the narratives, chronologies, and concepts that were once conceived without the history of women or gender. The outlook for a more generalized mainstreaming of gender history remains uncertain. While it is surely desirable that the kind of metanarratives represented by textbooks or synthetic histories of "high politics" incorporate scholarship on gender, this in itself does little to redefine key concepts or chronological frameworks. Yet it is worth considering whether the drive for acceptance into the mainstream might inhibit the potential of gender history to reconceive more fundamentally the terms and temporalities upon which prevalent historical narratives have relied. In fact, a premature embrace of the project of mainstreaming gender history may obscure from view the ways in which feminist history has accepted the limitations of its most productive terms, including, for purposes of this discussion, social citizenship.

CHAPTER 8 § CLAIMING CITIZENSHIP §
SUFFRAGE & SUBJECTIVITY IN GERMANY
AFTER THE FIRST WORLD WAR

In the aftermath of war and revolution in Germany citizenship emerged as a new political imaginary. In this essay I analyze through the lens of citizenship a prolonged moment of crisis and transformation in German history, in which a war was lost, an empire crumbled, and a revolution ushered in a decade of experiments in democracy, unprecedented in German history. I am concerned here with the rhetorical and legal processes that framed, instituted, and embodied women's citizenship during the early years of the Weimar Republic. I argue here that gender inflected both the symbolics and the subjectivities of this citizenship, which was imagined, desired, and claimed in new ways, particularly by those who lacked some of the most fundamental citizenship rights, such as the right to vote. The catastrophic conditions on the German home front and the deepening divide between militarized state and civic public opened spaces for citizenship claims that would have been unthinkable before the war. This work of envisioning and articulating new claims of citizenship began in the popular protests against expansionist war aims, and for peace, bread, and suffrage during the last two years of the war. Its fulfillment became the task of the revolutionary councils and assemblies that took power in November 1918, and then the foremost aim of the first democratically elected parliament in February 1919.

Charting the place of citizenship in the history of the transformations of war, revolution, and the founding of democracy requires, first, a brief assessment of definitions and historical placements of citizenship. I am particularly interested in the arenas beyond the juridical and formal prescriptions of citizenship and the ways in which citizenship was cast, redefined, and contested at different points in these years of crisis and change. One key question is how citizenship acquired a distinctive voice among several political languages and social identities that were jostled about during the ruptures in relations of state and society,

This essay took shape in privileged moments shared with the "Weimar group" at the University of Michigan. It is part of a larger research project: "Embodied Citizenships: Gender and the Crisis of the Nation in Germany, 1916–1930."

women and men. If a vocabulary of class characterized the political language of protest during the Kaiserreich, how did spaces for citizenship, both linguistic and social, coalesce amidst the collapse of the Kaiserreich and the German defeat? I hypothesize that the years from 1917 through 1924 marked the period of citizenship's greatest resonance and promise, at least for the period of German history from 1848 through 1933. It might be said that citizenship became a new object of desire, a social identity Germans *wanted* or aspired to fulfill, while class and perhaps *Stand* were social identities Germans already *had,* to paraphrase the social theorist David Held.[1] In this essay I am particularly interested in those languages of citizenship spoken by and about women, in how old and new ideologies of sexual difference inflected the ascription of citizenship rights to men and women, who were always implicitly embodied. This essay also pursues a historiographical point: namely to explore the reasons why the turning point in German history at which women became citizens has served as such a dead end in German gender history. Finally, the questions I pursue here about gender and citizenship should shed light on the resonances citizenship gained and lost in the course of founding and then defending democracy.

CITIZENSHIP IN GERMAN HISTORY

The specificities of German history, along with the fact that citizenship translates only awkwardly into German—its meaning in English is captured neither by *Staatsangehörigkeit* nor by *Staatsbürgerschaft*—may explain the relative absence of the term in most German historiography. Certainly the publication of Rogers Brubaker's *Citizenship and Nationhood in France and Germany* revitalized the interest in the history of German citizenships during the last decade. Yet his study has generated new interest mainly in ethnicity and citizenship law, fostering studies of citizenship in terms of its national boundedness rather than as a realm of experience or a form of social identity within civil societies.[2] In this study I understand citizenship as something transcending the

1. David Held, "Between State and Civil Society: Citizenship," in *Citizenship,* ed. Geoff Andrews (London, 1991), pp. 19–25.

2. Rogers Brubaker, *Citizenship and Nationhood in France and Germany* (Cambridge, Mass., 1992). Also see Andreas K. Fahrmeir, "Nineteenth-Century German Citizenships: A Reconsideration," *Historical Journal* 40/3 (1997): 721–52; and Dieter Gosewinkel, "Die Staatsangehörigkeit als Institution des Nationalstaats: Zur Entstehung des Reichs- und Staatsangehörigkeitsgesetzes vom 1913," in *Offene Staatlichkeit: Festschrift für Ernst-Wolfgang Böckenförde zum 65. Geburtstag,* ed. Rolf Grawert et al. (Berlin, 1995), pp. 359–78; and the monographs by Dieter Gosewinkel, *Einbürgern und Ausschließen: Die Nationalisierung*

terms of its containment within the strictures of formal, territorially grounded rights of *Staatsangehörigkeit* or *Staatsbürgerschaft,* which functioned not least to delineate national boundaries and national belonging. Taking citizenship in Bryan Turner's terms as a "set of practices—juridical, political, economic and cultural—which define a person or through which persons define themselves as competent members of society," helps to make a bit more concrete a term that is more contingent and indeterminate than class.[3] As a trope in a wide range of national or ethnic conflicts, in struggles for the rights of women, minorities, workers, or welfare recipients, contemporary uses of the term citizenship invoke distinct, even discordant catalogues of rights and claims. Narratives of citizenship can serve at times to buttress the integrative practices of states, while in other instances they might enunciate claims of those seeking access to citizenship rights.

If citizenship is understood more broadly as a political language that seeks to define the terms of political participation *within* nations and civil societies, the rhetorics or "narrative identities" of citizenship are also relevant for those on the margins of these formal rights.[4] So, for example, citizenship might have figured as a subversive discourse in Catholic and Social Democratic milieus, both in the wake of persecution by the Bismarckian state, and later as the cornerstone of the campaigns of workers' parties in Wilhelmine Prussia to repeal the three-class suffrage system, which remained a contentious issue during most of the Kaiserreich and gained new momentum on the eve of the First World War. German women's movements, both middle-class and Social Democratic, also asserted citizenship claims in their prewar campaigns for women's suffrage and their mobilizations against the German civil code at the turn of

der Staatsangehörigkeit vom Deutschen Bund bis zur Bundesrepublik Deutschland (Göttingen, 2001), and Andreas Fahrmeir, *Citizens and Aliens: Foreigners and the Law in Britain and the German States, 1789–1870* (New York, 2000).

3. Bryan Turner, "Contemporary Problems in the Theory of Citizenship," in *Citizenship and Social Theory,* ed. Turner (London, 1993).

4. The sociologist Margaret Somers analyzes citizenship as a "narrative identity," constituted "by a person's temporally and spatially-variable 'place' in culturally constructed stories . . . comprised of rules, practices, institutions, and the multiple lots of family, nation, or economic life." See Margaret R. Somers and Gloria D. Gibson, "Reclaiming the Epistemological 'Other': Narrative and the Social Constitution of Identity," in *From Persons to Nations: The Social Constitution of Identities,* ed. Craig Calhoun (London, 1994), p. 33. Also see Somers, "Citizenship and the Place of the Public Sphere: Law, Community, and Political Culture in the Transition to Democracy," *American Sociological Review* 58/5 (October 1993): 587–620.

the century, which granted husbands extensive and explicitly patriarchal rights over their wives in matters of child-rearing, employment, and property.[5]

Yet citizenship has had only a marginal place in the historiography of the Weimar Republic. It has also been relatively insignificant in the by now abundant historiography on women and gender in Weimar Germany, on family and welfare policies, on labor and/or body politics.[6] The absence of citizenship in feminist histories of Weimar Germany is symptomatic of the demarcations between gender and the study of politics, by which gender is relevant mainly in those realms remote from high politics, such as popular culture, consumption, or sexual reform. Eve Rosenhaft's contention of the mid-1990s that "it is still possible to write [or rewrite] a general account of German history that excludes women" has been reaffirmed in recent years as innovative new studies of Weimar political culture have remained impervious to the impulses of gender.[7] The persistence of these boundaries suggests a puzzling unevenness in the dissemination and reception of gender history across the more specialized thematic fields of modern German history. While scholarship on women and gender during the long nineteenth century has significantly revised understandings of civil society and public sphere, social discipline and social welfare, working-class and middle-class formation, German colonialism and imperialism, gender scholarship on the high-stakes histories of Weimar and Nazi Germany has not fundamentally challenged categories or temporalities. Few would dispute that contests over masculinities and femininities form a crucial part of the post–World War I "crisis of bourgeois Europe," but the work of making these links to the postwar period remains incomplete.[8] My exploration of the links between citizenship and gender, citizenship and bodies, is meant to challenge these historiographical borders and boundaries.

The citizenship that has been most salient in historical study of the demo-

5. Ann Taylor Allen, *Feminism and Motherhood in Germany, 1800–1914* (New Brunswick, N.J., 1991), pp. 48, 136–38; Dr. jur. Anna Schulz, "Frauenforderungen an die Gesetzgebung," in *Mutterschaft: Ein Sammelwerk für die Probleme des Weibes als Mutter,* ed. Adele Schreiber (Munich, 1912), pp. 672–87.

6. See Renate Bridenthal, Atina Grossmann, and Marion Kaplan, eds., *When Biology Became Destiny: Women in Weimar and Nazi Germany* (New York, 1984), which had a field-defining role.

7. Eve Rosenhaft, "Women, Gender, and the Limits of Political History," in *Elections, Mass Politics, and Social Change in Modern Germany: New Perspectives,* ed. James Retallack and Larry E. Jones (Cambridge, 1992), p. 148.

8. Charles Maier, *Recasting Bourgeois Europe: Stabilization in France, Germany, and Italy in the Decade after World War I* (Princeton, N.J., 1975).

cratic experiment of Weimar is typically encompassed in the rights of social citizenship located within the Weimar welfare state.[9] Despite the revolutionary proclamation of new suffrage laws in 1918 and the drafting of the first democratic constitution in 1919, the power of nationalism in the "spirit of August 1914," its resurgence in response to the "dictated peace" of Versailles, and the protracted civil strife between Socialists and Communists in the early years of the republic leave little space for citizenship in the narratives of Weimar. The Nazi *Volksgemeinschaft* usurped and racialized the civic spaces in which citizenship flourished during Weimar, so that the notions of claims and rights central to the practice of citizenship were silenced during the Third Reich. In modern German history, then, citizenship has been relevant mainly for the study of the Federal Republic since 1949, when democracy was sustained over a longer historical time span, and consumption, along with the successful postwar welfare state, expanded the terms of citizenship.

THE SPECIFICITY OF CITIZENSHIPS: THE WAR AND ITS AFTERMATH

In considering citizenship a critically important term for the period after the First World War, I understand it as a new legal or social identity, which became fixed in political culture as it was embraced by those who had long desired expanded legal and political rights. Moreover, in the volatile political culture of Weimar Germany citizenship also meant the emergence of new subjectivities within "a new language of democratic participation."[10] The citizenship I am interested in here is thus quite specific—it was born of not only of war, but also of defeat, not only of revolution, but also of the disintegration of the militarized state from within, torn apart by its relentless drive to both fulfill expansive war aims and provide for the population on the home front. This citizenship took shape precisely in the protests of women and youths on the home front against these contradictory goals of German total war. Second, this is citizenship in a different temporality than Brubaker's *jus sanguinis:* it was in-

9. Exceptions here include Julia Sneeringer, *Winning Women's Votes: Propaganda and Politics in Weimar Germany* (Chapel Hill, N.C., 2002), which examines the constructions of female citizenship by party political propaganda; and Heidemarie Lauterer's *Parlamentarierinnen in Deutschland 1918/19–1949* (Königstein, 2002).

10. Thomas Childers, "Languages of Liberalism: Liberal Political Discourse in the Weimar Republic," in *In Search of a Liberal Germany,* ed. Konrad Jarausch and Larry Eugene Jones (London, 1990), p. 326.

flected by struggles over rights and respectability in the last decades of the Kaiserreich, but its declaration in a moment of rupture suggests that it was not necessarily predetermined by earlier articulations of citizenship. In fact, no neat lines of continuity connect the prewar politics of class or *Stand* in the respective Social Democratic, Catholic, or liberal milieus, and the visions of citizenship that flourished in the streets and pubs and on the strike lines of the German home front during the war. The sudden inception of this citizenship, rather than its continuity or endurance over time, is of primary interest here. The citizenship of Weimar was not only defined in different temporal, but also in different spatial terms, as the borders of Germany were redrawn during the very years in which citizenship rights were written into law, so German citizenship of the interwar period was inscribed with loss of territory and longing for restitution of the borders of 1914.

Citizenship was a new juridical and legal status, first declared and then delimited at the highest levels of law and state, at a considerable distance from the realms in which it was imagined and fought over during the last years of the war. Citizenship on the German home front became a language in which new social groups mobilized and staked new claims upon the militarized state—the women of lesser means who feature in Belinda Davis's book, for example, or the war widows and veterans, who bore in their respective ways the "bitter wounds" of war.[11] Robert Whalen's estimate that some six million Germans belonged to the groups of war wounded, widows, or children orphaned by war, points to the potential for new mobilizations and new claims upon an expanded welfare state.[12] That newly congealed social groups held the state accountable for the human costs of the war and articulated claims to this effect (bread, suffrage, peace without annexations) meant that the political language of citizenship was distinct in important respects from prewar languages of class.

11. Belinda Davis, *Home Fires Burning: Food, Politics, and Everyday Life in World War I Berlin* (Chapel Hill, N.C., 2000); Robert Weldon Whalen, *Bitter Wounds: German Victims of the Great War, 1914–1939* (Ithaca, N.Y., 1984); Deborah Cohen, *The War Come Home: Disabled Veterans in Britain and Germany, 1914–1939* (Berkeley, Calif., 2001); and Sabine Kienitz, *Beschädigte Helden: Kriegsinvalide Körper in der Kultur. Deutschland 1914–1923* (Paderborn, forthcoming 2006). Also see Sabine Kienitz, "'Fleischgewordenes Elend': Kriegsinvalidität und Körperbilder als Teil einer Erfahrungsgeschichte des Ersten Weltkrieges," in *Die Erfahrung des Krieges: Erfahrungsgeschichtliche Perspektiven von der französischen Revolution bis zum zweiten Weltkrieg,* ed. Nikolaus Buschmann and Horst Carl (Paderborn, 2001). For a British comparison, see Joanna Bourke, *Dismembering the Male: Men's Bodies, Britain and the Great War* (Chicago, 1996).

12. Whalen, *Bitter Wounds,* p. 16.

Citizenship, at the time of its greatest resonance in the early years of the republic prior to the crisis of inflation in 1923–24, was a broader and more porous social identity than class, which remained anchored to notions of labor and skill that were themselves transformed by the militarization of the economy during the war. Indeed, four years of total war had cut a swath through an imagined working-class cohesion, dividing producers from consumers, soldiers from striking workers, veterans from war widows, those with work from the unemployed, those bearing the scars of war from those who survived unscathed. The declaration of citizenship rights—new suffrage rights for women over age twenty and the abolition of the Prussian three-class suffrage system—thus convened new communities, national and civic, in November 1918. The turning point I am most interested in here was the naming of women as members of this new civil community that was just taking shape. The conferral of suffrage upon women on November 12, 1918, stunned many suffrage advocates, not least because both civilian and military authorities had categorically rejected women's demands for the vote up to the very eve of the outbreak of revolution on November 9, notably a petition for suffrage submitted jointly by Social Democratic and liberal women's groups to the Reichstag on November 8.[13]

The proclamation of the democratic rights of citizenship for women, and the subsequent debates about its implications, drew unprecedented numbers of women into the realms of formal and informal politics between 1918 and 1921.[14] The particular power of citizenship rights to propel unprecedented levels of political participation and identification must be understood in the context of the profound reconfiguration of political space which took place as the militarized state disintegrated and the work of imagining and enacting the new "Reich as republic" began. Yet the desires and disorientations of this turbulent time at the end of the war, in which nearly every aspect of daily life and high politics was uncertain, and women's suffrage came as a shock, has not been marked as a turning point by either mainstream German history or more notably, by German gender history. Given the drama of the moment—the col-

13. International Institute of Social History, Amsterdam: Rat der Volksbeauftragten, Protokolle, 14.12.1918–31.12.1918. See especially "Aufruf des Rates der Volksbeauftragten an das deutsche Volk vom 12. November 1918." Also see Susanne Miller, ed., *Quellen zur Geschichte des Parlamentarismus und der politischen Parteien*, vol. 6: *Die Regierung der Volksbeauftragten 1918/19* (Düsseldorf, 1969).

14. The female membership of the Social Democratic Textile Workers' Union, for example, increased 450 percent (by 260,000 members) between December 1918 and the late fall of 1920. Some 90 percent of German women voters cast their ballots in the first democratic election in January 1919.

lapse of the imperial state, the convening of workers' and soldiers' councils, the negotiation of a major compromise between capital and labor (the Stinnes-Legien agreement of 1918) and the impending bargaining for peace—suffrage appears only fleetingly in the dramaturgy of Weimar history, as if it had no lasting implications for the doomed republic.

From this perspective the study of citizenship and gender can help us rethink the beginnings of Weimar as marking a rupture in the history of both German civil society and German gender relations. In the timeline of German history, in which continuities tend to overwhelm moments of abrupt change, the collapse of democracy usually overshadows the work of imagining and envisioning that shaped its founding. As the framing moment of Weimar, the November Revolution, for example, seldom escapes the categorizations of failure, stillbirth, or betrayal. Similarly, the tangled work of the *Nationalversammlung* in 1919, which mapped new relationships among the civic, family, and state in the name of democracy, and reconstituted the state to make space for the claims of a newly empowered citizenry, has most often been viewed in terms of its fateful compromises, such as Article 48, which Weimar's last stewards implemented to rule by emergency decree. Peter Fritzsche's provocative piece, "Did Weimar Fail?" highlights a new view of Weimar as "strikingly open-ended," "remarkably contingent," and shaped by "eclectic experimentalism" rather than circumscribed by failure.[15] Yet these terms refer mainly to the cultural promise of Weimar in the years of stabilization, rather than to the hopes of political democracy, which were undercut by the trauma of defeat and the unfinished revolution. While some historians have successfully captured the utopian desires and the topsy-turvy sense of displacement unleashed by the republic's recurrent crises, the revolutionary beginnings of Weimar are more often interpreted in terms of the drive to "return to normalcy," to restabilize relations of people and state, women and men.[16]

15. Peter Fritzsche, "Did Weimar Fail?" *Journal of Modern History* 68/3 (September 1996): 632–33.

16. Richard Bessel, *Germany after the First World War* (Oxford, 1993); and Elizabeth Domansky, "Militarization and Reproduction in World War I Germany," in *Society, Culture, and State in Germany, 1870–1930,* ed. Geoff Eley (Ann Arbor, Mich., 1996), pp. 427–63. Both Bessel and Domansky view much of the early history of Weimar in terms of the desire for a "return for normalcy," even if from very different standpoints. Martin Geyer's *Verkehrte Welt: Revolution, Inflation und Moderne* (Munich, 1998) is a notable exception to this viewpoint. For the period of the inflation, see Bernd Widdig, *Culture and Inflation in Weimar Germany* (Berkeley, Calif., 2001). On the conflicted visions of modernity in Weimar, see Mary Nolan, *Visions of Modernity: American Business and Modernization of Germany* (New York, 1994).

The widespread perception that gender ideologies and relations were broken in the immediate aftermath of war placed gender at the heart of the project of redefining and reinstating this so-called normalcy. Not only do the vast numbers of war dead and injured—the changing landscapes of masculinities, and their impingement on the visual and political culture of Weimar—suggest this, but also the transformations of self, state, and society experienced by women in the realms of work, family, and civic sphere during and after the war. Ute Daniel and Belinda Davis, among others, have drawn attention to the significance of these transformations during the last years of the war, but stopped short of analyzing their implications for the founding of the republic.[17] Thus the end of the war is usually disconnected from the framing moments of Weimar, while the shock of defeat, which lived on in the guise of the Versailles Treaty, serves as the definitive force in galvanizing sentiment against the republic throughout the 1920s.[18]

Another challenge of this study is explaining the relationship between the transformation of the gender order that took place during the war and the citizenship rights that were proclaimed after defeat. Did the wide-scale social protest of women on the home front, including their demands for suffrage, constitute a symptom of new (wartime) fissures in the gender order, or did their demands only become thinkable because the gender order was already breaking apart? Did the bestowal of citizenship rights on women in the heat of revolution attest to the recognition of profound differences in the ways men and women experienced or responded to the crisis of total war? Or was the instantiation of women's citizenship rights in the Weimar constitution the first step towards the restoration of a familiar set of gender hierarchies and ideologies? Most German historians would probably accept that some kind of deep change in the relations between the sexes took place during the war as women performed new kinds of labor, gained unprecedented authority in the family

17. Davis, *Home Fires Burning*, and Ute Daniel, *The War from Within: German Working-Class Women in the First World War*, trans. Margaret Ries (Oxford, 1997).

18. Benjamin Ziemann's recent essays on the memory of the war and on masculinity and militarism mark an important exception here. See, for example, his "'Gedanken eines Reichsbannermannes auf Grund von Erlebnissen und Erfahrungen': Politische Kultur, Flaggensymbolik und Kriegserinnerung in Schmalkalden 1926. Dokumentation," *Zeitschrift des Vereins für Thüringische Geschichte* 53 (1999): 201–32; and the useful essay collection edited by Benjamin Ziemann and Bernd Ulrich, *Krieg im Frieden: Die umkämpfte Erinnerung an den Ersten Weltkrieg: Quellen und Dokumente* (Frankfurt, 1997). Also see Ziemann, *Front und Heimat: Ländliche Kriegserfahrungen im südlichen Bayern 1914–23* (Essen, 1997).

and new visibility in public, and learned self-reliance in arenas as diverse as sex, scavenging, rationing, and mourning. But they would scarcely agree about how the profoundly new experiences of men in the trenches and women on the home front influenced the *postwar* gender order.

The debates about whether these changes represented a longer-term (modernizationist) emancipation or one merely "on loan," as Ute Daniel phrased it, were settled some years ago. The war experience of German women has not held up as emancipatory, not least because conditions on the home front and the loss of male family members were so disastrous as to belie most notions of emancipation.[19] In historical analyses of the aftermath of the First World War, German women's acquisition of new citizenship rights is usually viewed as scarcely resonating into the political culture of Weimar. Feminist historians have also regarded the declaration of formal citizenship rights for women as relatively insignificant, given the massive pressures in other realms of political life towards a restoration of prewar gender roles and ideologies. Women turned away from formal politics as early as 1919, so the argument goes, conceiving of their contribution to the new democracy in terms of "feminine and motherly expertise," practiced most commonly in the expanding realms of the welfare state. The fact that the numbers of women voters and of women elected to public office declined after an intense spurt of politicization between 1918 and 1920 has led many historians to conclude that the vote itself, as the centerpiece of citizenship, was without broader consequences for Weimar politics. In contrast to this view, I contend that the process of defining and delimiting the terms of female citizenship in the National Assembly of Weimar, and the new subjectivities it created, were formative of Weimar political culture, even if its outcome was not equal citizenship for women and men.

Even if more recent scholarship refrains from interpreting women's wartime experiences as emancipatory, a commonsense consensus prevails in much of the historiography that a restoration of gender roles and ideologies did take place after the war. The effects of women's suffrage and the election of women to Germany's first democratic parliament were soon reversed by the recurrent cycles of political turmoil and economic crisis that beset the republic from its founding through the crisis of 1923–24. As women gradually withdrew from the public sphere, traditional gender norms and roles were rapidly reinstated. According to one recent analysis: "Women's willing return to traditional gender roles was ultimately determined by their increased awareness of the limitations placed on their emancipation after the onset of the economic decline in

19. Daniel, *The War from Within*.

the mid 1920s that brought Weimar's intrinsically patriarchal structures to the fore."[20] In a similar vein, Ute Daniel has argued that "women's forms of spontaneous and unorganized collective action [found] no continuation beyond the world war." Although their sustained protests had a crucial role in dismantling the system of total war, Daniel views them as having no "observable, longer-term consequences for the forms of social relations and women's role in them" after the war because their subversive critique was intrinsic to the particular circumstances of Germany at war.[21] Feminist historians have thus conjured up patriarchal structures that were somehow inherent to German society—despite the dramatic transformations of masculinity and state in the course of the war—and that were quickly resuscitated in the years after the war. On the other hand, historians have drawn a line between the experiences and subjectivities of wartime and its aftermath, thus positing that women's participation in civil society and social protest diminished once the chief object of their discontent—the war itself—had ended. Women were thus able to return to their "natural" tasks of family and household, even if families and households were in no sense the same in 1918 as they had been in 1914.

This evocation of closure, of reversal, or a return to something preexistent soon after the end of the war raises interesting methodological questions about the different resonances of the categories of women and gender in historical analysis more generally and in the specific task of discerning the "observable consequences" of a moment of rupture like 1918–20. Confining our observations to the realms of formal politics and the question of women's quantitative participation might make it easy to conclude that women withdrew from or were driven out of public life, while following the lead of scholars in the visual arts and literature affords a rather different sense of the ways in which gender and the apparition of the "new woman" continued to preoccupy the public.[22]

20. Katharina von Ankum, ed., *Women in the Metropolis: Gender and Modernity in Weimar Culture* (Berkeley, Calif., 1997), p. 6.

21. Daniel, *The War from Within*, pp. 293–94.

22. Maria Tatar, *Lustmord: Sexual Murder in Weimar Germany* (Princeton, N.J., 1995); Brigid Doherty, "Figures of the Pseudorevolution," *October* 84 (Spring 1998), and "'We are all Neurasthenics!' or the Trauma of Dada Montage," *Critical Inquiry* 24/1 (Autumn 1997): 82–132; Dora Apel, "'Heroes' and 'Whores': The Politics of Gender in Weimar Antiwar Imagery," in *Art Bulletin* 79/3 (1997): 366–84; Patrice Petro, *Joyless Streets: Women and Melodramatic Representation in Weimar Germany* (Princeton, N.J., 1989); Kerstin Barndt, *Sentiment und Sachlichkeit: Der Roman der Neuen Frau in der Weimarer Republik* (Cologne, 2003); and Richard McCormick, *Gender and Sexuality in Weimar Modernity: Film, Literature, and "New Objectivity"* (New York, 2001).

The bitter struggles to reestablish familiar gender divisions and hierarchies form important threads of Weimar history, as state and social policy aimed to return men to intact families, to revitalize the family's reproductive function, to restrain and regulate sex, pleasure, birth control, and abortion. Both these positive and negative measures, and those aimed to contain women's participation in some of the newly significant publics—from cinema to consumption, parliaments to newly rationalized workplaces—formed part of a continuous project of restoring a broken patriarchy, one that required renewal and rejuvenation with each dramatic shift and turn of Weimar history. Examination of the arenas of contest over citizenship and gender suggests, however, that this rupture was not repaired in the course of the Weimar Republic and that gender relations never did quite go back to "normal" again. Forgoing the notion of this moment of closure at the end of the war might help explain, in part at least, the virulence of Nazi "family policies" that would later drive, uncompromisingly, to institute a revitalized and racialized patriarchy.

There is considerable historical evidence that the restoration of the gender order was indeed a primary project of Weimar democracy, and feminist historians have delivered much of it: the rapid implementation of the demobilization decrees in 1919, for example, literally stripped women both of their actual jobs and their right to work.[23] The Weimar constitution did institute political rights for women, but left restrictions on their civil rights in marriage and family in place, thus favoring protection of family and reproduction of nation over women's civil rights. Feminist studies of social work and welfare analyze the process by which female social reformers, who literally envisioned and staffed many branches of the Weimar welfare state, were kept out of the "male-dominated arena of social policy where so-called vital interests of state were being negotiated."[24] My aim is thus not to dispute these efforts to restore familiar gender ideologies and hierarchies, but to probe the ways in which the efforts remained incomplete, to challenge this sense of closure, and to explore the persistence of gender crisis into the later years of the Republic. Citizenship figures

23. Susanne Rouette, *Sozialpolitik als Geschlechterpolitik: Die Regulierung der Frauenarbeit nach dem Ersten Weltkrieg* (Frankfurt a. M., 1993).

24. Christiane Eifert, "Coming to Terms with the State: Maternalist Politics and the Development of the Welfare State in Germany," *Central European History* 30/1 (1997): 45–46. Also see the pathbreaking work of Young-sun Hong, "The Contradictions of Modernization in the German Welfare State: Gender and the Politics of Welfare Reform in First World War Germany," *Social History* 17 (1992): 251–70, and her *Welfare, Modernity, and the Weimar State, 1919–1933* (Princeton, N.J., 1998).

here, then, as one transformation—of women's legal status and subject position—that proved irreversible, at least until the Nazis seized power in 1933.

At first glance it appears that citizenship for women in Weimar Germany was confined to those rights which they "earned . . . in their role as mothers and house-workers," that is to a highly restricted kind of social citizenship.[25] Indeed, the power and pervasiveness of the German welfare state has meant that most explorations of women's citizenship in German history focus on precisely this arena, the only one in which female citizens were not only clients but also expert visionaries of social reform. In seeking to overcome the limitations of maternalist social citizenship, I probe women's entry into the "specifically political arena" in the last years of the war, during the revolution, and in the struggle for democracy. Following the lead of the feminist political theorist Anne Phillips, I consider that political arena one in which people transcend their "more private, localised interests and tackled what should be the community's common concerns."[26] An enormous archive of evidence exists on the manifold ways in which diverse and opposing groups of German women did precisely this during the years under study here, whether from nationalist, Catholic, liberal, or Social Democratic standpoints. Women experienced themselves becoming citizens as they entered debates on matters of indisputably "high" politics, from the consequences of Germany's defeat to the form and foundation of the new state.

FRAMING CITIZENSHIP

Much of the high drama of the Weimar Republic—its initial quest for legitimacy and its anguished struggle to survive—played out on the terrain of citizenship. Mass mobilizations on the home front around food shortages in 1916 spilled into protests against war and annexation and potent calls for full suffrage rights for women and male workers by 1917. This occurred in even more dramatic form by January 1918, when over one million workers threw off the last remnants of the *Burgfrieden* in their determined demands for peace without annexations and immediate suffrage reform. The strikes of 1917 and 1918, in which some half of the participants were women, mark a critical turning point in the relationship of women to state, one that is crucial to the history of the November Revolution and its immediate declaration of female

25. Hong, "Gender, Citizenship, and the Welfare State," p. 2.
26. Anne Phillips, "Citizenship and Feminist Theory," in *Citizenship*, ed. Andrews, pp. 76–88, esp. p. 79.

suffrage. Yet police and union reports reveal little about the demands, desires, and actions of female strikers in this volatile moment of transgressive citizenship.[27] We do know that women comprised a significant number of the strike participants and an oddly privileged segment therein, for the reprisals of the military state against striking workers took on highly gendered forms in 1917 and 1918. Male strikers, interpellated at this juncture as citizens by the militarized state, were stripped of their service exemptions and shipped off to the front or to military prisons, while female workers who figured in wartime discourses primarily as (embodied) mothers, war-wives or war-widows, were able to elude state sanctions. Indeed, already in the case of food protests in 1915–16, authorities had complained about the impossibility of effectively punishing female protesters, many whom were mothers with young children.[28] The participation of women, first in food protests in 1916 and 1917 and then in mass strikes, brought the governability of the cities into question and helped to dismantle military rule over civil society.

This moment of rupture was one in which the combined ordeals of women on the home front—hunger, cold, poverty, and sickness, next to fears of a prolonged annexationist war—galvanized new and vehement claims of women upon the militarized state. So, for example, war widows—some 533,000 by 1918—were propelled into a wholly new relationship with the state through their struggle for pensions.[29] Police reports attest to the "rage that drove women into public protest," along with the "urge for solidarity that widows felt with their 'sisters,'" and their growing consciousness of themselves "as a distinct group."[30] This distinction sharpened once the veterans returned home and widows recognized "how different [their] situation was from those families which had a husband and a father. . . ." Widows became bitterly aware of the inadequacy of their pensions and were forced to compete with men in the labor market. The words of one war widow describe the process by which this group of women embraced a new social identity of citizenship: "the war educated us, and now we begin to place our demands before the state."[31] As their

27. Bundesarchiv, Akten der Reichskanzlei (R43, nr. 22a): Streiks 20. November 1918–14. März 1919; Reichskanzlei Akte 548, Filme 12025/12026: Stammakten, 11 Handel & Gewerbe, Nr. 15 (9), Ausstände: Streikbewegung 10. Januar 1918–9. März 1918.

28. Daniel, *The War from Within*, pp. 235, 247, 292.

29. Whalen, *Bitter Wounds*, pp. 95–99.

30. Ibid., pp. 76–78, 109.

31. Martha Karnoss, "Organisation der Kriegerwitwen," *Reichsbund*, May 20, 1932, p. 106, as cited in Whalen, *Bitter Wounds*. I am in the process of completing my own evaluation of this valuable periodical.

experiences of war propelled them into open confrontation with the state, war victims' pensions would come to represent both a material and symbolic atonement of the state for the violence of war.[32]

While Kaiser Wilhelm II publicly conceded the need for suffrage reform in the spring of 1918, the military leaders Hindenburg and Ludendorff vowed that the pending German victory would prevent a dreaded turn towards democracy. At the same time, those who drove Germany onward in a fruitless war identified the protesters on the home front, whose demands for full and participatory citizenship rights were raised with increasing defiance in early 1918, as the very force responsible for the depletion of the German war effort. By implication at least, citizenship, its visionaries and advocates, once cast as outside of the nation, would also figure in the formulation of the infamous "stab in the back" legend.[33] The first and perhaps most consequential outcome of the November Revolution was the immediate extension of suffrage rights to women and the abolition of the Prussian three-class franchise system. The subsequent two-year period through the end of 1920 saw the mass political mobilization of new citizens, including women, as voters, members, even delegates of the new and reconstituted political parties and reinvigorated trade unions. The new political language of republican democracy permeated and recast the prewar languages of class and estate. This extraordinary moment of politicization coincided with the national humiliation of the Versailles Treaty, with the physical and political remapping of the German nation.

In the early days of November 1918 the war effort collapsed and the Kaiserreich crumbled amidst sailors' mutinies and the sprouting of workers' and soldiers' councils from Kiel to Munich. One of the first acts of the revolutionary Council of People's Representatives, which formed between November 9 and 12, was the proclamation of republican citizenship, including women's suffrage. The issues of women's suffrage and class-restricted suffrage in Prussia had been

32. Whalen describes an eerie demonstration of war victims in Berlin on December 22, 1918, with trucks of paraplegics leading the way, followed by the blind, guided by their dogs, and lastly, the widows and orphans, in *Bitter Wounds*, p. 124.

33. Gerald D. Feldman, *Army, Industry, and Labor in Germany, 1914–1918* (1966; Providence, R.I., 1992), pp. 337–41, 446–50; also see Geyer, *Verkehrte Welt*, pp. 48, 100. Feldman does not make a direct connection between calls for suffrage and the formulation of the *Dolchstoßlegende*; his analysis of the strikes of April 1917 and January 1918 suggests, however, that this connection is plausible. Geyer makes a somewhat different point about the implication of women in the "stab in the back" theory: he cites the views of the psychologist Emil Kraepelin on the failure of women to endure the long-term deprivation of war which "morally destabilized the home front" and left it unable to hold out.

acutely present in the last two years of the war, in the demands of the mass strikes and the maneuverings of the military authorities in response to civil unrest. Just ten days before this announcement, on November 2, 1918, women's associations of all political hues had called for an audience with the new chancellor, Prince Max von Baden, regarding the question of suffrage rights for women. On November 8, the day before the revolution, the Social Democrats proposed the formal adoption in the Reichstag of equal suffrage rights for women and men, but it was easily defeated by a coalition of bourgeois parties.[34] Given the refusal of civilian and military authorities, up to the very eve of the revolution, to grant women's demands for suffrage rights, middle-class feminists were stunned when suffrage rights "fell overnight from a storm cloud"[35] on November 12, making "women into citizens with a dash of a pen, with a mere announcement in the daily paper."[36]

A new electoral law went into effect on November 30, 1918, and the date for the election of the National Assembly was set for January 19, sparking a month of extraordinary political agitation and mobilization. In the words of one witness:

> Voters were showered with leaflets and every fence, empty shop windows, and street corners were covered with fliers. Political passions of all varieties were reawakened and party meetings were not the only place they were expressed. Groups assembled on streets and corners, where speeches were held and especially the Spartacus group was everywhere disseminating its viewpoints. Each party, each movement had the instinctive feeling that it was engaged in the final struggle, that this was a decisive moment in the future of German politics and of the German state.[37]

34. Eduard Heilfron, ed., *Die deutsche Nationalversammlung im Jahre 1919 [und 1920] in ihrer Arbeit für den Aufbau des neuen deutschen Volksstaates,* vol. 1 (Berlin, 1919–20), 12. Sitzung, 20. February 1919, p. 159.

35. Marie Bunsen, "Wir Wählerinnen," *Vossische Zeitung* 624/286 (Ausgabe A), December 6, 1918, p. 2.

36. Helene Lange Archiv, Berlin, Aktenzeichen 1062, Dr. Agnes von Harnack, "*Die Frauen und das Wahlrecht,*" in *Wahlhandbuch für Männer und Frauen zur Nationalversammlung,* ed. Deutscher Staatsbürgerinnen-Verband e.V. (Berlin, n.d). This pamphlet was likely published in the months between the proclamation of women's suffrage and the January 1919 elections to the National Assembly.

37. Wilhelm Ziegler, *Die deutsche Nationalversammlung 1919/1920 und ihr Verfassungswerk* (Berlin, 1932), pp. 29–30. Ziegler cites Ferdinand Runkel, *Die deutsche Revolution.*

When the National Assembly convened in Weimar in the early winter of 1919, it was clear to those who gathered that the real work of constituting women's citizenship had only begun.[38] The forty-one women deputies comprised 9.7 percent of the assembly and included eighteen Social Democrats and three Independent Social Democrats.[39] Between the months of February and August 1919 legislators deliberated over the draft of the constitution, which Hugo Preuß had authored in early January, including three articles that framed and delimited citizenship for women in the new republic. The formal ascription of citizenship rights to women in 1918–19 involved a complex of rights and duties, including: (1) active and passive suffrage for women over the age of twenty; (2) protection of the state for marriage and family and constriction of civil rights for women within these "private" institutions; (3) rights to social protection and social benefits within a refurbished welfare state, defined by men and staffed by women.

It is possible here to offer only a brief overview of the debates surrounding these articles. The centerpiece of the second section of the constitution, *Grundrechte und Grundpflichten der Deutschen* (Fundamental Rights and Fundamental Duties of German [Citizens]), Part I, "The Individual," was Article 109, which declared: "All Germans are equal before the law. Men and women have *in principle* the same rights and duties as citizens."[40] The controversy that ensued over this formulation highlighted the deep apprehension among legisla-

38. Ibid., p. 30. Not surprisingly, the Communist Party refused to participate in the election, which delegated and authorized the parties of Weimar to undertake the formation of the Republic: the Social Democratic Party (163 delegates); the Democratic Party (75 delegates) and the Catholic Center Party (90 delegates), held 338 of 421 seats in the Assembly, while the Independent Social Democrats (USPD) had 22 seats and the nationalist party (DNVP) 42 seats.

39. Christel Wickert, *Unsere Erwählten: Sozialdemokratische Frauen im Deutschen Reichstag und im Preußischen Landtag 1919 bis 1933*, vol. 2 (Göttingen, 1986), p. 64.

40. Article 109 reads: "Alle Deutsche sind vor dem Gesetz gleich. Männer und Frauen haben *grundsätzlich* dieselben staatsbürgerlichen Rechte und Pflichten" (emphasis added). It is worth noting that Hugo Preuß's draft of Part I, "Die Einzelperson," reads "Alle Deutschen sind vor dem Gesetze gleichberechtigt," without mention of women or men. See *Die Verfassung des Deutschen Reichs vom 11. August 1919* (Stuttgart, n.d.), pp. 36–37. For a comparison of Preuß's draft and the final version of the constitution, see Ziegler, *Die deutsche Nationalversammlung*. Also see the new collection edited by the Deutsche Nationalstiftung, *Weimar und die deutsche Verfassung: Geschichte und Aktualität von 1919* (Stuttgart 1999).

tors about the promised equality for women. According to this article, the realization of women's citizenship rights "would depend upon the natural limits" ("naturbedingte Grenzen") of sexual difference.[41] The qualifying phrase "in principle" also left open the possibility that local, provincial, or state laws might interpret the law differently, as its critics pointed out.[42] Women in the Independent and Majority Social Democratic delegations led the campaign to strike the term "grundsätzlich" ("in principle") from the constitution. The Independent Socialist Luise Zietz asserted passionately that women and men bore equal obligations in relation to the state: women's "Erfüllung der Mutterpflicht" (fulfillment of their duties as mothers) was comparable to the sacrifices soldiers made for their fatherland. Zietz contended creatively with the legacy of prewar maternalist feminism when she responded to an apparent barrage of arguments explicating the fundamental differences between the sexes. Equality, she observed somewhat ironically, did not mean that women would have to become soldiers, a prospect that was unlikely in any case given the foreseeable abolition of general conscription in Germany under the terms of the peace agreement. Gleichwertigkeit (equality), she noted sardonically, had not yet come to mean Gleichartigkeit (the same physical essence), particularly with respect to the distinct bodily capacities (körperliche Veranlagung) of men and women.[43] Although Zietz's remarks quite explicitly located citizenship in the real and imagined bodies of soldiers and mothers, the differences between them were not to stand in the way of full civil and political equality. Luise Zietz's much contested amendment to strike the word grundsätzlich from Article 109 was defeated on July 15, 1919, by a vote of 149 to 119.[44]

Under the rubric of Gemeinschaftsleben ("Community Life") Article 119 placed marriage, "the foundation of family life and the reproduction (Vermehrung) of the nation" under the special protection of the constitution. In an intriguing contrast to Article 109, marriage was to be "based on the equality (Gleichberechtigung) of both sexes. Reading these two articles in relation to one another reveals the willingness of legislators to locate full equality of the sexes in the private sphere of marriage, an irony that did not escape many of the crit-

41. Willibalt Apelt, Geschichte der Weimarer Verfassung (Munich, 1946), pp. 306–7.

42. Fritz Stier-Stomlo, "Artikel 109: Gleichheit vor dem Gesetz," in Die Grundrechte und Grundpflichten der Reichsverfassung: Kommentar zum zweiten Teil der Reichsverfassung, ed. Hans-Carl Nipperdey, 3 vols. (Berlin, 1929–30), 2:201–3.

43. For the debates on Article 109, see Heilfron, Die Nationalversammlung, vol. 6, 54. Sitzung, p. 3653; 57. Sitzung, Dienstag, den 15. Juli 1919, pp. 3812–26.

44. Ibid., pp. 3812–13.

ics of Article 109.[45] Nor could they overlook the disjuncture between this remarkable declaration of equality and the *Bürgerliches Gesetzbuch* (civil code), which favored husbands' dominance over wives with respect to property, employment, and child-rearing. In response feminist legislators moved to overturn the civil code, claiming that the two realms of law—constitutional and civil—were inherently contradictory. At the heart of this debate was an issue female activists had pursued in the late 1890s when the women's movement had mobilized to protest the enactment of the new civil code, specifically its denial of women's right to serve as guardians of their minor children. "Depriving a woman of the right to represent or protect her children is the bitterest injustice that one can do to a mother who has borne her children at the risk of her own life," argued Luise Zietz, once again aligning the sacrifices of motherhood with those of soldiers as citizens in service of the nation.[46] On the grounds that "men and women have the same rights," the Social Democrats proposed an amendment that would revise the civil code in light of the "new constitutional equality between the sexes," which was rejected on July 15, 1919, in a relatively close vote of 144 to 128.[47] The National Assembly contemplated not only the relations within families, but the meanings of the German family for the state, a question that weighed heavily on those who sought to repair the wounded nation in the aftermath of war. While Article 119 affirmed equality of the sexes as the foundation of the family in its first paragraph, in the next it spelled out the responsibility of state and communes for the "Reinerhaltung," "Gesundung," and "soziale Förderung der Familie" (for the preservation of the family's purity, health, and social advancement).[48]

The political meanings of the so-called *Frauenüberschuß* (excess of women) also resonated in the debates about women's new constitutional rights. Among these two million "excess" women were thousands of unmarried mothers who were likely to remain single given the high loss of life among men of their co-

45. Ziegler, *Die deutsche Nationalversammlung*, pp. 329–30. This article is in Part II of the "Basic Rights and Basic Duties of Germans."

46. Heilfron, *Die Nationalversammlung*, vol. 6, 54. Sitzung, Freitag, den 11. Juli 1919, p. 3653. For a discussion of this article, see "Die Frau im bürgerlichen Recht," *Gewerkschaftliche Frauenzeitung* 4/2 (January 29, 1919); Gertrud Lodahl, "Die Weimarer Verfassung und die Frauen," ibid., 4/17 (August 27, 1919); and Dr. jur. Anna Mayer, "Neue Rechte—Neue Pflichten," in *Die Frau in der Politik, Deutsche Stimmen*, no. 2 (January 18, 1920), suppl.

47. Heilfron, *Die Nationalversammlung*, 6:3825.

48. Dr. h.c. Alfred Wieruszowski, "Artikel 119: Ehe, Familie, Mutterschaft," in Nipperdey, *Grundrechte und Grundpflichten*, pp. 72–79.

hort. Also at stake were the military benefits for tens of thousands of illegitimate children of soldiers, whose support was terminated by the state at the end of the war. Fitting the fate of single mothers and their children into the new notion of citizenship based in marriage and family proved a challenging task for the assembly.[49] The intention of Article 121, for example, to establish "the same conditions for physical, spiritual, and social development for both legitimate and illegitimate children"[50] contradicted rather obviously the emphasis on marriage as the "foundation of family life." Thus, feminist delegates' call for the full integration of illegitimate children in the legal entity of family with respect to inheritance and child support failed on the grounds that it would violate the sanctity of marriage, which was at the heart of Article 119.[51] The constitution's extension of state protection of and provision for motherhood, articulated in Article 119, did not draw an explicit distinction between married and unwed mothers. Yet a Social Democratic amendment proposing that unwed mothers be permitted to call themselves "Frau" in their dealings with state bureaucracies, went through a third reading only to be "swept under the table."[52] The quest for parity between married and unmarried mothers in their encounters with the state sought to equalize the terms of new citizenship rights not only for women "of lesser means," but also for those single mothers whose lovers or fiancés would not return from the war.[53] The designation "Frau" was meant to recognize the sacrifices of single women and single mothers for the fatherland and to lend them a new kind of democratic respectability as they became claimants of widows' pensions and clients of the new system of child and maternal welfare. In this debate, then, the full impact of the *Frauenüberschuß* was revealed—its social, demographic implications for Germany's future as well as its political consequences for the new republic. Ultimately, the Weimar constitution's reaffirmation of marriage and its delineation of the social and reproductive tasks of the family worked to stabilize a nation at a point of profound crisis. In qualifying women's rights as citizens (in Article 109), the new legislation bound women to families (Article 119) and called upon German women to place their bodies in the service of state and nation.[54]

49. Christian J. Klumker, "Artikel 121: Stellung der unehelichen Kinder," in Nipperdey, *Grundrechte und Grundpflichten*, 2:107–9.

50. Ziegler, *Die deutsche Nationalversammlung*, pp. 329–30.

51. Wieruszowski, "Artikel 119," pp. 79–80.

52. Lodahl, "Die Weimarer Verfassung und die Frauen."

53. On women "of lesser means," see Davis, *Home Fires Burning*.

54. See the interesting commentary on these points in Wieruszowski, "Artikel 119," pp. 75–78, 89.

Swirling through the sources I examined here is a sense that the real work of defining citizenship and making it meaningful had only just begun in 1918: "The break with those who held power until now does not bring our task to an end," noted one contributor to the journal *Die Frauenbewegung*. "Rather we are standing at the edge of something totally new which we must now create."[55] The density and richness of political vision and debate that fills the pages of journals such as *Die Staatsbürgerin, Die Frauenbewegung,* the *Zeitschrift für Frauenstimmrecht, Die Frau,* and *Die Frau im Staat,* of the Social Democratic organs *Die Gleichheit* and its successor paper, *Die Genossin,* and of other remarkable accounts like those from the floor of the *Nationalversammlung* as it crafted the constitution, make clear that citizenship became a new imaginary. This was not least because of the extraordinary engagement of women who, as acting subjects, both intervened in discourses and involved themselves in the realms of citizenship practices.[56] This evidence points to the enormous capacity of new citizenship rights to inspire women's serious and systematic reimaginings of the political. Of course, the feminist press—a wide range of political journals published weekly or monthly by different, even opposing women's organizations—had debated the terms of women's political participation in the decades before the war.[57] Yet 1918–19 marks a turning point, not least because the spaces for citizenship widened within every political milieu and party, and also because feminists were eager to experience citizenship, to prove themselves

55. Elisabeth von Rotten, "Ansprache bei der Kundgebung zum Rechtsfrieden," in *Die Frauenbewegung* 23/1918, p. 19.

56. Regine Deutsch, Die politische Tat der Frau: Aus der Nationalversammlung (Gotha, 1920); ed. Buchhandlung Vorwärts (SPD), *Frauenstimmen aus der Nationalversammlung: Beiträge der sozialdemokratischen Volksvertreterinnen zu den Zeitfragen* (Berlin, 1920); Camilla Jellinek, *Die Frau im neuen Deutschland* (Stuttgart, 1920). Selected articles include Alice Salomon, "Der Ausschuß zur Vorbereitung der Frauen für die Nationalversammlung," *Die Frauenfrage* 21 (1919); Marianne Weber, "Parlamentarische Arbeitsformen," *Die Frau* 26 (1919); "Republik-Demokratie-Nationalversammlung," *Zeitschrift für Frauenstimmrecht* (November 1918); Gertrud Bäumer, "Die deutsche Verfassung und die Frau," *Die Frau* 26 (1919), and "Die Frauen und die Nationalversammlung," *Die Frauenfrage* 21 (1919), pp. 3–4.

57. *Die Frauenfrage, Zentralblatt des Bundes deutscher Frauenvereine,* ed. Marie Stritt; *Die Frau,* "theoretical organ" of the Bund Deutscher Frauen, ed. Helene Lange und G. Bäumer; *Die Staatsbürgerin,* published by the Deutscher Verband für Frauenstimmrecht, ed. Adele Schreiber, and later by Marie Stritt; *Die Frauenbewegung: Organ für das politische Leben der Frau,* and supplement: *Zeitschrift für Frauenstimmrecht,* published by the Berliner Verein Frauenwohl, ed. Minna Cauer. The women's supplement of the Indepen-

as citizens, at a time when the state had to be rebuilt and the nation had come apart at the seams. Indeed some feminists, disavowing all responsibility for the disastrous war and defeat, defined themselves as citizens who were unencumbered by the past and thus better able to envision a wholly new future than men.[58]

The apparent facts that women did not achieve equality or that these explicitly political arenas would become sites of bitter and violent strife, that many of the most engaged women turned their attention from the political to the social or were forced to do so, does not lessen the significance of their input and experiences within those arenas. Just as the transformations of the war years lived on in subjectivities well past 1918, so did the new experiences of citizenship resonate in, but also beyond these very realms of the political where they took shape.

CONCLUSION: THE SUBJECTIVITY OF CITIZENSHIP IN WEIMAR GERMANY

The arenas of citizenship which were established amidst the refounding of nation and state become an important site at which Weimar politics contended with the ruptures in gender ideologies that occurred during the war. Read as an attempt to repair these fractures represented by defeat and revolution, the declaration of women's citizenship can be made to fit the modern narratives of closure that measure short-term gains or losses only to conclude that these moments of transformation had no longer-term consequences for gender, women, or politics during the Weimar Republic. An alternative view is that women's acquisition of citizenship rights opened possibilities for the emergence of new female subjectivities and self-representations, which at the very least made gender a site of continuous contention throughout the history of the republic. The gulf between the official articulations of citizenship and women's own interpretation or experience of this contradictory catalogue of rights and duties demarcates the very space in which new subject positions were formed in the early years of the Weimar Republic.

One preliminary conclusion of this study is, then, that the subject position

---

dent Social Democratic Party was entitled *Aus der Frauenbewegung, Frauenbeilage der Freiheit, Berliner Organ der USPD.*

58. Adele Schreiber, "Revolution und Frauenrecht," in *Frauen! Lernt Wählen! Revolution und Frauenwahlrecht* (Berlin, 1918), p. 9. Her formulation was "Wir treten unbelastet in die Politik."

FIGURE 3. *Marianne Brandt,* Es wird marschiert, *1928.*
Montage of newspaper and magazine photographs (50.2 × 65.5 cm.),
Militärhistorisches Museum der Bundeswehr, Dresden.

FIGURE 4. *Marianne Brandt*, Helfen Sie mit! (die Frauenbewegte), *1926.*
Photomontage (68.3 × 50.3 cm.), Kupferstichkabinett, Dresden.

of citizen marked an abrupt and significant change in the volatile landscape of gender in postwar Germany. The work of female activists in fashioning and defending their new rights represents a critical chapter in the delimitation of Weimar democracy, at the level of both political discourses and day-to-day practices. And it is worth noting that despite the array of social and political institutions that worked vigorously to reinstate familiar gender relations and norms throughout the republic, neither citizenship rights nor the subjectivities they produced were reversible. To what extent, then, did the discourses about the "new woman" represent unease and apprehension about women as citizens who, in this one sense at least, could not be reassigned to the private sphere? There are many suggestions that women intellectuals, artists, and novelists played with this very ambiguity in their disparate representations of "new women." The coolly critical gazes of the female figures in Marianne Brandt's photo-collages *Helfen Sie mit* and *Es wird marschiert* depict women observing skeptically or bemusedly dissonant scenes. In *Es wird marschiert* (Figure 3), armies assemble and march in disparate clothing and directions across the page, juxtaposed with a tranquil lake where boats float on the water surface, and with the unsettling image of a child bending over toy weapons. In *Helfen Sie mit* (Figure 4), a graveyard is adjacent to boaters rowing across clam waters, while in the upper half of the collage bombs explode, a man boxes, and volcanoes appear to erupt. In each the woman is the most prominent figure who oversees, and thus assembles, the collage of disparate events and people.[59]

Or we might consider the controversy surrounding Irmgard Keun's novel, *Gilgi: Eine von uns,* which the Social Democratic newspaper *Vorwärts* serialized in 1932. Gilgi, a single working girl who eschewed identifications with either her job or her class background, also refused the prospect of marrying the man she loved, choosing instead to bear and raise her child alone.[60] The debates about the fate of girls like Gilgi that took place in the pages of *Vorwärts* not only attest to the popularity of this ambiguous figure of the "new woman," but also delineated arenas of acceptable and dangerous citizenship for women in the late years of the republic.[61] The fact that *flâneuses,* who mastered "the art of

59. See Elizabeth Otto, "Figuring Gender: Photomontage and Cultural Critique in Germany's Weimar Republic" (Ph.D. diss., University of Michigan, 2003).

60. Irmgard Keun, *Gilgi: Eine von uns* (1932) is discussed in Barndt, *Sentiment und Sachlichkeit,* pp. 150–165; Anke Gleber, *The Art of Taking a Walk: Flânerie, Literature, and Film in Weimar Culture* (Princeton, N.J., 1999). According to Barndt, the novel appeared in forty-nine installments between August 24, 1932, and October 25, 1932.

61. The novel was so popular that *Vorwärts* called upon its readers to compose essays

taking a walk" in the urban spaces of Weimar, or the "little shop girls," who flocked to the movies, were at one and the same time new *citizens* seems worthy of critical reflection, with respect to both the history of women and the history of Weimar's modernity and viability as a site of new democratic publics.[62]

These examples suggest the importance of exploring the ways in which consumption, leisure, and mass culture complicated the terrain of citizenship, which came to involve new "notions of the self, of collective identity, and of entitlement associated with the diffusion of mass consumption."[63] So the new legal category of female citizenship might be conceived as forming a stage for the "new woman of the metropolis," whose newness was defined not least by an explicitly embodied representation of self. While the *flâneuse,* as a specific kind of "new woman," may seem inherently depoliticized and far removed from parliament or political parties, the attention this female figure garnered in the literature and culture of Weimar Germany reveals a deep apprehension not only about women in public, but more specifically about women in public who were now endowed with the rights of citizenship. Tracing the thread of *gender* through the republic, rather than measuring the losses or gains of *women,* makes clear that the project of healing these ruptures lived on until the republic's collapse.

---

for prize competitions on "Scenes from Life and Career" with particular consideration of the "The Crisis of Our Time." Barndt, *Sentiment und Sachlichkeit,* pp. 150–52.

62. See, for example, Siegfried Kracauer, "Die kleinen Ladenmädchen gehen ins Kino," in *Das Ornament der Masse* (Frankfurt a. M., 1977), pp. 279–94; Gleber, *The Art of Taking a Walk;* Petro, *Joyless Streets,* esp. pp. 19–21, and Patrice Petro, "Perceptions of Difference: Woman as Spectator and Spectacle," in *Women in the Metropolis,* ed. von Ankum, pp. 41–66.

63. Victoria de Grazia, "Nationalizing Women: The Competition between Fascist and Commercial Cultural Models in Mussolini's Italy," in *The Sex of Things: Gender and Consumption in Historical Perspective,* ed. Victoria de Grazia with Ellen Furlough (Berkeley, Calif., 1996), p. 356. Also see Eve Rosenhaft, "Lesewut, Kinosucht, Radiotismus: Zur (geschlechter-)politischen Relevanz neuer Massenmedien in den 1920er Jahren," in *Amerikanisierung: Traum und Alptraum im Deutschland des 20. Jahrhunderts,* ed. Alf Lüdtke (Stuttgart, 1996), pp. 119–43.

SELECTED THEMATIC BIBLIOGRAPHY

CONTENTS

I. THEORY AND METHOD

I.1. Women, Gender, and Masculinity

Abrams, Lynn, and Elizabeth Harvey, eds. *Gender Relations in German History: Power, Agency and Experience from the Sixteenth to the Twentieth Century.* Durham, N.C.: Duke University Press, 1997.

Adams, Parveen, and Jeff Minson. "The 'Subject' of Feminism," in *The Woman in Question,* edited by Parveen Adams and Elizabeth Cowie. Boston: MIT Press, 1978.

Alcoff, Linda. "The Problem of Speaking for Others." *Cultural Critique,* no. 20 (Winter 1991–92): 5–32.

Alexander, Sally. "Women, Class, and Sexual Differences in the 1830s and 1840s: Some Reflections on the Writing of a Feminist History." *History Workshop* 17 (Spring 1984): 125–49.

Auslander, Leora. "Erfahrung, Reflexion, Geschichtsarbeit. Oder: Was es heißen könnte, gebrauchsfähige Geschichte zu schreiben." *Historische Anthropologie* 3/2 (1995): 222–41.

———. "Feminist Theory and Social History: Explorations in the Politics of Identity." *Radical History Review* 54 (1992): 158–76.

Barrett, Michèle, and Anne Phillips. *Destabilizing Theory: Contemporary Feminist Debates*. Stanford, Calif.: Stanford University Press, 1992.

Bederman, Gail. *Manliness and Civilization: A Cultural History of Gender and Race in the United States, 1880–1917*. Chicago: University of Chicago Press, 1996.

Berlanstein, Lenard. "Working with Language: The Linguistic Turn in French Labor History. A Review Article." *Comparative Studies of Society and History* 33/2 (1991): 426–40.

Bock, Gisela. "Challenging Dichotomies: Perspectives on Women's History," in *Writing Women's History: International Perspectives*, edited by Karen Offen, Ruth Roach Pierson, and Jane Rendall. Bloomington: Indiana University Press, 1991.

Bordo, Susan. "Feminism, Postmodernism, and Gender-Scepticism," in *Feminism/Postmodernism*, edited by Linda J. Nicholson. New York: Routledge, 1990.

Bos, Marguérite, Bettina Vincenz, and Tanja Wirz, eds. *Erfahrung: Alles nur Diskurs? Zur Verwendung des Erfahrungsbegriffs in der Geschlechtergeschichte*. Beiträge zur 11. Schweizerischen Historikerinnentagung 2002. Zürich: Chronos, 2004.

Brod, Harry, ed. *The Making of Masculinities: The New Men's Studies*. Boston: Allen & Unwin, 1987.

Brubaker, Rogers, and Frederick Cooper. "Beyond 'Identity.'" *Theory and Society* 29/1 (2000): 1–47.

Butler, Judith. "Contingent Foundations: Feminism and the Question of 'Postmodernism,'" in *Feminists Theorize the Political*, edited by Judith Butler and Joan W. Scott. New York: Routledge, 1992.

———. *Gender Trouble: Feminism and the Subversion of Identity*. New York: Routledge, 1990.

Butler, Judith, and Joan W. Scott, eds. *Feminists Theorize the Political*. New York: Routledge, 1992.

Canning, Kathleen. "Feminist History after the Linguistic Turn: Historicizing Discourse and Experience." *Signs* 19/2 (Winter 1994): 368–404.

Canning, Kathleen, Anna Clark, Sonya O. Rose, Marcia Sawyer, and Mariana Valverde. "Women's History–Gender History: Has Feminist Inquiry Lost Its Critical Edge?" *Journal of Women's History* 5/1 (Spring 1993): 89–128.

Caplan, Jane. "Postmodernism, Poststructuralism, and Deconstruction: Notes for Historians." *Central European History* 22 (1989): 279–300.

Caruth, Cathy. *Unclaimed Experience: Trauma, Narrative, and History*. Baltimore: Johns Hopkins University Press, 1996.

Chartier, Roger. *On the Edge of the Cliff: History, Languages, and Practices*, translated by Lydia G. Cochrane. Baltimore: Johns Hopkins University Press, 1997.

Clements, Barbara Evans, Rebecca Friedman, and Dan Healy, eds. *Russian Masculinities in History and Culture*. New York: Palgrave, 2002.

Connell, R. W. *Masculinities*. Berkeley: University of California Press, 1995.

Crew, David. "*Alltagsgeschichte:* A New Social History 'from Below?'" *Central European History* 22/3–4 (1989): 394–407.

Davidoff, Leonore. "Class and Gender in Victorian England," in *Sex and Class in Women's History*, edited by Judith L. Newton, Mary P. Ryan, and Judith R. Walkowitz. London: Routledge, 1983.

Davis, Natalie Zemon. "Women's History in Transition: The European Case." *Feminist Studies* 3/3–4 (1976): 83–103.

Ditz, Toby L. "The New Men's History and the Peculiar Absence of Gendered Power: Some Remedies from Early American Gender History." *Gender & History* 16/1 (April 2004): 1–35.

Downs, Laura Lee. "If 'Woman' Is Just an Empty Category, Then Why Am I Afraid to Walk Alone at Night? Identity Politics Meets the Postmodern Subject." *Comparative Studies in Society and History* 35/2 (April 1993): 414–37.

Dudink, Stefan, Karen Hagemann, and John Tosh, eds. *Masculinities in Politics and War: Gendering Modern History*. Manchester: Manchester University Press, 2004.

Eisenstein, Zillah. *Capitalist Patriarchy and the Case for Socialist Feminism*. New York: Monthly Review Press, 1978.

Eley, Geoff. "Labor History, Social History, *Alltagsgeschichte*: Experience, Culture, and the Politics of the Everyday—A New Direction for German Social History?" *Journal of Modern History* 61/2 (1989): 297–343.

Enstad, Nan. "Partners in Crime? Writing the Social History of Women and the Poststructural History of Gender." *Journal of Women's History* 14/3 (Autumn 2002): 177–86.

Felski, Rita. *The Gender of Modernity*. Cambridge, Mass.: Harvard University Press, 1995.

Fraser, Nancy. *Unruly Practices: Power, Discourse, and Gender in Contemporary Social Theory*. Minneapolis: University of Minnesota Press, 1989.

Fraser, Nancy, and Sandra Bartky. *Revaluing French Feminisms: Critical Essays on Difference, Agency, and Culture*. Bloomington: Indiana University Press, 1992.

Frevert, Ute. "Männergeschichte oder die Suche nach dem 'ersten' Geschlecht," in *Was ist Gesellschaftsgeschichte? Positionen, Themen, Analysen*, edited by M. Hettling, C. Huerkamp, P. Nolte, and H. W. Schmuhl. Munich: Beck, 1991.

Friedlander, Judith, Blanche W. Cook, Alice Kessler-Harris, and Carroll Smith-Rosenberg, eds. *Women in Culture and Politics: A Century of Change*. Bloomington: Indiana University Press, 1985.

Gagnier, Regenia. *Subjectivities: A History of Self-Representation in Britain, 1832–1920*. New York: Oxford University Press, 1991.

Gal, Susan, and Gail Kligman. *The Politics, of Gender after Socialism: A Comparative Essay*. Princeton, N.J.: Princeton University Press, 2000.

——, eds. *Reproducing Gender: Politics, Publics, and Everyday Life after Socialism*. Princeton, N.J.: Princeton University Press, 2000.

Glover, David, and Cora Kaplan. *Genders*. London: Routledge, 2000.

Grosz, Elizabeth. "Bodies and Knowledges: Feminism and the Crisis of Reason," in *Space, Time, and Perversion*, edited by Elizabeth Grosz. London: Routledge, 1995.

Hall, Catherine. "Politics, Post-Structuralism, and Feminist History." *Gender & History* 3/2 (1991): 204–10.

Haraway, Donna. *Simians, Cyborgs, and Women: The Reinvention of Nature*. New York: Routledge, 1991.

Harding, Sandra. "The Instability of the Analytical Categories of Feminist Theory," in *Sex and Scientific Inquiry*, edited by Sandra Harding and Jean E. O'Barr. Chicago: University of Chicago Press, 1987.

Harootunian, Harry. *History's Disquiet: Modernity, Cultural Practice, and the Question of Everyday Life*. New York: Columbia University Press, 2000.

Harvey, David. *The Condition of Postmodernity: An Enquiry into the Origins of Cultural Change*. Cambridge, Mass.: Blackwell, 1990.

Hausen, Karin. "Family and Role-Division: The Polarisation of Sexual Stereotypes in the Nineteenth Century," in *The German Family: Essays on the Social History of the Family in Nineteenth- and Twentieth-Century Germany*, edited by Richard J. Evans and W. R. Lee. London: Croom Helm; Totowa, N.J.: Barnes & Noble Books, 1981.

Hausen, Karin, and Heide Wunder. *Frauengeschichte/Geschlechtergeschichte*. Frankfurt a. M.: Campus Verlag, 1992.

Hirsch, Marilyn, and Evelyn Fox-Keller, eds. *Conflicts in Feminism*. New York: Routledge, 1990.

Honegger, Claudia. *Die Ordnung der Geschlechter: Die Wissenschaften vom Menschen und das Weib*. Frankfurt a. M.: Campus Verlag, 1991.

Honegger, Claudia, and Caroline Arni, eds. *Gender: Die Tücken einer Kategorie*. Zürich: Chronos, 2001.

Hull, Isabel. "Feminist and Gender History through the Literary Looking Glass: German Historiography in Postmodern Times." *Central European History* 22 (1989): 260–78.

Hunt, Lynn. *Beyond the Cultural Turn: New Directions in the Study of Society and Culture*. Berkeley: University of California Press, 1999.

——. "The Challenge of Gender: Deconstruction of Categories and Reconstruction of Narratives in Gender History," in *Geschlechtergeschichte und Allgemeine Geschichte*, edited by Hans Medick and Ann-Charlott Trepp. Göttingen: Wallstein Verlag, 1998.

——, ed. *The New Cultural History*. Berkeley: University of California Press, 1989.

Jay, Martin. *Cultural Semantics: Keywords of Our Time*. Amherst: University of Massachusetts Press, 1998.

Kelly, Joan. "The Doubled Vision of Feminist Theory." *Feminist Studies* 5/1 (1979): 216–27.

——. "The Social Relation of the Sexes: Methodological Implications of Women's History." *Signs* 1/4 (1976): 809–23.

——. *Women, History and Theory: The Essays of Joan Kelly*. Chicago: University of Chicago Press, 1984.

Kessel, Martina. "The 'Whole Man': The Longing for a Masculine World in Nineteenth-Century Germany." *Gender & History* 15/1 (April 2003): 1–31.

Kimmel, Michael, ed. *Changing Men: New Directions in Research on Men and Masculinity.* Newbury Park, Calif.: Sage Publications, 1987.

Kocka, Jürgen. "Zurück zur Erzählung? Plädoyer für historische Argumentation." *Geschichte und Gesellschaft* 10/3 (1984): 395–408.

Kruks, Sonia. *Retrieving Experience: Subjectivity and Recognition in Feminist Politics.* Ithaca, N.Y: Cornell University Press, 2001.

Kühne, Thomas. *Männergeschichte/Geschlechtergeschichte: Männlichkeit im Wandel der Moderne.* Frankfurt a. M.: Campus Verlag, 1996.

Laslett, Barbara, Ruth-Ellen Boettcher-Joeres, Mary Jo Maynes, and Evelyn Brooks Higginbotham, eds. *History and Theory: Feminist Research, Debates, Contestations.* Chicago: University of Chicago Press, 1997.

Lauretis, Teresa de. "Eccentric Subject: Feminist Theory and Historical Consciousness." *Feminist Studies* 16/1 (Spring 1990): 115–50.

Lüdtke, Alf. "Alltagsgeschichte: Aneignung und Akteure. Oder—es hat kaum begonnen!" *Werkstatt Geschichte* 17 (1997): 83–91.

———. "Introduction: What Is the History of Everyday Life and Who Are Its Practitioners?" in *The History of Everyday Life: Reconstructing Historical Experiences and Ways of Life,* edited by Alf Lüdtke and translated by William Templer. Princeton, N.J.: Princeton University Press, 1995.

———. "Organizational Order or *Eigensinn*? Workers' Privacy and Workers' Politics in Imperial Germany," in *Rites of Power: Symbolism, Ritual, and Politics since the Middle Ages,* edited by Sean Wilentz. Philadelphia: University of Pennsylvania Press, 1985.

MacKinnon, Catharine A. *Toward a Feminist Theory of the State.* Cambridge, Mass.: Harvard University Press, 1989.

Mansfield, Nick. *Subjectivity: Theories of the Self from Freud to Haraway.* New York: New York University Press, 2000.

Marks, Elaine, and Isabelle de Courtivron. *New French Feminisms.* New York: Schocken, 1981.

Maynes, Mary Jo, ed. *Gender, Kinship, Power: A Comparative and Interdisciplinary History.* New York: Routledge, 1996.

Medick, Hans. "'Missionäre im Ruderboot'? Ethnologische Erkenntnisweisen als Herausforderung an die Sozialgeschichte." *Geschichte und Gesellschaft* 10/3 (1984): 295–319.

Meehan, Joanna, ed. *Feminists Read Habermas: Gendering the Subject of Discourse.* London: Routledge, 1995.

Mohanty, Chandra Talpade. "Feminist Encounters: Locating the Politics of Experience," in *Destabilizing Theory: Contemporary Feminist Debates,* edited by Michèle Barret and Anne Phillips. Stanford, Calif.: Stanford University Press, 1992.

Moi, Toril. *What Is a Woman? And Other Essays.* New York: Oxford University Press, 1999.

Mosse, George L. *The Image of Man: The Creation of Modern Masculinity.* Oxford: Oxford University Press, 1996.

Newton, Judith L. "History as Usual? Feminism and the 'New Historicism,'" in *The New Historicism,* edited by H. Aram Veeser. New York: Routledge, 1989.

Nicholson, Linda J., ed. *Feminism/Postmodernism.* New York: Routledge, 1990.

——, ed. *The Second Wave: A Reader.* New York: Routledge, 1990.

Nye, Robert. *Masculinity and Male Codes of Honor in Modern France.* Oxford: Oxford University Press, 1993.

Opitz, Claudia. "Gender—eine unverzichtbare Kategorie der historischen Analyse. Zur Rezeption von Joan W. Scotts Studien in Deutschland, Österreich und der Schweiz," in *Gender: Die Tücken einer Kategorie,* edited by Claudia Honegger and Caroline Arni. Zürich: Chronos, 2001.

Ortner, Sherry. *Making Gender: The Politics and Erotics of Culture.* Boston: Beacon Press, 1996.

——. "Resistance and the Problem of Ethnographic Reversal," in *The Historic Turn in the Human Sciences,* edited by Terrence J. McDonald. Ann Arbor: University of Michigan Press, 1996.

Palmer, Bryan. *Cultures of Darkness: Night Travels in the Histories of Transgression.* New York: Monthly Review Press, 2000.

——. *Descent into Discourse: The Reification of Language and the Writing of Social History.* Philadelphia: Temple University Press, 1990.

Parr, Joy. "Gender History and Historical Practice." *Canadian Historical Review* 76 (1996): 354–76.

Poovey, Mary. "Feminism and Deconstruction." *Feminist Studies* 14/1 (Spring 1988): 51–65.

——. *Making a Social Body: British Cultural Formation, 1830–64.* Chicago: University of Chicago Press, 1995.

Rabine, Leslie Wahl. "A Feminist Politics of Non-Identity." *Feminist Studies* 14 (1988): 11–31.

Reid, Donald. *Paris Sewers and Sewermen: Realities and Representations.* Cambridge, Mass.: Harvard University Press, 1991.

Rhode, Deborah L., ed. *Theoretical Perspectives on Sexual Difference.* New Haven, Conn.: Yale University Press, 1991.

Riley, Denise. *Am I That Name? Feminism and the Category of "Women" in History.* Minneapolis: University of Minnesota Press, 1988.

Riot-Sarcey, Michelle. "The Difficulties of Gender in France: Reflections on a Concept." *Gender & History* 11/3 (1999): 489–98.

Rosaldo, Renato. *Culture and Truth: The Remaking of Social Analysis.* Boston: Beacon Press, 1989.

Rosenhaft, Eve. "Women, Gender, and the Limits of Political History," in *Elections, Mass Politics, and Social Change in Modern Germany: New Perspectives,* edited by James Retallack and Larry E. Jones. Washington, D.C.: German Historical Institute; Cambridge: Cambridge University Press, 1992.

Sawicki, Jana. *Disciplining Foucault: Feminism, Power and the Body.* London: Routledge, 1991.

Scott, Anne Firor, Sara M. Evans, Susan K. Cahn, and Elizabeth Faue. "Women's History in the New Millennium: A Conversation across Three Generations." *Journal of Women's History* 11/1 (1999): 9–30, 11/2 (1999): 199–220.

Scott, Joan W. "The Evidence of Experience." *Critical Inquiry* 17/3 (1991): 773–97.

———. "Feminism's History." *Journal of Women's History* 16/2 (2004): 10–29.

———. *Gender and the Politics of History.* New York: Columbia University Press, 1988.

———. "Gender: A Useful Category of Historical Analysis." *American Historical Review* 91/5 (1986): 1053–75.

Sewell, William H., Jr. "Gender, History, and Deconstruction: Joan Wallach Scott's *Gender and the Politics of History.*" CSST Working Papers 34 (1989). Ann Arbor, Mich.: Program in the Comparative Study of Social Transformation.

———. "Language and Practice in Cultural History: Backing Away from the Edge of the Cliff." *French Historical Studies* 21/2 (Spring 1988): 241–54.

Shapiro, Ann-Louise, ed. *Feminists Revision History.* New Brunswick, N.J.: Rutgers University Press, 1994.

Singer, Linda. "Feminism and Postmodernism," in *Feminists Theorize the Political,* edited by Judith Butler and Joan W. Scott. New York: Routledge, 1992.

Sinha, Mrinalini. *Colonial Masculinity: The "Manly Englishman" and the "Effeminate Bengali" in the Late Nineteenth Century.* Manchester: Manchester University Press, 1995.

Smith, Bonnie G. *The Gender of History: Men, Women, and Historical Practice.* Cambridge, Mass.: Harvard University Press, 1998.

———. *Global Feminisms since 1945.* London: Routledge, 2000.

Smith, Dorothy. *The Everyday World as Problematic: A Feminist Sociology.* Boston: Northeastern University Press, 1987.

———. *Texts, Facts, and Femininity: Exploring the Relations of Ruling.* New York: Routledge, 1990.

Smith-Rosenberg, Carroll. "The Female World of Love and Ritual: Relations between Women in Nineteenth-Century America." *Signs* 1/1 (1975): 1–29.

Somers, Margaret R., and Gloria D. Gibson. "Reclaiming the Epistemological 'Other': Narrative and the Social Constitution of Identity," in *From Persons to Nations: The Social Constitution of Identities,* edited by Craig Calhoun. London: Basil Blackwell, 1994.

Spiegel, Gabrielle M. "History, Historicism, and the Social Logic of the Text in the Middle Ages." *Speculum* 65 (1990): 59–86.

Spivak, Gayatri Chakravorty. "Can the Subaltern Speak?" in *Marxism and the Interpretation of Culture,* ed. Cary Nelson and Lawrence Grossberg. Urbana: University of Illinois Press, 1988.

Stallybrass, Peter, and Allon White. *The Politics and Poetics of Transgression.* Ithaca, N.Y.: Cornell University Press, 1986.

Stedman Jones, Gareth. "Anglo-Marxism, Neo-Marxism, and the Discursive Approach
  to History," in *Was bleibt von marxistischen Perspektiven in der Geschichtsforschung?*
  edited by Alf Lüdtke. Göttingen: Wallstein, 1997.

Strobel, Margaret, and Marjorie Bingham. "The Theory and Practice of Women's
  History and Gender History in Global Perspective," in *Women's History in Global
  Perspective,* edited by Bonnie G. Smith. Urbana: University of Illinois Press, 2004.

Terdiman, Richard. *Discourse/Counter-Discourse: The Theory and Practice of Symbolic
  Resistance in Nineteenth-Century France.* Ithaca, N.Y.: Cornell University Press, 1985.

Thompson, E. P. *The Making of the English Working Class.* New York: Vintage Books,
  1963.

——. *The Poverty of Theory and Other Essays.* London: Monthly Review Press, 1978.

Toews, John. "Intellectual History after the Linguistic Turn: The Autonomy of Meaning
  and the Irreducibility of Experience." *American Historical Review* 92 (October 1987):
  879–907.

Trouillot, Michel-Rolph. *Silencing the Past: Power and the Production of History.* Boston:
  Beacon Press, 1995.

Valverde, Mariana. "Poststructuralist Gender Historians: Are We Those Names?" *Labour/
  Le Travail* 25 (1990): 227–36.

Walkowitz, Judith R., Myra Jehlen, and Bell Chevigny. "Patrolling the Borders: Feminist
  Historiography and the New Historicism." *Radical History Review* 43 (1989):23–43.

Weedon, Chris. *Feminist Practice and Poststructuralist Theory.* Oxford: Basil Blackwell,
  1987.

Williams, Raymond. *Keywords: A Vocabulary of Culture and Society.* New York: Oxford
  University Press, 1976, reprinted 1983.

*Women's History in the New Millennium: Carroll Smith-Rosenberg's "The Female World
  of Love and Ritual" after Twenty-Five Years.* Forum with contributions by Molly
  McGarry, Kanchana Natarajan, Dasa Franciková, Tania Navarro Swain, and Karin
  Lützen, in *Journal of Women's History* 12/3 (Autumn 2000): 8–38.

I.2. Sexualities and Queer Studies

Boone, Joseph A., ed., *Queer Frontiers: Millennial Geographies, Genders, and Generations.*
  Madison: University of Wisconsin Press, 2000.

Bristow, Joseph. *Sexuality.* London: Routledge, 1997.

Butler, Judith. "Subjects of Sex/Gender/Desire," in *Gender Trouble: Feminism and the
  Subversion of Identity.* New York: Routledge, 1990. Reprinted in *Feminism and Politics,*
  edited by Anne Phillips. Oxford: Oxford University Press, 1998.

Burton, Antoinette, ed. *Gender, Sexuality, and Colonial Modernities.* London: Routledge,
  1999.

Chauncey, George. *Gay New York: Gender, Urban Culture, and the Makings of the Gay
  Male World, 1890–1940.* New York: Basic Books, 1994.

Clark, Anna. *Scandal: The Sexual Politics of the British Constitution.* Princeton, N.J.:
  Princeton University Press, 2004.

Corbin, Alan. *Women for Hire: Prostitution and Sexuality in France after 1850.* Cambridge, Mass.: Harvard University Press, 1996.

Dean, Carolyn. *Sexuality and Modern Western Culture.* New York: Twayne, 1996.

Duberman, Martin Bauml, Martha Vicinus, and George Chauncey, eds. *Hidden from History: Reclaiming the Gay and Lesbian Past.* New York: Meridian, 1990.

Duggan, Lisa. *Sapphic Slashers: Sex, Violence, and American Modernity.* Durham, N.C.: Duke University Press, 2000.

Eder, Franz X., Lesley A. Hall, and Gert Hekma, eds. *Sexual Cultures in Europe.* Vol. 1: *National Histories;* vol. 2: *Themes in Sexuality.* Manchester: Manchester University Press, 1999.

Engelstein, Laura. *The Keys to Happiness: Sex and the Search for Modernity in Fin-de-Siècle Russia.* Ithaca, N.Y.: Cornell University Press, 1993.

Evans, David T. *Sexual Citizenship: The Material Construction of Sexualities.* London: Routledge, 1993.

Fausto-Sterling, Anne. *Sexing the Body: Gender Politics and the Construction of Sexuality.* New York: Basic Books, 2000.

Foucault, Michel. *The History of Sexuality,* translated by Robert Hurley. 2 vols. New York: Pantheon, 1986.

Gibson, Mary. *Prostitution and the State in Italy, 1860–1915.* New Brunswick, N.J.: Rutgers University Press, 1986.

Grossmann, Atina. "The New Woman and the Rationalization of Sexuality in Weimar Germany," in *Powers of Desire: The Politics of Sexuality,* edited by Ann Snitow, Christine Stansell, and Sharon Thompson. New York: Monthly Review Press, 1983.

Halperin, David. "How to Do the History of Male Homosexuality." *Gay and Lesbian Quarterly* 6/1 (2000): 87–124.

———. "Is There a History of Sexuality?" in *The Lesbian and Gay Studies Reader,* edited by Henry Abelove, Michele Aina Barale, and David M. Halperin. New York: Routledge, 1993.

Healey, Dan. "(Homo)sex in the City Only? Finding Continuity and Change in the Gay Past." *Gender & History* 16/1 (April 2004): 198–204.

———. *Homosexual Desire in Revolutionary Russia: The Regulation of Sexual and Gender Dissent.* Chicago: University of Chicago Press, 2001.

Heinemann, Elizabeth. "Sexuality and Nazism: The Doubly Unspeakable?" in *Sexuality and German Fascism,* edited by Dagmar Herzog. Special issue of the *Journal of History of Sexuality* 11/1–2 (January/April 2002): 22–66.

Hershatter, Gail. *Dangerous Pleasures: Prostitution and Modernity in Twentieth-Century Shanghai.* Berkeley: University of California Press, 1997.

Herzog, Dagmar. "Hubris and Hypocrisy, Incitement and Disavowal: Sexuality and German Fascism," in *Sexuality and German Fascism,* edited by Dagmar Herzog. Special issue of the *Journal of History of Sexuality* 11/1–2 (January/April 2002): 1–21.

———. "'Pleasure, Sex, and Politics Belong Together': Post-Holocaust Memory and the Sexual Revolution in West Germany." *Critical Inquiry* 24 (Winter 1998): 393–444.

———, ed. *Sexuality and German Fascism.* Special issue of the *Journal of History of Sexuality* 11/1–2 (January/April, 2002).

Hull, Isabel V. *Sexuality, State, and Civil Society in Germany, 1700–1815.* Ithaca, N.Y.: Cornell University Press, 1996.

Kucich, John. "Heterosexuality Obscured." *Victorian Studies* 40/3 (Spring 1997): 475–88.

Lancaster, Roger N., and Michaela di Leonardo, eds. *The Gender Sexuality Reader: Culture, History, Political Economy.* London: Routledge, 1997.

McLaren, Angus. *The Trials of Masculinity: Policing Sexual Boundaries, 1870–1930.* Chicago: University of Chicago Press, 1997.

———. *Twentieth-century Sexuality: A History.* Oxford: Blackwell, 1999.

Mort, Frank. *Dangerous Sexualities: Medico-Moral Politics in England since 1830.* New York: Routledge, 1987.

Mosse, George. *Nationalism and Sexuality: Respectability and Abnormal Sexuality in Modern Europe.* New York: H. Fertig, 1985.

Murray, Stephen O. *Homosexualities.* Chicago: University of Chicago Press, 2000.

Naiman, Eric. *Sex in Public: The Incarnation of Early Soviet Ideology.* Princeton, N.J.: Princeton University Press, 1997.

Nye, Robert, ed. *Sexuality.* Oxford: Oxford University Press 1999.

Parker, Andrew, et al., eds. *Nationalisms and Sexualities.* London: Routledge, 1992.

Porter, Roy, and Mikuls Teich, eds. *Sexual Knowledge, Sexual Science: The History of Attitudes to Sexuality.* Cambridge: Cambridge University Press, 1994.

Prosser, Jay. *Second Skins: The Body Narratives of Transsexuality.* New York: Columbia University Press, 1998.

Puff, Helmut. "Männergeschichten/Frauengeschichten: Über den Nutzen einer Geschichte der Homosexualität," in *Geschlechtergeschichte und allgemeine Geschichte: Herausforderungen und Perspektiven,* edited by Hans Medick and Anne-Charlott Trepp. Göttingen: Wallstein, 1998.

Rubin, Gayle. "The Traffic in Women: Notes on the 'Political Economy' of Sex," in *Toward an Anthropology of Women,* edited by Rayna Rapp. New York: Monthly Review Press, 1975. Reprinted in *Feminism and History,* edited by Joan W. Scott. New York: Oxford University Press, 1996.

Schiebinger, Londa. *The Mind Has No Sex? Women in the Origins of Modern Science.* Cambridge, Mass.: Harvard University Press, 1989.

Thompson, Victoria. "Creating Boundaries: Homosexuality and the Changing Social Order in France, 1830–70," in *Feminism and History,* edited by Joan W. Scott. Oxford: Oxford University Press, 1996.

Vicinus, Martha. *Intimate Friends: Women Who Loved Women, 1778–1928.* Chicago: University of Chicago Press, 2004.

———. *Lesbian Subjects: A Feminist Studies Reader.* Bloomington: Indiana University Press, 1996.

Walkowitz, Judith. *City of Dreadful Delight: Narratives of Sexual Danger in Late Victorian London.* Chicago: University of Chicago Press, 1992.

———. *Prostitution and Victorian Society: Women, Class, and the State.* Cambridge: Cambridge University Press, 1980.

Weeks, Jeffrey. *Sexuality and Its Discontents: Meanings, Myths and Modern Sexualities.* London: Routledge, 1983.

White, Luise. *The Comforts of Home: Prostitution in Colonial Nairobi.* Chicago: University of Chicago Press, 1990.

I.3. Body History

Adelson, Leslie. *Making Bodies, Making History: Feminism and German Identity.* Lincoln: University of Nebraska Press, 1993.

Baecque, Antoine de. *The Body Politic: Corporeal Metaphor in Revolutionary France 1770–1800.* Stanford, Calif.: Stanford University Press, 1997.

Blakemore, Colin, and Sheila Jennett, eds. *The Oxford Companion to the Body.* Oxford: Oxford University Press, 2001.

Bourke, Joanna. *Dismembering the Male: Men's Bodies, Britain, and the Great War.* Chicago: University of Chicago Press, 1996.

Bowald, Beatrice, Alexandra Binnenkade, Sandra Büchel-Thalmeier, and Monika Jacobs, eds. *KörperSinne: Körper im Spannungsfeld von Diskurs und Erfahrung.* Luzern: Böhlau, 2002.

Butler, Judith. *Bodies That Matter: On the Discursive Limits of "Sex."* New York: Routledge, 1993.

Bynum, Caroline. "Why All the Fuss about the Body? A Medievalist's Perspective." *Critical Inquiry* 22 (1995): 1–33.

Canning, Kathleen. "The Body as Method? Reflections on the Place of the Body in Gender History." *Gender & History* 11/3 (November 1999): 499–513.

Caplan, Jane, ed. *Written on the Body: The Tattoo in European and American History.* Princeton, N.J.: Princeton University Press, 2000.

Doherty, Brigid. "Figures of the Pseudorevolution." *October* 84 (Spring 1998): 64–89.

———. "'We are all Neurasthenics!' or the Trauma of Dada Montage." *Critical Inquiry* 24/1 (Autumn 1997): 82–132.

Duden, Barbara. *The Woman beneath the Skin: A Doctor's Patients in Eighteenth-Century Germany,* translated by Thomas Dunlap. Cambridge, Mass.: Harvard University Press, 1991.

Duggan, Lisa. "The Theory Wars, or Who's Afraid of Judith Butler?" *Journal of Women's History* 10/1 (1998): 9–20.

Feher, Michael, with Ramona Nadoff and Nadia Tazi, eds. *Fragments for a History of the Human Body.* 3 vols. New York: Zone Books, 1989–1991.

Frader, Laura Levine. "From Muscles to Nerves: Gender, 'Race,' and the Body at Work in France, 1919–1939." *International Review of Social History* 44 (1999): suppl. pp. 123–47.

Frevert, Ute, ed. *Körpergeschichte.* Special issue of *Geschichte und Gesellschaft* 26/4 (2000).

Gatens, Moira. *Imaginary Bodies: Ethics, Power, and Corporeality.* London: Routledge, 1996.

Gilman, Sander. *Difference and Pathology: Stereotypes of Sexuality, Race, and Madness.* Ithaca, N.Y.: Cornell University Press, 1985.

Grossmann, Atina. "Abortion and Economic Crisis: The Campaign against Paragraph 218 in Germany," in *When Biology Became Destiny: Women in Weimar and Nazi Germany,* edited by Renate Bridenthal, Atina Grossmann, and Marion Kaplan. New York: Monthly Review Press, 1984.

——. *Reforming Sex: The German Movement for Birth Control and Abortion Reform, 1920–1950.* Oxford: Oxford University Press, 1995.

Grosz, Elizabeth. "Inscriptions and Body-Maps: Representations and the Corporeal," in *Feminine, Masculine and Representation,* edited by Terry Threadgold and Anne Cranny-Francis. Sydney: Allen & Unwin, 1990.

——. *Volatile Bodies: Toward a Corporeal Feminism.* Bloomington: Indiana University Press, 1994.

Halberstam, Judith. *Female Masculinity.* Durham, N.C.: Duke University Press, 1998.

Hall, Lesley A. "Women, Feminism and Eugenics," in *Essays in the History of Eugenics: Proceedings of a Conference Organised by the Galton Institute, London 1997,* edited by Robert A. Peel. London: The Galton Institute, 1998.

Haraway, Donna. *Simians, Cyborgs, and Women: The Reinvention of Nature.* New York: Routledge, 1991.

Hayles, N. Katherine. "The Materiality of Informatics." Unpublished paper, 1992.

Hewitt, Martin. "Bio-Politics and Social Policy: Foucault's Account of Welfare." *Theory, Culture and Society* 2/1 (1983): 67–84.

Hilman, David, and Carla Mazzio. *The Body in Parts: Fantasies of Corporeality in Early Modern Europe.* New York: Routledge, 1997.

Horn, David G. *Social Bodies: Science, Reproduction, and Italian Modernity.* Princeton, N.J.: Princeton University Press, 1994.

Hull, Isabel. "The Body as Historical Experience: Review of Recent Works by Barbara Duden." *Central European History* 28/1 (1995): 73–79.

Hunt, Lynn. *Eroticism and the Body Politic.* Baltimore: Johns Hopkins University Press, 1991.

Jacobus, Mary, Evelyn Fox Keller, and Sally Shuttleworth, eds. *Body/Politics: Women and the Discourses of Science.* New York: Routledge, 1990.

Jordanova, Ludmilla. *Sexual Visions: Images of Gender in Science and Medicine between the Eighteenth and the Twentieth Centuries.* Madison: University of Wisconsin Press, 1989.

Laqueur, Thomas W. "Bodies, Details, and the Humanitarian Narrative," in *The New Cultural History,* edited by Lynn Hunt. Berkeley: University of California Press, 1989.

——. *Making Sex: Body and Gender from the Greeks to Freud.* Cambridge, Mass.: Harvard University Press, 1990.

Laqueur, Thomas, and Catherine Gallagher, eds. *The Making of the Modern Body: Sexuality and Society in the Nineteenth Century.* Special issue of *Representations* 4 (Spring 1986).

Lawrence, Christopher, and Anna-K. Mayer, eds. *Regenerating England: Science, Medicine and Culture in Interwar Britain.* Wellcome Institute Series in the History of Medicine, vol. 60. Amsterdam: Rodopi, 2000.

Ko, Dorothy. *Every Step a Lotus: Shoes for Bound Feet.* Berkeley: University of California Press, 2001.

Martin, Emily. *The Woman in the Body: A Cultural Analysis of Reproduction.* Boston: Beacon Press, 1987.

Matus, Jill. *Unstable Bodies: Victorian Representations of Sexuality and Maternity.* Manchester: Manchester University Press, 1995.

Outram, Dorinda. *The Body and the French Revolution: Sex, Class, and Political Culture.* New Haven, Conn.: Yale University Press, 1989.

Planert, Ute. "Der dreifache Körper des Volkes: Sexualität, Biopolitik und die Wissenschaften vom Leben," in Körpergeschichte, edited by Ute Frevert. Special issue of *Geschichte und Gesellschaft* 26/4 (2000): 539–76.

Poovey, Mary. "Speaking of the Body: Mid-Victorian Constructions of Female Desire," in *Body/Politics: Women and the Discourses of Science,* edited by Mary Jacobus, Evelyn Fox Keller, and Sally Shuttleworth. New York: Routledge, 1990.

Price, Janet, and Margrit Shildrick, eds. *Feminist Theory and the Body: A Reader.* London: Routledge, 1999.

Rabinbach, Anson. "The European Science of Work: The Economy of the Body at the End of the Nineteenth Century," in *Work in France: Representations, Meaning, Organization, and Practice,* edited by Steven L. Kaplan and Cynthia J. Koepp. Ithaca, N.Y.: Cornell University Press, 1986.

——. *The Human Motor: Energy, Fatigue, and the Origins of Modernity.* Berkeley: University of California Press, 1990.

Sarasin, Philipp. "Mapping the Body: Körpergeschichte zwischen Konstruktivismus, Politik und 'Erfahrung.'" *Historische Anthropologie* 7/3 (1999): 437–51.

——. *Reizbare Maschinen: Eine Geschichte des Körpers 1765–1914.* Frankfurt a. M.: Suhrkamp, 2001.

Sarasin, Philipp, and Jakob Tanner, eds. *Physiologie und industrielle Gesellschaft: Studien zur Verwissenschaftlichung des Körpers im 19. und 20. Jahrhundert.* Frankfurt a. M.: Suhrkamp, 1998.

Scarry, Elaine. *The Body in Pain: The Making and Unmaking of the World.* Oxford: Oxford University Press, 1985.

Schiebinger, Londa. *Nature's Body: Gender in the Making of Modern Science.* Boston: Beacon Press, 1993.

——, ed. *Feminism and the Body.* Oxford: Oxford University Press, 2000.

Shilling, Chris. *The Body and Social Theory.* London: Sage, 1993.

Tanner, Jakob. "Körpererfahrung, Schmerz und die Konstruktion des Kulturellen." *Historische Anthropologie* 2/3 (1994): 489–502.

Turner, Bryan S. *The Body and Society.* 2d ed. London: Sage, 1996.

——. *Regulating Bodies: Essays in Medical Sociology.* London: Routledge, 1992.

Usborne, Cornelie. "Female Voices in Male Courtrooms—Abortion Trials in Weimar Germany," in *Coping with Sickness: Medicine, Law and Human Rights—Historical Perspectives,* edited by John Woodward and Robert Jütte. Sheffield: European Association for the History of Medicine and Health Publications, 2000.

——. *The Politics of the Body in Weimar Germany.* Ann Arbor: University of Michigan Press, 1992.

Verdery, Katherine. *The Political Lives of Dead Bodies: Reburial and Postsocialist Change.* New York: Columbia University Press, 1999.

II. REVISING CATEGORIES

II.1. Citizenship, Public Sphere, and Civil Society

Andrews, Geoff, ed. *Citizenship.* London: Lawrence & Wishart, 1991.

Appelt, Erna, ed. *Citizenship.* Special issue of *L'Homme: Zeitschrift für feministische Geschichtswissenschaft* 10/1 (1999).

Applewhite, Harriet, and Darlene Levy. *Women and Politics in the Age of the Democratic Revolution.* Ann Arbor: University of Michigan Press, 1990.

Berlant, Lauren. *The Queen of America Goes to Washington City: Essays on Sex and Citizenship.* Durham, N.C.: Duke University Press, 1997.

Blum, Carol. *Rousseau and the Republic of Virtue: The Language of Politics in the French Revolution.* Ithaca, N.Y.: Cornell University Press, 1986.

Boak, Helen. "Women in Weimar Germany: The 'Frauenfrage' and the Female Vote," in *Social Change and Political Development in Weimar Germany,* edited by Richard Bessel and E. J. Feuchtwanger. London: Croom Helm; Totowa, N.J.: Barnes & Noble, 1981.

Bock, Gisela, and Susan James, eds. *Beyond Equality and Difference: Citizenship, Feminist Politics, and Female Subjectivity.* London: Routledge, 1992.

Brubaker, Rogers. *Citizenship and Nationhood in France and Germany.* Cambridge, Mass.: Harvard University Press, 1992.

Calhoun, Craig. "Habermas and the Public Sphere," in *Habermas and the Public Sphere,* edited by Craig Calhoun. Cambridge, Mass.: Harvard University Press, 1992.

Camiscoli, Elisa. "Producing Citizens, Reproducing the 'French Race': Immigration, Demography and Pronatalism in Early Twentieth-Century France," in *Gender, Citizenships, and Subjectivities,* edited by Kathleen Canning and Sonya O. Rose. London: Blackwell, 2002.

Canning, Kathleen, and Sonya O. Rose, eds. *Gender, Citizenships, and Subjectivities.* London: Blackwell, 2002. First published as a special issue of *Gender & History* 13/3 (November, 2001).

Childers, Thomas. "Languages of Liberalism: Liberal Political Discourse in the Weimar Republic," in *In Search of a Liberal Germany: Studies in the History of German Liberalism from 1789 to the Present,* edited by Konrad H. Jarausch and Larry Eugene Jones. Oxford: Berg, 1990.

Conrad, Christoph, and Jürgen Kocka, eds. *Staatsbürgerschaft in Europa: Historische Erfahrungen und aktuelle Debatten*. Hamburg: Edition Körber-Stiftung, 2001.

Cott, Nancy. "Marriage and Women's Citizenship in the United States, 1830–1934." *American Historical Review* 103/5 (December 1998): 1440–74.

Davidoff, Leonore. "Gender and the Great Divide: Public and Private in British Gender History." *Journal of Women's History* 15/1 (Spring 2003): 11–27.

———. "Regarding Some Old Husbands' Tales: Public and Private in Feminist History," in *Worlds Between: Historical Perspectives on Gender and Class*. Cambridge: Polity Press, 1995.

Davis, Belinda. "Gender, Women, and the 'Public Sphere' in World War I Berlin," in *Society, Culture, and the State in Germany, 1870–1930*, edited by Geoff Eley. Ann Arbor: University of Michigan Press, 1996.

Eghigian, Greg. *Making Security Social: Disability, Insurance, and the Birth of the Social Entitlement State in Germany*. Ann Arbor: University of Michigan Press, 2000.

Eley, Geoff. "German History and the Contradictions of Modernity," in *Society, Culture, and the State in Germany, 1870–1930*, edited by Geoff Eley. Ann Arbor: University of Michigan Press, 1996.

———. "Nations, Publics, and Political Cultures: Placing Habermas in the Nineteenth Century," in *Habermas and the Public Sphere*, edited by Craig Calhoun. Cambridge, Mass.: Harvard University Press, 1992.

Eley, Geoff, and Atina Grossmann. "Maternalism and Citizenship in Weimar Germany: The Gendered Politics of Welfare." *Central European History* 30/1 (1997): 67–75.

Elshtain, Jean Bethke. *Public Man, Private Woman: Women in Social and Political Thought*. Princeton, N.J.: Princeton University Press, 1981.

Fahrmeir, Andreas K. "Nineteenth-Century German Citizenships: A Reconsideration." *Historical Journal* 40/3 (1997): 721–52.

Feinberg, Melissa. *Democracy and Its Limits: The Politics of Women's Citizenship in Czechoslovakia, 1918–1950*. Pittsburgh: University of Pittsburgh Press, forthcoming 2005.

Fletcher, Ian, Laura E. Nym Mayhall, and Philippa Levine, eds. *Women's Suffrage in the British Empire: Citizenship, Nation, and Race*. London: Routledge, 2000.

Fraser, Nancy. "Rethinking the Public Sphere: A Contribution to the Critique of Actually Existing Democracy," in *Habermas and the Public Sphere*, edited by Craig Calhoun. Cambridge, Mass.: MIT Press, 1992.

———. "Sex, Lies, and the Public Sphere: Reflections on the Confirmation of Clarence Thomas," in *Feminism, the Public and the Private*, edited by Joan Landes. Oxford: Oxford University Press, 1998.

Frevert, Ute. *A Nation in Barracks: Modern Germany, Military Conscription, and Civil Society*, translated by Andrew Boreham with Daniel Brückenhaus. Oxford: Berg, 2004. Originally published as *Die kasernierte Nation: Militärdienst und Zivilgesellschaft in Deutschland*. Munich: Beck, 2001.

Gal, Susan. "A Semiotics of the Public/Private Distinction." *Differences: A Journal of Feminist Cultural Studies* 13/1 (Spring 2002): 77–95.

Glenn, Evelyn Nakano. *Unequal Freedoms: How Race and Gender Shaped American Citizenship and Labor.* Cambridge, Mass.: Harvard University Press, 2004.

Godineau, Dominique. *The Women of Paris and Their French Revolution,* translated by Katherine Streip. Berkeley: University of California Press, 1998.

Goodman, Dena. "Public Sphere and Private Life: Towards a Synthesis of Current Historiographical Approaches to the Old Regime." *History and Theory* 31/1 (1992): 1–20.

Graham, Sandra Lauderdale. "Making the Private Public: A Brazilian Perspective." *Journal of Women's History* 15/1 (Spring 2003): 28–42.

Habermas, Jürgen. *The Structural Transformation of the Public Sphere: An Inquiry into a Category of Bourgeois Society,* translated by Thomas Burger with Frederick Lawrence. Cambridge, Mass.: MIT Press, 1989.

Harrison, Carol E. "Citizens and Scientists: Toward a Gendered History of Scientific Practice in Post-Revolutionary France," in *Gender, Citizenships, and Subjectivities,* edited by Kathleen Canning and Sonya O. Rose. London: Blackwell, 2002.

Healy, Maureen. "Becoming Austrian: Women, the State, and Citizenship in World War I." *Central European History* 35/1 (2002): 1–35.

Held, David. "Between State and Civil Society: Citizenship," in *Citizenship,* edited by Geoff Andrews. London: Lawrence & Wishart, 1991.

Hong, Young-Sun. "Gender, Citizenship, and the Welfare State: Social Work and the Politics of Femininity in the Weimar Republic." *Central European History* 30/1 (1997): 1–24, 67–75.

Hull, Isabel V. *Sexuality, State, and Civil Society in Germany, 1700–1815.* Ithaca, N.Y.: Cornell University Press, 1996.

Hunt, Lynn. *The Family Romance of the French Revolution.* Berkeley: University of California Press, 1992.

Kent, Susan Kingsley. *Sex and Suffrage in Britain, 1860–1914.* Princeton, N.J.: Princeton University Press, 1987.

Kerber, Linda. "The Meanings of Citizenship." *Journal of American History* 84/3 (December 1997): 833–54.

Landes, Joan, ed. *Feminism, the Public and the Private.* Oxford: Oxford University Press, 1998.

——. *Women and the Public Sphere in the Age of the French Revolution.* Berkeley: University of California Press, 1992.

Lauterer, Heidemarie. *Parlamentarierinnen in Deutschland 1918/19–1949.* Königstein: Ulrike Helmer Verlag, 2002.

Lister, Ruth. *Citizenship: Feminist Perspectives.* New York: New York University Press, 1997.

Marshall, T. H., with Tom Bottomore. *Citizenship and Social Class.* London: Pluto Press, 1992.

Mayhall, Laura E. Nym. *The Militant Suffrage Movement: Citizenship and Resistance in Britain 1860–1930.* Oxford: Oxford University Press, 2003.

——. "The Rhetorics of Slavery and Citizenship: Suffragist Discourse and Canonical

Texts in Britain, 1880–1914," in *Gender, Citizenship and Subjectivities,* edited by
  Kathleen Canning and Sonya O. Rose. London: Blackwell, 2002.

Maza, Sarah. *Private Lives and Public Affairs: The Causes Célèbres of Prerevolutionary
  France.* Berkeley: University of California Press, 1993.

McClelland, Keith. "Rational and Respectable Men: Gender, the Working Class, and
  Citizenship in Britain, 1850–1867," in *Gender and Class in Modern Europe,* edited by
  Laura Levine Frader and Sonya O. Rose. Ithaca, N.Y.: Cornell University Press, 1996.

Mehta, Uday. "Liberal Strategies of Exclusion," in *Tensions of Empire: Colonial Cultures in
  a Bourgeois World,* edited by Frederick Cooper and Ann Stoler. Berkeley: University
  of California Press, 1997.

Mouffe, Chantal. "Feminism, Citizenship, and Radical Democratic Politics," in *Feminists
  Theorize the Political,* edited by Judith Butler and Joan W. Scott. New York: Routledge,
  1992.

Ngai, Mae. *Impossible Subjects: Illegal Aliens and the Making of American Politics.*
  Princeton, N.J.: Princeton University Press, 2003.

Ong, Aihwa. "Cultural Citizenship as Subject Making: Immigrants Negotiate Racial and
  Cultural Boundaries in the United States," in *Race, Identity, and Citizenship: A Reader,*
  edited by Rodolfo D. Torres et al. Malden, Mass.: Blackwell, 1999.

———. *Flexible Citizenship: The Cultural Logics of Transnationality.* Durham, N.C.: Duke
  University Press, 1999.

Pateman, Carole. "The Fraternal Social Contract," in *Civil Society and the State,* edited by
  John Keane. London: Verso, 1988.

———. *The Sexual Contract.* Stanford, Calif.: Stanford University Press, 1988.

Phillips, Anne. "Citizenship and Feminist Theory," in *Citizenship,* edited by Geoff
  Andrews. London: Lawrence & Wishart, 1991.

Radcliff, Pamela B. "Imagining Female Citizenship in the 'New Spain': Gendering the
  Democratic Transition 1975–1978," in *Gender, Citizenship, and Subjectivities,* edited
  by Kathleen Canning and Sonya O. Rose. London: Blackwell, 2002.

Rendall, Jane. "Women and the Public Sphere," in *Gender & History: Retrospect and
  Prospect,* edited by Leonore Davidoff, Keith McClelland, and Eleni Varikas. Oxford:
  Blackwell, 2000.

Rose, Sonya O. *Which People's War? National Identity and Citizenship in Wartime Britain,
  1939–1945.* Oxford: Oxford University Press, 2003.

Ryan, Mary P. "Gender and Public Access: Women's Politics in Nineteenth-Century
  America," in *Habermas and the Public Sphere,* edited by Craig Calhoun. Cambridge,
  Mass.: MIT Press, 1992.

———. "The Public and the Private Good: Across the Divide in Women's History." *Journal
  of Women's History* 15/1 (Spring 2003): 10–27.

Scott, Joan W. "French Feminists and the Rights of 'Man': Olympe de Gouge's
  Declarations." *History Workshop* 28 (Autumn 1989): 1–21.

———. *Only Paradoxes to Offer: French Feminists and the Rights of Man.* Cambridge,
  Mass.: Harvard University Press, 1996.

Sewell, William H., Jr. "Le citoyen/la citoyenne: Activity, Passivity, and the Revolutionary Concept of Citizenship," in *The French Revolution and the Creation of Modern Political Culture,* vol. 2: *Political Culture of the French Revolution,* edited by Colin Lucas. Oxford: Pergamon, 1988.

Siim, Birthe. *Gender and Citizenship: Politics and Agency in France, Britain, and Denmark.* Cambridge: Cambridge University Press, 2000.

Sneeringer, Julia. "The Shopper as Voter: Women, Advertising, and Politics in Post-Inflation Germany." *German Studies Review* 27/3 (October 2004): 476–502.

———. *Winning Women's Votes: Propaganda and Politics in Weimar Germany.* Chapel Hill: University of North Carolina Press, 2002.

Somers, Margaret R. "Citizenship and the Place of the Public Sphere: Law, Community, and Political Culture in the Transition to Democracy." *American Sociological Review* 58 (1993): 587–620.

Thompson, Elizabeth. "Public and Private in Middle Eastern Women's History." *Journal of Women's History* 15/1 (Spring 2003): 52–68.

Turner, Bryan S. "Contemporary Problems in the Theory of Citizenship," in *Citizenship and Social Theory,* edited by Bryan S. Turner. London: Sage, 1993.

Turner, Bryan S., and Peter Hamilton, eds. *Citizenship: Critical Concepts.* London: Routledge, 1994.

Walby, Sylvia. "Is Citizenship Gendered?" *Sociology* 28/2 (May 1994): 379–95.

Werbner, Pnina, and Nira Yuval-Davis, eds. *Citizenship: Pushing the Boundaries.* Special issue of *Feminist Review* 57 (Autumn 1997).

Wildenthal, Lora. "Race, Gender, and Citizenship in the German Colonial Empire," in *Tensions of Empire: Colonial Cultures in a Bourgeois World,* edited by Frederick Cooper and Ann L. Stoler. Berkeley: University of California Press, 1997.

"Women, Work, and Citizenship." Forum in *International Labor and Working-Class History,* no. 52 (Fall 1997): 1–71.

Wood, Elizabeth. "The Trial of the New Woman: Citizens in Training in the New Soviet Republic," in *Gender, Citizenship, and Subjectivities,* edited by Kathleen Canning and Sonya O. Rose. London: Blackwell, 2002.

Young, Iris Marion. "Impartiality and the Civic Public," in *Feminism as Critique: Essays on the Politics of Gender in Late Capitalist Societies,* edited by Seyla Benhabib and Drucilla Cornell. Minneapolis: University of Minnesota Press, 1987.

———. "Polity and Group Difference: A Critique of the Ideal of Universal Citizenship," in *The Citizenship Debates: A Reader,* edited by Gershon Shafir. Minneapolis: University of Minnesota Press, 1998.

Yuval-Davis, Nira, and Pnina Werbner, eds. *Women, Citizenship and Difference.* New York: St. Martin's Press, 1999.

II.2. The Social, the Welfare State, and Social Movements

Allen, Ann Taylor. *Feminism and Motherhood in Germany, 1800–1914.* New Brunswick N.J.: Rutgers University Press, 1991.

Bock, Gisela, and Pat Thane, eds. *Maternity and Gender Policies: Women and the Rise of the European Welfare State.* London: Routledge, 1991.

Bridenthal, Renate. "'Professional Housewives': Stepsisters of the Women's Movement," in *When Biology Became Destiny,* edited by Renate Bridenthal, Atina Grossmann, and Marion Kaplan. New York: Monthly Review Press, 1984.

Caulfield, Sueann. "Getting into Trouble: Dishonest Women, Modern Girls, and Women-Men in the Conceptual Language of *Vida Policial, 1925–1927." Signs* 19/1 (1993): 146–76.

Cole, Joshua. *The Power of Large Numbers: Population, Politics, and Gender in Nineteenth-Century France.* Ithaca, N.Y.: Cornell University Press, 2000.

Crew, David F. *Germans on Welfare: From Weimar to Hitler.* Oxford: Oxford University Press, 1998.

Donzelot, Jacques. *The Policing of Families,* foreword by Gilles Deleuze, translated by Robert Hurley. New York: Pantheon Books, 1979.

Eifert, Christiane. "Coming to Terms with the State: Maternalist Politics and the Development of the Welfare State in Weimar Germany." *Central European History* 30/1 (1997): 25–47.

———. *Frauenpolitik und Wohlfahrtspflege: Zur Geschichte der sozialdemokratischen "Arbeiterwohlfahrt."* Frankfurt a. M.: Campus Verlag, 1993.

Evans, Richard J. *The Feminist Movement in Germany, 1894–1933.* London: Sage Publications, 1976.

———. *The Feminists: Women's Emancipation Movements in Europe, America and Australasia, 1840–1920.* London: Croom Helm, 1977.

Gerhard, Ute. *Debating Women's Equality: Toward a Feminist Theory of Law from a European Perspective,* translated by Allison Brown and Belinda Cooper. New Brunswick, N.J.: Rutgers University Press, 2001.

———. *Unerhört: Die Geschichte der deutschen Frauenbewegung.* Reinbek bei Hamburg: Rowohlt Taschenbuch, 1990.

Gerstenberger, Heide. "The Poor and the Respectable Worker: On the Introduction of Social Insurance in Germany." *Labour History* 48 (May 1985).

Gordon, Linda. "Social Insurance and Public Assistance: The Influence of Gender in Welfare Thought in the United States, 1890–1935." *American Historical Review* 97 (February 1992): 19–54.

———, ed. *Women, the State and Welfare.* Madison: University of Wisconsin Press, 1990.

Gray, Robert. "The Languages of Factory Reform in Britain c. 1830–1850," in *The Historical Meanings of Work,* edited by Patrick Joyce. Cambridge: Cambridge University Press, 1987.

———. "Medical Men, Industrial Labour, and the State in Britain, 1830–1850." *Social History* 16 (January 1991): 19–43.

Greven-Aschoff, Barbara. *Die bürgerliche Frauenbewegung in Deutschland 1894–1933.* Göttingen: Vandenhoeck & Ruprecht, 1981.

Hall, Lesley A. "Hauling Down the Double Standard: Feminism, Social Purity. and Sexual

Science in Late Nineteenth-Century Britain." *Gender & History* 16/1 (April 2004): 36–56.

Hobson, Barbara. "Feminist Strategies and Gendered Discourses in Welfare States: Married Women's Right to Work in the United States and Sweden," in *Mothers of a New World: Maternalist Politics and the Origins of Welfare States,* edited by Seth Koven and Sonya Michel. New York: Routledge, 1993.

Hong, Young-Sun. "The Contradictions of Modernization in the German Welfare State: Gender and the Politics of Welfare Reform in First World War Germany." *Social History* 17 (1992): 251–70.

———. *Welfare, Modernity, and the Weimar State, 1919–1933.* Princeton, N.J.: Princeton University Press, 1998.

Jenson, Jane. "Representations of Gender: Policies to 'Protect' Women Workers and Infants in France and the United States before 1914," in *Women, the State and Welfare,* edited by Linda Gordon. Madison: University of Wisconsin Press, 1990.

Koven, Seth, and Sonya Michel. "Gender and the Origins of the Welfare State." *Radical History Review* 43 (1989): 112–19.

———. "Womanly Duties: Maternalist Politics and the Origins of Welfare States in France, Germany, Great Britain, and the U.S., 1880–1920." *American Historical Review* 95/4 (October 1990): 1076–1108.

———, eds. *Mothers of a New World: Maternalist Politics and the Origins of Welfare States.* New York: Routledge, 1993.

Kraus, Alisa. "Depopulation and Race Suicide," in *Mothers of a New World: Maternalist Politics and the Origins of Welfare States,* edited by Seth Koven and Sonya Michel. New York: Routledge, 1993.

Kulawik, Theresa. *Wohlfahrtsstaat und Mutterschaft: Schweden und Deutschland 1870–1912.* Frankfurt a. M.: Campus Verlag, 1999.

Lees, Andrew. *Character Is Destiny: The Autobiography of Alice Salomon.* Ann Arbor: University of Michigan Press, 2004.

———. *Cities: Sin and Social Reform in Imperial Germany.* Ann Arbor: University of Michigan Press, 2002.

Offen, Karen. "Depopulation, Nationalism, and Feminism in Fin-de-Siècle France." *American Historical Review* 9/3 (June 1984): 648–76.

Pedersen, Susan. *Family, Dependence, and the Origins of the Welfare State: Britain and France, 1914–1945.* Cambridge: Cambridge University Press, 1993.

Poovey, Mary. "Domesticity and Class Formation: Chadwick's *Sanitary Report,*" in *Subject to History: Ideology, Class, Gender,* edited by David Simpson. Ithaca, N.Y.: Cornell University Press, 1991.

———. *Making a Social Body: British Cultural Formation, 1830–64.* Chicago: University of Chicago Press, 1995.

Quataert, Jean H. "A Source Analysis in German Women's History: Factory Inspectors' Reports and the Shaping of Working-Class Lives, 1878–1914." *Central European History* 16/2 (1983): 99–121.

——. "Woman's Work and the Early Welfare State in Germany: Legislators, Bureaucrats, and Clients before the First World War," in *Mothers of a New World: Maternalist Politics and the Origins of Welfare States,* edited by Seth Koven and Sonya Michel. New York: Routledge, 1993.

Reagin, Nancy R. *A German Women's Movement: Class and Gender in Hanover.* Chapel Hill: University of North Carolina Press, 1995.

Riley, Denise. "Some Peculiarities of Social Policy Concerning Women in Wartime and Postwar Britain," in *Behind the Lines: Gender and the Two World Wars,* edited by Margaret Randolph Higonnet, Jane Jenson, Sonya Michel, and Margaret Weitz. New Haven, Conn.: Yale University Press, 1987.

Rosenhaft, Eve, and W. R. Lee. "State and Society in Modern Germany: Beamtenstaat, Klassenstaat, Wohlfahrtsstaat," in *The State and Social Change in Germany, 1880–1980,* edited by Eve Rosenhaft and W. R. Lee. Oxford: Berg, 1990.

Rouette, Susanne. "Mothers and Citizens: Gender and Social Policy in Germany after the First World War." *Central European History* 30/1 (1997): 48–75.

Sachße, Christoph. *Mütterlichkeit als Beruf: Sozialarbeit, Sozialreform und Frauenbewegung 1871–1929.* Frankfurt a. M.: Suhrkamp, 1986.

Schultheiss, Katrin. *Bodies and Souls: Politics and the Professionalization of Nursing in France, 1880–1922.* Cambridge, Mass.: Harvard University Press, 2001.

Skocpol, Theda. *Protecting Soldiers and Mothers: The Political Origins of Social Policy in the United States.* Cambridge, Mass.: Belknap Press of Harvard University Press, 1992.

Scott, Joan W. "'L'ouvrière! Mot impie, sordide . . .' Women Workers in the Discourse of French Political Economy, 1840–1860," in *Gender and the Politics of History,* edited by Joan W. Scott. New York: Columbia University Press, 1988.

Steinmetz, George. *Regulating the Social: The Welfare State and Local Politics in Imperial Germany.* Princeton, N.J.: Princeton University Press, 1993.

Stewart, Mary Lynn. *Women, Work, and the French State: Labour Protection and Social Patriarchy, 1879–1919.* Kingston: McGill-Queen's University Press, 1989.

Stoehr, Irene. "'Organisierte Mütterlichkeit': Zur Politik der deutschen Frauenbewegung um 1900," in *Frauen suchen ihre Geschichte,* edited by Karin Hausen. Munich: Beck, 1983.

Wikander, Ulla, Alice Kessler-Harris, and Jane Lewis, eds. *Protecting Women: Labor Legislation in Europe, the United States and Australia, 1880–1920.* Urbana: University of Illinois Press, 1995.

II.3. Class, Gender, and Labor

Baron, Ava, ed. *Work Engendered: Toward a New History of American Labor.* Ithaca, N.Y.: Cornell University Press, 1991.

Berg, Maxine. *The Age of Manufactures: Industry, Innovation, and Work in Britain 1700–1820.* Oxford: Basil Blackwell in association with Fontana, 1985.

Berlanstein, Lenard, ed. *Rethinking Labor History: Essays on Discourse and Class Analysis.* Urbana: University of Illinois Press, 1993.

Bridenthal, Renate. "Beyond 'Kinder, Küche, Kirche': Weimar Women at Work." *Central European History* 6/2 (1973): 148–66.

Canning, Kathleen. "Gender and the Politics of Class Formation: Rethinking German Labor History." *American Historical Review* 97/3 (1992): 736–68.

———. *Languages of Labor and Gender: Female Factory Work in Germany, 1850–1914.* Ithaca, N.Y.: Cornell University Press, 1996. Paperback ed., Ann Arbor: University of Michigan Press, 2002.

Clark, Anna. "The Rhetoric of Chartist Domesticity: Gender, Language and Class in the 1830s and 1840s." *Journal of British Studies* 31 (1992): 62–88.

———. *The Struggle for the Breeches: Gender and the Making of the British Working Class.* Berkeley: University of California Press, 1995.

Clements, Barbara Evans, Barbara Alpern Engel, and Christine D. Worobec, eds. *Russia's Women: Accommodation, Resistance, Transformation.* Berkeley: University of California Press, 1990.

Coffin, Judith. *The Politics of Women's Work: The Paris Garment Trades, 1750–1915.* Princeton, N.J.: Princeton University Press, 1996.

———. "Social Science Meets Sweated Labor: Reinterpreting Women's Work in Late Nineteenth-Century France." *Journal of Modern History* 63/22 (1991): 230–70.

Cooper, Frederick. "Farewell to the Category-Producing Class?" *International Labor and Working-Class History,* no. 57 (Spring 2000): 60–68.

Crowston, Clare Haru. *Fabricating Women: The Seamstresses of Old Regime France, 1675–1791.* Durham, N.C.: Duke University Press, 2001.

Downs, Laura Lee. *Manufacturing Inequality: Gender Division in the French and British Metalworking Industries, 1914–39.* Ithaca, N.Y.: Cornell University Press, 1995.

Eley, Geoff, and Keith Nield. "Farewell to the Working Class?" *International Labor and Working-Class History,* no. 57 (Spring 2000): 1–30.

Engel, Barbara Alpern. *Between the Fields and the City: Women, Work, and Family in Russia, 1861–1914.* Cambridge: Cambridge University Press, 1994.

Frader, Laura Levine, and Sonya O. Rose, eds. *Gender and Class in Modern Europe.* Ithaca, N.Y.: Cornell University Press, 1996.

Franzoi, Barbara. *At the Very Least She Pays the Rent: Women and German Industrialization, 1871–1914.* Westport, Conn.: Greenwood Press, 1985.

Freifeld, Mary. "Technological Change and the 'Self-Acting' Mule: A Study of Skill and the Sexual Division of Labor." *Social History* 11/3 (October 1986): 319–43.

Green, Nancy L. *Ready-to-Wear and Ready-to-Work: A Century of Industry and Immigrants in Paris and New York.* Durham, N.C.: Duke University Press, 1997.

Gullickson, Gay. "Commentary: New Labor History from the Perspective of a Women's Historian," in *Rethinking Labor History: Essays on Discourse and Class Analysis,* edited by Lenard Berlanstein. Urbana: University of Illinois Press, 1993.

———. *Spinners and Weavers of Auffay: Rural Industry and the Sexual Division of Labor in a French Village, 1750–1850.* Cambridge: Cambridge University Press, 1986.

Hagemann, Karen. *Frauenalltag und Männerpolitik: Alltagsleben und gesellschaftliches Handeln von Arbeiterfrauen in der Weimarer Republik.* Bonn: Dietz, 1990.

Hanawalt, Barbara, Thomas Dublin, E. Patricia Tsurumi, and Louise A. Tilly. "*Women, Work, and Family* after Two Decades." *Journal of Women's History* 11/3 (Autumn 1999): 17–30.

Hausen, Karin, ed. *Geschlechterhierarchie und Arbeitsteilung: Zur Geschichte ungleicher Erwerbschancen von Männern und Frauen.* Göttingen: Vandenhoeck & Ruprecht, 1993.

Hilden, Patricia. *Working Women and Socialist Politics in France, 1880–1914: A Regional Study.* Oxford: Oxford University Press, 1986.

Joyce, Patrick. *Visions of the People: Industrial England and the Question of Class, 1848–1914.* Cambridge: Cambridge University Press, 1991.

———, ed. *The Historical Meanings of Work.* Cambridge: Cambridge University Press, 1987.

Kaplan, Temma. "Female Consciousness and Collective Action: The Case of Barcelona, 1910–18," in *Feminist Theory: A Critique of Ideology,* edited by Nannerl O. Keohane, Michelle Z. Rosaldo, and Barbara C. Gelpi. Chicago: University of Chicago Press, 1981.

———. *Taking Back the Streets: Women, Youth, and Direct Democracy.* Berkeley: University of California Press, 2004.

Kerchner, Brigitte. *Beruf und Geschlecht: Frauenberufsverbände in Deutschland 1848–1908.* Göttingen: Vandenhoeck & Ruprecht, 1992.

Kessler-Harris, Alice. "Gender and Work: Possibilities for a Global, Historical Overview," in *Women's History in Global Perspective,* edited by Bonnie G. Smith. Urbana: University of Illinois Press, 2004.

Kocka, Jürgen. *Arbeitsverhältnisse und Arbeiterexistenzen: Grundlagen der Klassenbildung im 19. Jahrhundert.* Bonn: Dietz, 1990.

———. *Weder Stand noch Klasse: Unterschichten um 1800.* Bonn: Dietz, 1990.

Liu, Tessie. *The Weaver's Knot: The Contradictions of Class Struggle and Family Solidarity in Western France, 1750–1914.* Ithaca, N.Y.: Cornell University Press, 1994.

Lown, Judy. *Women and Industrialization: Gender at Work in Nineteenth-Century England.* Cambridge: Polity Press, 1990.

Newton, Judith L., Mary P. Ryan, and Judith R. Walkowitz, eds. *Sex and Class in Women's History.* London: Routledge, 1983.

Nolan, Mary. "Economic Crisis, State Policy, and Working-Class Formation in Germany, 1870–1900," in *Working-Class Formation: Nineteenth-Century Patterns in Western Europe and the United States,* edited by Ira Katznelson and Aristide Zolberg. Princeton, N.J.: Princeton University Press, 1986.

Oertzen, Christine von. *Teilzeit und die Lust am Zuverdienen: Geschlechterpolitik und gesellschaftlicher Wandel in Westdeutschland, 1948–1969.* Göttingen: Vandenhoeck & Ruprecht, 1999.

Parr, Joy. "Disaggregating the Sexual Division of Labour: A Transatlantic Case Study." *Comparative Study of Society and History* 30/2 (1988): 511–33.

Patriarca, Silvana. "Gender Trouble: Women and the Making of Italy's 'Active Population,' 1861–1936." *Journal of Modern Italian Studies* 3/2 (1998): 144–63.

Paul, Kathleen, Marc W. Steinberg, and Ann Farnsworth-Alvear, eds. *What Next for Labor and Working-Class History?* Special issue of *International Labor and Working-Class History,* no. 46 (Fall 1994).

Quataert, Jean H. "The Shaping of Women's Work in Manufacturing: Guilds, Households, and the State in Central Europe, 1648–1870." *American Historical Review* 90 (December 1985): 1122–48.

Reddy, William. *Money and Liberty in Modern Europe: A Critique of Historical Understanding.* Cambridge: Cambridge University Press, 1987.

——. *The Rise of Market Culture: The Textile Trade and French Society, 1750–1900.* Cambridge: Cambridge University Press, 1984.

Rose, Sonya O. "'Gender at Work': Sex, Class, and Industrial Capitalism." *History Workshop* 21 (Spring 1986): 113–31.

——. "Gender Segregation in the Transition to the Factory: The English Hosiery Industry, 1850–1910." *Feminist Studies* 13/1 (Spring 1987): 163–84.

——. *Limited Livelihoods: Gender and Class in Nineteenth-Century England.* Berkeley: University of California Press, 1992.

Ross, Ellen. *Love and Toil: Motherhood in Outcast London, 1870–1918.* Oxford: Oxford University Press, 1993.

Rouette, Susanne. *Sozialpolitik als Geschlechterpolitik: Die Regulierung der Frauenarbeit nach dem Ersten Weltkrieg.* Frankfurt a. M.: Campus Verlag, 1993.

Schmitt, Sabine. *Der Arbeiterinnenschutz im deutschen Kaiserreich: Zur Konstruktion der schutzbedürftigen Arbeiterin.* Stuttgart: Metzler, 1995.

Scott, Joan W. "The 'Class' We Have Lost." *International Labor and Working-Class History,* no. 57 (Spring 2000): 69–75.

——. "On Language, Gender and Working-Class History." *International Labor and Working-Class History,* no. 31 (Spring 1987): 1–36. Reprinted in Scott, *Gender and the Politics of History.* New York: Columbia University Press, 1988.

Scott, Joan W., and Louise Tilly. *Women, Work, and Family.* New York: Holt, Rinehart and Winston, 1978.

Sewell, William H., Jr. "How Classes Are Made: Critical Reflections on E. P. Thompson's Theory of Working-Class Formation," in *E. P. Thompson: Critical Perspectives,* edited by Harvey Kaye and Keith McClelland. Philadelphia: Temple University Press, 1990.

——. "Toward a Post-materialist Rhetoric for Labor History," in *Rethinking Labor History: Essays on Discourse and Class Analysis,* edited by Lenard Berlanstein. Urbana: University of Illinois Press, 1993.

——. *Work and Revolution in France: The Language of Labor from the Old Regime to 1848.* Cambridge: Cambridge University Press, 1980.

Sowerwine, Charles. *Sisters or Citizens? Women and Socialism in France since 1876.* Cambridge: Cambridge University Press, 1982.

Stedman Jones, Gareth. *Languages of Class: Studies in English Working-Class History, 1832–1982.* Cambridge: Cambridge University Press, 1983.

Tabili, Laura. *"We Ask for British Justice": Workers and Racial Difference in Late Imperial Britain.* Ithaca, N.Y.: Cornell University Press, 1994.

Taylor, Barbara. *Eve and the New Jerusalem: Socialism and Feminism in the Nineteenth Century.* London: Virago, 1983.

Terdiman, Richard. "Is There Class in This Class?" in *The New Historicism,* edited by H. Aram Veeser. New York: Routledge, 1989.

Tröger, Annemarie. "The Creation of a Female Assembly-Line Proletariat," in *When Biology Became Destiny,* edited by Renate Bridenthal, Atina Grossmann, and Marion Kaplan. New York: Monthly Review Press, 1984.

Valenze, Deborah. *The First Industrial Woman.* Oxford: Oxford University Press, 1994.

Weinstein, Barbara. "Where Do New Ideas (about Class) Come From?" *International Labor and Working-Class History,* no. 57 (Spring 2000): 53–59.

III. GENDER HISTORY BY THEME AND HISTORICAL PERIOD

III.1. Middle-Class Formation, Domesticity, and Consumption

Armstrong, Nancy. *Desire and Domestic Fiction: A Political History of the Novel.* New York: Oxford University Press, 1987.

Auslander, Leora. "The Gendering of Consumer Practices in Nineteenth-Century France," in *The Sex of Things: Gender and Consumption in Historical Perspective,* edited by Victoria de Grazia and Ellen Furlough. Berkeley: University of California Press, 1996.

———. *Taste and Power: Furnishing Modern France.* Berkeley: University of California Press, 1996.

Benson, Susan Porter. *Counter Cultures: Saleswomen, Managers, and Customers in American Department Stores, 1890–1940.* Urbana: University of Illinois Press, 1986.

Breckman, Warren. "Disciplining Consumption: The Debate about Luxury in Wilhelmine Germany, 1890–1914." *Journal of Social History* 24/3 (Spring 1991): 485–505.

Carter, Erica. *How German Is She? Postwar West German Reconstruction and the Consuming Woman.* Ann Arbor: University of Michigan Press, 1997.

Christ, Carol. "Victorian Masculinity and the Angel in the House," in *A Widening Sphere: Changing Roles of Victorian Women,* edited by Martha Vicinus. Bloomington: Indiana University Press, 1977.

Coffin, Judith G. "Consumption, Production, and Gender: The Sewing Machine in Nineteenth-Century France," in *Gender and Class in Modern Europe,* edited by Laura Levine Frader and Sonya O. Rose. Ithaca, N.Y.: Cornell University Press, 1996.

——. "The Politics of Things: New Directions in the History of Consumption." *Journal of Modern History* 71/1 (March 1999): 177–81.

——. "A 'Standard' of Living? European Perspectives on Class and Consumption in the Early Twentieth Century," in *Class and Consumption,* edited by Victoria de Grazia and Lizabeth Cohen. Special issue of *International Labor and Working-Class History,* no. 55 (1999).

Cohen, Lizabeth. *A Consumer's Republic: The Politics of Mass Consumption in Postwar America.* New York: Knopf, 2003.

Crew, David F., ed. *Consuming Germany in the Cold War.* Leisure, Consumption and Culture Series. New York: Berg, 2003.

Crowston, Clare Haru. "The Queen and Her 'Minister of Fashion': Gender, Credit, and Politics in Pre-Revolutionary France." *Gender & History* 14/1 (April 2002): 92–116.

Davidoff, Leonore, and Catherine Hall. *Family Fortunes: Men and Women of the English Middle Class, 1780–1950.* Chicago: University of Chicago Press, 1987.

Einhorn, Barbara. *Cinderella Goes to Market: Citizenship, Gender, and Women's Movements in East Central Europe.* London: Verso, 1993.

Engel, Barbara Alpern. *Mothers and Daughters: Women of the Intelligentsia in Nineteenth-Century Russia.* Cambridge: Cambridge University Press, 1983.

Frank, Dana. "Consumerism and Consumption," in *Reader's Companion to U.S. Women's History.* Boston: Houghton Mifflin, 1998. Electronic resource: Electronic Data. Boulder, Colorado: Net Library, 2001.

Frevert, Ute, ed. *Bürgerinnen und Bürger: Geschlechterverhältnisse im 19. Jahrhundert.* Göttingen: Vandehoeck & Ruprecht, 1988.

Grazia, Victoria de. "Empowering Women as Citizen-Consumers," in *The Sex of Things: Gender and Consumption in Historical Perspective,* edited by Victoria de Grazia and Ellen Furlough. Berkeley: University of California Press, 1996.

Grazia, Victoria de, and Lizabeth Cohen. "Class and Consumption." *International Labor and Working-Class History,* no. 55 (1999): 1–5.

Grazia, Victoria de, and Ellen Furlough. *The Sex of Things: Gender and Consumption in Historical Perspective.* Berkeley: University of California Press, 1996.

Hall, Catherine. *White, Male and Middle-Class: Explorations in Feminism and History.* Cambridge: Polity, 1992.

Hausen, Karin. "Family and Role-Division: The Polarisation of Sexual Stereotypes in the Nineteenth Century," in *The German Family: Essays on the Social History of the Family in Nineteenth- and Twentieth-Century Germany,* edited by Richard J. Evans and W. R. Lee. London: Croom Helm; Totowa, N.J.: Barnes & Noble, 1981.

Israel, Kali. *Names and Stories: Emilia Dilke and Victorian Culture.* New York: Oxford University Press, 1999.

Joeres, Ruth-Ellen B., and Mary Jo Maynes, eds. *German Women in the Eighteenth and Nineteenth Centuries: A Social and Literary History.* Bloomington: Indiana University Press, 1986.

Kaplan, Marion A. *The Making of the Jewish Middle Class: Women, Family, and Identity in Imperial Germany.* New York: Oxford University Press, 1991.

Lewis, Jane, ed. *Labour and Love: Women's Experience of Home and Family, 1850–1940.* London: Blackwell, 1986.

Peiss, Kathy. *Cheap Amusements: Working Women and Leisure in New York City, 1880 to 1920.* Philadelphia: Temple University Press, 1986.

——. *Hope in a Jar: The Making of America's Beauty Culture.* New York: Metropolitan Books, 1998.

Pence, Katherine. "Labours of Consumption: Gendered Consumers in Post-War East and West German Reconstruction," in *Gender Relations in German History,* edited by Lynn Abrams and Elizabeth Harvey. Durham, N.C.: Duke University Press, 1997.

Petro, Patrice. "Perceptions of Difference: Woman as Spectator and Spectacle," in *Women in the Metropolis: Gender and Modernity in Weimar Culture,* edited by Katharina von Ankum. Berkeley: University of California Press, 1997.

Poovey, Mary. *Uneven Developments: The Ideological Work of Gender.* Chicago: University of Chicago Press, 1988.

Roberts, Mary Louise. *Disruptive Acts: The New Woman in Fin-de-Siècle France.* Chicago: University of Chicago Press, 2002.

Rosenhaft, Eve. "Lesewut, Kinosucht, Radiotismus. Zur (geschlechter-)politischen Relevanz neuer Massenmedien in den 1920er Jahren," in *Amerikanisierung: Traum und Alptraum im Deutschland des 20. Jahrhunderts,* edited by Alf Lüdtke. Stuttgart: Steiner, 1996.

Ross, Ellen. *Love and Toil: Motherhood in Outcast London, 1870–1918.* Oxford: Oxford University Press, 1993.

Scanlon, Jennifer. *The Gender and Consumer Culture Reader.* New York: New York University Press, 2000.

Schissler, Hannah, ed. *The Miracle Years: A Cultural History of West Germany, 1949–1968.* Princeton, N.J.: Princeton University Press, 2001.

Smith, Bonnie G. *Ladies of the Leisure Class: The Bourgeoisie of Northern France in the Nineteenth Century.* Princeton, N.J.: Princeton University Press, 1981.

Stewart, Mary Lynn. *For Health and Beauty: Physical Culture for Frenchwomen, 1880s–1930s.* Baltimore: Johns Hopkins University Press, 2001.

Strasser, Susan, Charles McGovern, and Matthias Judt, eds. *Getting and Spending: European and American Consumer Societies in the Twentieth Century.* Cambridge: Cambridge University Press, 1998.

Tosh, John. *A Man's Place: Masculinity and the Middle-Class Home in Victorian England.* New Haven, Conn.: Yale University Press, 1999.

Vicinus, Martha. *Suffer and Be Still: Women in the Victorian Age.* Bloomington: Indiana University Press, 1972.

——. *A Widening Sphere: Changing Roles of Victorian Women.* Bloomington: Indiana University Press, 1977.

Weckel, Ulrike. "A Lost Paradise of a Female Culture? Some Critical Questions Regarding the Scholarship on Late Eighteenth- and Early Nineteenth-Century German Salons." *German History* 18/3 (2000): 310–36.

Williams, Rosalind. *Dream Worlds: Mass Consumption in Late Nineteenth-Century France.* Berkeley: University of California Press, 1982.

III.2. Gender and Nation/Nationalism

Anderson, Benedict. *Imagined Communities: Reflections on the Origin and Spread of Nationalism.* London: Verso, 1983.

Baron, Beth. "The Making of the Egyptian Nation," in *Gendered Nations: Nationalism and Gender Order in the Long Nineteenth Century,* edited by Ida Blom, Karen Hagemann, and Catherine Hall. Oxford: Berg, 2000.

Blobaum, Robert. "The 'Woman Question' in Russian Poland, 1900–1914." *Journal of Social History* 35/4 (Summer 2002): 799–824.

Blom, Ida, Karen Hagemann, and Catherine Hall, eds. *Gendered Nations: Nationalism and Gender Order in the Long Nineteenth Century.* Oxford: Berg, 2000.

Chaterjee, Partha. *The Nation and Its Fragments: Colonial and Postcolonial Histories.* Princeton, N.J.: Princeton University Press, 1993.

Chickering, Roger. "'Casting Their Gaze More Broadly': Women's Patriotic Activism in Imperial Germany." *Past & Present* 118 (February 1988): 156–85.

Eley, Geoff, and Ronald G. Suny, eds. *Becoming National: A Reader.* New York: Oxford University Press, 1996.

Enders, Victoria Loree, and Pamela B. Radcliff, eds. *Constructing Spanish Womanhood: Female Identity in Modern Spain.* Albany: State University of New York Press, 1999.

Fidelis, Malgorzata. "'Participation in the Creative Work of the Nation': Polish Women Intellectuals in the Cultural Construction of Female Gender Roles, 1864–1890." *Journal of Women's History* 13/1 (Spring 2001): 108–31.

Hagemann, Karen. "Female Patriots: Women, War, and the Nation in the Period of the Prussian-German Anti-Napoleonic Wars." *Gender & History* 16/2 (August 2004): 397–424.

Hagemann, Karen. *"Mannlicher Muth und teutsche Ehre": Nation, Militär und Geschlecht zur Zeit der antinapoleonischen Kriege Preußens.* Paderborn: Schöningh, 2002.

Hagemann, Karen, and Ralf Pröve, eds. *Landsknechte, Soldatenfrauen und Nationalkrieger: Militär, Krieg und Geschlechterordnung im historischen Wandel.* Frankfurt a. M.: Campus Verlag, 1998.

Hall, Catherine, Keith McClelland, and Jane Rendall, eds. *Defining the Victorian Nation: Class, Race, and Gender and the British Reform Act of 1867.* Cambridge: Cambridge University Press, 2000.

Herminghouse, Patricia, and Magda Mueller, eds. *Gender and Germanness: Cultural Productions of Nation.* Providence, R.I.: Berghahn, 1997.

Jaworski, Rudolf, and Bianka Pietrow-Ennker, eds. *Women in Polish Society.* Boulder, Colo.: East European Monographs, 1992.

Landes, Joan. *Visualizing the Nation: Gender, Representation, and Revolution in Eighteenth-Century France.* Ithaca, N.Y.: Cornell University Press, 2001.

Malečková, Jitka. "Nationalizing Women and Engendering the Nation: The Czech National Movement," in *Gendered Nations: Nationalism and Gender Order in the Long Nineteenth Century,* edited by Ida Blom, Karen Hagemann, and Catherine Hall. Oxford: Berg, 2000.

Mosse, George. *Nationalism and Sexuality: Respectability and Abnormal Sexuality in Modern Europe.* New York: H. Fertig, 1985.

Novikova, Irina. "Constructing National Identity in Latvia: Gender and Representation during the Period of National Awakening," in *Gendered Nations: Nationalism and Gender Order in the Long Nineteenth Century,* edited by Ida Blom, Karen Hagemann, and Catherine Hall. Oxford: Berg, 2000.

Parker, Andrew, et al., eds. *Nationalisms and Sexualities.* London: Routledge, 1992.

Pierson, Ruth Roach. "Nations: Gendered, Racialized, Crossed with Empire," in *Gendered Nations: Nationalism and Gender Order in the Long Nineteenth Century,* edited by Ida Blom, Karen Hagemann, and Catherine Hall. Oxford: Berg, 2000.

Pierson, Ruth Roach, and Nupur Chaudhuri, eds. *Nation, Empire, Colony: Historicizing Gender and Race.* Bloomington: Indiana University Press, 1998.

Planert, Ute. *Antifeminismus im Kaiserreich: Diskurs, soziale Formation und politische Mentalität.* Göttingen: Vandenhoeck & Ruprecht, 1998.

——, ed. *Nation, Politik und Geschlecht: Frauenbewegungen und Nationalismus in der Moderne.* Frankfurt a. M.: Campus, 2000.

Ponichtera, Robert. "Feminists, Nationalists, and Soldiers: Women in the Fight for Polish Independence." *International History Review* 19/1 (February 1997).

Quataert, Jean H. *Staging Philanthropy: Patriotic Women and the National Imagination in Dynastic Germany, 1813–1916.* Ann Arbor: University of Michigan Press, 2001.

Sinha, Mrinalini. "Gender and Nation," in *Women's History in Global Perspective,* ed. Bonnie G. Smith. Urbana: University of Illinois Press, 2004.

Wildenthal, Lora. "'She is the Victor': Bourgeois Women, Nationalist Identities, and the Ideal of the Independent Woman Farmer in German Southwest Africa," in *Society, Culture and the State in Germany, 1870–1930,* edited by Geoff Eley. Ann Arbor: University of Michigan Press, 1996.

III.3. Empire, Colonialism, and Race

Amos, Vicky, and Pratibha Parmar. "Challenging Imperial Feminism." *Feminist Review* 17 (1984): 3–19.

Anzaldúa, Gloria, and Cherrie Moraga, eds. *This Bridge Called My Back: Writings of Radical Women of Color.* New York: Kitchen Table, Women of Color Press, 1982.

Bhavnani, Kum-kum, ed. *Feminism and "Race."* Oxford: Oxford University Press, 2001.

Brown, Elsa Barkley. "'What Has Happened Here': The Politics of Difference in Women's History and Feminist Politics." *Feminist Studies* 18 (Summer 1992): 295–312.

Burton, Antoinette. *At the Heart of the Empire: Indians and the Colonial Encounter in Late Victorian Britain*. Berkeley: University of California Press, 1998.

——. *Burdens of History: British Feminists, Indian Women, and Imperial Culture*. Chapel Hill: University of North Carolina Press, 1994.

——. *Dwelling in the Archive: Women, Writing, House, Home, and History in Late Colonial India*. Oxford: Oxford University Press, 2003.

——, ed. *After the Imperial Turn: Thinking with and through the Nation*. Durham, N.C.: Duke University Press, 2003.

——, ed. *Gender, Sexuality, and Colonial Modernities*. London: Routledge, 1999.

Camiscoli, Elisa. "Gender, Colonialism, and Citizenship in the Modern Middle East." *Gender & History* 16/1 (April 2004): 205–8.

Campt, Tina. "Blacks, Germans, and the Politics of Imperial Imagination, 1920–60," in *The Imperialist Imagination: German Colonialism and Its Legacies*, edited by Sarah Friedrichsmeyer, Sarah Lennox, and Suzanne Zantop. Ann Arbor: University of Michigan Press, 1998.

——. *Other Germans: Black Germans and the Politics of Race, Gender, and Memory in the Third Reich*. Ann Arbor: University of Michigan Press, 2004.

Chaudhuri, Nupur, and Margaret Strobel, eds. *Western Women and Imperialism: Complicity and Resistance*. Bloomington: Indiana University Press, 1992.

Chaterjee, Partha. "The Nationalist Resolution of the Women's Question," in *Recasting Women: Essays in Indian Colonial History*, edited by Kunkum Sangari and Sudesh Vaid. New Brunswick, N.J.: Rutgers University Press, 1990.

Collingham, E. M. *Imperial Bodies: The Physical Experience of the Raj, c. 1800–1947*. Cambridge: Polity Press, 2001.

Collins, Patricia Hill. "The Social Construction of Black Feminist Thought." *Signs* 14/4 (Summer 1989): 745–73.

Davin, Anna. "Imperialism and Motherhood." *History Workshop* 5 (1978): 9–65. Reprinted in *Tensions of Empire: Colonial Cultures in a Bourgeois World*, edited by Frederick Cooper and Ann Stoler. Berkeley: University of California Press, 1997.

Dawson, Graham. *Soldier Heroes: British Adventure, Empire, and the Imagining of Masculinities*. London: Routledge, 1994.

Dill, Bonnie Thornton. "Race, Class and Gender: Prospects for an All-Inclusive Sisterhood." *Feminist Studies* 9 (Spring 1983): 131–50.

Ferguson, Moira. *Subject to Others: British Women Writers and Colonial Slavery, 1670–1834*. London: Routledge, 1992.

Hall, Catherine. *Civilising Subjects: Metropole and Colony in the English Imagination, 1830–1867*. Oxford: Polity, 2002.

——. "The Rule of Difference: Gender, Class and Empire in the Making of the 1832 Reform Act," in *Gendered Nations: Nationalism and Gender Order in the Long Nineteenth Century*, edited by Ida Blom, Karen Hagemann, and Catherine Hall. Oxford: Berg, 2000.

——, ed. *Cultures of Empire: Colonizers in Britain and the Empire in the Nineteenth and Twentieth Centuries. A Reader.* New York: Routledge, 2000.

Higginbotham, Evelyn Brooks. "African-American Women's History and the Metalanguage of Race." *Signs* 17/2 (1992): 251–74.

Hooks, Bell. *Ain't I a Woman? Black Women and Feminism.* Boston: South End Press, 1981.

——. *Yearning: Race, Gender, and Cultural Politics.* Boston: South End Press, 1990.

Hunt, Nancy Rose. *A Colonial Lexicon of Birth Ritual, Medicalization, and Mobility in the Congo.* Durham, N.C.: Duke University Press, 1999.

Hurtado, Aida. "Relating to Privilege: Seduction and Rejection in the Subordination of White Women and Women of Color." *Signs* 14/4 (1989): 833–55.

McClintock, Anne. *Imperial Leather: Race, Gender, and Sexuality in the Colonial Movement.* New York: Routledge, 1995.

Mohanty, Chandra Talpade. *Feminism without Borders: Decolonizing Theory, Practicing Solidarity.* Durham, N.C.: Duke University Press, 2003.

——. "Feminist Politics: What's Home Got to Do with It?" in *Feminist Studies/Critical Studies,* edited by Teresa de Lauretis. Bloomington: Indiana University Press, 1986.

Mohanty, Chandra Talpade, Ann Russo, and Lourdes Torres, eds. *Third World Women and the Politics of Feminism.* Bloomington: Indiana University Press, 1991.

Pedersen, Susan. "National Bodies, Unspeakable Acts: The Sexual Politics of Colonial Policy-Making." *Journal of Modern History* 63 (December 1991): 647–80.

Pierson, Ruth Roach. "Nations: Gendered, Racialized, Crossed with Empire," in *Gendered Nations: Nationalism and Gender Order in the Long Nineteenth Century,* edited by Ida Blom, Karen Hagemann, and Catherine Hall. Oxford: Berg, 2000.

Pierson, Ruth Roach, and Nupur Chaudhuri, eds. *Nation, Empire, Colony: Historicizing Gender and Race.* Bloomington: Indiana University Press, 1998.

Scully, Pamela. "Race and Ethnicity in Women's and Gender History in Global Perspective," in *Women's History in Global Perspective,* ed. Bonnie G. Smith. Urbana: University of Illinois Press, 2004.

Sinha, Mrinalini. *Colonial Masculinity: The "Manly Englishman" and the "Effeminate Bengali" in the Late Nineteenth Century.* Manchester: Manchester University Press, 1995.

——. "Gender in the Critiques of Colonialism and Nationalism: Locating the 'Indian Woman,'" in *Feminists Revision History,* edited by Ann-Louise Shapiro. New Brunswick, N.J.: Rutgers University Press, 1994.

Smith, Barbara, ed. *Home Girls: A Black Feminist Anthology.* New York: Kitchen Table, Women of Color Press, 1983.

Smith, Julia Clancy, and Frances Gouda, eds. *Domesticating the Empire: Race, Gender, and Family Life in French and Dutch Colonialism.* Charlottesville: University of Virginia Press, 1998.

Spillers, Hortense. *Conjuring: Black Women, Fiction, and Literary Tradition.* Bloomington: Indiana University Press, 1985.

Stoler, Ann Laura. "Carnal Knowledge and Imperial Power: Gender, Race, and Morality in Colonial Asia," in *Feminism and History,* edited by Joan Wallach Scott. Oxford: Oxford University Press, 1996.

———. *Carnal Knowledge and Imperial Power: Race and the Intimate in Colonial Rule.* Berkeley: University of California Press, 2002.

———. "Making Empire Respectable: The Politics of Race and Sexual Morality in Twentieth-Century Colonial Cultures." *American Ethnologist* 16/4 (November 1989): 634–60.

Stoler, Ann Laura, and Karen Strassler. "Castings for the Colonial: Memory Work in 'New Order' Java." *Comparative Study of Society and History* 42/1 (2000): 4–48.

Stoler, Ann Laura, and Frederick Cooper, eds. *Tensions of Empire: Colonial Cultures in a Bourgeois World.* Berkeley: University of California Press, 1997.

Thomas, Lynn. *Politics of the Womb: Women, Reproduction, and the State in Kenya.* Berkeley: University of California Press, 2003.

Thompson, Elizabeth. *Colonial Citizens: Republican Rights, Paternal Privilege, and Gender in French Syria and Lebanon.* New York: Columbia University Press, 2000.

Trinh T. Minh-ha. "Not You/Like You: Post-Colonial Women and the Interlocking Questions of Identity and Difference." *Inscriptions* 3/4 (1988):71–76.

———, ed. *She, the Inappropriate/d Other.* Special issue of *Discourse* 8 (1986–87).

Weindling, Paul. *Health, Race, and German Politics between National Unification and Nazism, 1870–1945.* Cambridge: Cambridge University Press, 1989.

Wildenthal, Lora J. *German Women for Empire, 1884–1945.* Durham, N.C.: Duke University Press, 2001.

III.4. The First World War

Becker, Jean-Jacques. *The Great War and the French People.* Leamington Spa: Berg, 1986.

Berkin, Carol, and Clara Lovett. *Women, War, and Revolution.* New York: Holmes & Meier, 1980.

Bessel, Richard. *Germany after the First World War.* Oxford: Clarendon Press, 1993.

Braybon, Gail. *Women Workers in the First World War.* London: Croom Helm, 1981.

Chickering, Roger. *Imperial Germany and the Great War, 1914–1918.* Cambridge: Cambridge University Press, 1998.

———. "Total War: Use and Abuse of a Concept," in *Anticipating Total War: The German and American Experiences, 1871–1914,* edited by Manfred Boemeke. Cambridge: Cambridge University Press, 1999.

Cohen, Deborah. *The War Come Home: Disabled Veterans in Britain and Germany, 1914–1939.* Berkeley: University of California Press, 2001.

Damousi, Joy, and Marilyn Lake, eds. *Gender and War: Australians at War in the Twentieth Century.* Cambridge: Cambridge University Press, 1995.

Daniel, Ute. *The War from Within: German Working-Class Women in the First World War,* translated by Margaret Ries. Oxford: Berg, 1997.

Davis, Belinda. "Experience, Identity, and Memory: The Legacy of World War I." *Journal of Modern History* 75 (March 2003): 111–31.

——. *Home Fires Burning: Food, Politics, and Everyday Life in World War I Berlin*. Chapel Hill: University of North Carolina Press, 2000.

Domansky, Elizabeth. "Militarization and Reproduction in World War I Germany," in *Society, Culture, and the State in Germany, 1870–1930*, edited by Geoff Eley. Ann Arbor: University of Michigan Press, 1996.

Ecksteins, Modris. *Rites of Spring: The Great War and the Birth of the Modern Age*. New York: Anchor, 1990.

Engel, Barbara Alpern. "Not by Bread Alone: Subsistence Riots in Russia during World War I." *Journal of Modern History* 69/4 (1997): 696–721.

Fridenson, Patrick, ed. *The French Home Front*. Providence, R.I.: Berg, 1992.

Fussell, Paul. *The Great War and Modern Memory*. New York: Oxford University Press, 1975.

Grayzel, Susan R. *Women's Identities at War: Gender, Motherhood, and Politics in Britain and France during the First World War*. Chapel Hill: University of North Carolina Press, 1999.

Gullace, Nicoletta. *The Blood of Our Sons: Men, Women, and the Renegotiation of British Citizenship during the Great War*. New York: Palgrave, 2002.

——. "Women and War in Comparative Perspective." *Gender & History* 15/1 (April 2003): 140–45.

Hagemann, Karen, and Stefanie Schüler-Springorum. *Home/Front: The Military, War, and Gender in Twentieth-Century Germany*. Oxford: Berg, 2002. Originally published as *Heimat/Front: Militär und Geschlechterverhältnisse im Zeitalter der Weltkriege*. Frankfurt a. M.: Campus Verlag, 2002.

Harris, Ruth. "The 'Child of the Barbarian': Rape, Race, and Nationalism in France during the First World War." *Past & Present* 141 (November 1993): 170–206.

Hausen, Karin. "The 'Day of National Mourning' in Germany," in *Between History and Histories: The Making of Silences and Commemorations*, edited by Gerald Sider and Gavin Smith. Toronto: University of Toronto Press, 1997.

Higonnet, Margaret R. *Nurses at the Front: Writing the Wounds of the Great War*. Boston: Northeastern University Press, 2001.

Higonnet, Margaret Randolph, Jane Jenson, Sonya Michel, and Margaret Weitz, eds. *Behind the Lines: Gender and the Two World Wars*. New Haven, Conn.: Yale University Press, 1987.

Horne, John, ed. *State, Society, and Mobilization in Europe during the First World War*. Studies in the Social and Cultural History of Modern Warfare, vol. 3. Cambridge: Cambridge University Press, 1997.

Horne, John, and Alan Kramer. *German Atrocities, 1914: A History of Denial*. New Haven, Conn.: Yale University Press, 2001.

Kienitz, Sabine. *Beschädigte Helden: Kriegsinvalide Körper in der Kultur. Deutschland 1914–1923*. Paderborn: Schöningh, 2006 (forthcoming).

——. "Body Damage: War Disability and Constructions of Masculinity in Weimar Germany," in *Home/Front: The Military, War, and Gender in Twentieth-Century Germany,* edited by Karen Hagemann and Stefanie Schüler-Springorum. Oxford: Berg, 2002.

Köller, Christian, "Race and Gender Stereotypes in the Discussion on Colonial Troops: A Franco-German Comparison," in *Home/Front: The Military, War, and Gender in Twentieth-Century Germany,* edited by Karen Hagemann and Stefanie Schüler-Springorum. Oxford: Berg, 2002.

——. *"Von Wilden aller Rassen niedergemetzelt": Die Diskussion um die Verwendung von Kolonialtruppen in Europa zwischen Rassismus, Kolonial- und Militärpolitik (1914–30).* Stuttgart: Franz Steiner, 2001.

Kühne, Thomas, and Benjamin Ziemann. "Militärgeschichte in der Erweiterung: Konjunkturen, Interpretationen, Konzepte," in *Was ist Militärgeschichte?* edited by Thomas Kühne and Benjamin Ziemann. Paderborn: Schöningh, 2000.

Kundrus, Birthe. "The First World War and the Construction of Gender Relations in the Weimar Republic," in *Home/Front: The Military, War, and Gender in Twentieth-Century Germany,* edited by Karen Hagemann and Stefanie Schüler-Springorum. Oxford: Berg, 2002.

——. *Kriegerfrauen: Familienpolitik und Geschlechterverhältnisse im Ersten und Zweiten Weltkrieg.* Hamburg: Christians, 1995.

Leed, Eric. *No Man's Land: Combat and Identity in World War I.* Cambridge: Cambridge University Press, 1979.

Lerner, Paul. "Hysterical Cures: Hypnosis, Gender, and Performance in World War I and Weimar Germany." *History Workshop* 45 (1998): 79–99.

——. *Hysterical Men: War, Psychiatry, and the Politics of Trauma in Germany, 1890–1930.* Ithaca, N.Y.: Cornell University Press, 2003.

Marwick, Arthur. *The Deluge: British Society and the First World War.* Houndsmills: Macmillan, 1991.

Mosse, George. *Fallen Soldiers: Reshaping the Memory of the World Wars.* New York: Oxford University Press, 1990.

Nelson, Robert. "German Comrades—Slavic Whores: Gender Images in the German Soldier Newspapers of the First World War," in *Home/Front: The Military, War, and Gender in Twentieth-Century Germany,* edited by Karen Hagemann and Stefanie Schüler-Springorum. Oxford: Berg, 2002.

Shevin-Coetzee, Marilyn, and Frans Coetzee, eds. *Authority, Identity, and the Social History of the Great War.* Providence, R.I.: Berghahn, 1995.

——, eds. *World War I and European Society: A Sourcebook.* Lexington, Mass.: D. C. Heath, 1995.

Stites, Richard, and Aviel Roshwald. *European Culture in the Great War: The Arts, Entertainment and Propaganda, 1914–1918.* Studies in the Social and Cultural History of Modern Warfare, vol. 6. Cambridge: Cambridge University Press, 1999.

Thom, Deborah. *Nice Girls and Rude Girls: Women Workers in World War I.* New York: Palgrave, 1998.

Whalen, Robert Weldon. *Bitter Wounds: German Victims of the Great War, 1914–1939.* Ithaca, N.Y.: Cornell University Press, 1984.

Winter, Jay. *The Experience of World War I.* New York: Oxford University Press, 1989.

——. *Sites of Memory, Sites of Mourning: The Great War in European Cultural History.* Cambridge: Cambridge University Press, 1995.

Winter, Jay, and Jean-Louis Robert. *Capital Cities at War: Paris, London, Berlin, 1914–1919.* Cambridge: Cambridge University Press, 1997.

Wohl, Robert. *The Generation of 1914.* Cambridge, Mass.: Harvard University Press, 1979.

Woollacott, Angela. *On Her Their Lives Depend: Munitions Workers in the Great War.* Berkeley: University of California Press, 1994.

Ziemann, Benjamin, and Bernd Ulrich. *Krieg im Frieden: Die umkämpfte Erinnerung an den Ersten Weltkrieg: Quellen und Dokumente.* Frankfurt a. M.: Fischer Verlag, 1997.

III.5. Gender and Modernity: Interwar Period

Ankum, Katharina von, ed. *Women in the Metropolis: Gender and Modernity in Weimar Culture.* Berkeley: University of California Press, 1997.

Apel, Dora. "'Heroes' and 'Whores': The Politics of Gender in Weimar Antiwar Imagery." *Art Bulletin* 79/3 (1997): 366–84.

Barndt, Kerstin. *Sentiment und Sachlichkeit: Der Roman der Neuen Frau in der Weimarer Republik.* Cologne: Böhlau, 2003.

Fritzsche, Peter. "Did Weimar Fail?" *Journal of Modern History* 68/3 (September 1996): 632–33.

Geyer, Martin. *Verkehrte Welt: Revolution, Inflation und Moderne, München 1914–1294.* Göttingen: Vandenhoeck & Ruprecht, 1998.

Gleber, Anke. *The Art of Taking a Walk: Flânerie, Literature, and Film in Weimar Culture.* Princeton, N.J.: Princeton University Press, 1999.

Grossmann, Atina. "*Girlkultur* or Thoroughly Rationalized Female: A New Woman in Weimar Germany?" in *Women in Culture and Politics: A Century of Change,* edited by Judith Friedlander, Blanche W. Cook, Alice Kessler-Harris, and Carroll Smith-Rosenberg. Bloomington: Indiana University Press, 1986.

——. *Reforming Sex: The German Movement for Birth Control and Abortion Reform, 1920–1950.* Oxford: Oxford University Press, 1995.

Huyssen, Andreas. "Mass Culture as Woman: Modernism's Other," in *Studies in Entertainment: Critical Approaches to Mass Culture,* edited by Tania Modleski. Bloomington: Indiana University Press, 1986.

Kent, Susan Kingsley. *Making Peace: The Reconstruction of Gender in Interwar Britain.* Princeton, N.J.: Princeton University Press, 1993.

McCormick, Richard. *Gender and Sexuality in Weimar Modernity: Film, Literature, and "New Objectivity."* New York: Palgrave, 2001.

Nolan, Mary. "'Housework Made Easy': The Taylorized Housewife in Weimar Germany's Rationalized Economy." *Feminist Studies* 16 (1990): 549–77.

——. *Visions of Modernity: American Business and the Modernization of Germany.* New York: Oxford University Press, 1994.

Otto, Elizabeth. "Figuring Gender: Photomontage and Cultural Critique in Germany's Weimar Republic." Ph.D. diss., University of Michigan, 2003.

Petersen, Vibeke Rützou. *Women and Modernity in Weimar Germany: Reality and Representation in Popular Fiction.* Oxford: Berghahn, 2001.

Petro, Patrice. *Joyless Streets: Women and Melodramatic Representation in Weimar Germany.* Princeton, N.J.: Princeton University Press, 1989.

Reynolds, Sian. *France between the Wars: Gender and Politics.* London: Routledge, 1996.

Radcliff, Pamela B. *From Mobilization to Civil War: The Politics of Polarization in the Spanish City of Gijón, 1900–1937.* Cambridge: Cambridge University Press, 1996.

Roberts, Mary Louise. *Civilization without Sexes: Reconstructing Gender in Postwar France, 1917–1927.* Chicago: University of Chicago Press, 1994.

——. "'This Civilization No Longer Has Sexes': *La Garçonne* and Cultural Crisis in France after World War I." *Gender and History* 4/1 (1992): 49–69.

Scheck, Raffael. *Mothers of the Nation: Right-Wing Women in Weimar Germany.* Oxford: Berg, 2004.

——. "Women against Versailles: Maternalism and Nationalism of Female Bourgeois Politicians in the Early Weimar Republic." *German Studies Review* 22/1 (February 1999): 21–41.

Soland, Birgitte. *Becoming Modern: Young Women and the Reconstruction of Womanhood in the 1920s.* Princeton, N.J.: Princeton University Press, 2000.

Tatar, Maria. *Lustmord: Sexual Murder in Weimar Germany.* Princeton, N.J.: Princeton University Press, 1995.

Theweleit, Klaus. *Male Fantasies.* Vol. 1: *Women, Floods, Bodies, History;* vol. 2: *Male Bodies: Psychoanalyzing the White Terror;* translated by Stephen Conway. Minneapolis: University of Minnesota Press, 1987.

Widdig, Bernd. *Culture and Inflation in Weimar Germany.* Berkeley: University of California Press, 2001.

Wood, Elizabeth. *The Baba and the Comrade: Gender and Politics in Revolutionary Russia.* Bloomington: Indiana University Press, 1997.

III.6. Nazism, Fascism, and the Holocaust

Allen, Ann Taylor. "The Holocaust and the Modernization of Gender: A Historiographical Essay." *Central European History* 30/3 (1997): 349–64.

Baumel, Judith T. *Double Jeopardy: Gender and the Holocaust.* London: Vallentine Mitchell, 1998.

Beck, Birgit. "Rape: The Military Trials of Sexual Crimes Committed by Soldiers in the Wehrmacht, 1939–1944," in *Home/Front: The Military, War, and Gender in Twentieth-*

Century Germany, edited by Karen Hagemann and Stefanie Schüler-Springorum. Oxford: Berg, 2002.

Bergen, Doris. "Sex, Blood, and Vulnerability: Women Outsiders in German Occupied Europe," in *Social Outsiders in Nazi Germany*, edited by Robert Gellately and Nathan Stoltzfus. Princeton, N.J.: Princeton University Press, 2001.

Bock, Gisela. "Racism and Sexism in Nazi Germany: Motherhood, Compulsory Sterilization, and the State," in *When Biology Became Destiny*, edited by Renate Bridenthal, Atina Grossmann, and Marion Kaplan. New York: Monthly Review Press, 1984.

———. *Zwangssterilisation im Nationalsozialismus: Studien zur Rassenpolitik und Frauenpolitik.* Opladen: Westdeutscher Verlag, 1986.

Braybon, Gail, and Penny Summerfield, eds. *Out of the Cage: Women's Experiences in Two World Wars.* New York: Pandora Press, 1987.

Bridenthal, Renate, Atina Grossmann, and Marion Kaplan, eds. *When Biology Became Destiny: Women in Weimar and Nazi Germany.* New York: Monthly Review Press, 1984.

Browning, Christopher. *Ordinary Men: Reserve Police Battalion 101 and the Final Solution in Poland.* New York: Harper Perennial, 1993.

Burleigh, Michael, and Wolfgang Wippermann. *The Racial State. Germany 1933–1945.* Cambridge: Cambridge University Press, 1991.

Caldwell, Lesley. "Reproducers of the Nation: Women and the Family in Fascist Policy," in *Rethinking Italian Fascism: Capitalism, Populism, and Culture,* edited by David Forgacs. London: Lawrence & Wishart, 1986.

Czarnowski, Gabriele. *Das kontrollierte Paar: Ehe- und Sexualpolitik im Nationalsozialismus.* Weinheim: Deutscher Studien-Verlag, 1991.

———. "'The Value of Marriage for the *Volksgemeinschaft*': Policies towards Women and Marriage under National Socialism," in *Fascist Italy and Nazi Germany: Comparisons and Contrasts,* edited by Richard Bessel. Cambridge: Cambridge University Press, 1996.

David, Henry P., Jochen Fleischhacker, and Charlotte Höhn. "Abortion and Eugenics in Nazi Germany." *Population and Development Review* 14/1 (March 1988): 81–112.

Ettelson, Todd. "The Nazi 'New Man': Embodying Masculinity and Regulating Sexuality in the SA and SS, 1930–1939." Ph.D. diss., University of Michigan, 2002.

Feinberg, Melissa. "Gender and the Politics of Difference in the Czech Lands after Munich." *East European Politics and Societies* 17/2 (May 2003): 202–30.

Giles, Geoffrey J. "The Institutionalization of Homosexual Panic in the Third Reich," in *Social Outsiders in Nazi Germany,* edited by Robert Gellately and Nathan Stoltzfus. Princeton, N.J.: Princeton University Press, 2001.

———. "'The Most Unkind Cut of All': Castration, Homosexuality and Nazi Justice." *Journal of Contemporary History* 27 (1992): 41–61.

Gottlieb, Julie. *Feminine Fascism: Women in Britain's Fascist Movement, 1923–1945.* London: I. B. Tauris, 2000.

———. "'Motherly Hate': Gendering Anti-Semitism in the British Union of Fascists."
  Gender & History 14/2 (August 2002): 294–320.
Gravenhorst, Lerke, and Carmen Tatschmura, eds. *Töchter-Fragen: NS-Frauen-
  Geschichte*. Freiburg i. B.: Kore, 1990.
Grazia, Victoria de. *How Fascism Ruled Women: Italy 1922–1945*. Berkeley: University
  of California Press, 1992.
Grossmann, Atina. "Feminist Debates about Women and National Socialism." *Gender
  & History* 3/3 (Autumn 1991): 350–58.
———. "A Question of Silence: The Rape of German Women by Occupation Soldiers."
  October 72 (Spring 1995): 43–63. Reprinted in *West Germany under Construction:
  Politics, Society, and Culture in the Adenauer Era*, edited by Robert G. Moeller. Ann
  Arbor: University of Michigan Press, 1997.
Gubar, Susan. "'This Is My Rifle, This Is My Gun': World War II and the Blitz on
  Women," in *Behind the Lines: Gender and the Two World Wars*, edited by Margaret
  Randolph Higonnet, Jane Jenson, Sonya Michel, and Margaret Weitz. New Haven,
  Conn.: Yale University Press, 1987.
Guenther, Irene. *Nazi Chic? Fashioning Women in the Third Reich*. Oxford, Berg, 2004.
Harvey, Elizabeth. "Pilgrimages to the 'Bleeding Border': Gender and Rituals of
  Nationalist Protest in Germany, 1919–39." *Women's History Review* 9/2 (2000): 201–
  29.
———. *Women and the Nazi East: Agents and Witnesses of Germanization*. New Haven,
  Conn.: Yale University Press, 2003.
Jenson, Jane. "The Liberation and New Rights for French Women," in *Behind the Lines:
  Gender and the Two World Wars*, edited by Margaret Randolph Higonnet, Jane
  Jenson, Sonya Michel, and Margaret Weitz. New Haven, Conn.: Yale University Press,
  1987.
Jolluck, Katherine. *Exile and Identity: Polish Women in the Soviet Union during World
  War II*. Pittsburgh: University of Pittsburgh Press, 2002.
———. "'You Can't Even Call Them Women': Poles and 'Others' in Soviet Exile during the
  Second World War." *Contemporary European History* 10/3 (November 2001): 463–80.
Joshi, Vandana. *Gender and Power in the Third Reich: Female Denouncers and the Gestapo
  1933–1945*. Houndsmills: Palgrave, 2003.
Kaplan, Marion. *Between Dignity and Despair: Jewish Life in Nazi Germany*. New York:
  Oxford University Press, 1998.
Leck, Ralph M. "Conservative Empowerment and the Gender of Nazism: Paradigms of
  Power and Complicity in German Women's History." *Journal of Women's History* 12/2
  (Summer 2000): 147–69.
Maiwald, Stefan, and Gerd Mischler. *Sexualität unter dem Hakenkreuz: Manipulation und
  Vernichtung der Intimsphäre im NS-Staat*. Hamburg: Europa Verlag, 1999.
Koonz, Claudia. "The Competition for Women's *Lebensraum* 1928–1934," in *When
  Biology Became Destiny*, edited by Renate Bridenthal, Atina Grossmann, and Marion
  Kaplan. New York: Monthly Review Press, 1984.

———. "Eugenics, Gender, and Ethics in Nazi Germany: The Debate about Involuntary Sterilization 1933–1936," in *Reevaluating the Third Reich*, edited by Thomas Childers and Jane Caplan. New York: Holmes & Meier, 1993.

———. *Mothers in the Fatherland: Women, Family Life, and Nazi Ideology, 1919–1945*. New York: St. Martin's Press, 1986.

Krylova, Anna. "'Healers of Wounded Souls:' The Crisis of Private Life in Soviet Literature and Society, 1944–1946." *Journal of Modern History* 73/2 (June 2001): 307–32.

———. "Stalinist Identity from the Viewpoint of Gender: Rearing a Generation of Professionally Violent Women-Fighters in 1930s Stalinist Russia." *Gender & History* 16/3 (November 2004): 626–53.

Kühne, Thomas. "Comradeship: Gender Confusion and Gender Order in the German Military, 1918–1945," in *Home/Front: The Military, War, and Gender in Twentieth-Century Germany*, edited by Karen Hagemann and Stefanie Schüler-Springorum. Oxford: Berg.

Mason, Timothy. "Women in Germany 1925–1940: Family, Welfare, and Work." *History Workshop* 2 (1976): 5–32.

———. "Women in Nazi Germany." *History Workshop* 1 (1976): 74–113.

Milton, Sybil. "Women and the Holocaust: The Case of German and German Jewish Women," in *When Biology Became Destiny*, edited by Renate Bridenthal, Atina Grossmann, and Marion Kaplan. New York: Monthly Review Press, 1984.

Nash, Mary. *Defying Male Civilization: Women in the Spanish Civil War*. Denver, Colo.: Arden Press, 1995.

Nieden, Susanne zur. "Erotic Fraternization: The Legend of German Women's Quick Surrender," in *Home/Front: the Military, War, and Gender in Twentieth-Century Germany*, edited by Karen Hagemann and Stefanie Schüler-Springorum. Oxford: Berg, 2002.

Peto, Andrea. "Memory and the Narratives of Rape in Budapest and Vienna in 1945," in *Life after Death: Approaches to a Cultural and Social History of Europe during the 1940s and 1950s*, edited by Richard Bessel and Dirk Schumann. Washington, D.C.: German Historical Institute; Cambridge: Cambridge University Press, 2003.

Pollard, Miranda. *Reign of Virtue: Mobilizing Gender in Vichy France*. Chicago: University of Chicago Press, 1998.

Reichardt, Sven. *Faschistische Kampfbünde: Gewalt und Gemeinschaft im italienischen Squadrismus und in der deutschen SA*. Cologne: Böhlau, 2002.

Ringelheim, Joan. "The Split between Gender and the Holocaust," in *Women in the Holocaust*, edited by Dalia Ofer and Lenore Weitzman. New Haven, Conn.: Yale University Press, 1998.

———. "Women and the Holocaust: A Reconsideration of Research." *Signs* 10 (Summer 1985): 741–61.

Rose, Sonya O. *Which People's War? National Identity and Citizenship in Wartime Britain, 1939–1945*. Oxford: Oxford University Press, 2003.

Sachse, Carola. *Industrial Housewives: Women's Social Work in the Factories in Nazi Germany*, translated by Heide Kiessling and Dorothy Rosenberg, edited by Jane Caplan. New York: Institute for Research in History and Haworth Press, 1987.

Saldern, Adelheid von. "Victims or Perpetrators? Controversies about the Role of Women in the Nazi State," in *Nazism and German Society 1933–45*, edited by David F. Crew. London: Routledge, 1994.

Schoppmann, Claudia. "National Socialist Policies towards Female Homosexuality," in *Gender Relations in German History: Power, Agency, and Experience from the Sixteenth to the Twentieth Century*, edited by Lynn Abrams and Elizabeth Harvey. Durham, N.C.: Duke University Press, 1997.

Schoppmann, Claudia. *Nationalsoziastische Sexualpolitik und weibliche Homosexualität*. Pfaffenweiler: Centaurus, 1991.

Schwartz, Paula. "Redefining Resistance: Women's Activism in Wartime France," in *Behind the Lines: Gender and the Two World Wars*, edited by Margaret Randolph Higonnet, Jane Jenson, Sonya Michel, and Margaret Weitz. New Haven, Conn.: Yale University Press, 1987.

Seifert, Ruth. "The Second Front: The Logic of Sexual Violence in Wars," in *Violence and Its Alternatives: An Interdisciplinary Reader*, edited by Manfred B. Steger and Nancy S. Lind. New York: St. Martin's Press, 1999.

Stephenson, Jill. *The Nazi Organization of Women*. Totowa, N.J.: Croom Helm, 1981.

——. *Women in Nazi Germany*. Harlow: Longman, 2001.

——. *Women in Nazi Society*. New York: Barnes & Noble, 1975.

Summerfield, Penny. *Reconstructing Women's Wartime Lives: Discourse and Subjectivity in Oral Histories of the Second World War*. New York: St. Martin's, 1998.

Weitz, Margaret C. *Sisters in the Resistance: How Women Fought to Free France, 1940–1945*. New York: Wiley, 1995.

Willson, Perry R. *The Clockwork Factory: Women and Work in Fascist Italy*. Oxford: Clarendon Press, 1993.

——. *Gender, Family, and Sexuality: The Private Sphere in Italy, 1860–1945*. New York: Palgrave, 2003.

——. *Peasant Women and Politics in Fascist Italy: The Massale Rurali*. London: Routledge, 2002.

——. "Women in Fascist Italy," in *Fascist Italy and Nazi Germany: Comparisons and Contrasts*, edited by Richard Bessel. Cambridge: Cambridge University Press, 1996.

III.7. Postwar Europe and Historical Memory

Biess, Frank. "Men of Reconstruction—The Reconstruction of Men. Returning POWs in East and West Germany, 1945–1955," in *Home/Front: The Military, War, and Gender in Twentieth-Century Germany*, edited by Karen Hagemann and Stefanie Schüler-Springorum. Oxford: Berg, 2002.

Confino, Alon. "Collective Memory and Cultural History: Problems of Method." *History and Memory,* AHR Forum, *American Historical Review* 102/5 (December 1997): 1386–1403.

Crane, Susan A. "Writing the Individual Back into Collective Memory." *History and Memory,* AHR Forum, *American Historical Review* 102/5 (December 1997): 1372–1385.

Damousi, Joy. *The Labour of Loss: Mourning, Memory, and Wartime Bereavement in Australia.* Cambridge: Cambridge University Press, 1999.

Fehrenbach, Heide. "Rehabilitating Fatherland: Race and German Remasculinization." *Signs* 24/1 (Autumn 1998): 107–27.

Friedlander, Saul, ed. *Probing the Limits of Representation: Nazism and the "Final Solution."* Cambridge, Mass.: Harvard University Press, 1992.

Fritzsche, Peter. "The Case of Modern Memory." *Journal of Modern History* 73/1 (March 2001): 87–117.

Grossmann, Atina. "Trauma, Memory, and Motherhood: German and Jewish Displaced Persons in Post-Nazi Germany, 1945–1949," in *Life after Death: Approaches to a Cultural and Social History of Europe during the 1940s and 1950s,* edited by Richard Bessel and Dirk Schumann. Washington, D.C.: German Historical Institute; Cambridge: Cambridge University Press, 2003.

——. "Victims, Villains, and Survivors: Gendered Perceptions and Self-Perceptions of Jewish Displaced Persons in Occupied Postwar Germany," in *Sexuality and German Fascism,* edited by Dagmar Herzog. Special issue of *Journal of History of Sexuality* 11/1–2 (January/April, 2002): 291–318.

Heinemann, Elizabeth. "The Hour of the Woman: Memories of Germany's 'Crisis Years' and West German National Identity." *American Historical Review* 101/2 (April 1996): 354–95.

——. *What Difference Does a Husband Make? Women and Marital Status in Nazi and Postwar Germany.* Berkeley: University of California Press, 1999.

Herzog, Dagmar. "Desperately Seeking Normality: Sex and Marriage in the Wake of War," in *Life after Death: Approaches to a Cultural and Social History of Europe during the 1940s and 1950s,* edited by Richard Bessel and Dirk Schumann. Washington, D.C.: German Historical Institute; Cambridge: Cambridge University Press, 2003.

——. "'Pleasure, Sex, and Politics Belong Together': Post-Holocaust Memory and the Sexual Revolution in West Germany." *Critical Inquiry* 24 (Winter 1998): 393–444.

——. *Sex after Fascism: Memory and Morality in Twentieth-Century Germany.* Princeton, N.J.: Princeton University Press, 2005.

History and Memory. AHR Forum, *American Historical Review* 102/5 (December 1997): 1372–1412.

Höhn, Maria. *GIs and Fräuleins: The German-American Encounter in 1950s West Germany.* Chapel Hill: University of North Carolina Press, 2002.

Jerome, Roy, ed. *Conceptions of Postwar German Masculinity.* Albany, N.Y.: SUNY Press, 2001.

Kenney, Padraic. "The Gender of Resistance in Communist Poland." *American Historical Review* 104/2(April 1999): 399–425.

Moeller, Robert G. "The Homosexual Man Is a 'Man,' the Homosexual Woman Is a 'Woman': Sex, Society, and the Law in Postwar West Germany," in *West Germany under Construction: Politics, Society, and Culture in the Adenauer Era*, edited by Robert G. Moeller. Ann Arbor: University of Michigan Press, 1997.

———. "'The Last Soldiers of the Great War' and Tales of Family Reunions in the Federal Republic of Germany." *Signs* 24/1 (Autumn 1998): 128–46.

———. *Protecting Motherhood: Women and the Family in the Politics of Postwar West Germany.* Berkeley: University of California Press, 1993.

———. *War Stories: The Search for a Usable Past in the Federal Republic of Germany.* Berkeley: University of California Press, 2001.

Poiger, Uta. *Jazz, Rock, and Rebels: Cold War Politics and American Culture in a Divided Germany.* Berkeley: University of California Press, 2000.

———. "A New 'Western' Hero? Reconstructing German Masculinity in the 1950s." *Signs* 24/1 (Autumn 1998): 147–62.

Stoehr, Irene. "Cold War Communities: Women's Peace Politics in Postwar West Germany, 1945–52," in *Home/Front: The Military, War, and Gender in Twentieth-Century Germany*, edited by Karen Hagemann and Stefanie Schüler-Springorum. Oxford: Berg, 2002.

Tröger, Annemarie. "German Women's Memories of World War II," in *Behind the Lines: Gender and the Two World Wars*, edited by Margaret Randolph Higonnet, Jane Jenson, Sonya Michel, and Margaret Weitz. New Haven, Conn.: Yale University Press, 1987.

IV. OVERVIEWS, SYNTHESES, AND TEXTBOOKS

Anderson, Bonnie, and Judith P. Zinsser. *A History of Their Own: Women in Europe from Prehistory to the Present.* 2 vols. New York: Harper & Row, 1989.

Bock, Gisela. *Frauen in der europäischen Geschichte: Vom Mittelalter bis zur Gegenwart.* Munich: Beck, 2000. Published in English as *Women in European History*, translated by Allison Brown. London: Blackwell, 2001.

Boxer, Marilyn, and Jean H. Quataert, eds. *Connecting Spheres: Women in the Western World, 1500 to the Present.* Oxford: Oxford University Press, 1987.

Bridenthal, Renate, Claudia Koonz, and Susan Stuard, eds. *Becoming Visible: Women in European History.* 2d ed. Boston: Houghton Mifflin, 1987.

Bridenthal, Renate, Susan Stuard, and Merry Wiesner, eds., *Becoming Visible: Women in European History.* 3d ed. Boston: Houghton Mifflin, 1998.

Frevert, Ute. *Women in German History: From Bourgeois Emancipation to Sexual Liberation*, translated by Stuart McKinnon-Evans. Oxford: Berg, 1989.

Fraisse, Geneviève, and Michelle Perrot, eds. *Emerging Feminism from Revolution to*

World War. Vol. 4 of *A History of Women in the West,* ed. Georges Duby and Michelle
Perrot. Cambridge, Mass.: Belknap Press of Harvard University Press, 1993.

Good, David F., Margarete Gradner, and Mary Jo Maynes, eds. *Austrian Women in the
Nineteenth and Twentieth Centuries: Cross-Disciplinary Perspectives.* Providence, R.I.:
Berghahn, 1996.

Hunt, Lynn. *The Challenge of the West: Peoples and Cultures from the Stone Age to the
Global Age.* Vol. C: *Peoples and Cultures from 1787 to the Global Age.* Lexington: D.C.
Heath, 1995.

Kent, Susan Kingsley. *Gender and Power in Britain, 1640–1990.* London: Routledge, 1999.

Offen, Karen. *European Feminisms, 1700—1950: A Political History.* Stanford: Stanford
University Press, 2000.

Paletschek, Sylvia, and Bianka Pitrow-Ennker, eds. *Women's Emancipation Movements in
the Nineteenth Century: A European Perspective.* Stanford, Calif.: Stanford University
Press, 2004.

Panizza, Letizia, and Sharon Wood, eds. *A History of Women's Writing in Italy.*
Cambridge: Cambridge University Press, 2000.

Smith, Bonnie G. *Changing Lives: Women in European History since 1700.* Lexington,
Mass.: D. C. Heath, 1989.

——, ed., *Women's History in Global Perspective.* Urbana: University of Illinois Press,
2004.

Thébaud, Françoise, ed. *Toward a Cultural Identity in the Twentieth Century.* Vol. 5 of
A History of Women in the West, ed. Georges Duby and Michelle Perrot. Cambridge,
Mass.: Belknap Press of Harvard University Press, 1994.

INDEX